AFRICA'S
PEACEMAKERS

About the Editor

Adekeye Adebajo has been executive director of the Centre for Conflict Resolution in Cape Town, South Africa, since 2003. He obtained his doctorate from Oxford University, where he studied as a Rhodes Scholar. He has served on United Nations missions in South Africa, Western Sahara and Iraq. Dr Adebajo is the author of four books: *Building Peace in West Africa*; *Liberia's Civil War*; *The Curse of Berlin: Africa After the Cold War*; and *UN Peacekeeping in Africa: From the Suez Crisis to the Sudan Conflicts*. He is editor or co-editor of seven books, on managing global conflicts, the United Nations, the European Union, West African security, and South Africa's and Nigeria's foreign policies in Africa.

AFRICA'S PEACEMAKERS

NOBEL PEACE LAUREATES OF AFRICAN DESCENT

EDITED BY
ADEKEYE ADEBAJO

Centre for Conflict Resolution
CAPE TOWN

Zed Books
LONDON | NEW YORK

This book is dedicated to the memory of
Nelson Rolihlahla Mandela (18 July 1918–5 December 2013),
a Nobel Peace laureate, South African statesman, and one of
the greatest moral figures of the twentieth century.

Africa's Peacemakers: Nobel Peace Laureates of African Descent
was first published in 2014 by Zed Books Ltd, 7 Cynthia Street, London N1 9JF, UK
and Room 400, 175 Fifth Avenue, New York, NY 10010, USA

www.zedbooks.co.uk

Editorial Copyright © Centre for Conflict Resolution 2014
Copyright in this collection © Zed Books 2014

The right of Adekeye Adebajo to be identified as the editor of this work has been
asserted by him in accordance with the Copyright, Designs and Patents Act, 1988

Typeset in Monotype Bulmer by illuminati, Grosmont
Index by John Barker
Cover designed by Rogue Four Design
Printed and bound by TJ International Ltd, Padstow, Cornwall

Distributed in the USA exclusively by Palgrave Macmillan, a division of
St Martin's Press, LLC, 175 Fifth Avenue, New York, NY 10010, USA

A catalogue record for this book is available from the British Library
Library of Congress Cataloging in Publication Data available

ISBN 978 1 78032 942 0 hb
ISBN 978 1 78032 943 7 pb

CONTENTS

PART ONE

INTRODUCTION

ONE

OBAMA'S NOBEL ANCESTORS:
FROM BUNCHE TO BARACK AND BEYOND

ADEKEYE ADEBAJO

The political liberation of Africa was complete in May 1994 when Nelson Mandela became president of a democratic South Africa. In a speech to the US Congress five months later, Mandela quoted his fellow Nobel peace laureate Martin Luther King Jr's famous words from an old Negro spiritual, uttered during his 1963 speech commemorating the March on Washington DC: 'Free at last, free at last, thank God Almighty we are free at last!' Two of the twentieth century's greatest pan-African struggles – the civil rights and anti-apartheid battles – were thus inextricably linked. Both of these liberation struggles, in Africa and the United States, focused on combating racial injustice and social inequality. The black ghettos of the American civil rights struggle mirrored the black townships of the anti-apartheid struggle as the major cauldrons of these battles.

In 2013 the African Union (AU) commemorated fifty years since the birth of its predecessor, the Organisation of African Unity (OAU), which embodied the quest for pan-African unity. The AU has also designated the African diaspora a sixth subregion (along with Southern, Central, West, East and North Africa), thus recognising the continuing relevance of this historical relationship in which towering figures of the pan-African movement, like America's W.E.B. DuBois, Trinidad's

Henry Sylvester-Williams and George Padmore, Jamaica's Marcus
Garvey, and Martinique's Frantz Fanon played a major role[1] (see
Mazrui, Chapter 2 in this volume). The continent has also embarked
since 1960 on a quest for what Kenyan scholar Ali Mazrui famously
described in 1967 as a 'Pax Africana': creating and consolidating an
African-owned peace.[2] The thirteen Nobel peace laureates examined
in this volume are thus, in a real sense, prophets of Pax Africana.

This volume seeks to draw lessons for peacemaking, civil rights,
socio-economic justice, environmental protection, nuclear disarmament
and women's rights, based on the rich experiences of the thirteen Nobel
peace laureates of African descent who won the prize between 1950 and
2011. These Nobel laureates come from diverse backgrounds, but have
waged similar struggles for peace, justice and freedom. This collection of
lucid, jargon-free essays, written by an interdisciplinary team of fourteen
prominent African and African American scholars and practitioners, is
the first book comprehensively to address this important topic.

African Americans like Nobel peace laureates Ralph Bunche (who
won the prize in 1950) and Martin Luther King Jr (1964) played an
important role in the pan-African struggle, with Bunche leading the
creation of the United Nations Trusteeship Council by 1947 and King
championing decolonisation efforts. Both attended Kwame Nkrumah's
independence celebration in Accra in March 1957. South Africa was
the last African country to gain political independence from colonial
rule, in 1994, in this thirty-year struggle, and it is appropriate that four
of its citizens have won the Nobel Peace Prize: Albert Luthuli (1960),
Desmond Tutu (1984), Nelson Mandela (1993) and Frederik Willem de

---

1. I thank Kaye Whiteman, Chris Saunders and Ken Barlow for very useful comments on an
earlier draft of this chapter.
    See, for example, Tajudeen Abdul-Raheem (ed.), *Pan-Africanism: Politics, Economy, and Social
Change in the Twenty-First Century* (London: Pluto, 1996); Frantz Fanon, *The Wretched of the Earth*
(New York: Grove, 1963); Colin Grant, *Negro with a Hat: The Rise and Fall of Marcus Garvey and
His Dream of Mother Africa* (Oxford: Oxford University Press, 2008); Kwame Nkrumah, *Africa
Must Unite* (London: Panaf, 1963); George Padmore, *Pan-Africanism or Communism? The Coming
Struggle in Africa* (London: Dobson, 1956); Eric J. Sundquist (ed.), *The Oxford W.E.B. Du Bois
Reader* (New York: Oxford University Press, 1996); Immanuel Wallerstein, *Africa: The Politics of
Unity* (New York: Vintage, 1967).
    2. Ali A. Mazrui, *Towards a Pax Africana: A Study of Ideology and Ambition* (Chicago: University
of Chicago Press, 1967).

Klerk (1993). The ancient civilisation of Egypt has produced two Nobel peace laureates – Anwar Sadat (1978) and Mohamed ElBaradei (2005) – honoured for peacemaking and nuclear disarmament respectively.

Ghana, which produced one of the greatest prophets of Pax Africana in Kwame Nkrumah, has been honoured with the award of the Nobel Peace Prize to Kofi Annan (2001), the UN Secretary General between 1997 and 2006. Kenya, the site of one of Africa's greatest indigenous anti-colonial struggles, the Mau Mau resistance to British rule of 1952–1960, has produced a Nobel peace laureate in Wangari Maathai (2004), who devoted her life to environmental campaigning. Liberia, one of Africa's oldest republics, founded in 1847 by freed American slaves, has produced the two most recent African Nobel peace laureates: Ellen Johnson Sirleaf and Leymah Gbowee (both in 2011) for their role in the struggle for women's rights.

The first American president of African descent, Barack Obama (whose father was Kenyan), won the Nobel Peace Prize in 2009, and his career was inspired by Martin Luther King Jr's civil rights struggle.[3] Obama was also the direct beneficiary of this struggle, waged by King as well as Ralph Bunche. As a young student in the United States, Obama first became politically active when he engaged in the anti-apartheid struggle that sought to impose sanctions on the racist albinocracy in South Africa. He started a second and final presidential term in January 2013 in which he was expected to show more engagement with his ancestral continent. Obama therefore visited South Africa, Tanzania and Senegal six months into his second term.

This book will thus examine the contributions of three prominent African Americans, four South African priests and politicians, three peacemakers from Egypt and Ghana, and three women activists from Kenya and Liberia.

---

3. See, for example, Horace G. Campbell, *Barack Obama and Twenty-First Century Politics: A Revolutionary Movement in the USA* (New York: Pluto, 2010); David Mendell, *Obama: From Promise to Power* (New York: HarperCollins, 2007); Barack Obama, *Dreams from My Father: A Story of Race and Inheritance* (New York: Three Rivers, 1995); David Remnick, *The Bridge: The Life and Rise of Barack Obama* (New York: Random House, 2010).

The Nobel Peace Prize was established, ironically, by Alfred Nobel (1833–1896), the Swedish inventor of dynamite, who willed his fortune to the endeavour for peace in 1895. The first Peace Prize was awarded in 1901 (other prizes are awarded for literature, medicine, physics, chemistry and economics). Five individuals chosen by the Norwegian parliament elect the annual winner, based on nominations from previous Nobel laureates; current or former members of the Nobel Peace Committee; members of national assemblies and of organisations such as the International Court of Justice, the International Court of Arbitration and the Inter-Parliamentary Union; and university professors of political science, law, history and philosophy.[4] The decision is announced in October each year, and the award is presented in Oslo in December. India's politico-spiritual leader Mohandas 'Mahatma' Gandhi was nominated for the prize five times and shortlisted three times, but was controversially never awarded it due to the political clout of the British Empire (Britain has had close ties to Norway), against which he waged a successful liberation struggle.[5] Gandhi's non-violent struggle, however, served as an inspiration to eight of our thirteen Nobel peace laureates of African descent: Ralph Bunche, Albert Luthuli, Martin Luther King Jr, Anwar Sadat, Desmond Tutu, Nelson Mandela, Barack Obama and Leymah Gbowee (see also Mazrui, Chapter 2 in this volume.)

---

4. Øivind Stenersen, Ivar Libaek and Asle Sveen, *The Nobel Peace Prize: One Hundred Years for Peace* (Oslo: J.W. Cappelens Forlag, 2001, and addendum of laureates 2001–05), pp. 10–14. See also Tore Frängsmyr, *Alfred Nobel* (Stockholm: Swedish Institute, 1996).
5. See Adekeye Adebajo, 'The Heirs of Gandhi: How Africa and Asia Changed the World', in Adekeye Adebajo, *The Curse of Berlin: Africa After the Cold War* (New York: Columbia University Press, 2010), pp. 313–32; Judith M. Brown, *Gandhi: Prisoner of Hope* (New Haven CT: Yale University Press, 1989); Judith M. Brown and Martin Prozesky (eds), *Gandhi and South Africa: Principles and Politics* (Pietermaritzburg: University of Natal Press, 1996); M.K. Gandhi, *An Autobiography – or, The Story of My Experiments with the Truth* (London: Penguin, 2001 [1927]); Bhikhu Parekh, *Gandhi: A Very Short Introduction* (Oxford: Oxford University Press, 1997); Bill Sutherland and Matt Meyer, *Guns and Gandhi: Pan-African Insights on Nonviolence, Armed Struggle and Liberation* (Trenton NJ: Africa World Press, 2000).

Outline of the Book

The book begins with two introductory essays. The first, the present chapter, seeks to explain how the struggles for civil rights, peace-making, environmental protection, nuclear disarmament and women's rights link together, as well as identify the achievements of the thirteen Nobel peace laureates of African descent who led these struggles. The second framing chapter, by Kenyan scholar Ali Mazrui, explains the significance of Barack Obama being awarded the Peace Prize in the context of Mahatma Gandhi and the twelve Nobel peace laureates of African descent who came before and after him.

Next, in Part Two, three chapters by African American analysts Pearl Robinson (Chapter 3) and Lee Daniels (Chapter 5) and Sierra Leonean scholar-diplomat James Jonah (who was mentored by Ralph Bunche at the UN, Chapter 4) assess the three African-American Nobel peace laureates: Ralph Bunche, Martin Luther King Jr and Barack Obama. Both Bunche and King were involved in America's civil rights struggle, though Bunche won the prize chiefly for his peacemaking role in the Middle East with the United Nations. Connections between these struggles are made, while one of the chapters – by Pearl Robinson – innovatively compares and contrasts the perspectives of Bunche, King and Obama on war and peace, using their Nobel Peace Prize speeches and other sources.

In Part Three, the anti-apartheid and peacemaking legacies of four South African Nobel laureates are examined by four South African authors – Chris Saunders (Chapter 6), Maureen Isaacson (Chapter 7), Elleke Boehmer (Chapter 8) and Gregory Houston (Chapter 9). Albert Luthuli, the president of the African National Congress (ANC) between 1951 and 1967 and a traditional chief and former lay preacher, was the first African Nobel peace laureate, in 1960. In 1984, another 'troublesome priest', Archbishop Desmond Tutu, won the prize. Like Luthuli, Tutu used the Nobel platform in Oslo to protest against the repression of the racist government in Pretoria. Thus Saunders and Isaacson richly analyse the struggles of both Luthuli and Tutu.

Nelson Mandela, another ANC chieftain, became one of the twentieth century's greatest moral leaders. Boehmer's eloquent essay examines Mandela's use of oratory in waging the anti-apartheid struggle, offering a rich comparison with Barack Obama. Apartheid's last leader, Frederik Willem de Klerk, was a 'pragmatic peacemaker' who controversially shared the Nobel Peace Prize with Mandela in 1993. Houston's historical essay traces de Klerk's peacemaking contributions to South Africa's transformation into a democratic state by 1994.

In Part Four, two Egyptian authors – Boutros Boutros-Ghali (Chapter 10) and Morad Abou-Sabé (Chapter 11) – examine the legacy of the two Egyptian Nobel peace laureates. Boutros-Ghali, former Egyptian minister of state for foreign affairs and former UN Secretary General (1992–96), explains the significance of President Anwar Sadat's historic trip to Jerusalem in 1977, which led to his assassination four years later, having won the Nobel Peace Prize in 1978.[6] Egypt's second Nobel peace laureate, in 2005, was Mohamed ElBaradei, who headed the UN's International Atomic Energy Agency (IAEA) between 1997 and 2009, and has more recently been involved in civic struggles to promote democratic governance in Egypt, efforts that are analysed by Abou-Sabé in his essay.

Part Five assesses the environmental and peacemaking efforts of two Nobel laureates. South African scholar Janice Golding assesses the contributions of Kenyan environmental campaigner and 'Earth Mother' Wangari Maathai, who became the first African woman to be awarded the Nobel Peace Prize, in 2004 (Chapter 12). Another African-American scholar, Gwendolyn Mikell, examines the peacemaking legacy of Ghana's Kofi Annan, who served as UN Secretary General between 1997 and 2006 (Chapter 13).

Concluding the book, Part Six examines the two Liberian women who were jointly awarded the Nobel Peace Prize in 2011: President Ellen Johnson Sirleaf, dubbed the 'Iron Lady'; and civil society activist Leymah Gbowee, described as 'the prayerful peace warrior'. Both

---

6. See also Boutros Boutros-Ghali, *Egypt's Road to Jerusalem: A Diplomat's Story of the Struggle for Peace in the Middle East* (New York: Random, 1997).

fought actively for women's and civil rights in Liberia, and the two chapters here, by Nigerian analysts Adekeye Adebajo (Chapter 14) and Rosaline Daniel (Chapter 15) respectively, chronicle these struggles. Adebajo, however, is critical of Sirleaf being awarded the Peace Prize, due partly to her ambiguous role in Liberia's first civil war between 1989 and 1997.

Connections and Contrasts

These fifteen essays seek to make connections between the struggles for peace, justice and freedom and the thirteen individuals of African descent who have won the Nobel Peace Prize. Ralph Bunche and Martin Luther King Jr marched together during the civil rights struggles of the 1950s and 1960s; Albert Luthuli and King issued a joint declaration against apartheid in 1962; Luthuli and Nelson Mandela worked together against apartheid within the ANC in the 1950s and early 1960s; Mandela appointed Desmond Tutu head of South Africa's Truth and Reconciliation Commission (TRC), which submitted its report in 1996; Luthuli and Tutu were both priests who were forced into politics by the inequities of apartheid; King, Luthuli, Tutu and Mandela were all skilful performers who understood the importance of dramatic speeches and gestures; while F.W. de Klerk, as a young apartheid-supporting student leader, invited Luthuli to address fellow students at South Africa's Potchefstroom University in 1961.

There are other interactions and connections between our thirteen Nobel laureates. Barack Obama met Tutu in South Africa as a US senator in 2006, and as president honoured Tutu with America's Medal of Freedom in August 2009; Obama and Mandela both embodied a charismatic leadership style in pursuing their goals (see Boehmer, Chapter 8 in this volume); Kofi Annan and Mohamed ElBaradei were both self-effacing technocrats rather than politicians, who rose up the ranks to head their respective institutions, seeking to serve as a 'force for good' in the world and embody the principles of their organisations; Wangari Maathai, Ellen Johnson Sirleaf and Leymah

Gbowee all courageously pursued women's rights through methods that directly confronted authority; Maathai worked with fellow Nobel laureates Annan and Tutu to promote environmental issues. In 2006, then-senator Barack Obama planted a tree with Maathai in Nairobi's Uhuru Park. Both ElBaradei and his fellow Nobel peace laureate Maathai were involved in unorthodox struggles that sought to link nuclear disarmament and environmental protection to global security in a new framework of human security. Both became involved in domestic democracy struggles, in Egypt and Kenya respectively. Both ElBaradei and Obama shared the desire to rid the world of nuclear weapons.

Over two centuries ago, Jesus Christ had famously noted that 'A Prophet has no honour in his own country' (John 4:44). Six of our Nobel laureates who served as international civil servants or pursued global and regional issues suffered this fate. Ralph Bunche was recognised more in international circles than he was in the USA; Anwar Sadat was revered in the West, but shunned and isolated in the Middle East and Africa; Mohamed ElBaradei struggled in his bid to play a more prominent political role in Egypt after retiring from the UN in 2009; Ellen Johnson Sirleaf failed disastrously in her first bid to become Liberia's president in 1997; Kofi Annan spent only two years (1974–76) as head of the Ghanaian tourist board before returning to the UN; while Wangari Maathai's environmental activism was recognised more abroad than in Kenya. Five of our subjects – Sadat, de Klerk, Mandela, Sirleaf and Obama – were also heads of state burdened by state power, who sometimes took difficult decisions that did not always accord with the principles of the struggles they were waging.

Studies like these are naturally somewhat subjective by their very nature. Though these fifteen essays largely celebrate the heroic struggles waged by the thirteen Nobel peace laureates examined in this book, we have sought to avoid hagiography. The rest of this introduction thus provides an assessment of our Nobel peace laureates that diverges, in several cases, from the analyses of the chapter authors. Such differences will hopefully enrich the study and provide readers with a more rounded picture of our subjects.

Three African Americans

RALPH BUNCHE AND MARTIN LUTHER KING JR

Two African Americans won the Nobel Peace Prize before Obama: Ralph Bunche and Martin Luther King Jr.[7] Both were involved in America's civil rights struggle, which they linked to Africa's independence struggles. Bunche, the 'scholar–diplomat', was the first black person to win the prize, in 1950. His skilful mediation in the Middle East won him the award, and he served the UN for another two decades, contributing to peacemaking efforts in the Suez (1956) and Congo (1960–64) crises, though he had a terrible relationship with another pan-African icon, Patrice Lumumba, and was accused by some pan-Africanists as having pursued parochial American foreign policy interests in the Congo.[8] Bunche was also instrumental in establishing and directing the UN Trusteeship Council, which pushed for the liberation of Africa, beginning in 1947.[9] Significantly, in the 1950s he marched with the 'great provocateur' Martin Luther King Jr during America's civil rights struggle. King became the youngest winner of the Nobel Peace Prize in 1964, at the age of 35. Bunche and the civil rights establishment opposed King's anti-Vietnam stance, which they felt would harm the civil rights struggle, but they eventually agreed to disagree on this issue (see Robinson, Chapter 3, and Daniels, Chapter 5, in this volume). King famously noted – as quoted by Obama during the 'Arab Spring' of 2011 – that 'there is something in the soul that cries out for freedom'.[10] His personal life, however, was somewhat besmirched by reported adulterous affairs, and Lee Daniels notes in his essay that King was killed at 'precisely the right moment' to ensure his martyrdom.

---

7. See, for example, Robert A. Hill and Edmond J. Keller (eds), *Trustee for the Human Community: Ralph J. Bunche, the United Nations, and the Decolonisation of Africa* (Athens: Ohio University Press, 2010); Beverly Lindsay (ed.), *Ralph Johnson Bunche: Public Intellectual and Nobel Peace Laureate* (Urbana: University of Illinois Press, 2007); Brian Urquhart, *Ralph Bunche: An American Life* (New York: Norton, 1993).

8. See Crawford Young, 'Ralph Bunche and Patrice Lumumba: The Fatal Encounter', in Hill and Keller (eds), *Trustee for the Human Community*, pp. 128–47.

9. See Tor Sellström, 'The Trusteeship Council: Decolonisation and Liberation', in Adekeye Adebajo (ed.), *From Global Apartheid to Global Village: Africa and the United Nations* (Scottsville: University of KwaZulu-Natal Press, 2009), pp. 107–37.

10. Martin Luther King Jr, 'Birth of a New Nation', sermon delivered at the Dexter Avenue Baptist Church, Montgomery, Alabama, 7 April 1957 (www.modernghana.com).

BARACK OBAMA

As the first African-American US president was preparing to send more troops to wage war in Afghanistan, word came through in October 2009 that Obama had won the Nobel Peace Prize. Some of his early foreign policy actions unfortunately followed in the hawkish footsteps of his predecessor, George W. Bush: Obama's first military action as president, within days of taking office, was to sanction two missile strikes in Pakistan, which reportedly killed twenty-two people, including women and children. Three more US missile strikes a month later, in February 2009, killed another fifty-five people, drawing the ire of Pakistani officials.[11] In his first three years in office, Obama ordered targeted assassinations of suspected terrorists through an average of one drone strike every four days, compared to George W. Bush's average of one strike every forty days.[12] While Bush ordered about 50 drone strikes in eight years, Obama had ordered 375 strikes in four and a half years. These actions have mostly been conducted in the border area between Pakistan and Afghanistan, and by May 2013 had killed an estimated 3,500 people, including hundreds of innocent civilians, who accounted for an estimated 10–15 per cent of fatalities.[13] Obama also ordered the assassination of Saleh Ali Saleh Nabhan, the alleged ringleader of an al-Qaeda cell in Kenya in southern Somalia, by American commandos in September 2009.[14] As a consequence of these actions, some have been forced to ask whether Obama's foreign policy could come to represent 'Bush with a smile'.

Upon receiving news of the Nobel Peace Prize, Obama – in office for barely nine months at the time – seemed himself to admit that his award was more for aspirational rhetoric than for concrete accomplishments.

11. See Ewen MacAskill and Saeed Shah, 'US Casualties in Afghanistan to Rise, Says Biden', *Guardian*, 26 January 2009, p. 17; 'Saeed Shah, 'US Missiles Strike on Taliban Stronghold in Pakistan Tribal Area Kills 30', *Guardian*, 17 February 2009, p. 23.
12. 'Unmanned Aerial Warfare', *The Economist*, 8 October 2011, p. 32. See also 'Obama's Secret Wars', special report, *Foreign Policy*, March–April 2012.
13. Lexington, 'One Year of the One', *The Economist*, 29 October 2009 (www.economist.com); Micah Zenko, 'How Barack Obama Has Tried to Open up the One-Sided Drone War', *Financial Times*, 23 May 2013 (www.ft.com); David Carr, 'Debating Drones, in the Open', *New York Times*, 10 February 2013 (www.nytimes.com).
14. Jeffrey Gettleman and Eric Scmitt, 'American Raid in Somalia Kills Qaeda Militant', *New York Times*, 15 September 2009, pp. A1, A11.

The jury is still out on whether Obama can live up to the ideals of the prize. His Nobel acceptance speech in Oslo in December 2009 was disappointing, showing more of the pragmatic politician than the idealist prophet. He fittingly acknowledged the legacy of Martin Luther King Jr and Gandhi, noting: 'I am living testimony to the moral force of non-violence.' But in much of his speech – delivered in the shadow of two American foreign wars, in Afghanistan and Iraq – Obama explained why it was 'necessary' to use force to bring about peace. A celebration of peace thus turned into a justification for war. Obama used the concept of 'just wars'[15] to explain why he could not be guided by King's example alone, since non-violence could not have halted tyrants like Adolf Hitler. In stark contrast to his earlier recognition of the historical imperial actions of the United States,[16] he glorified his country for having 'helped underwrite global security for more than six decades ... and enabled democracy to take hold in places like the Balkans'.[17] Obama went on, rather inappropriately in the context of a Nobel speech, to criticise Iran's and North Korea's nuclear ambitions, while reserving his own country's right to act unilaterally, echoing Bush's doctrine of 'pre-emptive' use of force. (For another perspective on the speech, see Robinson, Chapter 3 in this volume.)

The African references in Obama's Nobel speech also perpetuated negative stereotypes of the continent, with the Kenyan–Kansan referring to Somalia as a 'failed state' of terrorism, piracy and famine, as well as talking of genocide in Darfur, rape in the Democratic Republic of the Congo (DRC) and repression in Zimbabwe (though referring to the bravery of citizens in resisting it). This speech was, unsurprisingly, well received in the United States, with Obama clearly trying to avoid charges that he was pandering to an international global audience who had had no hand in his election as president in 2008. In the same Nobel speech, Obama also controversially referred to fellow Nobel peace

15. See, for example, Michael Walzer, *Just and Unjust Wars: A Moral Argument with Historical Illustrations*, 2nd edn (New York: Basic Books, 1992).

16. Barack Obama, *The Audacity of Hope: Thoughts on Reclaiming the American Dream* (New York: Crown, 2006), p. 281.

17. The quotations in this paragraph are from Barack Obama's Nobel Peace Prize speech delivered in Oslo on 10 December 2009 (www.nobelprize.org).

laureate Albert Schweitzer (who won the prize in 1952) as among the 'giants of history', alongside previous peace laureates Martin Luther King Jr, Nelson Mandela and American war hero General George Marshall. Schweitzer was a French–German doctor who had set up a mission hospital in Gabon in 1913 to help the local population cure diseases and convert African 'pagans' to Christianity. He worked tirelessly in Gabon – with some spells in Europe – until his death in 1965.

Schweitzer, however, is widely viewed as a racist who referred frequently to black Africans as 'primitives' and 'savages'. As he put it: 'The native moves under patriarchal authority. He does not understand dealing with an office, but dealing with a man.'[18] Schweitzer also despised Islam – the religion of Obama's grandfather,[19] which Barack sought as president to reach out to – dismissing it as having 'never produced any thinking about the world and mankind which penetrated to the depths'.[20] As Ali Mazrui – himself, paradoxically, the Albert Schweitzer Professor at the State University of New York – noted about the German doctor: 'He could be accused of behaving as if the only good African was a sick one.'[21]

Despite the pretty poetry heard during the 2008 US presidential campaign by the most cosmopolitan and worldly of the forty-four individuals to occupy the White House, Obama has ruled in pragmatic prose. He is very much a dyed-in-the-wool politician, cut from the same cloth as his Democratic Party predecessor, Bill Clinton. Both men consistently demonstrated a willingness to sacrifice core principles at the altar of political survival. A line in Obama's Nobel speech may unwittingly provide what could well become the epitaph to his own presidency: 'Even those of us with the best of intentions will at times fail to right the wrongs before us.' Obama's instincts to be a force for good in the world have often been diverted by his country's imperial temptations, as again underlined by the 2011 intervention in Libya led

---

18. Quoted in Ali A. Mazrui, 'Dr. Schweitzer's Racism', *Transition* 53 (1991), p. 101.
19. See Peter Firstbrook, *The Obamas: The Untold Story of an African Family* (New York: Random House, 2011); David Maraniss, *Barack Obama: The Story* (New York: Simon & Schuster, 2012).
20. Quoted in Mazrui, 'Dr. Schweitzer's Racism', p. 99.
21. Quoted in ibid., p. 101.

by the North Atlantic Treaty Organization (NATO).[22] After all, the road to hell is famously paved with good intentions.

Obama's Africa policy has comprised four pillars: to support democratic governance, to foster economic growth and development, to increase access to quality health and education, and to help manage conflicts. However, he has continued several of the truculent George W. Bush's most egregious policies. These have militarised American engagement with Africa, despite Obama's pledge during a July 2009 speech in Accra to promote 'strong institutions, not strong men'. 'Extraordinary rendition' of suspected terrorists abroad continued, with reports of torture; 1,500 American soldiers remained in Djibouti to track terrorists; autocratic regimes in oil-rich Gabon and Equatorial Guinea remained staunch US clients; and officials of America's Germany-based Africa Command (AFRICOM) still roamed the continent in search of 'mad mullahs'. The Obama administration also dispatched drones to Somalia and Mali, missiles of death that have notoriously killed scores of innocent civilians wherever they have been deployed. Washington, however, provided $355 million to the African Union Mission in Somalia (AMISOM), though many African armies continued to complain that they needed more logistics and equipment, and not counterterrorism training. Obama drastically cut AIDS funding to Africa by $200 million in 2012,[23] one of the few successes of US policy towards the continent under George W. Bush. It is important to note that Obama was obstructed at every turn by Republican opponents who vowed from the start to make him a 'one-term president'. The racism that still afflicts American society scarcely dissipated with the historic election of the country's first black president. However, despite Obama's sporadic diplomatic safaris to Africa, his Africa policy represented more continuity with, rather than change from, a discredited past.

---

22. For a more detailed critique, see Tariq Ali, *The Obama Syndrome: Surrender at Home, War Abroad* (London: Verso, 2010).

23. Cited in Sarah Boseley, 'US Grapples with Neglect of HIV', *Mail and Guardian* (South Africa), 13–19 July 2012, p. 30.

Four South African Priests and Politicians

Four South Africans have won the Nobel Peace Prize; three of them contributed to promoting socio-economic justice, while all were peace-makers. While Albert Luthuli, Desmond Tutu and Nelson Mandela all shared the same Christian education and were titans in the anti-apartheid struggle, F.W. de Klerk was in many ways the very antithesis of this struggle. De Klerk was instead the very embodiment of the very apartheid system he helped to destroy in a pragmatic act of politicide.

ALBERT LUTHULI

The president of the African National Congress, Albert Luthuli was the first African peace laureate, in 1960 (he received the prize in December 1961). Coming shortly after the Sharpeville massacre in South Africa, the award was an attempt to highlight apartheid's brutalities. Luthuli – the 'Black Moses' who titled his autobiography *Let My People Go* – was president of the ANC from 1951 until his death in 1967. This title was taken from a civil rights-era American Negro spiritual: 'Go down, Moses, Way down in Egypt's land; Tell old Pharaoh to Let My people go!' (quoted in Saunders, Chapter 6 in this volume.) Luthuli was a traditional chief from rural KwaZulu-Natal who uniquely was able to bridge the divide between the urban and rural masses of Africa's oldest liberation movement. He was involved in the Defiance Campaign of 1952 and led several acts of civil disobedience, for which he was jailed and 'banned'. However, he stuck doggedly to his principles of Gandhian non-violent passive resistance (though he noted that he was not a pacifist), advocated economic sanctions against the apartheid regime, and consistently pushed for the inclusion of whites, Indians and 'Coloureds' (mixed-race populations) in the struggle to ensure democratic majority rule and an end to apartheid. For Luthuli, who was steeped in Christian religious beliefs, the road to freedom lay through the cross, and sacrifices and suffering would be required in order to translate Jesus' love ethic into concrete achievements. The cross thus had to come before the crown. Like Gandhi, the point of the struggle for Luthuli was to transform the enemy's hatred through love and human dignity. As Chris Saunders notes in his essay, Luthuli and Nelson Mandela disagreed on the ANC's approach to armed struggle, with the priest showing understanding for the cause, but personally maintaining a commitment to non-violence.

Luthuli's Nobel speech in Oslo in December 1961, titled 'Africa and Freedom', was one of the most powerful statements ever delivered in this forum.[24] It was an elegant, dignified and defiant speech that exposed the evil criminality of apartheid, citing examples of the shooting of protestors, oppressive pass laws, bannings and prohibitions, imprisonment and land dispossession. Luthuli described apartheid as a 'museum piece', a sort of giant Jurassic Park of massive injustice full of political dinosaurs who would ultimately become extinct. It was a speech that Martin Luther King Jr could have delivered about apartheid America; both prophets shared an undying belief in non-violent struggle, as well as in the ultimate triumph of the human spirit over oppression. Luthuli's magnanimity towards his oppressors, his continued calls for reconciliation, and his building of bridges with progressive white South Africans were the torch that his fellow ANC chieftain and Nobel laureate Nelson Mandela would take up four decades later in liberating his country from the bondage of white apartheid pharaohs.

This speech was also the *cri de cœur* of a committed pan-African prophet linking Africa's independence struggle to that of apartheid South Africa and calling for a united continent that must abandon its oppressive past and build democratic societies based on humane values. Luthuli demonstrated that his Christian faith was the foundation for all his political actions, employing evocative biblical allusions and calling for churches across the globe to join the anti-apartheid struggle. He appealed to his European audience in Oslo and beyond to see the world as one humanity in the spirit of *ubuntu* – the gift of discovering our shared humanity – and cited examples from Europe's blood-strewn history to win support for Africa's liberation. In the words of one of

---

24. Albert Luthuli's Nobel Peace Prize speech is available at www.nobelprize.org/nobel_prizes/ peace/laureates/1960/lutuli-acceptance.html.

Luthuli's favourite poets, Henry Wadsworth Longfellow, the ANC
stalwart left his 'footprints on the sands of time'.

DESMOND TUTU

In 1984 the Anglican archbishop of Cape Town, Desmond Tutu, a
'troublesome priest' like Luthuli, won the Nobel Peace Prize for his
quest for socio-economic justice in apartheid South Africa. Tutu was a
fearless anti-apartheid activist who not only challenged the evil system
but also waded into crowds in his purple cassock in volatile black
townships to save alleged apartheid collaborators from being burnt alive
through 'necklacing'. Like Luthuli, Tutu preached non-violence, though
both men sympathised with the armed struggle's ultimate objectives
of freedom and justice. Like Luthuli's Nobel speech, Tutu's was also a
searing indictment of apartheid, which he compared to Adolf Hitler's
treatment of Jews in Nazi Germany. Like Luthuli, Tutu decried the
injustices of curfews and bans, and of the killing of more than 500 black
schoolchildren during the Soweto uprising of 1976. Some believe that
Tutu's Nobel Prize helped to galvanise the global sanctions movement
between 1985 and 1989. His cause was also pan-African: he travelled
to Mobutu Sese Seko's Zaire to preach a liberation theology against
oppression; he visited and criticised Marxist governments in Ethiopia
and Angola; and he would later criticise human rights abuses in Robert
Mugabe's Zimbabwe and General Sani Abacha's Nigeria. Tutu also
visited Rwanda shortly after its 1994 genocide to preach a sermon
of forgiveness and reconciliation. Fellow Nobel laureate Kofi Annan
described Tutu as a 'voice for the voiceless'.[25]

After South Africa's independence in 1994, Tutu became the 'face' of
the country's Truth and Reconciliation Commission, which he chaired.
The TRC sought – through the testimony of victims and perpetrators
– to uncover the truth about apartheid. But some criticised Tutu for
Christianising the process, and noted that neither blacks nor whites felt

---

25. John Allen, *Rabble-Rouser for Peace: The Authorised Biography of Desmond Tutu* (London
and Johannesburg: Random House, 2006), p. 394.

that the commission had delivered justice.[26] Tutu's 'rainbow nation of God' depiction of South Africa has also often been ridiculed as naive. The 'Arch' himself has sometimes taken controversial positions. He compared the struggle against apartheid to that against Communism and Nazism, seemingly ignoring the incredible role that such Communist Party stalwarts as Chris Hani and Joe Slovo had played in the ANC's liberation struggle. Tutu also often displayed a strangely obsessive need for publicity, even signing up with a lucrative American speakers' agency.[27] He has sometimes shown signs of being an unguided missile, as when he threatened to pray against the democratically elected South African government – which had denied Tibet's spiritual leader, the Dalai Lama, a visa to attend Tutu's eightieth birthday in October 2011 – noting histrionically that the ANC-led government was worse than the apartheid regime. Critics have also highlighted Tutu's celebration of the cult of celebrity, hobnobbing with stars like Bono (who serenaded the 'Arch' during his eightieth birthday) who patronise and trivialise African causes. (For another view of Tutu, see Isaacson, Chapter 7 in this volume.)

NELSON MANDELA

Nelson Mandela, another ANC chieftain like Luthuli, emerged from twenty-seven years in jail preaching a message of reconciliation with his former enemies.[28] The ANC consciously used Mandela to represent the face of its struggle. 'Madiba' (Mandela's clan name) personally embodied his people's aspirations for a democratic future. Like an 'avuncular saint', he emerged from prison without any apparent bitterness towards his former enemies, and tirelessly promoted national

---

26. See, for example, Yasmin Sooka, 'Race and Reconciliation: *E Pluribus Unum?*', in Adekeye Adebajo, Adebayo Adedeji and Chris Landsberg (eds), *South Africa in Africa: The Post-Apartheid Era* (Scottsville: University of KwaZulu-Natal Press, 2007), pp. 78–91.

27. Allen, *Rabble-Rouser for Peace*.

28. See, for example, Kofi Annan, foreword to *Mandela: The Authorised Portrait* (London: Bloomsbury, 2006); Elleke Boehmer, *Nelson Mandela: A Very Short Introduction* (Oxford: Oxford University Press, 2008); Tom Lodge, *Mandela: A Critical Life* (Oxford: Oxford University Press, 2006); Xolela Mangcu (ed.), *The Meaning of Mandela: A Literary and Intellectual Celebration* (Cape Town: Human Sciences Research Council, 2006); Anthony Sampson, *Mandela: The Authorised Biography* (London: HarperCollins, 1999).

reconciliation. As president, he came to symbolise his country's racial reconciliation. The charisma of this 'founding father' helped South Africa's young democratic institutions to flower between 1994 and 1999, and gave the country an international stature of which a former global pariah could never have dreamed. In contrast to Africa's other post-independence 'founding fathers', such as Ghana's Kwame Nkrumah, Zambia's Kenneth Kaunda, Kenya's Jomo Kenyatta, Senegal's Léopold Senghor and Tanzania's Julius Nyerere, Mandela bowed out gracefully at the end of his first presidential term in 1999, setting a standard for future African leaders aspiring to greatness.

One of Madiba's lasting legacies will be his efforts – not always successful – at promoting national and international peacemaking. He tirelessly reached out to his former enemies at home, and led peacemaking efforts in Burundi, the DRC and Lesotho.[29] During his presidency from 1994 to 1999, South Africa largely shunned a military role for fear of arousing allegations of hegemonic domination, since the apartheid army had been particularly destructive in Southern Africa, causing an estimated 1 million deaths, as well as $60 billion of damage in the 1980s alone.[30] A botched intervention in Lesotho in 1998 – led by a former apartheid officer – revived unpleasant historical memories of this past. However, in what came to be known by some as the 'Mandela Doctrine', the Nobel laureate told his fellow leaders at the OAU summit in Ouagadougou, Burkina Faso, in 1998:

> Africa has a right and a duty to intervene to root out tyranny.... [W]e must all accept that we cannot abuse the concept of national sovereignty to deny the rest of the continent the right and duty to intervene when behind those sovereign boundaries, people are being slaughtered to protect tyranny.[31]

29. See Kristina Bentley and Roger Southall, *An African Peace Process: Mandela, South Africa, and Burundi* (Cape Town: Human Sciences Research Council, 2005). See also James Barber, *Mandela's World: The International Dimension of South Africa's Political Revolution, 1990–99* (Cape Town: David Philip, 2004); Chris Landsberg, 'Promoting Democracy: The Mandela–Mbeki Doctrine', *Journal of Democracy* 11(3) (July 2000), pp. 107–21.

30. Adebayo Adedeji (ed.), *South Africa and Africa: Within or Apart?* (London: Zed Books, 1996), p. 9.

31. Quoted in Eboe Hutchful, 'Understanding the African Security Crisis', in Abdel-Fatau Musah and J. Kayode Fayemi (eds), *Mercenaries: An African Security Dilemma* (London: Pluto, 2000), p. 218.

Critics have noted, however, that Mandela may have ended up doing more long-term damage as president by papering over racial differences and not forcing whites to show more contrition to their largely black victims of apartheid. Many of South Africa's 5 million whites continue to enjoy their privileged lifestyle, while the national high priest, Madiba, appears to have absolved them of their sins without proper confession and penance. Mandela's legacy in liberating his country is secure, but the success of his efforts at national reconciliation will only endure if rapid progress can be made to narrow the grotesque socio-economic inequalities in the most unequal society on earth. Also requiring comment is the controversial co-joining of two very different historical figures under the Mandela Rhodes Foundation in 2002: nineteenth-century imperialist Cecil Rhodes and twentieth-century liberation hero Nelson Mandela. Surely Jews would not have created a Herzl (founder of the Zionist movement) Hitler Foundation – so why have Africans accepted this monstrosity? Has Mandela perhaps taken reconciliation too far, in rehabilitating a malevolent figure that Africans really should have condemned to the pit-latrine of history?[32]

FREDERIK WILLEM DE KLERK

In a television interview with Christiane Amanpour on the Cable News Network (CNN) in May 2012, apartheid's last president, F.W. de Klerk, caused widespread outrage when he appeared to defend the apartheid system which had legalised racism in South Africa between 1948 and 1990 and been condemned by the United Nations as a 'crime against humanity'. South African cartoonists lampooned him as a political dinosaur, while other critics called on him to return the Nobel Peace Prize he had won alongside Mandela in 1993. On closer inspection, the greater outrage may actually be that so many people were so surprised by de Klerk's comments, much of which he had consistently put on the public record for decades. A close reading of this history shows that repudiating apartheid would have represented an act of political

---

32. See Adekeye Adebajo, 'Mandela and Rhodes: A Monstrous Marriage', in Adebajo, *The Curse of Berlin*, pp. 215–32.

parricide for de Klerk, as his entire family history was based on the implementation of this ideology. De Klerk did not help end apartheid because it was morally repugnant, but because – in his own words – 'it failed' as a system of political control and socio-economic engineering. One of the most famous conversions since Saint Paul tumbled off his horse on the road to Damascus was thus undertaken more out of political pragmatism than moral conviction.

During the 2012 CNN interview, de Klerk acknowledged that the fact that apartheid trampled human rights 'was and remains morally indefensible', but then noted that he could only say in 'a qualified way' that apartheid had been morally wrong. He argued that the idea of the black majority being herded into Bantustans was 'not repugnant' and was historically inaccurate since, in his view, the homelands had always been there. He then fatuously compared the Bantustans favourably with the democratic 'velvet divorce' of Czechoslovakia in 1993, and further noted that blacks 'were not disenfranchised, they voted'. By this jaundiced view of history, a system that had reserved less than 15 per cent of land for 80 per cent of South Africans, restricted the freedom of movement of blacks, and stripped them of their human dignity was somehow defensible. The black majority must also have been consistently electing racist rulers to oppress themselves between 1948 and 1990. Sensing the outrage caused by his comments and the immense damage it had done to his reputation, de Klerk sought to backtrack, claiming that his statements had been 'misinterpreted'. His record, however, suggests otherwise.

De Klerk was the scion of a conservative Afrikaner family and a dyed-in-the-wool National Party (NP) member. Both his father and his grandfather had been senators for the party of apartheid, and his father had actually served in the government of apartheid's 'grand wizard' and architect, Hendrik Verwoerd (1958–66). F.W. de Klerk held seven ministerial posts before becoming president in 1989, but never showed any signs of a commitment to reforming the evils of the apartheid system. He was a staunch defender of white privilege who, as education minister in the 1980s, pushed to introduce a quota system to limit the number of black students in universities. Even as late as November 1989, de Klerk opposed common political institutions for all South Africans. He embarked on a remarkable political reversal three months later – releasing Mandela from twenty-seven years of incarceration – under the pressure of continuing black protests and a plummeting economy wracked by increasingly devastating economic sanctions. However, de Klerk does deserve some credit for his role in South Africa's democratic transition.

Much to Desmond Tutu's annoyance, de Klerk refused to take proper responsibility for the crimes of apartheid governments in which he had served. In his perversely self-justifying 1999 memoir *The Last Trek – A New Beginning*, de Klerk sought to portray the Truth and Reconciliation Commission as a witchhunt against Afrikaners, and dismissed apartheid's crimes as having been committed by a small group of securocrats without the knowledge of most National Party politicians. He refused to acknowledge that one side's struggle had been morally superior in the conflict, describing the ANC's armed struggle as 'unnecessary and counter-productive'. He insultingly sought to portray his party as reformers spawned by the ANC, claiming disingenuously that the National Party had accepted the vision of a united South Africa by the time the ANC accelerated its armed struggle in the early 1960s. De Klerk also incredibly claimed that most of the politically related deaths in South Africa had not been committed by apartheid's securocrats.[33] In a reckless abdication of responsibility, this was a stout defence of the apartheid system that de Klerk had never unambiguously repudiated.

One wonders in retrospect whether Mandela should perhaps not have rejected the Nobel Peace Prize in 1993 rather than accepting a moral equivalence between a pragmatic politician of apartheid and the political prophet who ensured its destruction. As Maureen Isaacson notes in her essay (Chapter 7), Desmond Tutu expressed regret at having nominated de Klerk for the Nobel Peace Prize.

---

33. F.W. de Klerk, *The Last Trek – A New Beginning: The Autobiography* (London: Pan, 2000 [1999]), pp. 376–7.

Three Peacemakers from Egypt and Ghana

Anwar Sadat, Mohamed ElBaradei and Kofi Annan were all active peacemakers. Where Sadat was a head of state, ElBaradei and Annan were American-trained international civil servants who both fell foul of their former US patron after disagreeing over how to deal with Iraq and Iran. All three men were idealists, with Sadat and Annan sometimes displaying a naive faith in the goodness of Uncle Sam. Washington was instrumental in the election of ElBaradei and Annan to the head of their organisations before later turning against them. Sadat died a martyr to his cause in 1981, while Annan suffered a political crucifixion by his former American patron.

ANWAR SADAT

The president of Egypt from 1970 to 1981, Anwar Sadat,[34] – the 'tragic peacemaker' – whose mother was the descendant of a black African slave and who as a child dressed himself up like Gandhi and meditated on the roof of his home in Cairo, was awarded the Nobel Peace Prize after his historic trip to Jerusalem in 1977. Following this visit, Sadat made peace with Israel in a series of meetings with its prime minister, Menachem Begin, at Camp David, in a process facilitated by US president Jimmy Carter. (Sadat felt that Carter should also have been awarded the prize in 1978, but the American president had not been nominated; Carter would eventually win the prize in 2002 after years of transparently campaigning for it.) In his essay (Chapter 10), Boutros Boutros-Ghali, Sadat's minister of state for foreign affairs during this period, provides a balanced but candid first-hand portrait of Sadat during these negotiations.

Sadat had gambled that going to war against Israel in 1973 would secure peace. He thus paradoxically waged war to promote peace. When he made his historic visit to Israel in 1977, he drew from his experiences of traditional leaders in Egyptian villages sitting together to eat and resolve issues. True to his peasant roots, he felt the need

---

34. See Anwar el-Sadat, *In Search of Identity* (London: Collins, 1978).

to break bread with the enemy and talk. Sadat was single-minded and stubborn. He took risks for peace, but his arrogance, naivety and exaggerated trust in Washington sometimes turned out to be reckless. A US-mediated peace agreement was eventually reached in 1979 in which Israel returned the Sinai to Egypt. Sadat's rapprochement with Tel Aviv led to his diplomatic isolation in the Arab world, and eventually resulted in his assassination by Islamist extremists (domestic opponents he had treated harshly) in October 1981. Sadat and Begin were jointly awarded the Nobel Peace Prize, an act that some considered to be as controversial as Mandela and de Klerk being jointly nominated in 1993.

MOHAMED ELBARADEI

Egypt's second Nobel peace laureate, in 2005, was Mohamed ElBaradei – the 'Rocket Man' – who was director general of the Vienna-based International Atomic Energy Agency between 1997 and 2009. The agency was founded in 1957 to inspect nuclear facilities and ensure that peaceful nuclear activities were not used to develop weapons of mass destruction. ElBaradei consistently called for the peaceful use of atomic energy and a nuclear-free world, and worried incessantly about nuclear weapons falling into the hands of terrorist groups. In stark contrast, Alfred Nobel himself had hoped to rid the world of war by developing advanced weapons.

ElBaradei showed himself to be a man of great integrity and inde-pendence. As head of the IAEA, he repeatedly noted that he had found no evidence of Saddam Hussein's Iraq restarting a nuclear weapons programme. The warmongering George W. Bush administration – bent on 'regime change' in Iraq – sought, however, to ignore the truth, and attempted to discredit ElBaradei, criticising him for being too soft on Iran and too hard on Israel. In his 2011 memoir *The Age of Deception* ElBaradei noted how the IAEA exposed American deceit in seeking to use forged documents to prove that Saddam Hussein had sought to purchase uranium from Niger. The Egyptian technocrat criticised Washington's belligerent approach in refusing to negotiate with Iran while seeking domineeringly to set the terms of a solution. He also exposed the twisted logic in the irrational American approach: attacking a country (Iraq) without nuclear weapons, and vacillating while another (North Korea) acquired them.[35]

The Egyptian doggedly fought and won a third term as head of the IAEA in 2005 in the face of strong and petty opposition from Uncle Sam, reminiscent of the vindictively prejudiced American campaign that had denied ElBaradei's compatriot Boutros Boutros-Ghali a second term as UN Secretary General in 1996.[36] A few months later, ElBaradei and his IAEA won the Nobel Peace Prize for 'their efforts to prevent nuclear energy from being used for military purposes'. In his Nobel Prize speech, the Egyptian technocrat sought to link the nuclear threat to problems of poverty and underdevelopment. He warned against the nuclear hypocrisy of certain countries arrogating to themselves the right to possess weapons that they sought to deny to others, and argued that global nuclear disarmament was the only viable solution to this problem: the nuclear genie could clearly not be put back in the bottle. Following his retirement from the IAEA in 2009, the Egyptian technocrat returned home to play an important role in pro-democracy efforts, as described by Morad Abou-Sabé in his essay (Chapter 11).

The fact that ElBaradei agreed to serve an illegitimate military-installed interim regime in Egypt as vice president following a coup against the elected government of Mohamed Morsi in July 2013, however, spoke volumes about the opportunism of Egypt's political class. His call for the 'rectification of the revolution' echoed the language employed by the head of state of Burkina Faso, Blaise Compaoré, following his brutal 1987 coup that assassinated the charismatic military ruler Thomas Sankara. ElBaradei's plea for the international community to provide aid was heeded by autocratic sheikhdoms such as Kuwait, Saudi Arabia and the United Arab Emirates, which offered $12 billion. Following

35. Mohamed ElBaradei, *The Age of Deception: Nuclear Diplomacy in Treacherous Times* (New York: Holt, 2010), pp. 4–8.

36. See Adekeye Adebajo, 'The Pharaoh and the Prophet: Boutros Boutros-Ghali and Kofi Annan', in Adebajo, *The Curse of Berlin*, pp. 77–97.

the killing of about 1,000 pro-Morsi demonstrators by security forces, ElBaradei resigned from his post in protest in August 2013.

KOFI ANNAN

Ghana's Kofi Annan served as UN Secretary General between 1997 and 2006, and shared the 2001 Nobel Peace Prize with his organisation. During his ten-year tenure, Annan courageously, but perhaps naively, acted as a 'secular pope' in championing the cause of 'humanitarian intervention'. After a steep decline in the mid-1990s, UN peacekeeping increased again by 2005 to around 80,000 troops with a budget of $3.2 billion. African countries like Sudan, the Congo, Liberia, Ethiopia, Eritrea and Côte d'Ivoire were the main beneficiaries. Annan also dislodged the UN bureaucracy from its creative inertia to embrace views and actors from outside the system. He reached out for advice from civil society groups, organising seminars with policy institutes and encouraging the United Nations to work more with these actors in the field. Annan also promoted the cause of women in UN institutions, appointing Canada's Louise Fréchette as his deputy, and Ireland's Mary Robinson as his High Commissioner for Human Rights.[37]

One lingering accusation that Kofi Annan has not quite been able to shake off is that, while serving as UN Undersecretary General for Peacekeeping in 1994, he did not respond appropriately to a cable warning of an impending genocide in Rwanda. Much controversy still remains over his failure to report the contents of this cable – sent three months before the massacres begun in January 1994 from Canadian UN force commander General Roméo Dallaire, who asked for authorisation to take military action to forestall the impending genocide – to both UN Secretary General Boutros Boutros-Ghali and the Security Council. A subsequent UN inquiry report published in December 1999 criticised Annan and his deputy, Iqbal Riza, for this shortcoming.[38]

---

37. See ibid.
38. See *Report of the Independent Inquiry into the actions of the United Nations during the 1994 genocide in Rwanda*, 16 December 1999, S/1999/1257. See also Linda Melvern, *A People Betrayed: The Role of the West in Rwanda's Genocide* (London: Zed Books, 2000), p. 93.

Right-wing British politician Enoch Powell once famously noted that all political careers end in failure. This appeared to be particularly apt as one observed the tragic twilight of Annan's tenure as UN Secretary General. (Gwendolyn Mikell's essay, Chapter 13 in this volume, offers a kinder verdict on Annan's tenure.)[39] In retrospect, the 2001 Nobel citation that praised the Ghanaian technocrat for being 'pre-eminent in bringing new life to the organisation'[40] sounded anachronistic by 2006 in light of the Rwandan genocide, the oil-for-food scandal in Iraq (in which Annan's son, Kojo, was implicated in questionable business dealings), and the failure of UN reform in 2005. The Ghanaian failed fundamentally to transform the UN or to achieve a durable legacy. Annan's troubled exit from the post could yet transform him, in the hands of future historians, into a prophet without honour, embroiled in scandal during his final years and rendered a lame duck by the USA – the country that had done the most to anoint him UN Secretary General in 1996. Annan finally and painfully discovered the ancient wisdom: that one needs a long spoon to sup with the devil.

Three Women Activists from Kenya and Liberia

Wangari Maathai, Ellen Johnson Sirleaf and Leymah Gbowee all fought for the emancipation and equality of women in Kenya and Liberia. All three had prophesies and watershed moments that seemed to push them towards their destinies. All three strong-willed women separated from their partners due to abuse. Maathai and Gbowee largely waged their struggles through acts of civil disobedience involving civil society groups, while Sirleaf fought her battles first as a senior civil servant, and then in various political formations before becoming Africa's first elected female leader in 2006.

---

39. For Annan's defence of his own record, see Kofi Annan, *Interventions: A Life in War and Peace* (New York: Penguin, 2012).

40. Nobel Peace Committee, 'Nobel Peace Prize 2001', 12 October 2001, http://nobelprize.org/peace/laureates/2001/press.html.

WANGARI MAATHAI

Kenyan environmental campaigner Wangari Maathai died from cancer at the age of 71 in September 2011, a month before two African women joined the elite ranks of Nobel peace laureates. She was born in the village of Ihithe against the backdrop of the cloud-covered majesty of Mount Kenya. She drank water from the stream, but became conscious at an early age of the destruction of the country's forests by commercial plantations. As if by a prophetic vision, she resigned her professorship at the University of Nairobi in 1977 in a bid to save the country's forests and fight for the plight of rural women. She would eventually lead the Green Belt Movement to plant 30 million trees across Africa. Since deforestation and soil erosion were making it difficult for women to find firewood, the Green Belt Movement paid them to plant trees. Wangari fought consistently for women's and human rights, developing a citizen education programme. Her husband, however, left her for being 'too educated, too strong, too stubborn, and too hard to control'.[41] She was head of Kenya's National Council of Women, and successfully protested the corrupt and autocratic regime of Daniel arap Moi's effort in 1989 to build a high-rise office park in the green belt of Nairobi's Uhuru Park. As she defiantly noted: 'Our forefathers shed blood for our land.'[42] The government harassed and jailed Maathai during the 1990s as she extended her battle to advocating for the release of Kenya's political prisoners. Throughout these struggles, the tree remained the symbol of democratic contestation and conflict resolution.[43]

Maathai became the first African woman to be awarded the Nobel Peace Prize, in 2004, for her contributions to 'sustainable development, democracy and peace'. Many found it odd that an environmentalist could be awarded the prize, but this victory helped to reinforce the link between the environment, poverty, governance and conflict.

---

41. Quoted in Stenersen, Libaek and Sveen, *The Nobel Peace Prize*, in the addendum of laureates 2001–05, 'Wangari Maathai', p. 13.
42. Quoted in *The Take Away*, 'Wangari Maathai Discusses "The Challenge of Africa"', 10 April 2009 (www.the takeaway.org).
43. See Wangari Maathai, *The Green Belt Movement: Sharing the Approach and the Experience* (New York: Lantern, 2004); Wangari Maathai, *Unbowed: A Memoir* (New York: Knopf, 2006); Wangari Maathai, *The Challenge for Africa: A New Vision* (London: Heinemann, 2009).

Remarkably, only twelve of the 116 Nobel peace laureates had been women at the time of this award.[44] Wangari identified totally with Africa. At the traditional waving to the crowd on the balcony while receiving the Nobel Prize in Oslo, she danced a joyous African dance. At her Nobel lecture, she was resplendent in an orange and black African dress with headgear to match, saying: 'I am especially mindful of women and the girl child. I hope it [the prize] will encourage them to raise their voices and take more space for leadership.'[45]

In 2002, Wangari was elected to the Kenyan parliament, and a year later became assistant minister for the environment. In 2005 she became the first president of the African Union's Economic, Cultural and Social Council (ECOSOCC).[46] This was a controversial appointment, as Wangari was a Kenyan politician, purportedly representing the main civil society organ of the continental body. She also had her critics, who accused her of lacking intellectual *gravitas* and lambasted her for a statement that the AIDS virus may have been created in Western laboratories as a 'biological weapon' to annihilate African populations, a statement that Wangari denied having made.[47] As Maathai noted in her Nobel peace lecture in 2004: 'We are called to assist the Earth to heal her wounds.'[48] With her life's struggles complete, the world bid farewell to Africa's indomitable 'Earth Mother' in 2011.

ELLEN JOHNSON SIRLEAF

Two Liberian women were awarded the Nobel Peace Prize in 2011: President Ellen Johnson Sirleaf and civil society's Leymah Gbowee (Yemeni activist Tawakul Karman also shared the award). The awarding of the Peace Prize to Sirleaf for championing women's rights, in October 2011, four days before a presidential election, must, however,

---

44. See Judith Hicks Stiehm, *Champions for Peace: Women Winners of the Nobel Peace Prize* (Lanham MD: Rowman & Littlefield, 2006).

45. See Wangari Maathai's Nobel Peace Prize speech, www.nobelprize.org.

46. See, for example, Charles Mutasa, 'A Critical Appraisal of the African Union–ECOSOCC Civil Society Interface', in John Akokpari, Angela Ndinga-Muvumba and Tim Murithi (eds), *The African Union and Its Institutions* (Johannesburg: Jacana, 2008), pp. 291–306.

47. See Jeffrey Gettleman, 'Wangari Maathai, Nobel Peace Prize Laureate, Dies at 71', *New York Times*, 26 September 2011 (www.nytimes.com).

48. See Wangari Maathai's Nobel Peace Prize speech.

count as one of the most political acts in the history of the prize. It would be hard to imagine the prize being awarded to a sitting American or European leader less than a week before an election. This prize also demonstrated the enormous gulf between international perceptions of Liberia's 'Iron Lady' and the more critical view that many Liberians and West Africans had of Sirleaf based on her six years in office and past political record.

Under the leadership of the 75-year-old 'Ma Ellen'[49] – one of Africa's most accomplished technocrats – Liberia made some impressive progress. The country's external debt of $5.8 billion was largely forgiven. About $16 billion in foreign direct investment flowed into the country. Some infrastructure was repaired. An inherited budget of $80 million was quadrupled. Yet many of Sirleaf's domestic critics questioned her somewhat messianic and sometimes selectively ruthless approach to leadership. In what was clearly the biggest misjudgement of her career, Sirleaf helped raise $10,000 to support Charles Taylor's National Patriotic Front of Liberia (NPFL) rebel movement, which launched a war against Samuel Doe's brutal regime in December 1989. She went to visit the warlord in his bush hideout in 1990. Taylor, who was tried between 2008 and 2012 for alleged war crimes committed in Sierra Leone (and jailed for fifty years), later claimed that Sirleaf had been the international coordinator of his movement between 1986 and 1994.

The problems inherited by Sirleaf's administration clearly overwhelmed her. Unemployment stood at 95 per cent six years into her presidency, while foreign aid of $425 million exceeded the country's $370 million annual budget. Former combatants were not being provided with jobs quickly enough, leading to instability and crime. In December 2010, Berlin-based Transparency International, in its Global Corruption Barometer, named Liberia the most corrupt country in the world. As African governments vociferously opposed the presence of an American military Africa Command on their territory, Sirleaf, as president, uniquely called for the Command to be located in her

---

49. For her own perspective on her record, see Ellen Johnson Sirleaf, *This Child Will Be Great: Memoirs of a Remarkable Life by Africa's First Woman President* (New York: HarperCollins, 2009).

country, opportunistically and short-sightedly demonstrating greater faith in American arms than in Liberian institutions. The slow pace of change in the eight years of her presidency made Liberians wary of Sirleaf's lofty rhetoric. She broke her promise to serve only a single term, thus spurning the example of her professed hero and fellow Nobel laureate Nelson Mandela. Given the timing of this award and her political track record, the ennobling of Liberia's 'Iron Lady' must count as one of the most controversial acts in the history of the prize.

LEYMAH GBOWEE

Leymah Gbowee, a 41-year-old Liberian former social worker, has been a key figure in West Africa's women's movement. Citing Gandhi and fellow Nobel laureate Marin Luther King Jr as among her key influences, Gbowee served until December 2012 as the executive director of the Accra-based Women Peace and Security Network (WIPSN–A), which works across the West African subregion in Liberia, Nigeria, Sierra Leone and Côte d'Ivoire to promote peace, political participation and literacy. She previously coordinated the Women in Peacebuilding Programme/West African Network for Peacebuilding (WIPNET/WANEP). She also served on Liberia's Truth and Reconciliation Commission and was a staunch supporter of fellow laureate Ellen Johnson Sirleaf, helping to mobilize Liberian women to vote for her in presidential elections in 2005 and 2011.[50] This relationship spectacularly soured in 2012 when Gbowee resigned as head of the Commission, charging Sirleaf with nepotism and with neglecting to address the widening gap between rich and poor. Gbowee made a name for herself during Liberia's second civil war in April 2003 (based apparently on a dream in which she heard a voice urging her to rally the women of her church to the cause of peace) when she mobilised Liberian women – across religious and social backgrounds – to push then warlord-president Charles Taylor

---

50. See, for example, Tamasin Ford, 'Leymah Gbowee: Profile', *Guardian*, 7 October 2011 (www.theguardian.com); Bob Herbert, 'A Crazy Dream', *New York Times*, 31 January 2009 (www.nytimes.com).

and the Liberians United for Reconciliation and Democracy (LURD) rebels to sign a peace accord in Accra.

These events were well captured in the 2008 documentary *Pray the Devil Back to Hell* and passionately recounted in Gbowee's 2011 memoir *Mighty Be Our Powers*.[51] Galvanised by radio messages, thousands of Liberian women protested every day near an open-air fish market in Monrovia, praying, picketing and fasting for peace. They eventually forced Taylor to meet with them, with Gbowee presenting a petition as leader of the group and demanding an end to the war. She then led about 200 women to occupy the negotiation hall in Accra in July 2003, acting as their eloquent and determined spokeswoman in demanding that a peace deal be signed. Her protest methods were sometimes unorthodox: threatening to strip naked in the negotiation hall, and urging women to embark on a 'sex strike' to pressure their husbands to support peace efforts. The women also contributed to disarmament efforts, sometimes winning the trust of child soldiers, who regarded them as their 'mothers'.

Though Gbowee and her courageous female activists clearly made a significant contribution to peace efforts through their 'mass action' in Liberia over a period of two and a half years, it is important not to exaggerate this role – as some have done, for example, in the documentary *Pray the Devil Back to Hell* – as having directly halted the conflict. Such an interpretation would ignore more important variables such as the military successes of the LURD rebel movement; Taylor's indictment for war crimes in June 2003 and subsequent departure into Nigerian exile three years later through assurances from regional leaders; and American pressure on the warlord-president to leave power on account of allegations of a link with al-Qaeda through diamonds sold by Sierra Leonean rebels.

---

51. Leymah Gbowee and Carol Mithers, *Mighty Be Our Powers: How Sisterhood, Prayer, and Sex Changed a Nation at War – A Memoir* (New York: Beast, 2011).

Concluding remarks

It is worth briefly noting the irony that the first African Nobel Peace
Prize went to a country – South Africa – that would be the last to gain
its independence, in 1994. The most recent Nobel peace laureates, in
2011, went to two remarkable women from a country – Liberia – that
had enjoyed freedom from foreign rule since 1847.

US president Barack Obama followed in the footsteps of ten
illustrious laureates of African descent, while two African women
have been awarded the prize since his 2009 nomination for the Nobel
Peace Prize. Obama's own achievements will be measured by how he
builds on the legacy of those who came before and after him: from the
civil rights struggle of Bunche and King to the anti-apartheid struggle
of Luthuli, Tutu and Mandela; from the peacemaking of Sadat, Annan
and de Klerk to the environmental activism of Maathai, the nuclear
disarmament of ElBaradei and the women's rights struggle of Sirleaf
and Gbowee.

None of Obama's ten Nobel predecessors of African descent, nor the
two that came after him, were in a powerful enough position to secure
world peace. The young 'Afro-Saxon'[52] president of the most powerful
nation on earth is the first Nobel peace laureate of African descent who
has a chance to leave an indelible mark on global peace and security:
supporting UN and regional peacekeeping efforts in Africa, securing
peace in the Middle East, promoting nuclear disarmament, confronting
domestic and international racism, and championing environmental
and women's rights. The most deserving Nobel peace laureate not to
have won the prize, Mahatma Gandhi, noted in 1936 that it was 'maybe
through the Negroes that the unadulterated message of non-violence
will be delivered to the world'.[53] Through the example of the thirteen
prophets of Pax Africana examined in this book, could this prophecy
yet be fulfilled?

---

52. This expression is borrowed from Ali Mazrui.
53. Quoted in Ali Mazrui, 'Africa and Other Civilizations: Conquest and Counter-Conquest', in
John W. Harbeson and Donald Rothchild (eds), *Africa in World Politics: The African State System
in Flux*, 3rd edn (Boulder CO: Westview, 2000), p. 127.

Bibliography

Abdul-Raheem, Tajudeen (ed.), *Pan-Africanism: Politics, Economy, and Social Change in the Twenty-First Century* (London: Pluto, 1996).

Adebajo, Adekeye, *The Curse of Berlin: Africa after the Cold War* (New York: Columbia University Press, 2010).

Adedeji, Adebayo (ed.), *South Africa and Africa: Within or Apart?* (London: Zed Books, 1996).

Ali, Tariq, *The Obama Syndrome: Surrender at Home, War Abroad* (London: Verso, 2010).

Allen, John, *Rabble-Rouser for Peace: The Authorised Biography of Desmond Tutu* (London and Johannesburg: Random House, 2006).

Annan, Kofi, foreword to *Mandela: The Authorised Portrait* (London: Bloomsbury, 2006).

Annan, Kofi, *Interventions: A Life in War and Peace* (New York: Penguin, 2012).

Barber, James, *Mandela's World: The International Dimension of South Africa's Political Revolution, 1990–99* (Cape Town: David Philip, 2004).

Bentley, Kristina, and Roger Southall, *An African Peace Process: Mandela, South Africa, and Burundi* (Cape Town: Human Sciences Research Council, 2005).

Boehmer, Elleke, *Nelson Mandela: A Very Short Introduction* (Oxford: Oxford University Press, 2008).

Boseley, Sarah, 'US Grapples with Neglect of HIV', *Mail and Guardian* (South Africa), 13–19 July 2012, p. 30.

Boutros-Ghali, Boutros, *Egypt's Road to Jerusalem: A Diplomat's Story of the Struggle for Peace in the Middle East* (New York: Random, 1997).

Brown, Judith M., *Gandhi:Prisoner of Hope* (New Haven CT: Yale University Press, 1989).

Brown, Judith M., and Martin Prozesky (eds), *Gandhi and South Africa: Principles and Politics* (Pietermaritzburg: University of Natal Press, 1996).

Campbell, Horace G., *Barack Obama and Twenty-First Century Politics: A Revolutionary Movement in the USA* (New York: Pluto, 2010).

Carr, David, 'Debating Drones, in the Open', *New York Times*, 10 February 2013 (www.nytimes.com).

de Klerk, F.W., *The Last Trek – A New Beginning: The Autobiography* (London: Pan, 2000 [1999]).

The Economist, 'Unmanned Aerial Warfare', *The Economist*, 8 October 2011, p. 32.

ElBaradei, Mohamed, *The Age of Deception: Nuclear Diplomacy in Treacherous Times* (New York: Holt, 2010).

Fanon, Frantz, *The Wretched of the Earth* (New York: Grove, 1963).

Firstbrook, Peter, *The Obamas: The Untold Story of an African Family* (New York: Random House, 2011).

Ford, Tamasin, 'Leymah Gbowee: Profile', *Guardian,* 7 October 2011 (www.guardian.co.uk).

Foreign Policy, 'Obama's Secret Wars', special report, *Foreign Policy*, March–April 2012.

Frängsmyr, Tore, *Alfred Nobel* (Stockholm: Swedish Institute, 1996).

Gandhi, M.K., *An Autobiography – or, The Story of My Experiments with the Truth* (London: Penguin, 2001 [1927]).

Gbowee, Leymah, and Carol Mithers, *Mighty Be Our Powers: How Sisterhood, Prayer, and Sex Changed a Nation at War – A Memoir* (New York: Beast, 2011).

Gettleman, Jeffrey, 'Wangari Maathai, Nobel Peace Prize Laureate, Dies at 71', *New York Times*, 26 September 2011 (www.nytimes.com).

Gettleman, Jeffrey, and Eric Schmitt, 'American Raid in Somalia Kills Qaeda Militant', *New York Times*, 15 September 2009, pp. A1, A11.

Grant, Colin, *Negro with a Hat: The Rise and Fall of Marcus Garvey and His Dream of Mother Africa* (Oxford: Oxford University Press, 2008).

Herbert, Bob, 'A Crazy Dream', *New York Times*, 31 January 2009 (www.nytimes.com).

Hill, Robert A., and Edmond J. Keller (eds), *Trustee for the Human Community: Ralph J. Bunche, the United Nations, and the Decolonisation of Africa* (Athens: Ohio University Press, 2010).

Hutchful, Eboe, 'Understanding the African Security Crisis', in Abdel-Fatau Musah and J. Kayode Fayemi (eds), *Mercenaries: An African Security Dilemma* (London: Pluto, 2000).

King Jr, Martin Luther, 'Birth of a New Nation', sermon delivered at the Dexter Avenue Baptist Church, Montgomery, Alabama, 7 April 1957 (www.modernghana.com).

Landsberg, Chris, 'Promoting Democracy: The Mandela–Mbeki Doctrine', *Journal of Democracy* 11(3) (July 2000), pp. 107–21.

Lexington, 'One Year of the One', *The Economist*, 29 October 2009 (www.economist.com).

Lindsay, Beverly (ed.), *Ralph Johnson Bunche: Public Intellectual and Nobel Peace Laureate* (Urbana: University of Illinois Press, 2007).

Lodge, Tom, *Mandela: A Critical Life* (Oxford: Oxford University Press, 2006).

Luthuli, Albert, Nobel Peace Prize speech, www.nobelprize.org/nobel_prizes/peace/laureates/1960/lutuli-acceptance.html.

Maathai, Wangari, *The Green Belt Movement: Sharing the Approach and the Experience* (New York: Lantern, 2004).

Maathai, Wangari, *Unbowed: A Memoir* (New York: Knopf, 2006).

Maathai, Wangari, *The Challenge for Africa: A New Vision* (London: Heinemann, 2009).

MacAskill, Ewen, and Saeed Shah, 'US Casualties in Afghanistan to Rise, Says Biden', *Guardian*, 26 January 2009, p. 17.

Mangcu, Xolela (ed.), *The Meaning of Mandela: A Literary and Intellectual Celebration* (Cape Town: Human Sciences Research Council, 2006).

Maraniss, David, *Barack Obama: The Story* (New York: Simon & Schuster, 2012).

Mazrui, Ali A., *Towards a Pax Africana: A Study of Ideology and Ambition* (Chicago: University of Chicago Press, 1967).

Mazrui, Ali A., 'Dr. Schweitzer's Racism', *Transition* 53 (1991).

Mazrui, Ali, 'Africa and Other Civilizations: Conquest and Counter-Conquest', in John W. Harbeson and Donald Rothchild (eds), *Africa in World Politics: The African State System in Flux*, 3rd edn (Boulder CO: Westview, 2000).

Melvern, Linda, *A People Betrayed: The Role of the West in Rwanda's Genocide* (London: Zed Books, 2000).

Mendell, David, *Obama: From Promise to Power* (New York: HarperCollins, 2007).

Mutasa, Charles, 'A Critical Appraisal of the African Union–ECOSOCC Civil Society Interface', in John Akokpari, Angela Ndinga-Muvumba and Tim Murithi (eds), *The African Union and Its Institutions* (Johannesburg: Jacana, 2008), pp. 291–306.

Nkrumah, Kwame, *Africa Must Unite* (London: Panaf, 1963).

Nobel Peace Committee, 'Nobel Peace Prize 2001', 12 October 2001, http://nobelprize.org/peace/laureates/2001/press.html.

Obama, Barack, *Dreams from My Father: A Story of Race and Inheritance* (New York: Three Rivers, 1995).

Obama, Barack, *The Audacity of Hope: Thoughts on Reclaiming the American Dream* (New York: Crown, 2006).

Obama, Barack, Nobel Peace Prize speech, Oslo, 10 December 2009 (www.nobelprize.org).

Padmore, George, *Pan-Africanism or Communism? The Coming Struggle in Africa* (London: Dobson, 1956).

Parekh, Bhikhu, *Gandhi: A Very Short Introduction* (Oxford: Oxford University Press, 1997).

Remnick, David, *The Bridge: The Life and Rise of Barack Obama* (New York: Random House, 2010).

Report of the Independent Inquiry into the Actions of the United Nations during the 1994 Genocide in Rwanda, 16 December 1999, S/1999/1257.

el-Sadat, Anwar, *In Search of Identity* (London: Collins, 1978).

Sampson, Anthony, *Mandela: The Authorised Biography* (London: HarperCollins, 1999).

Sellström, Tor, 'The Trusteeship Council: Decolonisation and Liberation', in Adekeye Adebajo (ed.), *From Global Apartheid to Global Village: Africa and the United Nations* (Scottsville: University of KwaZulu-Natal Press, 2009), pp. 107–37.

Shah, Saeed, 'US Missiles Strike on Taliban Stronghold in Pakistan Tribal Area Kills 30', *Guardian*, 17 February 2009, p. 23.

Sirleaf, Ellen Johnson, *This Child Will Be Great: Memoirs of a Remarkable Life by Africa's First Woman President* (New York: HarperCollins, 2009).

Sooka, Yasmin, 'Race and Reconciliation: *E Pluribus Unum*?', in Adekeye Adebajo, Adebayo Adedeji and Chris Landsberg (eds), *South Africa in Africa: The Post-Apartheid Era* (Scottsville: University of KwaZulu-Natal Press, 2007), pp. 78–91.

Stenersen, Øivind, Ivar Libaek and Asle Sveen, *The Nobel Peace Prize: One Hundred Years for Peace* (Oslo: J.W. Cappelens Forlag, 2001, and addendum of laureates 2001–05), pp. 10–14.

Stiehm, Judith Hicks, *Champions for Peace: Women Winners of the Nobel Peace Prize* (Lanham MD: Rowman & Littlefield, 2006).

Sundquist, Eric J. (ed.), *The Oxford W.E.B. Du Bois Reader* (New York: Oxford University Press, 1996).

Sutherland, Bill, and Matt Meyer, *Guns and Gandhi: Pan-African Insights on Nonviolence, Armed Struggle and Liberation* (Trenton NJ: Africa World Press, 2000).

The Take Away, 'Wangari Maathai Discusses "The Challenge of Africa"', 10 April 2009 (www.the takeaway.org).

Urquhart, Brian, *Ralph Bunche: An American Life* (New York: Norton, 1993).

Wallerstein, Immanuel, *Africa: The Politics of Unity* (New York: Vintage, 1967).

Walzer, Michael, *Just and Unjust Wars: A Moral Argument with Historical Illustrations*, 2nd edn (New York: Basic Books, 1992).

Young, Crawford, 'Ralph Bunche and Patrice Lumumba: The Fatal Encounter', in Robert A. Hill and Edmond J. Keller (eds), *Trustee for the Human Community: Ralph J. Bunche, the United Nations, and the Decolonisation of Africa* (Athens: Ohio University Press, 2010), pp. 128–47.

Zenko, Micah, 'How Barack Obama Has Tried to Open up the One-Sided Drone War', *Financial Times*, 23 May 2013 (www.ft.com).

TWO

BARACK OBAMA: BETWEEN RACIAL
COMPATRIOTS AND NOBEL ANCESTORS

ALI A. MAZRUI

The term 'Afro-pessimism' is now familiar in Africanist circles.[1] It refers to the widespread tendency to expect mainly bad news out of Africa. Less frequently used is the term 'Afro-optimism', indicating a strong readiness to give Africa the benefit of the doubt. In 2008, two historical prophecies, both of them Afro-optimistic, were still seeking fulfilment in the struggle to elect the first black president of the United States. The first was made by Mohandas 'Mahatma' Gandhi in 1936, who prophesied that 'it may be through the Negroes that the unadulterated message of non-violence will be delivered to the world'.[2] The second was made by Robert F. Kennedy in 1968, the year of his assassination. In an interview on *Voice of America*, he prophesied that around the year 2008 the United States would elect its first 'Negro president'. Both Gandhi and Kennedy were speaking at a time when it was still politically correct to use the word 'Negro' when referring to

1. For some of the research for this chapter, I am indebted to Seifudein Adem and Ravenna Narizzano-Bronson of the Institute of Global Cultural Studies at Binghamton University in New York.
2. See *Harijan*, 14 March 1936.

a black person. Kennedy formulated his prophecy as follows: '[Things are] moving so fast in race relations a Negro could be president in 40 years.... There is no question about it. In the next 40 years a Negro can achieve the same position that my brother [John F. Kennedy] had.'[3]

The election of Barack Hussein Obama to the US presidency in the election of November 2008 fulfilled Robert Kennedy's prophecy with staggering precision. Nostradamus, the sixteenth-century Renaissance astrologer, would have been envious. But what has that got to do with Mahatma Gandhi's prophecy seventy-two years earlier that the torch of *satyagraha* (soul force) would be passed to black people and make them the vanguard of global non-violence? Let us deal with the fate of Gandhi's prophecy prior to the election of Barack Obama before we explore the implications of Obama's election for both prophecies.

In the Shadow of Gandhi

It is one of the curious facts of history that, outside India itself, the torch of Gandhi came to be passed most prominently not to his fellow Asians but to blacks both in the New World and in Africa. It is not without significance that among the first non-white winners of the Nobel Peace Prize – Obama's Nobel ancestors – were Ralph Bunche, Chief Albert Luthuli, Martin Luther King Jr and Archbishop Desmond Tutu.

Perhaps Gandhi himself would not have been surprised. Having lived in South Africa for twenty-one years, until 1914, quite early in his life he saw non-violent resistance as a method that would be well suited for the African as well as the Indian. In 1924, Gandhi said that if the black people 'caught the spirit of the Indian movement, their progress must be rapid'.[4] The most impressive progress of all has been Obama's

---

3. Robert Kennedy's brother, John F. Kennedy, had broken the de facto American taboo against electing a Roman Catholic as president of the United States. Robert Kennedy thought the taboo against a black president would be broken forty years from 1968. See *Washington Post*, 27 May 1968. The late Tim Russert reminded American television audiences in June 2008 of Robert Kennedy's prophecy.

4. *Young India, 1924–1926* (Madras: Ganesan, 1927), pp. 839–40. See also Pyarelal Nayyar, 'Gandhiji and the African Question', *Africa Quarterly* 2(2) (July–September 1962). See also the selection from Gandhi titled 'Mahatma Gandhi on Freedom in Africa', *Africa Quarterly* 1(2) (July–September 1961). For a more extensive discussion by Gandhi on non-violence, see Gandhi, *Non-Violence in Peace*

rise to the American presidency. And yet to understand Gandhi's claim, one should perhaps link it to something later said by his disciple Jawaharlal Nehru, India's first prime minister and the intellectual father of 'non-alignment': 'Reading through history I think the agony of the African continent ... has not been equalled anywhere.'[5]

Thus to the extent that the black man or woman had more to be angry about than other men or women, he or she would need greater self-discipline than others to be 'passive' in his or her resistance. But, by the same token, to the extent that black people in the past four centuries had suffered more than any other people, passive but purposeful self-sacrifice for the cause should come easier to them. And to the extent that blacks had more to forgive the rest of the world for, this forgiveness, when it came, should be all the more weighty. Perhaps in response to the sum of these considerations, Gandhi came to the conclusion by 1936, as noted earlier, that 'it may be through the Negroes that the unadulterated message of non-violence will be delivered to the world'.[6] Would Mohandas be more accurately vindicated than Nostradamus?

Certainly in America, the torch came to be passed to Martin Luther King Jr. And in South Africa, where Gandhi first experimented with his methods of *satyagraha*, the torch passed to Albert Luthuli and later to Desmond Tutu. In Northern Rhodesia (Zambia before independence), its founding leader, Kenneth Kaunda, became a vigorous Gandhian, arguing: 'I reject absolutely violence in any of its forms as a solution to our problems.'[7] But, like Gandhi himself, Kaunda never won the Nobel Peace Prize. Is there a paradox in Gandhi's prophecy that it may be through black people that the unadulterated message of 'soul force' and passive resistance will be realised?[8] If Gandhi was correct,

and War, 2nd edn (Ahmedabad: Navajivan, 1944).

5. Jawaharlal Nehru, 'Portuguese Colonialism: An Anachronism', *Africa Quarterly* 1(3) (October–December 1961), p. 9. See also Jawaharlal Nehru, 'Emergent Africa', *Africa Quarterly* 1(1) (April–June 1961), pp. 7–9.

6. *Harijan*, 14 March 1936.

7. See Kenneth Kaunda, *Black Government?* (Lusaka: United Society for Christian Literature, 1960).

8. See Sudarshan Kapur, *Raising up a Prophet: The African-American Encounter with Gandhi* (Boston MA: Beacon, 1992), pp. 89–90.

this would be one more illustration of a culture that gives birth to an idea that it does not necessarily fulfil itself.

The Oslo-based Nobel Peace Committee seems to have shared some of Gandhi's optimism about the 'soul force' of black people. Thirteen Africans or people of African descent have won the Nobel Peace Prize since the middle of the twentieth century: Ralph Bunche (1950), Albert Luthuli (1960), Martin Luther King Jr (1964), Anwar Sadat (1978), Desmond Tutu (1984), Nelson Mandela (1993), Frederik Willem de Klerk (1993), Kofi Annan (2001), Wangari Maathai (2004), Mohamed ElBaradei (2005), Barack Obama (2009), Ellen Johnson Sirleaf (2011) and Leymah Gbowee (2011) – to each of whom a chapter in this volume is devoted. Neither Gandhi himself nor any of his compatriots in India seem to have been seriously considered for the Nobel Peace Prize for much of the twentieth century. Was the Indian political-spiritual leader vindicated in his view that the so-called Negro was going to be the best exemplar of 'soul force'? Was this a case of African culture being empirically more Gandhian than Indian culture?

In reality, Africans have perpetrated just as much violence as Indians. What is distinctive about Africans is their short memory of hate. In Kenya – the land of Barack Obama's father – Jomo Kenyatta was unjustly imprisoned by the British colonial authorities in 1952 on charges of having founded the Mau Mau resistance movement. A British governor, Patrick Renison, denounced Kenyatta as 'a leader unto darkness and death'.[9] And yet when Kenyatta was released from jail in 1961, he not only forgave the white settlers but turned the whole country towards a pro-Western orientation, to which it has remained committed ever since. Kenyatta even published a book in 1968 titled *Suffering Without Bitterness*.[10]

Ian Smith, the white settler leader of Rhodesia, unilaterally declared independence in 1965 and unleashed a civil war on the country. Thousands of people, mainly black, died as a result of racist policies

9. This was the appellation given to Jomo Kenyatta by British governor Patrick Renison, according to the Kenyan Ministry of External Affairs. See www.mfa.go.ke/kenyatta.html, accessed 28 December 2005.
10. Jomo Kenyatta, *Suffering Without Bitterness* (Nairobi: East African Publishing House, 1968).

pursued by Smith for fifteen years. Yet when the war ended in 1980, Smith and his cohorts were not subjected to a Nuremberg-style trial. On the contrary, the Rhodesian leader himself became a member of parliament in a black-ruled Zimbabwe that busied itself in criticising its post-Smith black leaders – foremost of all Robert Mugabe – as incompetent and dishonest. Where else but in Africa could such tolerance occur?[11] India's memory of hate may not be as short as Africa's, but India appointed a Sikh – Manmohan Singh – as prime minister in 2008, even though Sikhs had assassinated a Hindu prime minister, Indira Gandhi, in 1984.

We have also witnessed the phenomenon of South Africa's Nelson Mandela, Obama's racial compatriot. Mandela lost twenty-seven of the best years of his life in prison under the laws of the apartheid regime. Yet when released in 1990, he not only promoted a policy of reconciliation, but also often went beyond the call of duty. On one occasion before he became president in 1994, white men were fasting to death after being convicted of terrorist offences by their own white government; Mandela went out of his way to beg them to eat, and thus spare their own lives. When Mandela became president of South Africa in 1994, it was surely enough that his government would leave the architects of apartheid unmolested. Yet he went out of his way to pay a social call and have tea with the unrepentant widow of Hendrik F. Verwoerd, the supreme architect of the worst forms of apartheid, who had shaped the whole racist order from 1958 to 1966.[12]

Was Mahatma Gandhi correct, after all, that his torch of *satyagraha* might find its brightest manifestations among black people? The latest test is now at hand. A black man has been elected, and re-elected, president of the United States. Is Barack Obama likely to manifest Gandhian 'soul force'? He is preceded by an American tradition that salutes warrior-presidents. Being 'presidential' has been equated with

11. See also Anthony Parsons, 'From Southern Rhodesia to Zimbabwe, 1965–1985', *International Affairs* 9(4) (November 1988); Victor de Waal, *The Politics of Reconciliation: Zimbabwe's First Decade* (London: Hurst, 1981).
12. On Nelson Mandela's meeting with Verwoerd, see Anthony Sampson, *Mandela: The Authorized Biography* (New York: Knopf, 1999), p. 514.

being ready to order military action (see Robinson, Chapter 3 in this volume).

Less than a year after assuming office as US president in January 2009, Obama won the Nobel Peace Prize. He was the fourth American president to win the prize – preceded by Theodore Roosevelt (1905), Woodrow Wilson (1919) and Jimmy Carter (2002, twenty-two years after leaving office). For some, it is easier to understand how Obama became US president than why he won the Nobel Prize so soon after election. Did Oslo provide the right reasons?

The Hidden Agenda behind Obama's Nobel Prize

Although the conscious rationale of the Oslo Foundation for awarding Barack Obama the Nobel Peace Prize was based on his diplomatic efforts, the hidden agenda among those who nominated Obama was almost certainly race relations. The issue of race as an aspect of peace has obsessed the Oslo Foundation for more than half a century. Of the six Nobel Peace Prizes awarded to sub-Saharan Africans, four have been awarded for achievements in race relations, to laureates Albert Luthuli, Archbishop Desmond Tutu, Nelson Mandela and F.W. de Klerk (who was, of course, a white South African). But there have been two notable Nobel exceptions to racial peace: Wangari Maathai (2004), whose best achievements were in development and environment, and Kofi Annan (2001), who shared the prize with the United Nations on issues of international peace.

But even race relations are surely broader than relations between blacks and whites. The Literature Prize has, in some respects, been more multiracial than the Peace Prize. The first breakthrough of a man of colour came in 1913 with the Literature Prize, awarded to Rabindranath Tagore of what was at the time British India. Since then, the geographical distribution of the Literature Prize has been quite wide. Its winners have indeed included Obama's racial compatriots.

In literature and economics, the African diaspora has produced fewer Nobel laureates than has the African continent itself. Diaspora

winners of the Literature Prize have included Derek Walcott of Saint
Lucia (1992) and Toni Morrison of the United States (1993). The
diaspora has also produced the black world's only Nobel Prize winner
for economics – Saint Lucia's William Arthur Lewis in 1964. Egypt's
Naguib Mahfouz won the Literature Prize in 1988. In black Africa south
of the Sahara, the only Nobel literature winner has been Wole Soyinka
of Nigeria in 1986. Two white South Africans – Nadine Gordimer (1991)
and John M. Coetzee (2003) – have also won the Literature Prize.

Obama's African-American Ancestors

Let us now turn to Obama's American legacy. We begin with what
W.E.B. DuBois, the famous African American intellectual (1868–1963),
and Obama had in common. Both were products of intermarriage
between black and white. Both carried names that betrayed their bi-
cultural descent. Barack Obama's name betrayed his Luo ancestry on
the side of his Kenyan father. William Edward Burghardt DuBois's
name betrayed his French legacy. Both suffered a crisis of identity in
their earlier years. In personal visage, DuBois was much fairer in skin
colour than Obama. However, over time, DuBois identified himself
with black identity more passionately than has Obama. Indeed, DuBois
came to see himself as first and foremost an African, and he eventually
naturalised as a citizen of Ghana. Obama, on the other hand, saw
himself as less and less of an African, despite the fact that his father
had been born an African and had died as a citizen of Kenya in 1982.
In terms of preferred policy, W.E.B. DuBois was a black Atlanticist.[13]
He dreamt of the unification of the African diaspora in the Americas,
with black Africa as a new racial commonwealth in the world system.
Barack Obama saw himself as fundamentally an American, and forever
a citizen of the United States.

In 1895, DuBois became the first African American to receive a
doctorate (in history) from Harvard University. In 1990, Obama became

---

13. On the concept of the 'black Atlantic', see Paul Gilroy, *The Black Atlantic: Modernity and Double Consciousness* (Cambridge MA: Harvard University Press, 1993).

the first African American to be elected president of the *Harvard Law Review*, and he later obtained a law degree from DuBois's alma mater. DuBois, in his younger years, was often regarded as 'not Negro enough', partly because he was fair-skinned, and partly because of his upper-social-class demeanour. Obama, throughout much of his career, was demeaned by some fellow African Americans as 'not black enough', more because he was brought up in a white family by his grandmother in Hawaii than simply because his Kansan mother had been white. In later years, Obama's brilliant Harvard career earned him the political stigma of 'elitist'.

Dubois's vision of the proper destiny for African Americans had two contemporary rivals. Booker T. Washington wanted African Americans temporarily to forgo political power, civil liberties and higher education in the liberal arts and the liberal professions. Through his 'Tuskegee Machine', Washington recommended that black youth focus on 'industrial education' instead. He was at the peak of his influence from 1895 to 1910. In contrast, DuBois's vision of education for black youth focused on cultivating what he called the 'Talented Tenth' in preparation for black entry into 'modern civilization'. Obama's world-view has almost never been Afro-centric in this way.

Another rival vision of black destiny in DuBois's era was that champthe-pioned by Marcus Garvey, a Jamaican immigrant to the United States who succeeded in mobilising many thousands of African Americans in the 1920s to pursue private enterprise, and aspire to migrate back to Africa en masse.[14] Garvey and DuBois debated each other in vitriolic terms and even exchanged racial epithets. In contrast, Obama has tried to avoid debating race with fellow African Americans – except his former radical pastor, Reverend Jeremiah Wright, during the presidential election campaign of 2008.

In their different ways, both DuBois and Garvey were black Atlanticists. But while DuBois aspired to send to Africa some members of the diaspora's 'Talented Tenth', to help develop and even 'civilise' the

---

14. See, for example, Colin Grant, *Negro with a Hat: The Rise and Fall of Marcus Garvey and His Dream of Mother Africa* (Oxford: Oxford University Press, 2008).

continent, Garvey believed in a kind of black Zionism. To Garvey, all African people in the diaspora were entitled to the 'right of return' to Africa. But since most of Africa was still colonised in the first half of the twentieth century, Garvey's dream was even more remote than DuBois's 'Talented Tenth'. Early in his presidency, in July 2009, Obama addressed the African continent from Accra, Ghana, where DuBois had become a citizen and lies buried.

While in policy terms DuBois limited himself to the unity of the black Atlantic, his own de facto concept of 'global Africa' included a version of the black Indian Ocean. Indeed, DuBois went to the extent of claiming that black-skinned South Asians, such as the Tamils of India and Sri Lanka, were descended from the black Africans of pre-recorded history. Obama's dream of a 'post-racial' America also had rival paradigms among African Americans. Civil rights stalwarts Jesse Jackson and Andrew Young believed in the integration of African Americans into mainstream American culture, but they still retained and defended black race-consciousness. Jackson and Young tried to promote a *multiracial* America, while Obama championed a *non-racial* America.

The third black school of thought in Barack Obama's life was that represented by his pastor for twenty years, Reverend Jeremiah Wright of Trinity United Church of Christ in Chicago. Reverend Wright's America was far from Obama's dream of a *non-racial* America. Nor was Wright's preferred America *multiracial* like that of Andrew Young and Jesse Jackson. Essentially, Wright sought *racial separatism*, although the wider church to which he belonged was committed to multiracialism and racial integration.

Obama's Global Compatriots

With regard to the wider range of Obama's racial compatriots, let us now deal with the distinction between 'Africans of the blood' and 'Africans of the soil'. Africans of the blood belong to the black race; Africans of the soil belong to the African continent, but are not necessarily of the black race. The first African Secretary General of the United Nations was Boutros Boutros-Ghali of Egypt, who is an African of the soil. He was succeeded by Kofi Annan of Ghana, who is an African of the blood.

Most Egyptians are not immigrants, and are therefore Africans of the soil by *ancestry*. Most white South Africans, on the other hand, are Africans of the soil by *adoption*. Ghanaians and Nigerians are, in reality, both Africans of the blood (as black people) and Africans of the soil (as children of Africa). On the other hand, diaspora black people, such as Barack Obama and Toni Morrison, are Africans of the blood (racially black), but are no longer Africans of the soil (they are now children of the diaspora instead).

Within the African continent itself, Africans of the soil have won more Literature Prizes than have Africans of the blood. Africans of the soil who have won the Literature Prize are Naguib Mahfouz of Egypt (1988), Nadine Gordimer of South Africa (1991) and John M. Coetzee of South African birth and now of Australia (2003), while Nigeria's Wole Soyinka (1986) is the only African of the blood who has won the Literature Prize. In contrast, Africans of the blood have won more Peace Prizes than have Africans of the soil. The former are Albert Luthuli of South Africa (1960), Archbishop Desmond Tutu of South Africa (1984), Nelson Mandela of South Africa (1993), Kofi Annan of Ghana (2001), Wangari Maathai of Kenya (2004), and Ellen Johnson Sirleaf and Leymah Gbowee of Liberia (2011). Africans of the soil include Egypt's Anwar Sadat (1978), South Africa's Frederik Willem de Klerk (1993) and Egypt's Mohamed ElBaradei (2005).

Let us now turn to the linguistic bias in the history of the Nobel Prize. Unless one regards Arabic as an African language, none of the Literature Prizes won by black authors has been awarded for literature in indigenous African languages (such as Hausa, Kiswahili or Wolof). None has been awarded for oral literature, such as the elaborate oral traditions of the Somali people. What is more surprising is that all the Nobel Literature Prizes won by black authors have been awarded exclusively for literature written in the English language. Three of these authors – a Nigerian, an American and a West Indian (from Saint Lucia) – have won the Literature Prize for creative writing, while a fourth – Arthur Lewis (also of Saint Lucia) – has won the prize for economics.

This English-language bias extends to black Nobel peace laureates. Of the black Peace Prize winners, three are South Africans, three are Americans, one is Ghanaian, two are Liberian and one is a Kenyan. There is not a single black Nobel peace laureate from francophone Africa or lusophone Brazil. The only rival language among all Nobel laureates in global Africa is Arabic, with all three Arab winners being Egyptian – two for peace and one for literature.

The most surprising coincidence of all is that out of the twenty Nobel laureates who are from Africa or of African descent – Obama's racial compatriots – almost all come from countries previously ruled by Britain at some stage in history. These countries of origin include the United States, as well as South Africa, Egypt, Nigeria, Ghana, Saint Lucia, Kenya, and Britain itself. A diaspora Egyptian also won the Nobel Prize for Chemistry (Ahmed Zewail, 1999).

Perhaps one of the reasons for this Anglophilia is once again the relative preoccupation of the Nobel prize judges with issues of race. More than a third of the Peace Prizes have been awarded to countries with a difficult history in race relations – South Africa and the United States. Apart from Wole Soyinka (Nigerian) and Naguib Mahfouz (Egyptian), all Literature Prizes have been awarded to South Africans, Americans or West Indians – all from countries, again, with a tortuous history of race relations. Indeed, the writings for which these individuals won these prizes were all, to one degree or another, informed by the history of race in their respective countries. In the Oslo Foundation's response to black candidates, is there a convergence between Anglocentrism and Afrocentrism?

Is there also a territorial size bias in Nobel Prizes awarded to Africans and their descendants? Although the overwhelming majority of Obama's racial compatriots live in small countries, about half of the Nobel Prizes won by blacks have gone to four big countries: the

United States, South Africa, Nigeria and Egypt. Brazil, the second largest 'African' country after Nigeria, has yet to produce a black laureate. Brazil is home to more of Obama's racial compatriots than is the United States, with 92.6 million citizens classified as mixed race or black, compared to 37.6 million African Americans.

From Colour Line to Culture Line

At the beginning of the twentieth century, W.E.B. DuBois – already regarded as a great African-American thinker and leader – predicted that the central problem of the century would be the 'colour line'. DuBois presciently foresaw the century engulfed by racism, lynching, the 'white man's burden' and what came to be subsequently known as apartheid. The twentieth century was also overwhelmed by refugees on the run from racially and nationalistically instigated conflicts. And now in the twenty-first century, is it the 'culture line' that will be the central problem? Has a transition occurred, from a clash of identities (such as races) to a clash of values (such as cultural norms in conflict)? Are the refugees of the twenty-first century already disproportionately *cultural* refugees?

The late American political scientist Samuel Huntington was not, of course, a latter-day W.E.B. DuBois. However, on the eve of the twenty-first century, Huntington predicted that humanity was headed for a 'clash of civilisations'. He argued that, since the Cold War was over, future conflicts in the world would be fought less and less between states and ideological blocs, and more and more between civilisations and cultural coalitions. Huntington launched this debate with his 1993 article in the US establishment journal *Foreign Affairs* – an article that reverberated around the world. He followed this with a major book on the same subject.[15]

---

15. For the relevant article and early responses, see Samuel P. Huntington et al., 'The Clash of Civilizations: The Debate', *Foreign Affairs* 72(3) (Summer 1993). The book-length expansion of Huntington's argument can be found in *The Clash of Civilizations and the Remaking of World Order* (New York: Simon & Schuster, 1996).

While another distinguished scholar at the time, African American William Julius Wilson at the University of Chicago, had earlier predicted the declining significance of race,[16] which would become increasingly overshadowed by class and economics, Huntington predicted the rising salience of culture, which would overshadow both race and class. In a strange twist of fate, pan-Africanism took the lead in the transition from the politics of colour identity to the politics of shared cultural experience. Was the intercultural experience of African Americans preparation for building bridges between civilisations? Early in his presidency, Obama extended an olive branch to the Muslim world as a whole, from the Egyptian capital of Cairo, in a speech in June 2009.

Within the black Atlantic, this bridge-building began with the ultimate contradiction of W.E.B. DuBois. He was a man whose family name was French, whose actual physical appearance was virtually white, but whose allegiance was indisputably African. He was the reverse of William Blake's poem about the African child, 'The Little Black Boy'. For Blake (1757–1827), the child was black, but the boy insists 'O! my soul is white'.[17] For DuBois, one could proclaim the reverse: this man was white, but his soul was black. As intimated earlier, DuBois's actual skin colour defied his real cultural allegiance. What the DuBois paradox taught us was that 'blackness' could be a cultural identity rather than a physical appearance. As for Barack Obama, he was culturally brought up in a white home under his maternal grandmother. Even in multiracial Hawaii, Barack went to a school that was disproportionately white. During his early childhood, he was psychologically caught between a black skin and a white culture. Was this paradox a psychological preparation for bridging civilisations?

Then there was the phenomenon of the Trinidadian prophet of pan-Africanism George Padmore, and his fascination with Marxism, alongside DuBois's response to historical materialism. Padmore was a black West Indian. Here were two major pan-African thinkers who

---

16. See William Julius Wilson, *The Declining Significance of Race: Blacks and Changing American Institutions* (Chicago: University of Chicago Press, 1978).

17. William Blake, *Songs of Innocence and Experience* (Oxford: Oxford University Press, 1970 [1794]).

were involved in the politics of black identity, and were at the same time drawn towards the ideas of an ethnic German Jew named Karl Marx. Padmore's most influential book, published in 1956, was titled *Pan-Africanism or Communism? The Coming Struggle in Africa.*[18] It was an illustration of the huge ideological ambivalence regarding the politics of blackness, on the one hand, and the politics of class – regardless of race – on the other. The black Atlantic was particularly exposed to the ideological winds of Western civilisation. But were such black Westernisers like DuBois and Padmore destined to become bridge-builders between cultures? Were they more earnest in their global bridge-building than Obama has been so far?

On the whole, almost without realising it, DuBois and Padmore were products of the 'dual heritage': two converging civilisations. These prominent pan-Africanists were products of left-wing Western civilisation, on the one hand, and left-wing pan-Africanism, on the other. Without fully realising it, they constituted a transition from the politics of black identity to the politics of multicultural ideologies.

Then came Ghana's Kwame Nkrumah. He constituted the next stage of the transition from the 'dual heritage' of leftist Westernism and leftist pan-Africanism to the new 'triple heritage' of Africanity, Islam and Western civilisation. Nkrumah called this convergence 'consciencism' in 1964, identifying it as a synthesis of African tradition, Islamic heritage and what he described as 'Euro-Christian values'.[19] Barack Obama, when he was very young, was briefly influenced by both Islam and Westernism. Was a multicultural upbringing a good counterculture to the tradition of presidential militarism?

The concept of 'global Africa' did not emerge until the 1980s. Was it I who first proclaimed this concept, in my 1986 television series *The Africans: A Triple Heritage*? I titled the concluding programme 'Global Africa', and promoted it as a synthesis of three civilisations: Africanity, Islam and Westernism. Was this a prelude to cultural globalization?

18. George Padmore, *Pan-Africanism or Communism? The Coming Struggle in Africa* (London: Dobson, 1956).
19. Kwame Nkrumah, *Consciencism: Philosophy and Ideology for Decolonisation and Development* (New York: Monthly Review Press, 1964).

Had Barack's Kenyan father not abandoned him, the young Obama might have become a product of that 'triple heritage'.

Though it was I who put forward the concept of Africa's 'triple heritage', in the 1980s, the fusion of three civilisations had originated with Edward Blyden's *Christianity, Islam, and the Negro Race* in 1887.[20] It was then reincorporated into Kwame Nkrumah's 'Consciencism', before being consummated in my aforementioned television series and companion book.[21] The struggle for an alliance of civilisations has continued. Barack Obama, by becoming president of a white-majority country, has set a precedent for other white-majority countries. Is a black prime minister of Britain now on the horizon?

Concluding Reflections:
Between Nostradamus and Mister Obama

Michel de Nostredame, better known as Nostradamus (1503–1566), has gone down in history as the most famous seer of the European Renaissance. Even today, the Frenchman's prophecies are still being debated in books, articles and television documentaries. Nostradamus is credited with having forecast aspects of the French Revolution of 1789, the rise of Hitler in 1933, and even the 11 September 2001 attack on the World Trade Center in New York. Yet Nostradamus did not predict either Obama's election as US president or his winning of the Nobel Peace Prize.

This essay has placed two prophecies about black people within the tradition of Nostradamus. The first was made by Robert F. Kennedy, who prophesied that the United States would elect a black president by 2008. The election of Barack Obama to the presidency in 2008 fulfilled this prophecy, outshining contemporary predictions as well as those of the French astrologer of the sixteenth century.

The second prophesy was made by Indian political-spiritual leader Mahatma Gandhi, who predicted that the torch of his 'soul force'

20. Edward Blyden, *Christianity, Islam, and the Negro Race* (London: Whittingham, 1887).
21. Ali A. Mazrui, *The Africans: A Triple Heritage* (New York: Little, Brown, 1986).

(non-violent resistance) would be passed on to black people. Gandhi's prophecy lacks the precision of Kennedy's and is therefore closer to the ambiguous prophecies of Nostradamus. However, in support of Gandhi's Afro-optimism about blacks becoming a future vanguard of 'soul force' is the phenomenon of Africa's short memory of hate. Africans are just as violent as any other people, but they have historically tended to move towards forgiveness much faster than other groups. Also, Africa has produced an impressive number of Nobel peace laureates since the second half of the twentieth century. Although Gandhi himself was never awarded the Nobel Peace Prize, some of his disciples in the black world (including Martin Luther King Jr and Archbishop Desmond Tutu) have been among the most famous of Nobel peace laureates. The population of India (about 1.2 billion) is larger than the populations of all fifty-five African countries combined. But Africa has won many more Nobel Prizes than has India. Mahatma Gandhi was nominated five times for the Peace Prize, but the influence of the British Empire in the 1930s and 1940s was still too strong to permit the awarding of the prize to a leader of an anti-colonial movement like India's.

Now the world is dealing with the staggering novelty of the first black president of the United States. As an American president, Barack Obama has become the most powerful black person in the history of civilisation. This does not mean that Obama is greater than Shaka Zulu of South Africa, Menelik II of Ethiopia, Usman Dan Fodio of Nigeria, or Ramses II of ancient Egypt. Obama is not yet so great, but since January 2009 he has been exercising the immense leverage of the United States as a superpower. He is already more powerful than Africa's great icons combined.

But will Obama's performance eventually make him a great president? And will that greatness come through 'soul force' and avoidance of war? Every American president since Franklin D. Roosevelt in 1933 has initiated either a full-scale war or at least an armed conflict. Indeed, presidents Ronald Reagan (1980–88) and the two Bushes (1989–92 and 2001–08) unleashed more than one war each. The minimum test for Obama as an embodiment of Gandhi's 'soul force' continues to be whether he can become the first US president since the Second World War (1939–45) to refrain from initiating any major conflicts. Does the more restrained American participation in the Anglo-French-led war against Muammar Gaddafi's Libya in 2011 constitute enough of a Gandhian acceptance of *limited* warfare?

Of course, Obama had already inherited two wars – one in Iraq, from which he withdrew most American troops in 2010, and one in Afghanistan, which he may have escalated but from which he has promised to withdraw most US troops by 2014. Neither war was started by Obama. Can he avoid initiating a military conflict with Iran, or North Korea or Syria? Has Obama failed the test of 'soul force'? In addition to the Libyan conflict, he has escalated drone attacks against Pakistan, Afghanistan, Yemen and Somalia, making him one of the most homicidal presidents in recent US history. The Nobel judges had probably hoped that Obama would be the first US president in seven decades to refrain from making a decision to start a new war. They probably hoped that Obama would avoid the temptation of equating 'acting presidential' with a readiness to use military force.

Mohandas Gandhi's prophecy about black non-violence was issued in 1936, when Franklin D. Roosevelt was president of the United States. Is Obama, when compared with other American presidents, the most peace-loving US president since Gandhi uttered that prophecy? Obama has already publicly declared his ambition to help promote a militarily nuclear-free world. Gandhi's prophecy about black 'soul force' hangs in the balance with the election of the most powerful black person in history. Equipped with the power to destroy the world, would this particular black man – Barack Obama – start the process of trying truly to save the world? There is no room for complacency, but is there still room for Afro-optimism and hope?

Indeed there are hopeful signs. These include Obama's ambition (thwarted by Republicans) to change the nature of domestic politics in the United States and to transcend some of the deep divisions between parties, social classes and generations. Another Gandhian hope is manifested in Obama's remarkable record so far in initiating post-racial politics in the United States. One measure of progress towards a post-racial America is Obama's own election as president. And yet, is a post-racial America – in the words of Langston Hughes, the African American poet of the Harlem renaissance of the 1920s – a 'dream deferred'?

As Barack Obama enters a second presidential term following his re-election in November 2012, a third hopeful sign is his background as a product of at least three civilisations (America, Africa and Islam), against a wider background of multiculturalism in Indonesia, where he lived during part of his childhood, and in Hawaii, where he was born and spent much of his childhood. Obama is the first American president who is the son and grandson of Muslims on the paternal side. Indeed, he has a Swahili first name (Baraka), a Muslim middle name (Hussein) and an African family name (Obama). Does he stand a chance of embodying Gandhian 'soul force'?

Bibliography

Blake, William, *Songs of Innocence and Experience* (Oxford: Oxford University Press, 1970 [1794]).

Blyden, Edward, *Christianity, Islam, and the Negro Race* (London: Whittingham, 1887).

de Waal, Victor, *The Politics of Reconciliation: Zimbabwe's First Decade* (London: Hurst, 1981).

Gandhi, M.K., *Young India, 1924–1926* (Madras: Ganesan, 1927).

Gandhi, M.K., *Non-Violence in Peace and War*, 2nd edn (Ahmedabad: Navajivan, 1944).

Gandhi, M.K., 'Mahatma Gandhi on Freedom in Africa', *Africa Quarterly* 1(2) (July–September 1961).

Gilroy, Paul, *The Black Atlantic: Modernity and Double Consciousness* (Cambridge MA: Harvard University Press, 1993).

Grant, Colin, *Negro with a Hat: The Rise and Fall of Marcus Garvey and His Dream of Mother Africa* (Oxford: Oxford University Press, 2008).

Harijan, 14 March 1936.

Huntington, Samuel P., et al., 'The Clash of Civilizations: The Debate', *Foreign Affairs* 72(3) (Summer 1993).

Huntington, Samuel P., *The Clash of Civilizations and the Remaking of World Order* (New York: Simon & Schuster, 1996).

Kapur, Sudarshan, *Raising up a Prophet: The African-American Encounter with Gandhi* (Boston MA: Beacon, 1992).

Kaunda, Kenneth, *Black Government?* (Lusaka: United Society for Christian Literature, 1960).

Kenyatta, Jomo, *Suffering Without Bitterness* (Nairobi: East African Publishing House, 1968).

Mazrui, Ali A., *The Africans: A Triple Heritage* (New York: Little, Brown, 1986)

Nayyar, Pyarelal, 'Gandhiji and the African Question', *Africa Quarterly* 2(2) (July–September 1962).

Nehru, Jawaharlal, 'Emergent Africa', *Africa Quarterly* 1(1) (April–June 1961), pp. 7–9.

Nehru, Jawaharlal, 'Portuguese Colonialism: An Anachronism', *Africa Quarterly* 1(3) (October–December 1961).

Nkrumah, Kwame, *Consciencism: Philosophy and Ideology for Decolonisation and Development* (New York: Monthly Review Press, 1964).

Padmore, George, *Pan-Africanism or Communism? The Coming Struggle in Africa* (London: Dobson, 1956).

Parsons, Anthony, 'From Southern Rhodesia to Zimbabwe, 1965–1985', *International Affairs* 9(4) (November 1988).

Sampson, Anthony, *Mandela: The Authorized Biography* (New York: Knopf, 1999).

Washington Post, 27 May 1968.

Wilson, William Julius, *The Declining Significance of Race: Blacks and Changing American Institutions* (Chicago: University of Chicago Press, 1978).

PART TWO

THE THREE AFRICAN AMERICANS

THREE

RALPH BUNCHE, MARTIN LUTHER KING JR AND BARACK OBAMA: THREE AFRICAN-AMERICAN NOBEL LAUREATES DEBATE WAR AND PEACE

PEARL T. ROBINSON

Winning the Nobel Peace Prize in 2009 posed a conundrum for Barack Obama. As a sitting president of the United States, presiding over two active wars, how was he to respond? The Nobel Peace Committee's decision to honour a national political leader less than a year into his first term – before he had scored any significant foreign policy victories – drew praise, scepticism and even a degree of scorn. The announcement from Oslo lauded Obama for his 'extraordinary efforts to strengthen international diplomacy and cooperation between peoples'. In further details, the press release accorded 'special importance' to the awardee's 'vision of and work for' a world free of nuclear arms.[1] But speaking in the White House Rose Garden on the day of the announcement in October 2009, Obama remarked, 'To be honest, I do not feel that I deserve to be in the company of ... the transformative figures who've been honoured by this prize.' He then gave notice of his intention to accept the award as 'a call to action' – a call for all nations to confront the common challenges of the twenty-first century.[2]

---

1. 'The Nobel Peace Prize 2009 – Press Release', 9 October 2009, www.nobelprize.org/nobel_prizes/peace/laureates/2009/press.html.
2. 'Remarks by the President on Winning the Nobel Peace Prize', 9 October 2009, www.whitehouse.gov/the_press_office/Remarks-by-the-President-on-Winning-the-Nobel-Peace-Prize.

Granted, President Obama was an unlikely peace laureate for the class of 2009. Yet, even then he had the earmarks of a contender. His inaugural address as president of the United States, delivered in January 2009, prefigured a transformative foreign policy agenda. To the curious millions who tuned in at home and abroad, the new president proclaimed that America would 'play its role in ushering in a new era of peace'.[3] Speaking directly to 'the Muslim world', Obama signalled a willingness to 'seek a new way forward, based on mutual interest and mutual respect'. Regarding the dreaded spectre of a global catastrophe posed by atomic weapons, he declared that his new administration would 'work tirelessly' with 'old friends and former foes' to reduce the threat of nuclear war. For a leader generally considered to be risk-averse, this bold commitment to the imperatives of a just and lasting peace was a remarkable display of the 'audacity of hope': the title of Obama's 2006 book.[4]

Speaking in Oslo city hall barely two months later as a Nobel laureate, president Obama acknowledged that the timing of his award was inconvenient – coming, as he said, 'at the beginning, and not the end, of my labours on the world stage'.[5] Feigned humility? Perhaps. But Obama's Nobel lecture left little doubt that the new president had set his sights on becoming a transformative world leader.

By 2009, only two other African Americans had won the coveted Nobel Peace Prize: Ralph Bunche (1950) and Martin Luther King Jr (1964).[6] Bunche was a member of the United Nations Secretariat, honoured for his successful mediation of an armistice agreement between Palestine and seven Arab states in 1949 (see Jonah, Chapter 4 in this volume); King was an ordained Baptist minister with a doctorate in theology, honoured for his courageous leadership of a non-violent campaign to bring racial justice to the American South (see Daniels, Chapter 5 in

---

3. 'President Barack Obama's Inaugural Address', 21 January 2009, www.whitehouse.gov/blog/inaugural-address.

4. Barack Obama, *The Audacity of Hope: Thoughts on Reclaiming the American Dream* (New York: Crown, 2006). See also Barack Obama, *Dreams from My Father: A Story of Race and Inheritance* (New York: Three Rivers, 1995).

5. 'Barack H. Obama Nobel Lecture: A Just and Lasting Peace', 10 December 2009, www.nobelprize.org/nobel_prizes/peace/laureates/2009/obama-lecture_en.html.

6. The writer Toni Morrison, an African American, won the 1993 Nobel Prize for Literature.

this volume). Even before being awarded the Nobel Peace Prize, all three of these African Americans – Bunche, King and Obama – were already, by any standard, extraordinarily accomplished human beings.[7] Each was on record as a theorist and practitioner of peacemaking. Each had developed a deeply personal and highly sophisticated understanding of racial bigotry and religious stereotyping as impediments to peace. Each insisted that in modern war victory is illusory. Yet they did not see eye to eye on the relationship between war and peace.

A good deal of evidence of the contrasting visions of these three peace laureates can be found in formal statements made during the Nobel award ceremonies in Oslo. Indeed the acceptance speeches and Nobel lectures of these three African-American laureates flesh out the major themes and subtle distinctions of their respective positions on war and peace. Likewise, the Oslo statements of Theodore Roosevelt (1910) and Woodrow Wilson (1919) – the only other American presidents so far to have been awarded the Nobel Peace Prize while still in office – are instructive. Lessons drawn from their respective experiences with peacemaking force a reconsideration of Obama's contention that the occupant of the White House is obliged to defend the *necessity* of war.

The Situational Peace Activist

President Barack Obama's 2009 Nobel lecture, 'A Just and Lasting Peace', targets two audiences: global humanity and his domestic constituency. The carefully crafted narrative chronicles a persistent struggle for peace, despite inherent political constraints and limits on presidential power. After expressing profound gratitude to the Nobel Peace Committee for its endorsement of his administration's highest aspirations in the pursuit of peace, Obama pivots. Abruptly shifting tone, he proceeds to delineate his solemn responsibilities as a commander-in-chief who must order troops to kill and be killed. This

---

7. All three earned graduate degrees in the Boston–Cambridge area. Bunche was the first black American to receive a doctorate in government from Harvard University (1934). King earned a doctorate in systematic theology from Boston University (1955). And Obama graduated from Harvard Law School (1991), where he was the first African American to serve as president of the *Harvard Law Review*.

juxtaposition of life-affirming and life-denying power is jarring. The
claim that his administration was working to replace war with peace
does not obscure the contradictions. We are left with the portrait of
a president who is a situational peace activist – both empowered and
constrained by his relationship to the state:

> OBAMA: [W]e are not mere prisoners of fate. Our actions matter, and
> can bend history in the direction of justice.... Still, we're at war, and
> I'm responsible for the deployment of thousands of young Americans to
> battle in a distant land.... And so I come here with an acute sense of the
> costs of armed conflict.[8]

As Obama cautiously navigates the thin line between war and peace,
he seems to be guided by the dictum of nineteenth-century Prussian
military theorist Carl von Clausewitz: 'War is a mere continuation of
politics by other means.'[9]

President Barack Obama is indeed a master politician. And he
touts a willingness to use his commander-in-chief powers to expand
the hegemony of the 'free world': ordering unprecedented numbers of
predator drone strikes in Pakistan, Yemen, Somalia and Mali; assassinations of foreign nationals and even American citizens suspected of
terrorist activities in Yemen; special operations against terrorist leaders
in Pakistan, Yemen, Afghanistan and North Africa; and an armed intervention to protect endangered civilian populations in Libya.[10] However,
few were aware that 'when he accepted the Peace Prize in December
2009 the new president had already authorised more drone strikes
than George Bush approved during his entire eight-year presidency'.[11]

---

8. 'Barack H. Obama Nobel Lecture'.
9. Carl von Clausewitz, *On War*, abridged version, trans. Michael Howard and Peter Paret,
edited with an introduction by Beatrice Heuser (Oxford: Oxford University Press, 2007).
10. Micah Zenk, *Between Threats and War: U.S. Discrete Military Operations in the Post-Cold
War World* (Palo Alto CA: Stanford University Press, 2010); David Rhode, 'The Obama Doctrine:
How the President's Drone War is Backfiring', *Foreign Policy*, March–April 2012 (www.foreignpolicy.
com/articles/2012/02/27/the_obama_doctrine?print=yes&hidecomments=yes&page=full); *Guardian*, 'US Drone Strikes Listed and Detailed in Pakistan, Somalia, and Yemen', 2 August 2012 (www.
guardian.co.uk/news/datablog/2012/aug/02/us-drone-strikes-data); Kimberly Dozier, 'U.S. Special
Forces Setting up Strike Teams in N. Africa', 3 October 2012, www.msnbc.msn.com/id/49271035/ns/
world_news-mideast_n_africa/#.UHHodLRpuqQ.
11. Daniel Klaidman, 'Drones: The Silent Killers', *Newsweek*, 4–11 June 2012, p. 40.

Perhaps this is why Obama's Oslo lecture included explicit references to the 'human tragedy' associated with the pursuit of peace:

> OBAMA: So yes, the instruments of war do have a role to play in preserving the peace. And yet this truth must coexist with another – that no matter how justified, war promises human tragedy.[12]

But the prize was awarded for efforts to advance the cause of *peace*, and president Obama's task in Oslo in December 2009 was to convince the global community that its most powerful military leader could also become an apostle in the struggle for global peace.

Ralph Bunche and Martin Luther King Jr – the two of Obama's African-American ancestors who had stood on that Oslo platform five and six decades earlier – had also wrestled with similar issues of war and peace during their labours on the world stage. But neither Bunche nor King was a professional politician – let alone a sitting head of state. Their respective institutional affiliations – one an international civil servant, the other the leader of a domestic social movement – freed them from the obligation to justify the wages of war. Nevertheless, both left practical legacies that could serve as sounding boards as Obama struggled to articulate his own path to peace.

One can well imagine that in order to prepare for Oslo, the first black president of the United States might have consulted the lectures of his predecessors for wisdom and direction. In fact, his Nobel text includes six references to King, including a quotation from the civil rights leader's 1964 Nobel lecture. Although Bunche is not mentioned by name, two of his signature concerns – international peacekeeping[13] and nuclear disarmament – feature prominently in Obama's prescriptive 'agenda for peace'. Bunche, in his pioneering role as one of the architects of United Nations peacekeeping, had developed professional expertise in raising armies for peace (see Chapter 4 in this volume).

---

12. 'Barack H. Obama Nobel Lecture'.
13. Ralph Bunche was one of the principal architects of UN peacekeeping operations. For a detailed discussion, see Brian Urquhart, *Ralph Bunche: An American Odyssey* (New York: Norton, 1993).

BUNCHE: In each instance of a threat to the peace, the United Nations projects itself into the area of conflict by sending United Nations representatives to the area for the purpose of mediation and conciliation.[14]

KING: It is not enough to say 'We must not wage war'. It is necessary to love peace and sacrifice for it.[15]

As president, Obama has tended to use Martin Luther King's fierce dedication to non-violence as a foil that contrasts with his own toughness and willingness to do whatever it takes to fulfil the obligations of an American commander-in-chief. Yet we learn in the David Mendell biography *Obama: From Promise to Power* that as a young man in his early twenties Obama was drawn to King's powerful political message of non-violence after reading Taylor Branch's riveting account of the civil rights struggle.[16] The US president's 2009 Nobel lecture retains a prominent moral thread, but diverges radically from King's anti-war philosophy. Earlier versions of this divergence are visible in the way that the young politician had framed his opposition to American intervention in Iraq.

Speaking in 2002 at an anti-war rally in Chicago, then-Illinois state senator Barack Obama declared that, while not being a pacifist, he opposed the impending American intervention in Iraq because it was 'a dumb war' based 'not on principle but on politics'.[17] In a 2007 presidential campaign video, then-US senator Barack Obama reminded his compatriots that he had long 'opposed going to war in Iraq' and had cautioned that invading a country that showed 'no imminent threat to the US' would play to extremism and 'distract us from the fight against al-Qaeda and the Taliban'.[18] By evoking basic tenets of preventive war theory, Obama thus managed to affirm his belief in war as a patriotic option, while disparaging the attack on Iraq as neither practical nor

14. 'Ralph J. Bunche Nobel Lecture: Some Reflections on Peace in our Time', 11 December 1950, www.nobelprize.org/nobel_prizes/peace/laureates/1950/bunche-lecture.html.
15. 'Martin Luther King Jr. Nobel Lecture: The Quest for Peace and Justice', 11 December 1964, www.nobelprize.org/nobel_prizes/peace/laureates/1964/king-lecture.html.
16. David Mendell, *Obama: From Promise to Power* (New York: HarperCollins, 2007), p. 74.
17. 'Barack Obama's Full Speech on 26 October 2002', Liberalscum Buster, http://liberalscum-buster.wordpress.com/2008/01/26/barack-obamas-full-speech-on-october-26-2002.
18. Barack Obama, 'Blueprint for Change: Iraq', 21 October 2008, www.youtube.com/watch?v=wDhOxNeOj4U.

morally justifiable. Two years later, when accepting the Nobel Peace Prize, the president paid homage to Mahatma Gandhi and Martin Luther King as visionaries who had set a high moral standard, even as he portrayed himself as a politician whose actions were tempered by their wisdom:

> OBAMA: The non-violence practiced by men like Gandhi and King may not have been practical or possible in every circumstance, but the love that they preached – their fundamental faith in human progress – that must always be the North Star that guides us on our journey.[19]

Obama's finely calibrated political compass is programmed to seek a middle path to retain political viability. Randall Kennedy's insightful analysis of his dual-track approach to racial issues can be extended to other policy spheres. As a rule, Obama the politician first finds a way to signal that he identifies with a problem. Then, when ready to advance a solution, he does so 'cautiously, within the boundaries of what he perceives to be conducive to his [own] political well-being'.[20] In Oslo, the issue was war and peace:

> OBAMA: I do not bring with me today a definitive solution to the problems of war. What I do know is that meeting these challenges will require the same vision, hard work, and persistence as those men and women who acted so boldly decades ago. And it will require us to think in new ways about the notions of just war and the imperatives of a just peace.[21]

Unable to stand at the podium and renounce war, the Nobel peace laureate instead offered an ethical framework for determining *when* war is morally acceptable. As he put it, 'There will be times when nations – acting individually or in concert – will find the use of force not only necessary but morally justified.'[22]

19. 'Barack H. Obama Nobel Lecture'.
20. Randall Kennedy, *The Persistence of the Color Line: Racial Politics and the Obama Presidency* (New York: Pantheon, 2011), p. 264.
21. 'Barack H. Obama Nobel Lecture'.
22. Ibid.

Reflections on Peace in Our Time

Ralph Bunche did not equivocate when accepting his Nobel Peace Prize in Oslo in December 1950. Instead, he sought to articulate a set of principles, practices and mechanisms that could serve to resolve interstate conflicts without resort to war. While careful to note 'the vital differences and wide areas of conflict among nations', Bunche insisted that 'there is virtually none that could not be settled peacefully – by negotiation and mediation', were it not for recalcitrant political leaders who lack 'a genuine will for peace'.[23] He lamented the widely held belief that war was inevitable. Countering the idea that 'narrow, self-centered nationalism' drives international relations and thus stands as an enduring obstacle to peace, Bunche reserved his most scathing critique for the advocates of preventive war:

> BUNCHE: To suggest that war can prevent war is a base play on words and a despicable form of warmongering.

He further ventured that the preventive doctrine is sometimes used to mask a belief in the inevitability of war:

> BUNCHE: There are some ... who, in their resignation to war, wish merely to select their own time for initiating it.

Ironically, fifty-nine years later, Barack Obama's Nobel lecture included an updated version of the preventive war argument – expanded and reformulated as 'just war' theory. This was Obama's rationale for the two wars, in Afghanistan and Iraq – inherited from the George W. Bush administration (2001–08) – being waged on his watch. President Obama, however, withdrew most US troops from Iraq by 2010, and pledged to withdraw American troops from Afghanistan in 2014.

'Preventive war' is a pre-emptive doctrine.[24] It holds that a country, sensing vulnerability and an imminent threat, might possibly be justified in making the first strike. But for proponents of 'just war' theory,

---

23. 'Ralph J. Bunche Nobel Lecture'.
24. Neta Crawford, 'The Slippery Slope to Preventive War', *Ethics and International Affairs* 17(1) (2003), p. 30.

the pre-emptive rationale is insufficient. They call for additional ethical obligations to minimise harm – particularly to civilian populations – and to avoid unnecessary use of violence. Secular theorists and theologians who hold that morality has a place in international politics have contributed to the development of 'just war' theory for centuries.[25] Some contemporary international relations theorists seek to update the metrics of minimal harm and unnecessary violence in order to account for the changing technology of warfare and to recalibrate acceptable thresholds of harm.[26] Obama's 2009 Nobel lecture builds on this literature:

> OBAMA: The concept of a 'just war' emerged, suggesting that war is justi-fied only when certain conditions were met: if it is waged as a last resort or in self-defense; if the force used is proportional; and if, whenever possible, civilians are spared from violence.[27]

After carefully considering the nature of terrorism and examining the metrics of contemporary warfare, Neta Crawford concludes that 'it is extremely difficult to fight a just counterterror war'.[28] Anticipating such calculations, even as early as 1950, Bunche posed a rhetorical question:

> BUNCHE: Who indeed, could be so unseeing as not to realize that in modern war victory is illusory; that the harvest of war can be only misery, destruction, and degradation?[29]

Believing that only the United Nations could make the world secure, Bunche used the Oslo platform in 1950 to advance a three-pronged agenda for peace: establishment of a UN-supervised military force sufficient in strength to check the aggressive use of force by belligerent governments; creation of international bodies to mediate conflicts, keep the peace and avoid nuclear war; and the provision of international guarantees of human rights (economic, social and political) for racial,

---

25. Leading theorists of 'just war' include Saint Augustine, Hugo Grotius, Immanuel Kant, Michael Walzer, and even the US Catholic bishops. See Neta Crawford, 'Just War Theory and the U.S. Counterterror War', *Perspectives on Politics* 1(1) (March 2003), pp. 6–7.
26. Ibid., pp. 8–12.
27. 'Barack H. Obama Nobel Lecture'.
28. For a discussion, see Crawford, 'Just War Theory', p. 5.
29. 'Ralph J. Bunche Nobel Lecture'.

ethnic and religious minorities. But as the Cold War gained sway by 1950, the two dominant superpowers – the United States and the Soviet Union – stubbornly refused to subject their sovereignty to a world body managed by international civil servants.

Frustrations notwithstanding, Bunche spent another two decades working on the requirements for building the apparatus of UN peace-keeping, promoting peaceful uses of atomic energy, and establishing institutions to control nuclear weapons and avoid nuclear war. His elevation to the post of UN Undersecretary General for Political Affairs in 1968 translated into assignments as a UN troubleshooter in hotspots around the world.

In 1970, as the United Nations prepared to celebrate its twenty-fifth anniversary, its first Nobel peace laureate and most senior American staff member sat down with BBC radio for an interview.[30] True to form, Bunche reaffirmed his conviction that the 'foremost purpose of [the] UN … is to maintain peace [and] human advance'. Reflecting on the legacy of the twenty-five years of the world body, he singled out UN interventions in Suez, Congo[31] and Cyprus as operations that might possibly have saved the world from cataclysmic nuclear war. Bunche counted among his greatest frustrations the failure of UN efforts to negotiate a settlement of the Vietnam War (1964–73). Looking forward, he shed a light on the danger of a world in which 'the destructive power in the hands of man has become unlimited'. One wonders what Bunche might have said about the 2009 Nobel peace laureate's new metrics for calibrating a 'just war'.

The Quest for Peace and Justice

On the evening of 4 April 1968, the world was stunned by the news of Martin Luther King Jr's assassination in the city of Memphis in

---

30. 'BBC Interview', June 1970, typescript notes for interview with Ralph Bunche on the twenty-fifth anniversary of the United Nations, Ralph Bunche Additions, Box 17, Folder 13, Schomburg Center for Research on Black Culture, New York.

31. Despite Bunche's efforts to portray the 1960 UN intervention in the Congo as a success, he is often blamed for the failure of the UN peacekeeping force to prevent the overthrow and assassination of popular pan-African Congolese prime minister Patrice Lumumba in 1961.

the American South. A despondent Ralph Bunche lamented the loss of 'one of [the] most earnest, respected and commanding voices in the allied causes of peace, freedom and the dignity of man'.[32] More than forty years later, in presidential remarks spoken at the dedication of the Martin Luther King memorial in Washington DC, Barack Obama marvelled at how 'a black preacher with no official rank or title' somehow 'gave voice to our deepest dreams and our most lasting ideals'.[33] Both men singled out the power of King's magnificent voice. Bunche associated the power of that voice with practical work in the service of peace and human dignity. Obama connected the voice to dreams and ideals. One can almost sense the US president distancing himself from the moral certitude of King's convictions. On matters of state-sanctioned war and peace, the distance looms large:

> KING: [W]isdom born of experience should tell us that war is obsolete. There may have been a time when war served as a negative good by preventing the spread and growth of an evil force, but the destructive power of modern weapons eliminated even the possibility that war may serve as a negative good.[34]

> OBAMA: [A]s a head of state sworn to protect and defend my nation, I cannot be guided by [the] examples of [Gandhi and King] alone. I face the world as it is, and cannot stand idle in the face of threats to the American people.[35]

But, as we have seen, this jangling discord was not always the case. When opposing intervention in Iraq, the young Obama's anti-war rhetoric echoed King's critique in his famous 1967 Riverside Church address in New York to the 'Clergy and Laymen Concerned About Vietnam':

> OBAMA: [A]n invasion of Iraq without a clear rationale and without strong international support will only fan the flames of the Middle East, ... and strengthen the recruitment arm of al-Qaeda.[36]

32. 'Personal Statement by Dr. Ralph J. Bunche', 5 April 1968, Ralph Bunche Additions, Box 17, Folder 13, Schomburg Center for Research on Black Culture, New York..
33. 'Remarks by President Barack Obama at the Martin Luther King, Jr. Memorial Dedication, the National Mall, Washington, D.C.', 16 October 2011, www.whitehouse.gov/the-press-office/2011/10/16/remarks-president-martin-luther-king-jr-memorial-dedication.
34. 'Martin Luther King Jr. Nobel Lecture'.
35. 'Barack H. Obama Nobel Lecture'.
36. 'Barack Obama's Full Speech on October 26, 2002'.

KING: War is not the answer. Communism will never be defeated by the use of atomic bombs or nuclear weapons. Let us not join those who shout war and, through their misguided passions, urge the United States to relinquish its participation in the United Nations.[37]

The enemy had changed, but the message was largely the same:

OBAMA: [T]he battles that we need to fight ... are ... battles against ignorance and intolerance. Corruption and greed. Poverty and despair.

KING: We must with positive action seek to remove those conditions of poverty, insecurity, and injustice which are the fertile soil in which the seed of communism grows and develops.

Could it be that the Reverend King's stature as the leader of a non-violent social movement gave him a peculiar kind of agency not available to the black resident of the White House? Maybe. Whatever the case, the Vietnam War of 1964–73 precipitated excruciatingly difficult choices, as the young minister weighed his practical responsibilities to the civil rights community and the pull of moral conscience. After wrestling with that dilemma for nearly two years, King chose to follow his conscience.

That Martin Luther King's decision to embrace the peace option fully in 1967 would prove problematic for Ralph Bunche came as a surprise – and made headline news. King's 1967 Riverside address had demonised the Vietnam War and questioned the motivations of the American people. While giving new impetus to the peace movement, this dramatic turn of events also drew a firestorm of criticism from opinion-makers, who challenged King's patriotism, accused him of 'going red', and branded him a turncoat to the Lyndon Johnson administration, which had supported civil rights legislation.[38] Bunche, speaking as a citizen and as a director of the National Association for the Advancement of Colored People (NAACP), publicly criticised King for failing to subjugate his personal views to his obligations as a civil

---

37. Martin Luther King Jr, 'Beyond Vietnam', address delivered at Riverside Church, New York, 4 April 1967, www.stanford.edu/group/King/liberation curriculum/speeches/beyondvietnam.htm.
38. Michael Eric Dyson, *I May Not Get There with You: The True Martin Luther King, Jr.* (New York: Free Press, 2000), pp. 51–62.

rights leader.[39] In effect, mainstream civil rights organisations such
as the NAACP and the Urban League feared collateral damage from
these strident criticisms.

King often brushed aside naysayers who insisted that he should
confine his activities to the area of civil rights:

> KING: [M]any persons have questioned me about the wisdom of my path:
> ... 'Why are you speaking about war, Dr. King?' ... 'Peace and civil
> rights don't mix.' ... [S]uch questions mean that the inquirers have not
> really known me, my commitment, or my calling.[40]

But coming from Ralph Bunche, a man whom King respected and
admired, the criticism stung. After all, the Riverside address of 1967
had linked the reverend's personal decision to speak out against the
Vietnam War to 'the burden of responsibility' that came with having
won the Nobel Peace Prize three years earlier. More to the point, King's
1964 Nobel lecture had raised concern about three interdependent
problems that plagued the modern world and that were, in his view,
undermining the quality of moral and spiritual life:

> KING: Each of these problems, while appearing to be separate and
> isolated, is inextricably bound to the other. I refer to racial injustice,
> poverty, and war.[41]

Among those who understood the depths and complexity of King's
analysis of the human condition, few were more attuned to these
perspectives than his fellow Nobel peace laureate, Ralph Bunche.

King's Riverside narrative of militant anti-war resistance was situated
in a particular historical moment. Passage of the 1964 Civil Rights Act
and the 1965 Voting Rights Act had delivered the lion's share of the
legislative agenda called for by the 1963 March on Washington DC,
where King had delivered his famous and eloquent 'I Have a Dream'
speech. But the fracturing of the civil rights coalition along racial,

39. William Otis, 'King–Vietnam', *Associated Press*, 12 April 1967, Ralph Bunche Additions, Box
17, Folder: Bunche's Remarks About MLKing re Civil Rights and Vietnam, Schomburg Center for
Research on Black Culture, New York.
40. King, 'Beyond Vietnam'.
41. 'Martin Luther King Jr. Nobel Lecture'.

programmatic and ideological lines, together with the wave of violent black revolts in the nation's inner cities, had engendered a loss of focus and a reduction in financial support for the movement as a whole. King's militant anti-war rhetoric put him at odds with the civil rights establishment as well as with the Lyndon Johnson administration.

Bunche attempted to do some damage control by drafting a narrative of reconciliation. Parsing his personal objection to the war and his responsibilities as a long-time NAACP board member, he agreed to work with three other directors on a public statement. The result was a resolution, unanimously adopted by the NAACP national board in 1967, that distanced the organisation from King and the anti-war movement. As the NAACP's 'Statement on Vietnam' noted:

> To attempt to merge the civil rights movement with the peace movement, or to assume that one is dependent upon the other, is, in our judgment, a serious tactical mistake. It will serve the case neither of civil rights nor of peace. The NAACP knows that civil rights battles will have to be fought and won on their own merits, irrespective of the state of war or peace in the world.... We are not a peace organisation nor a foreign policy Association. We are a civil rights organisation... We are, or course, for a just peace.[42]

Behind this carefully balanced language was the hand of a skilled diplomat well honed in the art of high-stakes conflict resolution.[43] The board's resolution did not mention King by name.

What followed was a brief exchange of statements and counter-statements issued by Bunche and King through the media. King accepted the language but not the substance of the NAACP statement, reiterating his view that the Vietnam War was killing the civil rights movement. Bunche was heavily criticised for supporting the civil rights establishment rather than King over this issue. Meanwhile, the scholar-diplomat continued quietly to express personal opposition to the war,

---

42. 'NAACP Board Minutes', 10 April 1967, Ralph Bunche Additions, Box 17, Folder: Remarks About MLKing, Schomburg Center. New York; statement abridged by author.

43. Bunche served on another ad hoc NAACP board committee to work out financial issues with the Association's Legal Defence and Educational Fund, which was beginning to eat into the veteran institution's fund-raising base. This fund, formerly the legal arm of the NAACP, became autonomous in 1957. 'NAACP Board Minutes', 10 April 1967.

while working behind the scenes with Burmese UN Secretary General U Thant on efforts to negotiate a ceasefire in the conflict. Bunche even received King, Benjamin Spock and several other leaders of the peace movement for a brief meeting in his office at the UN Secretariat in New York before they addressed an anti-war demonstration outside the building. The press covered both the meeting and the rally.[44]

At least for a short while, Bunche's diplomatic fix seemed to have moved the two peace laureates towards common ground:

> KING: We do not believe in any merger or fusion of movements, but we can equally believe that no one can pretend that the existence of the war is not profoundly affecting the destiny of civil rights progress.[45]

> BUNCHE: Dr. King ... most emphatically confirmed to me ... that he was not advocating a fusion or merger or marriage of the civil rights movement.... This was my sole concern – I am not concerned with his position on Vietnam.... [S]o far as I am concerned this takes care of the issue to which my critical statement had been directed.[46]

> KING: I shall remain president of the Southern Christian Leadership Conference and do all I can in this role. But I deem it my responsibility to speak out positively and forthrightly on the war in Vietnam.[47]

Constraints of the Presidency Revisited

So, are there lessons for Barack Obama to learn from Theodore Roosevelt (1906) and Woodrow Wilson (1919), the two other American presidents to have won the Nobel Peace Prize while still in office? Roosevelt was honoured for mediating the Russo-Japanese war and successfully concluding the Treaty of Portsmouth, signed by Moscow and Tokyo in 1905.[48] Wilson was recognised for his Fourteen Point Programme for World Peace of 1918 and his work in achieving inclusion of

---

44. Charles Henry and Ralph Bunche, *Model Negro or American Other?* (New York: New York University Press, 1999), p. 237.

45. 'Dr. King Disavowal Accepted by Bunche', *New York Times*, 14 April 1967, Ralph Bunche Additions, Box 17, Folder: Remarks About MLKing, Schomburg Center, New York.

46. 'Statement Given by Mr. Ralph J. Bunche to CBS Radio', 13 April 1967, Ralph Bunche Additions, Box 17, Folder: Remarks About MLKing, Schomburg Center, New York.

47. Lawrence E. Davis, 'Dr. King's Response', *New York Times*, 13 April 1967, Ralph Bunche Additions, Box 17, Folder: Remarks About MLK, Schomburg Center, New York, p. 32.

48. 'The Nobel Peace Prize 1906 – Presentation Speech', 10 December 1906, www.nobelprize.org/nobel_prizes/peace/laureates/1906/press.html.

the Covenant of the League of Nations in the 1919 Treaty of Versailles, which ended the First World War (1914–18).[49]

When presenting President Roosevelt with the Nobel Peace Prize in 1906, Norwegian statesman Gunnar Knudsen explained that the Nobel Peace Committee was seeking to change global public opinion on the prospects for peace – a goal that required reaching beyond utopian idealists to real-world practitioners. The United States was among the first nations 'to infuse the ideal of peace into practical politics', and it was especially reassuring to find an American leader who was willing to take the fight on the road.[50]

Theodore Roosevelt was neither shy nor reticent about using the power of his office to pursue peace, and his 'rough rider' attitude must have been particularly gratifying to the Nobel Foundation. Interestingly, he waited until a year after leaving the White House to travel to Oslo, delivering his Nobel lecture in 1910. Speaking with the assurance of an activist president who understood both the power and the limitations of the office, Roosevelt noted the 'peculiar pleasure' of being able to lead life on a somewhat higher plane:

> ROOSEVELT: In this case, while I did not act officially as President of the United States, it was nevertheless only because I was President that I was enabled to act at all.[51]

Certainly no pacifist, Roosevelt pressed the need 'to check a cruel and unhealthy militarism in international relationships'. He advocated the use of arbitration and mediation, development of a more robust Hague Tribunal, and the creation of a League of Peace to deal with international disputes. All of these suggestions were solidly grounded in policies that could be undertaken by a leader bound to uphold the national interest:

> ROOSEVELT: I speak as a practical man, and whatever I now advocate I actually tried to do when I was ... the head of a great nation and keenly jealous of its honour and interest.

---

49. 'Woodrow Wilson – Acceptance Speech', 10 December 1920, www.nobelprize.org/nobel_prizes/peace/laureates/1919/wilson-acceptance.html.
50. 'The Nobel Peace Prize 1906 – Presentation Speech'.
51. Ibid.

Acknowledging the 'limitations' and the 'qualifications to be borne in mind', Roosevelt insisted that great advances in the cause of international peace could nevertheless be made by a continuous accretion of small steps. When effectively combined with the 'bully pulpit' of the American presidency and the establishment of some form of international policing power, such efforts might eventually aggregate sufficient 'power necessary to command peace throughout the world':

> ROOSEVELT: [I]n striving for a lofty ideal we must use practical methods; and if we cannot attain all at one leap, we must advance towards it step by step, reasonably content so long as we do actually make some progress in the right direction.

For Woodrow Wilson, who defeated Theodore Roosevelt in the presidential election of 1912 and presided over his country's entry into the First World War, the honour of winning the Nobel Peace Prize was bitter-sweet. Wilson had attempted to convince a nation with isolationist tendencies that war could be fought for a moral cause, and that the post-war peace could be won. He introduced his Fourteen Point Programme for World Peace, which eventually became the basis for treaty negotiations in Versailles at the end of the war.[52] The plan rested on the principle of justice for the peoples and nations of the world. Its fourteenth point proposed the establishment of a League of Nations: an idea that Theodore Roosevelt had advanced in his own Nobel lecture eight years earlier. Alas, neither the victorious European Allies nor the largely isolationist American Senate warmed to all of Wilson's proposals.

Wilson had put the prestige of his office on the line, and in 1919 travelled to Versailles, where he personally headed the American delegation at the peace table. French prime minister Georges Clemenceau and British premier Lloyd George joined in pressing for harsh punishment, territorial changes and crippling reparations to be imposed on Germany. However, the American president managed to get the idea

---

52. 'President Wilson's Message to Congress', 8 January 1918, Records of the United States Senate, Group 46, National Archives, www.ourdocuments.gov/doc.php?flash=true&doc=62.

of a League of Nations written into the final treaty that ended the First World War.

A politically diminished and physically ailing Woodrow Wilson returned home to a country that was ready to shrug off European entanglements. Defying his doctor's orders, he undertook a gruelling whistle-stop speaking tour across America to sell his fourteen-point programme, but suffered a paralysing stroke while on the road. Wilson never fully recovered. The US Senate refused ratification of the deal, America did not join the League of Nations, and the country settled back comfortably into 'splendid isolation'. A political rout followed, as the Republican Party won a landside victory in the 1920 presidential election by denouncing Wilson's policies, and Warren Harding became president of the United States.

The denouement of President Wilson's 'earnest effort in the cause of peace'[53] carries short-term and long-term lessons. In the short term it is not the office but rather the political viability of the office-holder that determines the ability to act. As for the longer term, Woodrow Wilson, in his Nobel Peace Prize address, said it best:

> WILSON: If there were but one such [Nobel Peace] prize, ... I could not of course accept it. For mankind has not yet been rid of the unspeakable horror of war.... It is the better part of wisdom to consider our work as one begun. It will be a continuing labour. In the indefinite course of [the] years before us there will be abundant opportunity for others to distinguish themselves in the crusade against hate and fear and war.

The weight of the evidence suggests that Barack Obama has learned this lesson well. As for the longer term, this must be left for historians to determine.

Concluding Reflections

In 1950, Ralph Bunche ended his Nobel peace lecture in Oslo with an appeal to *reason*:

> There will be no security in our world, no release from agonising tension, no genuine progress, no enduring peace, until, in Shelley's fine

---

53. 'Woodrow Wilson – Acceptance Speech'.

words, 'reason's voice, loud as the voice of nature, shall have waked the nations'.

Fourteen years later, Martin Luther King Jr ended his Nobel lecture with an appeal to *moral authority*:

> Here and there an individual or group dares to love and rises to the majestic heights of moral maturity. So in a real sense this is a great time to be alive.

Barack Obama, unwilling – indeed unable – to concede the futility of war, concluded his 2009 Nobel message with a plea for *practical actions to advance human progress*:

> Clear-eyed, we can understand that there will be war and still strive for peace. We can do that – for that is the story of human progress; that's the hope of all the world; and at this moment of challenge, that must be our work here on earth.

Regrettably, president Obama did not take the opportunity to push the argument about the need to end the interventions in Iraq and Afghanistan by non-violent means.[54] Instead, he surged his way out, then negotiated transitional arrangements based on the retention of residual US forces in both countries.

Viewed through the lens of positions taken by Bunche and King, it is clear that Commander-in-Chief Obama falls short as a peacemaker. One is left wondering whether Woodrow Wilson, or even Theodore Roosevelt, might have concluded that the 2009 Nobel Peace Prize Committee made a good wager.

Bibliography

Bunche, Ralph J., 'Ralph J. Bunche Nobel Lecture: Some Reflections on Peace in our Time', 11 December 1950, www.nobelprize.org/nobel_prizes/peace/laureates/1950/bunche-lecture.html.
Crawford, Neta, 'Just War Theory and the U.S. Counterterror War', *Perspectives on Politics* 1(1) (March 2003).
Crawford, Neta, 'The Slippery Slope to Preventive War', *Ethics and International Affairs* 17(1) (2003).

54. I thank Ambassador Thomas Pickering for this insight. Pers. comm., Medford MA, 13 October 2011.

Davis, Lawrence E., 'Dr. King's Response', *New York Times*, 13 April 1967.

Dozier, Kimberly, 'U.S. Special Forces Setting up Strike Teams in N. Africa', 3 October 2012, www. msnbc.msn.com/id/49271035/ns/world_news-mideast_n_africa/#.UHHodLRpuqQ.

Dyson, Michael Eric, *I May Not Get There with You: The True Martin Luther King, Jr.* (New York: Free Press, 2000).

Guardian, 'US Drone Strikes Listed and Detailed in Pakistan, Somalia, and Yemen', 2 August 2012 (www.guardian.co.uk/news/datablog/2012/aug/02/us-drone-strikes-data).

Henry, Charles, and Ralph Bunche, *Model Negro or American Other?* (New York: New York University Press, 1999).

Kennedy, Randall, *The Persistence of the Color Line: Racial Politics and the Obama Presidency* (New York: Pantheon, 2011).

King Jr, Martin Luther, 'Martin Luther King Jr. Nobel Lecture: The Quest for Peace and Justice', 11 December 1964, www.nobelprize.org/nobel_prizes/peace/laureates/1964/king-lecture.html.

King Jr, Martin Luther, 'Beyond Vietnam', address delivered at Riverside Church, New York, 4 April 1967, www.stanford.edu/group/King/liberation curriculum/speeches/beyondvietnam.htm.

Klaidman, Daniel, 'Drones: The Silent Killers', *Newsweek*, 4–11 June 2012.

Mendell, David, *Obama: From Promise to Power* (New York: HarperCollins, 2007), p. 74.

New York Times, 'Dr. King Disavowal Accepted by Bunche', 14 April 1967.

Nobel Prize, 'The Nobel Peace Prize 1906 – Presentation Speech', 10 December 1906, www. nobelprize.org/nobel_prizes/peace/laureates/1906/press.html.

Nobel Prize, 'The Nobel Peace Prize 2009 – Press Release', 9 October 2009, www.nobelprize.org/ nobel_prizes/peace/laureates/2009/press.html.

Obama, Barack, *Dreams from My Father: A Story of Race and Inheritance* (New York: Three Rivers, 1995).

Obama, Barack, 'Barack Obama's Full Speech on 26 October 2002', Liberalscum Buster, http:// liberalscumbuster.wordpress.com/2008/01/26/barack-obamas-full-speech-on-october-26-2002.

Obama, Barack, *The Audacity of Hope: Thoughts on Reclaiming the American Dream* (New York: Crown, 2006).

Obama, Barack, 'Blueprint for Change: Iraq', 21 October 2008, www.youtube.com/ watch?v=wDhOxNeOj4U.

Obama, Barack, 'Remarks by the President on Winning the Nobel Peace Prize', 9 October 2009, www. whitehouse.gov/the_press_office/Remarks-by-the-President-on-Winning-the-Nobel-Peace-Prize.

Obama, Barack, 'Barack H. Obama Nobel Lecture: A Just and Lasting Peace', 10 December 2009, www.nobelprize.org/nobel_prizes/peace/laureates/2009/obama-lecture_en.html.

Obama, Barack, 'Remarks by President Barack Obama at the Martin Luther King, Jr. Memorial Dedication, the National Mall, Washington, D.C.', 16 October 2011, www.whitehouse.gov/ the-press-office/2011/10/16/remarks-president-martin-luther-king-jr-memorial-dedication.

Rhode, David, 'The Obama Doctrine: How the President's Drone War is Backfiring', *Foreign Policy*, March–April 2012 (www.foreignpolicy.com/articles/2012/02/27/the_obama_doctrine?print=yes &hidecomments=yes&page=full).

Urquhart, Brian, *Ralph Bunche: An American Odyssey* (New York: Norton, 1993).

von Clausewitz, Carl, *On War*, abridged version, trans. Michael Howard and Peter Paret, ed., with an introduction by Beatrice Heuser (Oxford: Oxford University Press, 2007).

Wilson, Woodrow, 'President Wilson's Message to Congress', 8 January 1918, Records of the United States Senate, Group 46, National Archives, www.ourdocuments.gov/doc. php?flash=true&doc=62.

Wilson, Woodrow, 'Woodrow Wilson – Acceptance Speech', 10 December 1920, www.nobelprize. org/nobel_prizes/peace/laureates/1919/wilson-acceptance.html.

Zenk, Micah, *Between Threats and War: U.S. Discrete Military Operations in the Post-Cold War World* (Palo Alto CA: Stanford University Press, 2010).

FOUR

RALPH BUNCHE:
THE SCHOLAR–DIPLOMAT

JAMES O.C. JONAH

Ralph Bunche was the first person of African descent to be awarded the Nobel Peace Prize, in 1950, for his peacemaking efforts for the United Nations in the Middle East. He served the UN Secretariat from its birth in 1945 until his death in 1971. This essay first explores Bunche's early efforts in the creation of the UN and his role in its decolonisation efforts. It then traces his peacemaking efforts in the Middle East, his relationship with three UN Secretaries General (Norway's Trygve Lie, Sweden's Dag Hammarskjöld and Burma's U Thant), his contributions to the birth and evolution of UN peacekeeping, and his role in specific cases such as the Suez Crisis of 1956 and the Congo Crisis of 1960–64, as well as his broader activities as the UN's principal 'troubleshooter'. This essay is, in a sense, an 'insider's perspective', as I served the UN for thirty years beginning in 1963, rising to Undersecretary General for Political Affairs, and I was mentored by Bunche at the beginning of my career.

A Life in War and Peace

Ralph Bunche came to the UN Secretariat in New York almost by accident. A distinguished scholar before the Second World War, he had proved himself in conducting excellent research on the mandate system of the French in Togoland (now Togo) and French colonial rule in Dahomey (now Benin). Accordingly, he was very well placed when the US government was looking for an African expert to assist it in its evolving work on the continent, particularly when allied troops were about to be deployed in North Africa. Owing to his performance and achievements in this area, Bunche was later brought into the planning for the United Nations at the Dumbarton Oaks conversations in 1944. For domestic political reasons, the trusteeship principles were never discussed at the Dumbarton Oaks talks, though Bunche later made a tremendous contribution in transforming the mandate system of the League of Nations system to the trusteeship system under the United Nations. At the San Francisco conference of 1945, the African-American scholar–diplomat almost single-handedly formulated the UN Charter provisions on the trusteeship system. With his wealth of experience, it was not surprising that the UN Secretariat needed Bunche's guidance, particularly in the establishment of its Trusteeship Department.

It is significant that, as a member of the US delegation to the first UN General Assembly session in London, in January 1946, Bunche had been approached by Ping Chia Kuo, the secretary of the Assembly's Trusteeship Council, to join the UN Secretariat as assistant director of the Trusteeship Department. Bunche had not responded. However, when Victor Hoo, UN Assistant Secretary General for Trusteeship, had to spend the summer of 1946 in hospital, it was the US delegation that proposed that Bunche be loaned to the new Secretariat to work on setting up the Trusteeship Council and the Trusteeship Department.

Bunche was passionate in ensuring that the trusteeship system become effective. In that endeavour, he teamed up with a British colleague, Wilfred Benson, director of the division of non-self-governing territories. Both men fervently believed that colonialism had no future. Bunche came on temporary loan to the UN Secretariat in April 1946 for six weeks as acting director of the Trusteeship division. The loan was prolonged several times, and in the end, in December 1946, the UN Secretary General, Norwegian lawyer Trygve Lie, on the recommendation of Hoo, requested the US government to release Bunche to become a permanent member of the UN Secretariat. Bunche was happy at the UN Secretariat in New York, because he did not want to go back to Washington DC, due to 'Jim Crow' racist laws in the US capital. Bunche, however, remained with the UN not only because of the racism in Washington DC, but also because he found his job at the world body fulfilling.[1]

His extensive travels and acquaintances before the Second World War (1939–45) in Europe, Africa and Asia gave Bunche rich insights into the workings of the international community. Apart from wide contacts with prominent political and diplomatic personalities in London, Bunche consulted with Jomo Kenyatta, future president of Kenya, and the great Trinidadian pan-Africanist George Padmore. Bunche's 1934 doctoral dissertation at Harvard University had focused on a comparison of French colonial administration in its colony of Dahomey and in the French-administered League of Nations Mandate of Togoland, and he kept a lively interest in the question of mandated territories and dependent peoples. Shortly after he joined the US State Department in 1943, Bunche was invited to be part of a team exploring issues related to international security organisations: part of US efforts to plan for the post-war era. Bunche's main preoccupation was, however, how best to transform the mandate system into something more dynamic. Before the San Francisco UN conference in 1945, Bunche and his colleagues reviewed the issues of trusteeship and dependent peoples. His decisive contributions to the formulations of principles for a trusteeship system as well as his drafting of the specific provisions on the same matter in the UN Charter made him the clear choice to work on the question of Palestine when the UN assumed responsibility for the Palestine mandate from the British government in May 1948.

When the UN established its Special Committee on Palestine (UNSCOP), its Secretary General, Trygve Lie, made Bunche his representative, and he became the heart and soul of the committee. Due to his grasp of the issues involved and his writing and analytical skills, he drafted both the majority and the minority reports, but he

---

1. Brian Urquhart, *Ralph Bunche: An American Life* (New York: Norton, 1993), pp. 133–6.

saw his task as a technical one. Bunche was not pleased with the result of UNSCOP's deliberations.[2]

When the UN General Assembly adopted the partition plan contained in the report and the state of Israel was declared in 1948, war broke out. The UN made efforts to bring about a ceasefire and to promote peace between the conflicting parties. Sweden's Count Bernadotte was appointed as the mediator to assist the parties in reaching a peaceful settlement. Lie also appointed Bunche as his personal representative to the mediator. Thus began a cordial and fruitful relationship between Bernadotte and Bunche. Both men worked tirelessly on the problem on the island of Rhodes until the mediator was ready to submit his report: a document that would have changed, in substantial ways, the UN partition plan on Palestine.

The belief that the mediator would assign the Negev and Jerusalem to Transjordan, while compensating the Jewish state with the greater part of Galilee, triggered Bernadotte's assassination by Zionist extremists in Jerusalem in September 1948. Here was the original concept of a 'territorial land swap' in the Arab–Israeli dispute if one were needed. Bunche was scheduled to have been with Bernadotte, but did not arrive on time to sit beside him in his car, and was informed about the assassination while he was negotiating with border guards to get his British secretary through the Israeli checkpoint. When the report of Bernadotte's death reached New York, the UN Security Council decided to appoint Bunche as acting mediator, vesting him – a member of the UN Secretariat – with executive responsibilities never before granted to any other official except the UN Secretary General.[3] Bunche immediately took charge of the mediator's staff and endeavoured to enhance their morale. The manner in which he managed that critical transition after Bernadotte's death was clear testimony to his leadership skills.

Having completed his reporting responsibilities to the UN Secretary-General and Security Council regarding the assassination of Bernadotte,

    2. Ibid., pp. 148–51.
    3. J.C. Hurewitz, 'Ralph Bunche as an Acting Mediator: The Opening Phase', in Benjamin Rivlin (ed.), *Ralph Bunche: The Man and His Times* (New York: Holmes & Meier, 1990), p. 158.

Bunche turned his attention to his mediation efforts. When he was satisfied that the time was ripe, he began formal talks between Egypt and
Israel on Rhodes island in January 1949. The skilful manner in which
Bunche conducted the armistice talks has been fully documented. In
this context, it is important to observe that Bunche broke new ground
in making arrangements for the talks between Israeli and Egyptian
delegations: it was a mix of 'shuttle diplomacy', direct negotiation and
old-fashioned arm-twisting. The initial pattern that Bunche established,
which was used in the other armistice talks – between Jordan and
Israel and subsequently between Israel and Lebanon, and Israel and
Syria – has been meticulously followed by other UN representatives
who have been requested to conduct negotiations aimed at promoting
the peaceful settlement of disputes.

It serves no useful purpose here to rehash the details of Bunche's
negotiating strategy. Brian Urquhart – the British UN Undersecretary
General for Special Political Affairs between 1974 and 1986 – in his
excellent biography of Ralph Bunche has exhaustively dealt with this
matter.[4] The successful conclusion of agreements between Egypt and
Israel, Israel and Jordan, Israel and Syria, and Israel and Lebanon –
constituting the armistice regime – earned Bunche the Noble Peace
Prize in 1950. In his conduct of the armistice talks in 1949, Bunche was
conscious and proud of the role that the UN Secretariat had played.
He told his colleagues in the Secretariat:

> What is most significant about this entire operation since 17 September
> [1948] … is the fact that since that date it has been exclusively a Sec-
> retariat operation in so far as the mediation and truce supervision is
> concerned.… [We] have been proud of the fact that there was sufficient
> confidence in the Secretariat, on the part of the Members of the United
> Nations, to leave a task as responsible and difficult as this one entirely in
> the hands of the Secretariat.[5]

The tradition of the UN Security Council granting executive responsibilities to a few of its officials other than the Secretary General,

---

4. Urquhart, *Ralph Bunche*, pp. 199–220.
5. Hurewitz, 'Ralph Bunche as an Acting Mediator', p. 158.

begun only three years after the establishment of its Secretariat in 1948, continued over the years, though today, with the steady erosion of the international civil service,[6] senior Secretariat officials are rarely called upon to perform troubleshooting roles. The current preference is to appoint outside officials from governments to perform these vital functions.

Bunche's concept of an independent international civil service may appear to some to be overtly rigid, quixotic and antiquated. His initial reaction when the announcement was made in September 1950 that he had won the Nobel Peace Prize was to reject it. He knew the strict provisions of the UN's staff regulations and rules. However, when he consulted Trygve Lie, the Norwegian urged him to accept the award. When Swedish technocrat Dag Hammarskjöld became UN Secretary General in 1953, Bunche recounted his dilemma and Lie's advice. Hammarskjöld made clear to Bunche that he would not have advised acceptance of the award. Bunche himself came to be hesitant to nominate candidates for the Nobel Peace Prize, although he was under pressure many times to do so. He made very few exceptions. One of them was his nomination of Hammarskjöld, who won the Peace Prize posthumously in 1961.

After Bunche was awarded the Nobel Peace Prize for his spectacular achievement in the Egyptian–Israeli armistice talks, he became the guru of high-stakes diplomatic activities in the UN Secretariat. Hammarskjöld, upon his appointment as the second UN Secretary General, in 1953, recognised this by appointing Bunche as one of two Undersecretaries General without portfolio – the other was the senior Soviet official in the Secretariat, Ilya Tchernychev, the man whom Hammarskjöld had known in Stockholm as Soviet ambassador prior to his appointment as UN Secretary General. Bunche thus transferred from the Trusteeship Department to the Office of the Secretary General, on the thirty-eighth floor of the UN's headquarters in

6. See James O.C. Jonah, 'Secretariat Independence and Reform', in Thomas G. Weiss and Sam Daws (eds), *The Oxford Handbook on the United Nations* (Oxford: Oxford University Press, 2007), pp. 160–74.

New York, where he remained until his death in December 1971. The African-American scholar–diplomat overshadowed all of his Soviet colleagues who joined him in the office over the years: Ilya Tchernychev, Anatoly Dobrynin and V.P. Susloo (a hard-line Soviet apparatchik). Bunche became virtually the pre-eminent political adviser to three UN Secretaries General, and the *eminence grise* of the UN Secretariat. It is important to note that Hammarskjöld's change in the top echelons in the Secretariat was intended to emphasise that, contrary to the arrangements made in the London 'gentlemen's agreement', these senior officials would henceforth cease to be representatives of their governments, but instead become more active members of an independent Secretariat.

Bunche's Commitment to the International Civil Service

Ralph Bunche remained totally committed to the UN Secretariat and the ideals of the international civil service. Had he wanted to, he could have gone on to greener pastures. In April 1948, US president Harry Truman sent his secretary of state, Dean Rusk, to New York to try to persuade Bunche to accept the post of assistant secretary of state for Near Eastern, South Asian, and African affairs. Even with his strong academic credentials and his devotion to Harvard University, Bunche – due to the pressure of events at the UN – had been unable to take up his appointment as professor of government, announced in 1950, at Harvard University. After Dwight Eisenhower was elected US president in 1952, he offered Bunche the position of deputy to Ambassador Henry Cabot Lodge at the US Mission to the UN, but Bunche, noting that he loved his job in the Secretariat, politely declined. In 1956, Eisenhower wanted to appoint Bunche as a member of the US Commission on Civil Rights. In June 1960, Robert F. Kennedy – in support of his brother John F. Kennedy's presidential campaign – went to see Bunche to ask him to join the campaign as a foreign policy expert. Bunche declined, with the observation that he had refused a similar offer from Adlai

Stevenson, the Democratic candidate, when Stevenson was running for president in 1952. Bunche preferred to stay at the UN.

With respect to the UN Secretariat as a whole, Bunche had a strong commitment to staff welfare and advancement, as well as justice and anti-discrimination. It came to his knowledge in July 1952 that a black staff member named Edith Jones was being dismissed from the Secretariat on orders from the Secretary General, Trygve Lie. Her 'crime' was that she was dating a young man and compatriot of the UN Secretary General from Norway, whose parents had complained to Lie. The UN Secretary General had then ordered Jones to be fired. Incensed, Bunche confronted Lie and had the dismissal rescinded.

While at the United Nations, Bunche witnessed the travails of the Korean War (1950–53) and the Soviet Union's withdrawal of recognition of the UN Secretary General and refusal to work with him. Trygve Lie had antagonised Moscow by strongly supporting UN action in Korea under an American flag (made possible by the temporary absence of the protesting Soviets from the Security Council). Owing to Moscow's boycott of the Council, UN Secretary General Lie instructed all senior officials not to accept invitations extended by Soviet-bloc countries. Needless to say, this made life very difficult for senior Secretariat officials. Bunche also witnessed a tragic period in the history of the UN: the witch-hunt in the McCarthy period of 1952–53, which was the first serious challenge to the independence of the international civil service. Owing to the strong support of UN staff and other member states, the world body was able to survive these travails, but lost some of its best staff members. Bunche himself was distressed at the death of a brilliant legal counsel and international civil servant – his friend Abraham Feller – a victim of the cruel attack on the international civil service.

In January 1953, US president Harry Truman, in one of his last official acts, issued Executive Order 10422, which required that every American citizen working for international organisations be subjected to a loyalty investigation. Under that provision, Bunche appeared before the Loyalty Board in 1954. Happily, he was vindicated. The charges against him had been based on false information by people who either were envious of him or did not like him. Essentially Bunche was charged, mainly in the right-wing US media, of subversive activities based on the alleged close relationship between the National Negro Congress – of which Bunche was a member – and the Communist Party.[7]

Two months before the end of his term as UN Secretary General in November 1952, Trygve Lie made arrangements with the US government that made it possible for the Federal Bureau of Investigation to commence the finger-printing of American UN staff members on UN premises. This unfortunate decision by Lie plunged a dagger into the heart of the international civil service. Once Bunche had been cleared of all subversive charges, Hammarskjöld remarked: 'Bunche has always had my unreserved confidence as a man of outstanding integrity. He is an honour to the organisation he serves.'[8]

After a brief period of relative unease resulting from a misunderstanding of the shyness of Hammarskjöld, the relationship between Bunche and Hammarskjöld became exceedingly warm. They were intellectual soulmates and Hammarskjöld trusted Bunche's judgement. Bunche equally respected the integrity and steadfastness of U Thant, the Burmese UN Secretary General between 1961 and 1971. However, at times, Bunche could not fathom the mode of U Thant's spiritual thinking. Bunche was in the hall of the UN General Assembly in October 1960 when Dag Hammarskjöld refused to resign as Soviet leader Nikita Khrushchev had demanded. The Swede went on to oppose Khrushchev's proposal of a troika of Secretaries General, the second serious challenge to the concept of an independent international civil service. Bunche understood clearly that had Hammarskjöld conceded to Khrushchev's demand, this would have dealt a fatal blow to the credibility of the UN. When U Thant returned from a trip in September 1965, he was rattled by Soviet ambassador Nikolai Federenko's criticisms. Bunche noted: 'The Secretary General is thin-skinned and

7. Urquhart, *Ralph Bunche*, pp. 243–56.
8. Quoted in Brian Urquhart, *Hammarskjöld* (New York: Knopf, 1972), p. 73.

takes attacks hard.... Hammarskjöld was more of a fighter – he got
angry and belligerent as well as hurt.'[9]

Bunche's Contributions to UN Peacekeeping

Notwithstanding the vital contributions of Lester Pearson (Canada's
foreign minister), Andrew Cordier and Dag Hammarskjöld, Bunche
can arguably be considered the 'father' of United Nations peacekeeping. Even though Hammarskjöld himself was the initial drafter of the
concept and principles of the UN Emergency Force in the Middle
East (UNEF) of 1956, Bunche, on the basis of the model of the UN
Truce Supervision Organisation (UNTSO) of the same year, made a
major contribution to UNEF. The African American was almost always
alongside Hammarskjöld in the planning and deployment of UNEF.
Subsequently, Bunche became a key member of the Secretariat Study
Group set up by Hammarskjöld to examine the UNEF experience for
the future.[10]

From his office on the thirty-eighth floor of the UN's headquarters
in New York – later called the Office of the Undersecretaries General
for Special Political Affairs – Bunche blossomed as the UN's principal
troubleshooter. From there, too, he actively collaborated with Hammarskjöld in planning for the first major UN peacekeeping mission in
the Middle East, in 1956 – the aforementioned UN Emergency Force.[11]
Though UNTSO observers were unarmed, this experience helped
when the time came to formulate the principles and guidelines for
UNEF. Once UNEF had been deployed, Hammarskjöld decided to
assign its day-to-day supervision and management to Bunche's office.
From then until his death in 1971, Bunche was the executive manager

9. Urquhart, *Ralph Bunche*, p. 378.
10. Urquhart, *Hammarskjöld*, p. 228.
11. See, for example, Adekeye Adebajo, *UN Peacekeeping in Africa: From the Suez Crisis to the Sudan Conflicts* (Boulder CO: Lynne Rienner, 2011); Mona Ghali, 'United Nations Emergency Force I: 1956–1967', in William Durch (ed.), *The Evolution of UN Peacekeeping: Case Studies and Compara- tive Analysis* (New York: St. Martin's Press, 1993); William Roger Louis and Roger Owen (eds), *Suez 1956: The Crisis and Its Consequences* (Oxford: Oxford University Press, 1989).

of all peacekeeping operations on behalf of the UN Secretary General. The African American was primarily responsible for the requirement that all national contingents in a peacekeeping force must serve only under the UN flag. Initially, troop-contributing countries wanted to fly their own individual national flags. While stressing the international nature of UN peacekeeping, Bunche insisted – despite strong opposition from UNEF's advisory committee – that only the UN flag should be flown. Hammarskjöld gave Bunche strong support and the practice became the norm for all peacekeeping operations around the globe.[12]

As is usually the case, the establishment of a UN peacekeeping force in the field involves delicate negotiations with the parties concerned, as well as with potential troop-contributing countries. Hammarskjöld requested Bunche to recommend which countries should be part of UNEF. With many countries wishing to participate, this turned out to be a difficult exercise, but Bunche was firm in ensuring a balanced composition of troop contributors. He accompanied Hammarskjöld on his visits to the Middle East to finalise arrangements for the proper functioning of UNEF and to engage in difficult negotiations with regard to the clearing of the Suez Canal, the deployment of UNEF forces in Gaza, and arrangements on Aqaba.

Bunche also travelled to Latin America and Europe to examine UN offices in those areas, and was a valued member of the Secretary General's team that produced the report for the major reorganisation of the UN Secretariat in 1955. In carrying out these duties, Bunche was a strong defender of the independence of the Secretariat and its international character. Hammarskjöld's confidence in Bunche was such that he showed no hesitation in delegating to him the task of managing UN efforts on the peaceful uses of atomic energy. US president Dwight Eisenhower, in his address before the UN General Assembly in December 1953, had made a number of proposals regarding the new field of the peaceful uses of atomic energy. Among these proposals were two of great importance to Hammarskjöld: the creation of an International

12. Urquhart, *Ralph Bunche*, pp. 271–2.

Atomic Energy Agency (IAEA), and the convening of an international conference on the peaceful uses of atomic energy, to be held in 1955. Hammarskjöld and Bunche devoted much time to these issues, but Bunche played the role of midwife.[13] He worked closely with the group of distinguished international scientists that had been assembled to prepare for the international conference, and participated at the conference when it convened in Geneva in 1955. Bunche further contributed to the establishment of the IAEA. In fulfilling Hammarskjöld's wishes, he made certain that the new institution was brought into a close relationship with the UN. Bunche also presided over the conference, in September 1956, that finalised the statute of the IAEA.

The Congo Crisis

Ralph Bunche had participated in Ghana's historic independence celebration in 1957 (also attended by Martin Luther King Jr) and warmly welcomed Africa's decade of decolonisation in the 1960s. He was therefore pleased when Hammarskjöld requested him to be his representative at the independence ceremonies of the Belgian Congo. Bunche arrived in the Congolese capital of Léopoldville (Kinshasa) in June 1960 after a stopover in Brussels for consultations. His arrival in the Congo meant that the UN Secretary General had a reliable adviser and observer on the ground. Bunche was soon reporting to Hammarskjöld about the situation in the country and the impending dangers. He was worried about the unhelpful attitude of Belgian officials towards the Congolese, although Belgian officials in Léopoldville showed relatively better understanding than those in Brussels.

Bunche was in Léopoldville when the Belgian-officered Force Publique – rechristened the Armée Nationale Congolaise (ANC) – mutinied in Thysville in July 1960. The evolving situation was so chaotic that Bunche wrote to his wife: 'This is the toughest spot I've ever been

---

13. Ibid., p. 261.

in – even Palestine was safe by comparison.'[14] Against Bunche's advice, Belgian troops intervened, with disastrous consequences.[15]

Bunche also did not have a good relationship with the young and in-experienced Congolese leaders, particularly the radical prime minister, Patrice Lumumba. With the fear expressed by the Western powers of a communist takeover in the Congo, Bunche had to maintain a delicate balance in his dealings with the US ambassador, Clare Timberlake. He anticipated that both President Joseph Kasavubu and Prime Minister Patrice Lumumba would request UN peacekeeping troops. When they finally did, Hammarskjöld convened a meeting of the Security Council. The Congo was not yet a member of the UN. When the Council authorised the deployment of a United Nations force, the UN Opera-tion in the Congo (ONUC), in July 1960, Bunche was already on the ground and so was able to help Hammarskjöld to establish the force. In the early months of ONUC, even bitter critics of the UN applauded the speed and skill with which Hammarskjöld and Bunche had set the force in motion.[16]

Later, the situation in the Congo deteriorated in the face of intense East–West rivalries. The UN was caught in the middle, and Bunche found himself under pressure from all sides. When he felt that his impartiality was being questioned by Patrice Lumumba, he asked Hammarskjöld to recall him to headquarters in New York. There, Bunche became an active participant in the so-called Congo Club, a small group of senior Secretariat officials with whom Hammarskjöld regularly consulted on policy towards the Congo and the state of politi-cal, military and civil administration in the country. Besides Bunche, there were two other senior American officials – Andrew Cordier and Henry Labouisse – in the Congo Club, which was a favourite target of Soviet abuse during the zenith of the Cold War. Bunche was criticised

14. Ibid., p. 308.
15. See Georges Abi-Saab, *The United Nations Operation in the Congo, 1960–1964* (Oxford: Oxford University Press, 1978); Catherine Hoskyns, *The Congo Since Independence, January 1960–December 1961* (London: Oxford University Press, 1965); Conor Cruise O'Brien, *To Katanga and Back: A UN Case History* (London: Hutchinson, 1962); Indar Jit Rikhye, *Military Adviser to the Secretary-General: UN Peacekeeping and the Congo Crisis* (London: Hurst, 1993).
16. Urquhart, *Ralph Bunche*, p. 319.

for his membership of the club, as well as for his activities in the Congo when he served as the special representative of the Secretary General from June to August 1960.

Bunche and the United States Government

For the greater part of his career in the UN Secretariat, Bunche, like other senior Americans in the Secretariat such as Andrew Cordier, was dogged by the suspicion that he was an executor of American foreign policy – a notion that was anathema to him as a bona fide international civil servant. While it is accurate to note that Bunche, as well as Hammarskjöld, shared the same world-view as many Western policymakers – particularly during the intense period of the Cold War – he was never subservient to US policy and goals. This would become evident during the Congo Crisis and in the events that led to the withdrawal of UNEF from the Sinai in 1967. In the Congo, for example, Bunche's light-skinned complexion posed considerable problems for the Congolese leadership. They could not make up their minds as to whether they should relate to him as an African American or as part of the Western 'imperialist' group. In July 1960, when security was breaking down in Léopoldville, the US ambassador, Clare Timberlake, urged the French ambassador to ready French troops in Brazzaville for intervention in the Congo. Bunche was strongly opposed to such a move. Furthermore, in July 1960 Bunche had refused a recommendation by the Swedish force commander, General Carl von Horn, to disarm the Congolese troops, which Timberlake had strongly recommended. Bunche's view was that the Congolese troops could be disarmed only with the consent of the government, which was denied by the Congolese prime minister.[17]

In July 1960, Hammarskjöld appointed Bunche as the commander of ONUC, pending the arrival from Jerusalem of the Swedish chief of staff of UNTSO, General Carl von Horn, who was to command the peacekeeping force in the Congo. At the initial stage of the Congo

---

17. Ibid., p. 312.

operation, Bunche was obliged to work closely with Clare Timberlake, which inevitably made Moscow suspicious. But Bunche was always conscious of his role as an independent civil servant, and on occasion made decisions that Timberlake opposed.[18] The Congo, then, was a major test of the authority and independence of the UN Secretary General and its Secretariat. Bunche clashed with von Horn, who later wrote critically about Bunche in his book recounting his experience in the Congo.[19] Von Horn wanted to use military force in the Congo, while Bunche believed in resolving problems through patient negotiations.

Even a patient Bunche found the going rough when dealing with the mercurial Congolese premier Patrice Lumumba.[20] He felt that he could not agree to Lumumba's request that the Congolese government should take charge of Léopoldville airport. In his anger, Lumumba refused to meet with Bunche to discuss the matter further, and Bunche, having realised that his impartiality was being questioned, asked to return to headquarters in New York. Despite his difficulties with Lumumba, Bunche was saddened when he learned of his murder in Katanga in February 1961. Yet in a demonstration by African-American members of the public in the UN Security Council following the death of Lumumba, Bunche was criticised, along with Dag Hammarskjöld and Adlai Stevenson, the US permanent representative to the UN, as 'stooges' of the white man.

Bunche had, however, gone to great lengths to preserve his impartiality and objectivity. For example, during his first visit to Katanga he realised that he would have to rely on the coding facilities of the Belgian officials to communicate with Hammarskjöld, who was in Léopoldville. Bunche quickly arranged to communicate with the UN Secretary General using a prearranged code system. This caused some confusion with the UN team in Léopoldville, but the Belgians had no clue of what Bunche was reporting to Hammarskjöld. After Hammarskjöld's tragic

18. Ibid., p. 312.
19. Carl von Horn, *Soldiering for Peace* (London: Cassell, 1996).
20. See Crawford Young, 'Ralph Bunche and Patrice Lumumba: The Fatal Encounter', in Robert A. Hill and Edmond J. Keller (eds), *Trustee For the Human Community: Ralph J. Bunche, the United Nations, and the Decolonisation of Africa* (Athens: Ohio University Press, 2010), pp. 128–47.

death in a plane crash over Zambia in September 1961 while pursuing efforts to resolve the Congo Crisis, Bunche continued to be the main adviser to the next UN Secretary General, U Thant. Since the Burmese diplomat was new to the problems in the Congo, Bunche carried a heavy burden in tackling the highly controversial UN operation. But he persevered, and in the end the UN's 20,000 peacekeepers were able to prevent the secession of Katanga and thereby preserve the unity of the Congo. The mission left the country in 1964 after four years of tortuous peacekeeping.

After the Congo

Towards the end of his career at the UN, Bunche turned his attention to negotiation and conciliation. To help resolve the 1962 dispute in Yemen involving Saudi Arabia and Egypt, Bunche was requested by U Thant to travel to Yemen in February 1963. Following his talks and further consultations with Washington, a plan of disengagement was worked out, and a UN observer force was deployed to ensure implementation of the agreement. The UN Yemen Observer Mission (UNYOM), which began its operation in July 1963, was managed by Bunche's office. He also played a critical role in settling a dispute between Britain and Iran over Bahrain in 1969–70. The negotiations were conducted through 'quiet diplomacy' without much fanfare. Both Teheran and London accepted Bunche's recommendation calling for the people of Bahrain to decide their own future. The British and Iranians gave full credit to Bunche for the successful negotiations, which were endorsed by the UN Security Council.

   The dramatic events leading up to the Six Day War between Egypt and Israel in 1967 and its aftermath were troubling to Bunche. Despite his and U Thant's best efforts to arrest the worsening situation in the Middle East – after Egypt had requested the withdrawal of UNEF in May 1967 – they were unsuccessful. Bunche himself came under severe criticism from many quarters. The most disappointing was the accusation from Egypt that he was colluding with Washington to embarrass

Cairo. There appeared to be a conflict within the Egyptian government itself. Strong evidence showed that its popular leader Gamal Abdel Nasser was considering the redeployment of UNEF forces in Sinai and Gaza rather than complete withdrawal, but the Egyptian military brass preferred total withdrawal. In fact, the action on the ground by the Egyptian forces left no other options. Nevertheless, Bunche was clear in his mind that even the redeployment of UNEF was unacceptable. He firmly believed that the UN could not stand aside while the Egyptian army attacked Israel. It was due to this principled position that Bunche was criticised by the Egyptians for being inflexible.

Bunche and U Thant were further criticised by some Western governments and media for not being firm with Nasser. Critics argued that they should have used diplomacy to prevent the withdrawal of UNEF. These allegations, however, did not take fully into account the fact that U Thant had gone to Cairo to seek to change Nasser's position, and that the matter had been discussed with the UNEF advisory committee, which Hammarskjöld had set up in 1957. Far more compelling was the fact that two of the largest UNEF contingents – India's and Yugoslavia's – had already indicated that their troops would be withdrawn. In addition, the legal argument was strong: once Egypt had withdrawn its consent from UNEF, there was no longer any legal basis to maintain the force.

When war finally and inevitably broke out in June 1967, Bunche and U Thant were blamed by a section of the world media, but neither allowed this to deter the UN from undertaking actions to bring a rapid end to the fighting. Bunche worked tirelessly on two major documents for U Thant that set the record straight: notes on the withdrawal of UNEF, and a report prepared for the special emergency session of the UN General Assembly that met in June 1967.[21] That the prestige of the organisation he loved was at one its lowest ebbs was one of the main reasons why Bunche expended so much time and effort to demonstrate that he and the UN Secretary General had done everything

---

21. Urquhart, *Ralph Bunche*, pp. 410–12.

within their power to avert war in the Middle East. As the key adviser to U Thant, Bunche was blamed by some for wrongly advising the Secretary General to accede to Nasser's request to withdraw UNEF from Sinai, but both men had exhausted every possibility to avert the war. The Egyptian government was so convinced that Bunche had made a blunder that U Thant was advised not to take him with him on his trip to Cairo to meet with Nasser. Bunche, however, soldiered on as U Thant's trusted adviser on matters in the Middle East and other issues. Until the end of his life in 1971, he shared U Thant's deep regret that the UN Secretary General's role in the crisis had been so misunderstood.

Concluding Reflections

Throughout his diplomatic career, Ralph Bunche shunned publicity and showed a preference for 'quiet diplomacy'. He was a modest and humble man who never hesitated to stand up for what he believed was right and proper. He was not thin-skinned, and could fight back if he felt he had been unreasonably challenged. Regrettably, Bunche was not blessed with robust health, and for most of his professional life he was bothered by various ailments such as kidney problems and pinched nerves in his neck.[22] However, his deep sense of duty allowed him to persevere under often difficult circumstances. He was extremely resistant to pressure from outside, particularly from his own country, the United States, and was insistent on the highest possible professional and ethical standards.

While Bunche was conscious of his rank within the UN Secretariat and the privileges that went with it, he was equally aware of the world body's responsibilities. It was this balancing act that constrained his involvement in the US Civil Rights Movement in the 1950s. In a eulogy delivered at Bunche's funeral service at the Riverside Church in New York on 11 December 1971, Roy Wilkins, executive secretary

---

22. Ibid., pp. 454–5.

of the National Association for the Advancement of Coloured People (NAACP), said the following about his friend: 'He conceived it to be a matter of honour not to allow his title or his activities in the United Nations to intrude in any official way into the internal affairs of a member nation – the United States of America.'[23] But Bunche was totally committed to the civil rights struggle. He was a member of the NAACP's board of directors, and kept in close touch with the leading civil rights leaders, including Martin Luther King Jr, whom Bunche had joined in the March on Washington DC in 1963 (see Robinson, Chapter 3, and Daniels, Chapter 5, in this volume.) An overarching character trait that commended Bunche to many international leaders was his trustworthiness. Following Bunche's death at the age of 68, U Thant's tribute to him in the UN General Assembly on 9 December 1971 reflected on what he called Bunche's 'unshakable integrity'. Brian Urquhart, the British Undersecretary General for Special Political Affairs between 1974 and 1986 and Bunche's biographer, referred to his 'ingrained and unshakable integrity and sense of principle'.[24] The UN Charter of 1945 specifically mentions 'integrity' as a requirement for an international civil servant. In the conduct of delicate negotiations as well as in the operations of an international secretariat with diverse cultures, ideologies, races, religions and historical experiences, the common ground ought to be the trust that UN staff and member states have for each other.

Bunche's was a 'transforming leadership' in the sense used by James MacGregor Burns.[25] In his lifetime, he demonstrated both moral and intellectual leadership, though Brian Urquhart recounted an incident at a lunch for top UN Secretariat officials during which Secretary General Trygve Lie yelled down the table to Bunche: 'Ralph, you are a great number two man, but not a number one.'[26] When the UN Security Council was considering the recommendation of its Secretary General

23. Roy Wilkins eulogy, Riverside Church, New York, 11 December 1971.
24. Brian Urquhart, 'Ralph Bunche and the Development of UN Peacekeeping', in Benjamin Rivkin (ed.), *Ralph Bunche: The Man and His Times* (Boulder CO: Lynne Rienner, 1990), p. 209. See also Urquhart, *Ralph Bunche.*
25. James MacGregor Burns, *Leadership* (New York: Harper & Row, 1978).
26. Urquhart, *Ralph Bunche*, p. 197.

to appoint Bunche as acting mediator following the assassination of
Count Bernadotte in September 1948, John Troutbeck, the British
ambassador in Cairo, opposed the appointment on the grounds that
Bunche was 'a competent official rather than a statesman'.[27] But most of
those who came into contact with him recognised Bunche as a genuine
international leader of the highest rank.

The special time reserved by the UN General Assembly on 9
December 1971 for its tribute to the memory of Ralph Bunche was
also significant for the fact that the Assembly that afternoon had before
it an agenda item on the situation in the Middle East. Throughout
his career in the UN Secretariat, Bunche had devoted much of his
time and energy to tackling the problems of this region. The last official meeting he had from his office on the thirty-eighth floor of UN
headquarters, before being admitted to the New York hospital where
he died in December 1971, was related to the situation in the Middle
East. In the tributes to Bunche in the UN General Assembly, frequent
references were made to his extraordinary memory and analytical
powers. The US permanent representative to the UN, George H.W.
Bush – who later became US president, from 1989 and 1992 – noted:
'In the constellation of the United Nations leaders, the name of Ralph
Bunche holds a unique place of honour. His death marks the end of
a United Nations era. His example will be permanent inspiration to
all of us who care about the future of the United Nations as a World
Organization for peace.'[28] Due to his prodigious accomplishments as
the world body's pre-eminent 'troubleshooter', Bunche's name became
inseparable from the achievements of the UN Secretariat during his
lifetime. His biographer, Brian Urquhart, observed that Bunche's international stature and ability were vital factors in the work of the world
body, particularly in the work of the UN Secretary General.[29]

It may be recalled that U Thant, the third Secretary General of the
United Nations, agreed to stay on in his job in November 1962 only if

27. Ibid., p. 179.
28. Ibid., pp. 3–4.
29. Ibid., p. 455.

he could count on Bunche's support. It is thus fitting to conclude this essay with U Thant's eloquent tribute to his departed colleague in the hall of the UN General Assembly in December 1971:

> Ralph Bunche transcends both nationality and race in a way that is achieved by very few. He was the most effective and best known international civil servant to my knowledge, and his record of achievement as an individual member of the Secretariat was unsurpassed. He was an outstanding example of that new twentieth-century breed of international officials who devote all their gifts and their lives to the service of the community of mankind.[30]

Bibliography

Abi-Saab, Georges, *The United Nations Operation in the Congo, 1960–1964* (Oxford: Oxford University Press, 1978).

Adebajo, Adekeye, *UN Peacekeeping in Africa: From the Suez Crisis to the Sudan Conflicts* (Boulder CO: Lynne Rienner, 2011).

Burns, James MacGregor, *Leadership* (New York: Harper & Row, 1978).

Ghali, Mona, 'United Nations Emergency Force I: 1956–1967', in William Durch (ed.), *The Evolution of UN Peacekeeping: Case Studies and Comparative Analysis* (New York: St. Martin's Press, 1993).

Hoskyns, Catherine, *The Congo Since Independence, January 1960–December 1961* (London: Oxford University Press, 1965).

Hurewitz, J.C., 'Ralph Bunche as an Acting Mediator: The Opening Phase', in Benjamin Rivlin (ed.), *Ralph Bunche: The Man and His Times* (New York: Holmes & Meier, 1990).

Jonah, James O.C., 'Secretariat Independence and Reform', in Thomas G. Weiss and Sam Daws (eds), *The Oxford Handbook on the United Nations* (Oxford: Oxford University Press, 2007), pp. 160–74.

Louis, William Roger, and Roger Owen (eds), *Suez 1956: The Crisis and Its Consequences* (Oxford: Oxford University Press, 1989).

O'Brien, Conor Cruise, *To Katanga and Back: A UN Case History* (London: Hutchinson, 1962).

Rikhye, Indar Jit, *Military Adviser to the Secretary-General: UN Peacekeeping and the Congo Crisis* (London: Hurst, 1993).

United Nations, U Thant address, UN General Assembly, 9 December 1971.

Urquhart, Brian, *Hammarskjöld* (New York: Knopf, 1972).

Urquhart, Brian, 'Ralph Bunche and the Development of UN Peacekeeping', in Benjamin Rivkin (ed.), *Ralph Bunche: The Man and His Times* (Boulder CO: Lynne Rienner, 1990), p. 209.

Urquhart, Brian, *Ralph Bunche: An American Life* (New York: Norton, 1993).

von Horn, Carl, *Soldiering for Peace* (London: Cassell, 1996).

Young, Crawford, 'Ralph Bunche and Patrice Lumumba: The Fatal Encounter', in Robert A. Hill and Edmond J. Keller (eds), *Trustee For the Human Community: Ralph J. Bunche, the United Nations, and the Decolonisation of Africa* (Athens: Ohio University Press, 2010), pp. 128–47.

---

30. U Thant address, UN General Assembly, 9 December 1971.

FIVE

MARTIN LUTHER KING JR:
THE GREAT PROVOCATEUR

LEE A. DANIELS

> The only thing we did wrong,
> Stayed in the wilderness a day too long
> Keep your eyes on the prize,
> Hold on, hold on
>
> from the traditional freedom song
> 'Keep Your Eyes on the Prize'

Comparatively speaking, the following were some of the kinder comments that came pouring into newspapers and blogs from ordinary
Americans in August 2011 when the massive 30-foot-tall statue of Martin
Luther King Jr, set on the National Mall in Washington DC – America's
most sacred historical ground – was unveiled for public viewing days
before the dedication ceremonies:[1]

---

1. For the rich literature on Martin Luther King Jr, see Taylor Branch, *Parting the Waters: America
in the King Years, 1954–63* (New York: Simon & Schuster, 1989); Taylor Branch, *Pillar of Fire: America
in the King Years, 1963–65* (New York: Simon & Schuster, 1999); Taylor Branch, *At Canaan's Edge:
America in the King Years, 1965–68* (New York: Simon & Schuster, 2007); Rebecca Burns, *Burial for
a King: Martin Luther King, Jr.'s Funeral and the Week That Rocked the Nation* (New York: Scribner,
2011); Clayborn Carson, David J. Garrow, Gerald Gill, Vincent Harding and Darlene Clark Hine
(eds), *The Eyes on the Prize Civil Rights Reader: Documents, Speeches, and Firsthand Accounts from
the Black Freedom Struggle* (New York: Penguin, 1991); Clayborne Carson and Kris Shepard (eds),
A Call to Conscience: The Landmark Speeches of Dr. Martin Luther, Jr. (New York: Grand Central,
2002); David J. Garrow, *Bearing the Cross: Martin Luther King, Jr. and the Southern Christian
Leadership Conference* (New York: Morrow, 1987); Clarence B. Jones and Stuart Connelly, *Behind the
Dream: The Making of a Speech that Transformed a Nation* (New York: Palgrave Macmillan, 2011);
Diane McWhorter, *Carry Me Home: Birmingham, Alabama – The Climatic Battle of the Civil Rights*

'Appalling.'

'This memorial is a disaster. It looks like something the Russians put up to honour Lenin or Stalin in Moscow.'

'The MLK memorial … joins the short list of truly bad art works dedicated to great men.'

'His memorial conveys none of his love of people and justice; rather, it stands as an emotionless piece of granite and crossed arms, closing out the world around him. What a travesty.'

The ceremonies were originally scheduled for 28 August 2011, to mark the anniversary of the 1963 March on Washington, at which King delivered his iconic 'I Have a Dream' speech. However, a massive hurricane that spread over nearly the entire US east coast forced its postponement. The dedication thus took place on 16 October 2011.

The massive white granite block containing the statue of King – half emerging from it with his arms folded across his chest and a stern visage, looking towards the Jefferson Memorial across the gentle pond of the Tidal Basin – is set about 50 feet in front of its twin sister blocks. The effect is as if the monument had been wrenched from their centre. They, flanked on either side by a low wall of green granite containing some of King's more famous quotations, form a dramatic gateway into the plaza. The concept is meant to reflect the hope that King expressed in the soaring phrases of his watershed 'Dream' speech at the 1963 march: that he was returning to the South 'with this faith [that] we will be able to hew out of the mountain of despair a stone of hope'.[2]

Initially, it seemed that everyone found something to dislike about the statue of Martin Luther King, the 'apostle of non-violence', whose strategy for black Americans' civil rights campaign had been inspired by Mahatma Gandhi's civil rights campaigns in South Africa and India between 1894 and 1947. The focus of the individual complaints varied, but there was wide agreement expressed that this first tribute on the

Revolution (New York: Simon & Schuster, 2002); Bruce Watson, Freedom Summer: The Savage Season that Made Mississippi Burn and Made America a Democracy (New York: Viking, 2010); John A. Williams, The King God Didn't Save: Reflections on the Life and Death of Martin Luther King, Jr. (New York: Coward–McCann, 1970).
    2. Martin Luther King Jr, 'I Have a Dream,' speech delivered 28 August 1963, www.americanrhetoric.com/speeches/mlkihaveadream.htm.

Mall to an African American – pointedly set on an axis between the memorial to Thomas Jefferson, the president many consider to be American democracy's intellectual progenitor, and that of Abraham Lincoln, the president who saved the Union and emancipated the millions of enslaved Africans and African Americans – was a disappointment.

'A Mirror of Greatness, Blurred', declared the headline atop the review by Edward Rothstein, the chief cultural critic of the *New York Times*.[3] His counterpart at the *Washington Post*, Phillip Kennicott, declared the statue the 'unfortunate' result of the plan for the entire 4-acre memorial being 'stuck between the conceptual and the literal' – the upshot being that 'once it was decided that there had to be a monumental, lifelike image of King, the concept and its literal execution were both doomed to failure'.[4]

As one who was at the site the day it was dedicated, I appreciated the criticism – not because I agreed or disagreed with it, but simply for the controversy. That – the controversy – is what was fitting and healthy. It was a metaphorical breath of fresh air, blowing away at least some of the clouds of stultifying hero-worship and religiosity that have continually threatened to distort who and what the real Martin Luther King was, and what it was he was fighting for and against. It was a reminder of what King was in life, and what he remains in death: a provocateur.

Controversy surrounded the man at every stage of his thirteen-year odyssey from his twenty-sixth to thirty-ninth birthdays, from youthful, highly educated black Baptist preacher to the world's greatest provocateur for justice. And why would it not have? The mission King undertook was enormous: to bring into being the final stage of American democracy's legal commitment to the rights of black Americans, to guide African Americans through the final stage of claiming their right to be full citizens, and to challenge white Americans to help make their country a just nation.

---

3. Edward Rothstein, 'A Mirror of Greatness, Blurred', *New York Times*, 25 August 2011, www.nytimes.com/2011/08/26/arts/design/martin-luther-king-jr-national-memorial-opens-in-washington.html?pagewanted=all.
4. Philip Kennicott, 'MLK Memorial Review: Stuck Between the Conceptual and Literal', *Washington Post*, 26 August 2011, www.washingtonpost.com/lifestyle/style/mlk-memorial-review-stuck-between-the-conceptual-and-literal/2011/08/05/gIQAv38JgJ_print.html.

The Prophet of the Civil Rights Struggle

Provoking controversy was the only way to shake white America out of its self-induced racial complacency. The only way to change the status quo that had confined black Americans to a small corner of American life was through the 'marvelous new militancy' King referenced in his 'Dream' speech. King fulfilled the role of a militant beyond anyone's expectations – in provoking not only the furious opposition of many whites, but also, in the last years of his life, the considerable exasperation of many of his fellow blacks.

Martin Luther King Jr was a revolutionary of the most profound kind: he was a provocateur for peace. He believed that peace could be achieved not by embracing war but by embracing non-violence. This was the first underestimation that many Americans – many whites, and some blacks – made about King. They thought that he intended his preaching of the power of non-violence to bring about fundamental social change only in the 'American dilemma' of race relations in the United States, that he was confining himself to 'just' the black American freedom struggle.

Surely that seemed in the 1950s and early 1960s a difficult enough challenge. After all, the United States then was a country that had institutionalised a pervasive apartheid. Not as vicious as that in apartheid South Africa and Ian Smith's Rhodesia, to be sure, but brutal nonetheless, especially in the American South. In one sense, America's colour line was comparatively the more shocking, because the country's white majority endlessly boasted of its love for freedom and democracy. In reality, its racially exclusive civic life was shameful. Then suddenly, in the middle of the 1950s, there appeared this small, slight, black Baptist preacher, only in his middle twenties and chosen by a small group of churchgoers and civil rights activists in one of the most virulently racist cities in the South – Montgomery, Alabama – to lead a mass movement to get rid of the seemingly picayune rule requiring blacks to sit at the back of city-run (and therefore taxpayer-supported) buses.[5]

5. *Martin Luther King, Jr., and the Global Freedom Struggle* (Stanford CA: Martin Luther King, Jr.

What the black and white citizens of Montgomery and then the whole of America soon discovered, however, was the preacher's peculiar inner fire and charisma, a magnetism born in part of his ability to use his rich baritone voice powerfully to articulate both the pragmatic and the transcendent personal effect of combining the black religious social gospel tradition and the profound altruism of *agape*.[6] That was the core of King's genius: he persuaded America's black masses that his personal beliefs were theirs, too; that they also could achieve *agape*'s seemingly otherworldly requirement of disinterested, unconditional love for all human beings – even those who denied their own humanity – and use its powerful positiveness directly to confront the murderous, state-sponsored regime of Southern racial segregation.

In fact, King had captured the zeitgeist among African Americans. American blacks – excepting the few revolts involving appreciable numbers of enslaved blacks – had, from their earliest efforts in the seventeenth-century British colonies, always used reformist, non-violent means of petitioning the political system to try to overcome their de-graded political status. However, as late as the 1950s, they had very little to show for these efforts. Indeed, their quickness in adapting themselves to the American political and educational system after emancipation from the two-and-a-half-century gulag of Negro slavery so threatened whites' own sense of identity that the latter embarked on a series of anti-black political actions and court decisions that culminated in the US Supreme Court's 1896 decision in *Plessy* v. *Ferguson*.[7] That ruling fully established racism as law in the American South, and as custom that had the force of law in the North. The amazing thing is that, despite the terrible treatment of African Americans, after *Plessy* they undertook a seven-decade journey – simultaneously geographical, spiritual and intellectual – that vindicated their faith in the idea of democracy.[8]

Research and Education Institute, Stanford University, 13 December 2011), http://mlk-kpp01.stanford.edu/index.php/encyclopedia/encyclopedia/enc_montgomery_bus_boycott_1955_1956.

6. Albert J. Raboteau, 'A Hidden Wholeness: Thomas Merton and Martin Luther King, Jr.', *Spirituality Today*, 13 December 2011 (www.spiritualitytoday.org/spir2day/884057raboteau.html).

7. '*Plessy* v. *Ferguson*', Wikipedia, http://en.wikipedia.org/wiki/Plessy_v._Ferguson; accessed 13 December 2011.

8. 'Great Migration (African American)', Wikipedia, http://en.wikipedia.org/wiki/Great_Migration_%28African_American%29; accessed 13 December 2011.

King came to maturity in the late 1940s and early 1950s, just as black Americans – with a critical minority now in the North's urban centres, and having sufficiently recovered psychologically and materially from *Plessy*'s devastating setback – were ready to apply what the black American intellectual Martin L. Kilson described as a full 'challenge-demeanour' mode to all aspects of Jim Crow,[9] the widely used eponym for the laws and customs that composed the South's legalised racism. African Americans were ready to use the tactics of non-violent resistance to confront white racism directly. A series of carefully plotted legal victories in the 1930s and 1940s, won by the intrepid band of lawyers working for, and allied with, the National Association for the Advancement of Colored People (NAACP), through its Legal Defense and Educational Fund,[10] had forged the legal assault on Jim Crow that led to the landmark school desegregation decision of *Brown* v. *Board of Education* in 1954.[11] Now the struggle had to be taken to the streets.[12] Although the tradition of black protest against segregation on public transportation was actually a century old by then, the Montgomery bus boycott of 1955–56 became the first battleground of the new 'direct mass-action' phase of the black American freedom struggle.[13]

King, born and raised in nearby Atlanta, Georgia, as the namesake of one of the South's most powerful black preachers, had just arrived in the capital of the Old Confederacy[14] in 1954 as the new pastor of the prestigious Dexter Avenue Baptist Church.[15] The city's vibrant,

---

9. 'Jim Crow Laws', Wikipedia, http://en.wikipedia.org/wiki/Jim_Crow_laws; accessed 13 December 2011.

10. Jack Greenberg, *Crusaders in the Courts: How a Dedicated Band of Lawyers Fought for the Civil Rights Revolution* (New York: Basic, 1995), pp. 267–9.

11. '*Brown* v. *Board of Education*', Wikipedia, http://en.wikipedia.org/wiki/Brown_v._Board_of_Education; accessed 13 December 2011.

12. 'We Worked with Martin', Defenders Online: A Civil Rights Blog, 14 October 2011, www.thedefendersonline.com/2011/10/14/we-worked-with-martin.

13. Lee A. Daniels, 'The Montgomery Bus Boycott: It Wasn't the First', Defenders Online: A Civil Rights Blog, 11 November 2010, www.thedefendersonline.com/2010/11/30/the-montgomery-bus-boycott-it-wasn%e2%80%99t-the-first.

14. 'Montgomery, Alabama', Wikipedia, http://en.wikipedia.org/wiki/Montgomery,_Alabama; accessed 13 December 2011.

15. 'Dexter Avenue Baptist Church (Montgomery, Alabama)', in *Martin Luther King, Jr., and the Global Freedom Struggle*, http://mlk-kpp01.stanford.edu/index.php/encyclopedia/encyclopedia/enc_dexter_avenue_baptist_church.

politically astute civil rights community chose him as the boycott's public leader precisely because he was new in town and unknown to its intransigent white political and civic establishment. Within three years of the victory of the Montgomery bus boycott, King was universally acknowledged as the chief spokesperson of the entire fledgling mass movement of black Americans and their (relatively few) white allies who had shown that they were prepared to endure economic privation, jailings, beatings and even death to overthrow America's regime of legalised segregation.[16]

King's performance in that role, in a movement whose leadership and mass base were in fact diffuse and had many 'independent operators' and selfless heroes and heroines, was extraordinary. He therefore richly deserved the Nobel Peace Prize he was awarded in 1964 at the age of 35. He deserved another one even more for the work he carried on after receiving the prize in Oslo. It was during those latter years that King demonstrated to the world that, for him, being a provocateur for peace knew no boundaries.

The Ideology of Non-Violence

[N]onviolence is not sterile passivity, but a powerful moral force which makes for social transformation.

Martin Luther King Jr, Acceptance Speech,
Nobel Peace Prize, 1964

It is of course no accident that the King Memorial stands on America's most hallowed ground, where homage is paid to the (mostly) men and the ideas they espoused that have been sanctified as part of the country's intellectual and spiritual treasure. The King Memorial, in both symbolic and real terms, stands where it does between the Jefferson and Lincoln Memorials, and in close proximity to the obelisk of the Washington Monument, as a provocation: a stark, implicitly de facto refutation of both the centuries of racial wrongs that sacrificed

---

16. David Lisker, 'A Brief History, 1961 Freedom Riders 40th Reunion', Freedom Riders Foundation, 10 November 2001, www.freedomridersfoundation.org/id16.html.

the 'inalienable rights'[17] of non-white Americans, and today's at best naive notion that the United States has entered a 'post-racial' era (see Mazrui, Chapter 2 in this volume, for another perspective.) Instead, the monument constitutes a demand to intensify the dialogue about the relation of the ideas and actions of all four men – King, Washington, Jefferson and Lincoln – to the *idea* of America.

George Washington and Thomas Jefferson, the soldier-statesman and the statesman-intellectual, are unquestionably first among equals among the nation's 'Founding Fathers'. Washington was the stoic, inspiring saviour of the American Revolution of 1776, and, as its first president, America's Cincinnatus;[18] Jefferson was the great creative thinker who penned soaring oratory about freedom. And yet both fully embodied the twisted complexities of the founding of the United States of America. For each derived his wealth and status from 'ownership' of hundreds of enslaved Africans and African Americans. Both were peers of the prominent men who gathered in Philadelphia in 1787 to engineer a constitution[19] for the new nation that exalted the idea of freedom and opportunity *for white men* – and tried to disguise the fact that this was to be based on the theft of freedom and opportunity from those in the land who were not white, most of all the blacks.

Abraham Lincoln would be forced to wrestle with and finally resolve the legality of that nefarious bargain. He was the one who had to salvage the liberal ideals that Jefferson and his colleagues had set down on parchment and then ignored for their own psychological comfort and material profit. The result was the violent confrontation in the 1860s – profoundly traumatic to whites – between morality and immorality, one driven in equal measure by the fierce economic demands of industrial capitalism to obliterate the wasteful, feudalistic regime of slavery. The forces of morality and industrial capitalism, of course, won the military phase of the war. But the white South, capitalizing

---

17. Thomas Kindig, 'The Declaration of Independence: Unalienable/Inalienable', US History, www.ushistory.org/declaration/unalienable.htm; accessed 13 December 2011.

18. 'Cincinnatus', Wikipedia, http://en.wikipedia.org/wiki/Cincinnatus; accessed 13 December 2011.

19. 'Constitutional Convention (United States)', Wikipedia, http://en.wikipedia.org/wiki/Constitutional_Convention_%28United_States%29; accessed 13 December 2011.

on white Northerners' antipathy towards treating blacks as equals, won
the political phase, and for the next century took its revenge against
the sons and daughters of the former slaves.

Martin Luther King Jr was America's guide out of that ethical
morass. He was not really the movement's field general – he rarely
dictated overall strategy, and he directly commanded few troops. But
he was what we might call the convener of the movement, the guardian
of its 'soul force', because in a movement full of powerful thinkers and
strategists, skilled organisers and charismatic orators he was the one
who could best preach its words and promote its vision. That vision
was of a society where African Americans – the first people who could
be said to have been 'made in America' – could lay peaceful claim to
the full measure of their American citizenship.

That is where non-violence came in. King did not 'discover' the idea.
Non-violence sprang from the religious faith of black Americans and
their secular faith in the democratic ideal. But King became the chief
spokesman for its use, not merely as a tactic, but as an ennobling way
of life that enabled blacks to resist the hatred of white racists, even
the murderers, and that gave whites the time and the means to find
a way out of their psychological degradation and to discover that the
American community should have no colour line.

By no means did all blacks within and certainly outside the movement see things the same way. However, non-violence had two major
other effects that cemented the black masses' remarkable, unswerving
loyalty to it for more than a decade. One was that it made whole the
psyche of black Americans. The second was that it was a superb strategy to provoke the white South to reveal to the world the callousness
and horrific violence of the American version of apartheid. The strategy
of non-violence implicitly proclaimed the movement's invincibility to
violence. 'Ain't gonna let nobody turn me 'round, turn me 'round, turn
me 'round/ Ain't gonna let nobody turn me 'round/ Gonna keep on
a-walkin', keep on a-talkin'/ Marching down to Freedomland' went the
words of one movement anthem. And those in the movement meant it.
The civil rights demonstrators expected to be arrested and jailed. Many

were beaten to the point of being hospitalised. Some were murdered. But the movement declared – which proved to be true – that others would come the next day and the day after that to take their place. Through its use of non-violence as a teaching tool, the movement held up a mirror to white America, and many whites outside the South who had rarely thought about their society's racial inequality were shocked at what they saw reflected.

Of course, it helped tremendously that the post–Second World War period, after 1945, was consumed with issues of freedom and opportunity on a global scale: the tense Cold War stand-off between the United States, the Soviet Union and China; the spread of victorious independence movements of coloured peoples in Africa and Asia; the growing material affluence of American society, which helped foster greater racial tolerance as well as the resources for expanding opportunity; the burgeoning interest of newspapers and the general public in news; and the realisation of some within the still-primitive television industry that this was an excellent medium for telling the story of real life in a clear, understandable and dramatic fashion. The Civil Rights Movement's stark juxtaposition of *good* – peaceful demonstrators, wreathed in dignity, seeking rights that were supposed to belong to every American – and *evil* – the enraged, yelling white mobs, the beatings, the murders – provided an excellent vehicle for testing that latter realisation, which would prove so crucial through the 1960s to the development of television and the news industry as a whole.[20] In that regard, the Civil Rights Movement, not the war in Vietnam, was America's first 'living room war'.

All these developments combined to help the movement underscore the wide gap between white Americans' rhetoric about their society and its reality. And yet racism was so deeply embedded in the American system, and in the psyche of most white Americans, that even after the movement endured a concentrated explosion of violence in the

20. Lee A. Daniels, 'When the Whole World Was Watching: The First Time', Defenders Online: A Civil Rights Blog, 15 February 2011, www.thedefendersonline.com/2011/02/15/when-the-whole-world-was-watching-the-first-time.

South during the first three years of the John F. Kennedy administration (1961–63), substantial numbers of Northern as well as Southern whites opposed such bedrock civil rights measures as federal legislation guaranteeing Southern blacks the right to vote.

This opposition, evident in one national poll after another during that period, was a major reason why Kennedy spent the first two and a half years of his abruptly terminated administration 'going slow' on civil rights. His own lifelong lack of acquaintance with black Americans, and lack of interest in America's racial situation until he had become president, accurately reflected that same lack in the huge majority of his white compatriots. It was only in June 1963, when an assassin's bullet claimed the life of Medgar Evers,[21] the charismatic president of the Mississippi state chapter of the NAACP, that Kennedy – who himself would be assassinated five months later – fully committed his administration to the civil rights struggle. He pledged, during a national television address on the very night of Evers's martyrdom, to submit a comprehensive civil rights bill (which became the Civil Rights Act of 1964) to the US Congress. Within days, according to a July 1963 article in the *New York Times*, national polls began to show 'the longest, steepest downgrade of his administration, with no evidence that his reputation as a national leader is doing anything but dropping steadily'.[22] The news report went on to note the obvious explanation, as put forth by both pollsters and politicians, for Kennedy's loss of popularity with the public: his vigorous civil rights programme.

Martin Luther King, speaking at the Lincoln Memorial on that beautiful sun-splashed day in August 1963, did what he was so good at: he couched black America's demand – and its rebuke, one might well say, of Washington and Jefferson and the rest – in an appeal to the idealism of his compatriots. 'In a sense', noted King,

---

21. 'Medgar Evers', Wikipedia, http://en.wikipedia.org/wiki/Medgar_Evers; accessed 13 December 2011.
22. Warren Weaver Jr, 'At Home: The President's Popularity Seems to Be Slipping', *New York Times*, 7 July 1963.

we've come to our nation's capital to cash a check. When the architects of our republic wrote the magnificent words of the Constitution and the Declaration of Independence, they were signing a promissory note to which every American was to fall heir. This note was a promise that all men, yes, black men as well as white men, would be guaranteed the 'unalienable Rights' of 'Life, Liberty and the pursuit of Happiness'. It is obvious today that America has defaulted on this promissory note, insofar as her citizens of colour are concerned. Instead of honouring this sacred obligation, America has given the negro people a bad check, a check which has come back marked 'insufficient funds'.

Over the joyous laughter and applause of the throng, King went on:

But we refuse to believe that the bank of justice is bankrupt. We refuse to believe that there are insufficient funds in the great vaults of opportunity of this nation. And so, we've come to cash this check, a check that *will* give us upon demand the riches of freedom and the security of justice.[23]

As mentioned earlier, King's role as the 'apostle of non-violence' was critical in another way, one that is rarely remarked upon: King, as black America's most prominent advocate, helped the country complete its decades-long project of self-psychoanalysis – its reality-check. That self-diagnosis had begun in earnest after the *Plessy* decision of 1896 stripped blacks of their newly won status as American citizens, and marooned them in a vast sea of cruelty. It required blacks to ask themselves an extraordinary question, as put forth succinctly by the great African-American intellectual W.E.B. DuBois: 'How does it feel to be a problem?'[24] DuBois understood that white America's profound mistreatment of blacks left African Americans no choice but to doubt themselves. 'This', he wrote in his 1903 classic *The Souls of Black Folk*, 'was a strange experience – peculiar even for one who has never been anything else.'[25]

DuBois continued:

23. King Jr, 'I Have a Dream'.
24. W.E.B. DuBois, *The Souls of Black Folk* (New York: Dover Publications, 1994 [1903]), p. 1.
25. Ibid., p. 2.

The Negro American was born with a veil and gifted with second
sight in this American world – a world which yields him no true self-
consciousness, but only lets him see himself through the revelation of the
other world. It is a peculiar sensation, this double-consciousness, this
sense of always looking at one's self through the eyes of others, of meas-
uring one's soul by the tape of a world that looks on in amused contempt
and pity. One ever feels his two-ness – an American, a Negro; two souls,
two thoughts, two unreconciled strivings; two warring ideals in one dark
body, whose dogged strength alone keeps it from being torn asunder.
This history of the American Negro is the history of this strife.[26]

Black America's only hope of solving this crisis was to *think* as well
as act its way out of it. That meant, above all, considering whether the
white racist ideology was right: were blacks inferior? That question
could be answered in the negative only by forging a place of comfort
and opportunity for blacks in American society, despite the barriers
they faced. The success of blacks in making social progress from the
1920s through the 1950s enabled them, then, to expand DuBois's
definition of double-consciousness. At first, this had been a tool for
self-diagnosis and questioning their own capability. Soon, however,
blacks found that this 'second sight' helped them not only to navigate
the discordant, wrenching paths of a modernising America, but also to
examine white America itself. The result was the next stage of double-
consciousness – the 'challenge-demeanour' and its mass expression: the
civil rights movement of the 1950s and 1960s.

In other words, black Americans refashioned double-consciousness
from a burden into a compass and a gyroscope to steady themselves
and plot their course along the seventy-year trek from *Plessy* to the civil
rights victories of the 1960s. Their commitment to non-violence, with
its demand for discipline, stoic courage and self-sacrifice if necessary for
the good of the community, together with their pledge of allegiance to
America itself, hardly ever acknowledged, was the final test that black
Americans undertook to prove – to themselves and above all to others
– their worthiness as human beings and as full American citizens.

---

26. Ibid.

Containing Black Rage

There is a definite effort on the part of America to change Martin
Luther King, Jr. from what he was really about – to make him the
Uncle Tom of the century. In my mind, he was the militant of the
century.[27]

Reverend Hosea Williams, a chief lieutenant
to Martin Luther King Jr

Yet, amid the progress towards full citizenship that the March on
Washington in 1963 had made apparent, a shocking three-year spasm
of violence was still to course through the arteries of America's body
politic – as signalled three weeks after the March by the infamous
bombing of the Sixteenth Street Baptist Church in Birmingham,
Alabama, which killed four young black girls.[28] The trail to freedom
grew bloodier still the next summer, with another racial crime that
again shocked the world: the murder of civil rights workers Michael
Schwerner, Andrew Goodman and James Chaney in Mississippi.[29]
Still more were to die on the civil rights battlefront in the coming
years before King's own martyrdom. And many blacks regarded the
February 1965 assassination of Malcolm X – on the heels of Kennedy's
assassination – as further evidence that the dynamic of political violence
spreading through American society was a by-product of the racist
violence used against the Civil Rights Movement.

Indeed, one could argue that it was this stretch of time as much
as any other that cast a quality of heroic tragedy over the Movement.
Tragedy attends all great historical struggles. In the fight for the
freedom of black Americans, the road to salvation would be hallowed
by the blood of the righteous. Some would lose their lives. This was
the destiny of a great endeavour.

---

27. Garrow, *Bearing the Cross*.
28. '16th Street Baptist Church', Wikipedia, accessed 13 December 2011, http://en.wikipedia.org/wiki/16th_Street_Baptist_Church.
29. Bruce Watson, 'Freedom Summer: The Savage Season That Made America a Democracy', *Defenders Online: A Civil Rights Blog*, 2 July 2010, www.thedefendersonline.com/2010/07/02/freedom-summer-the-savage-season-that-made-america-a-democracy.

But it was also clear that with the passage of the two landmark civil rights laws – the Civil Rights Act of 1964[30] and the Voting Rights Act of 1965[31] – many Americans, black as well as white, felt that the usefulness of non-violence and of the Civil Rights Movement – and perhaps of King himself – was at an end. It was not only the enactment of these laws under the presidency of Lyndon Johnson, with their outlawing of the stark forms of racial injustice and their emphasis on the use of 'process' and 'politics' in traditional terms to address the needs of black America, that was significant. There was also a clear sense among the nation's white majority that they had done all they could reasonably be asked to do. That black Americans insisted that the federal laws were just the beginning of the changes needed, on the other hand, produced a new palpable tension across the colour line.

That was soon to be sharpened to a fever pitch when the black ghettos of the country's North and West began to explode, beginning with the Harlem ghetto of New York City in 1964. The furious conflagration in the Watts ghetto of Los Angeles the following year – the more stunning because of the neighbourhood's seemingly benign palm-treed, single-family-home character – set the pattern that was to be followed through the rest of the decade in large cities, most notably Detroit and Newark, and small alike: wholesale violence confined to the ghettos that was to leave substantial sections of many of them scarred for decades to come.

Martin Luther King, along with many of the civil rights leaders, had seen this uncapping of explosive, destructive anger coming. He had warned America at several points during his 1963 'Dream' speech 'of the fierce urgency of Now' and that 'the whirlwinds of revolt will continue to shake the foundations of our nation until the bright day of justice emerges'. He had made it clear to all who were willing to listen that black Americans lived 'on a lonely island of poverty in the midst of a vast ocean of material prosperity' all over the country, and not just

---

30. 'Civil Rights Act of 1964', Wikipedia, http://en.wikipedia.org/wiki/Civil_Rights_Act_of_1964; accessed 13 December 2011.
31. 'The Voting Rights Act of 1965', US Department of Justice, www.justice.gov/crt/about/vot/intro/intro_b.php; accessed 13 December 2011.

in the South. And King had declared that 'we cannot be satisfied as long as the Negro's basic mobility is from a smaller ghetto to a larger one ... [nor] as long as a Negro in Mississippi cannot vote and a Negro in New York believes he has nothing for which to vote.'[32] Did America think that these were mere rhetorical flourishes?

King spent the last three years of his life (1965–68) casting about for a strategy to reorient the Civil Rights Movement to resolve the issues he had warned America about at the Lincoln Memorial in 1963, the issues that the rioters in the ghettos had put before the nation in much starker fashion. The practice of traditional politics was one way, and the explosion of black political activism along those lines would bear tremendous fruit in the coming years. Perhaps the most extraordinary of the facts that showed how readily blacks took to traditional politics was that in 1972 – merely seven years after the Voting Rights Act had opened American politics to meaningful black participation throughout the country, not just in the South – Shirley Chisholm, a black Democratic congresswoman from Brooklyn, New York, mounted, with no help from the traditional white political establishment and precious little from her black male office-holding colleagues, a surprising and credible campaign for the presidency of the United States. Chisholm made it all the way to the first days of the Democratic National Convention before making way for the eventual nominee, South Dakota senator George McGovern. Her campaign set the model for audacity and smartly played politics which would become the hallmark of black politics to the present, ultimately producing the triumph of America's first black president in November 2008: Barack Obama (see Mazrui, Chapter 2, and Robinson, Chapter 3, in this volume).

But traditional political activism was not the path that Martin Luther King was interested in. His vision of the economic needs of the masses of black Americans, and of the moral health of the country, was much broader. In fact, King's own belief in non-violence as a means of eliminating injustice – social, political and economic – had intensified. Many

---

32. King Jr, 'I Have a Dream'.

in America were so intent on writing King off as a social force that they did not realise he had saved his greatest work for the final act of his life.

Concluding Reflections

Well I don't know what will happen now; we've got some difficult days ahead. But it really doesn't matter with me now because I've been to the mountaintop.

                                                        Martin Luther King Jr

Martin Luther King Jr died on 4 April 1968, slain by an assassin's bullet. He was murdered because he had become even more of a disturber of the unjust peace once he moved beyond the fight to destroy the stark, legalised racism of the Jim Crow South during the 1950s and early 1960s. It was after being awarded the Nobel Peace Prize in 1964 that King began directly to attack not only anti-black racism in the North but also the structural foundations of economic inequality that had made it so effective. He soon began to lose support among Northern politicians, both white and black, and among the editorial boards of Northern white newspapers.

It was after King spoke out against the Vietnam War in 1967, exactly one year prior to his assassination, in his brilliant 'Beyond Vietnam' speech at New York's Riverside Church – infuriating President Lyndon Johnson and much of the liberal establishment – that the leadership of the established civil rights organisations began openly to criticise him. Liberal and conservative pundits also began to excoriate him for involving himself in foreign policy. In early 1968, King immersed himself in a complex strike by black sanitation workers in Memphis for better pay and working conditions, and announced plans to bring a multiracial 'Poor People's Campaign' to Washington DC, to lobby the US Congress and the White House. Critics declared that he had made an immense strategic mistake and largely expended his political capital as a leader.

In fact, in retrospect, those years were King's finest hours. He never submitted to the seductive post–Nobel Prize offers from the

Johnson White House and the establishment, and never compromised his reformist rhetoric and activism for the sake of conventional bounds. He never backed down when erstwhile allies abandoned him and government operatives, taping his telephone calls and shadowing his every move, threatened to expose his great personal weakness: his apparently relentless philandering.

King pressed on, despite knowing that financial contributions to his organisation, the Southern Christian Leadership Conference, were drying up; that more black Americans themselves were questioning the relevance of non-violent activism; and that the exposure of his sexual wanderlust would surely wreck his reputation. Yet his work over the last three years of his life is just as admirable as his work during the civil rights struggle. Reverend Hosea Williams, one of King's closest aides throughout the years of struggle, described him as 'the militant of the century'. Williams was referring to the twentieth century. But King may hold this title for a good part of the twenty-first as well.

Martin Luther King Jr – the 'apostle of non-violence' – was shadowed by violence his entire life. Of course, at first it was the impersonal kind of violence that shadowed every black Southerner, living in a region where any white man, woman or child could, with impunity, kill, or cause to be killed, any black man, woman or child. But once King joined the movement and became its most prominent voice, violence moved closer to him. It began to stalk him, until it finally caught and destroyed him. But the engineers of his murder forgot, as had the violent white resistance to the Movement in the South once the activists had taken to the streets, that although people can be killed, ideas and inspiration cannot. Did the architects of his death ever understand that they had killed King at precisely the right moment that would guarantee his martyrdom and ensure that his legacy would live on, burning brightly at the centre of consciousness throughout America and around the world?

References

Branch, Taylor, *Parting the Waters: America in the King Years, 1954–63* (New York: Simon & Schuster, 1989).

Branch, Taylor, *Pillar of Fire: America in the King Years, 1963–65* (New York: Simon & Schuster, 1999).

Branch, Taylor, *At Canaan's Edge: America in the King Years, 1965–68* (New York: Simon & Schuster, 2007).

Burns, Rebecca, *Burial for a King: Martin Luther King, Jr.'s Funeral and the Week That Rocked the Nation* (New York: Scribner, 2011).

Carson, Clayborn, David J. Garrow, Gerald Gill, Vincent Harding and Darlene Clark Hine (eds), *The Eyes on the Prize Civil Rights Reader: Documents, Speeches, and Firsthand Accounts from the Black Freedom Struggle* (New York: Penguin, 1991).

Carson, Clayborne, and Kris Shepard (eds), *A Call to Conscience: The Landmark Speeches of Dr. Martin Luther, Jr.* (New York: Grand Central, 2002).

DuBois, W.E.B., *The Souls of Black Folk* (New York: Dover Publications, 1994 [1903]).

Garrow, David J., *Bearing the Cross: Martin Luther King, Jr. and the Southern Christian Leadership Conference* (New York: Morrow, 1987).

Greenberg, Jack, *Crusaders in the Courts: How a Dedicated Band of Lawyers Fought for the Civil Rights Revolution* (New York: Basic, 1995).

Jones, Clarence B., and Stuart Connelly, *Behind the Dream: The Making of a Speech that Transformed a Nation* (New York: Palgrave Macmillan, 2011).

Kennicott, Philip, 'MLK Memorial Review: Stuck Between the Conceptual and Literal', *Washington Post*, 26 August 2011 (www.washingtonpost.com/lifestyle/style/mlk-memorial-review-stuck-between-the-conceptual-and-literal/2011/08/05/gIQAv38JgJ_print.html).

King Jr, Martin Luther, 'Dexter Avenue Baptist Church (Montgomery, Alabama)', in *Martin Luther King, Jr., and the Global Freedom Struggle*, http://mlk-kpp01.stanford.edu/index.php/encyclopedia/encyclopedia/enc_dexter_avenue_baptist_church.

King Jr, Martin Luther, 'I Have a Dream', speech delivered 28 August 1963, www.americanrhetoric.com/speeches/mlkihaveadream.htm.

King Jr, Martin Luther, *Martin Luther King, Jr., and the Global Freedom Struggle* (Stanford CA: Martin Luther King, Jr. Research and Education Institute, Stanford University, 13 December 2011), http://mlk-kpp01.stanford.edu/index.php/encyclopedia/encyclopedia/enc_montgomery_bus_boycott_1955_1956.

Lisker, David, 'A Brief History, 1961 Freedom Riders 40th Reunion', Freedom Riders Foundation, 10 November 2001, www.freedomridersfoundation.org/id16.html.

McWhorter, Diane, *Carry Me Home: Birmingham, Alabama – The Climatic Battle of the Civil Rights Revolution* (New York: Simon & Schuster, 2002).

Raboteau, Albert J., 'A Hidden Wholeness: Thomas Merton and Martin Luther King, Jr.', *Spirituality Today*, 13 December 2011 (www.spiritualitytoday.org/spir2day/884057raboteau.html).

Rothstein, Edward, 'A Mirror of Greatness, Blurred,' *New York Times*, 25 August 2011 (www.nytimes.com/2011/08/26/arts/design/martin-luther-king-jr-national-memorial-opens-in-washington.html?pagewanted=all).

Watson, Bruce, *Freedom Summer: The Savage Season that Made Mississippi Burn and Made America a Democracy* (New York: Viking, 2010).

Weaver Jr, Warren, 'At Home: The President's Popularity Seems to Be Slipping', *New York Times*, 7 July 1963.

Williams, John A., *The King God Didn't Save: Reflections on the Life and Death of Martin Luther King, Jr.* (New York: Coward–McCann, 1970).

PART THREE

THE FOUR SOUTH AFRICANS

SIX

ALBERT LUTHULI:
THE BLACK MOSES

CHRIS SAUNDERS

Albert John Mvumbi Luthuli (1898–1967), who was sometimes called 'Madlanduna' – his Zulu clan name – was the first African, and the first South African, to be awarded the Nobel Peace Prize.[1] He was awarded the prize in 1961 as leader of the African National Congress (ANC), for its non-violent opposition to the racial policy of apartheid. A man of great dignity and presence, he was the key figure in that struggle in the years before the award of the prize. Let us first consider those years, before turning to the award of the prize itself, what happened after it was awarded, and Luthuli's links with other Nobel peace laureates.

Before the Nobel Peace Prize

The African National Congress, Africa's oldest liberation movement, had been in existence for almost fifty years when Luthuli was awarded the Nobel Peace Prize in 1961 (for 1960). Since 1912 the party had opposed racial segregation and then apartheid in non-violent ways: first by petitions and deputations, and then, after 1949, by using direct action and more confrontational methods. In 1951, Luthuli was elected

---

1. While Luthuli used to sign his surname 'Lutuli', most members of his family and others retain the 'h', and so I follow that spelling of the name.

president of the ANC in what was then Natal province. His public support for the 1952 Defiance Campaign of the Congress Alliance, led by the ANC, caused South Africa's apartheid government to demand that he either resign from the party or be dismissed from his post as chief of the Umvoti Reserve in what is now the province of KwaZulu-Natal. Luthuli, who was known in the ANC as 'the Chief', refused to resign from the organisation which elected him as its new president-general in December 1952. The government responded to the election by prohibiting Luthuli from travelling, a ban that was renewed the following year, and again after his visit to Cape Town in 1959. By the time he was awarded the Nobel Prize a year later, Luthuli had been confined to a small area around Groutville, his home in Natal province.

Groutville, where Luthuli was raised as a child, was a small village that had been founded a century earlier by missionaries of the American Board of Missions, the proselytising arm of the Congregational Church. He attended the local Congregational School before moving to other mission-led institutions, eventually completing a higher teachers' training course at Adams College, where he then taught for fifteen years. Luthuli's leadership qualities were demonstrated when he became secretary of the African Teachers' Association in 1928, and then president of that organisation in 1933. A lay preacher in his church, he rose to become chair of the South African Board of the Congregational Church of America, president of the Natal Mission Conference, and an executive member of the Christian Council of South Africa. Luthuli attended the International Missionary Conference in Madras, India, in 1938. In 1948 he spent nine months on a lecture tour of the United States that was sponsored by two missionary organisations.[2]

It was not until he was in his mid-forties that Luthuli became active politically. From early 1936, he was the elected chief of the Umvoti Reserve, which meant that he had to perform judicial and executive functions. Disillusioned with the role of the churches in opposition to

---

2. See, for example, Anthony Sampson, 'The Chief', in *The Treason Cage: The Opposition on Trial in South Africa* (London: Heinemann, 1958); Nadine Gordimer, 'Chief Luthuli', *Atlantic Monthly*, April 1959; 'The Lutuli Story' (1961), available at www.anc.org.za; Gerald Pillay (ed.), *Voices of Liberation*, Volume 1: *Albert Luthuli*, 2nd edn (Cape Town: Human Sciences Research Council Press, 2012).

racial segregation, he joined the ANC in 1944. He was soon elected to the committee of its Natal division, and in 1951 he became provincial president of the organisation. The next year he joined other ANC leaders in helping to organise the Defiance Campaign against unjust apartheid laws. Confined to Groutville, and after suffering a minor stroke, he could not attend the Congress of the People held outside Johannesburg in June 1955 (where the famous 'Freedom Charter' was drafted), but he was nevertheless among those who were arrested in its aftermath and charged with treason. After being held in custody for a year during the preliminary hearings in the case, he was released in December 1957, when the charges against him and sixty-four others were dropped. Luthuli later testified in the ongoing treason trial on the ANC's adherence to non-violence, and his testimony helped secure the eventual acquittal of the remaining persons charged. Six days after anti-pass demonstrators at Sharpeville were massacred by the apartheid police in March 1960, Luthuli publicly burnt his pass (which all blacks were forced to carry as a form of identification and control) during a protest in Pretoria, South Africa's administrative capital, and called for a national day of mourning. When a state of emergency was declared by the apartheid regime on 30 March 1960, he was among those who were detained. On that occasion, Luthuli was slapped by policemen, an incident recorded in his 1962 autobiography *Let My People Go*.[3] He was held in jail until August 1960, then tried and given a six-month suspended sentence.

Back at his home in Groutville, Luthuli was in 1961 involved in secret meetings with other members of the ANC's national executive at which the issue of adopting the armed struggle was raised. Though he remained a firm advocate of non-violent means to oppose apartheid, Luthuli came to realise the inevitability of the turn to violence, and he agreed not to criticise those who, like Nelson Mandela (see Boehmer, Chapter 8 in this volume), wished to take that path, providing that they formed a separate organisation to pursue violent means to secure

---

3. Albert Luthuli, *Let My People Go: An Autobiography* (Johannesburg: Collins, 1962).

the end of apartheid. Much later, Mandela recalled what Luthuli had said at that time: 'Let us not embark on violence; let us continue with non-violence.' But Mandela added that when Luthuli and others 'couldn't resist the argument I was putting forward, they said, "You go and start that organisation. We will not discipline you because we understand why you have taken this line. But don't involve us; we are going to continue with non-violence".'[4]

Luthuli's Political and Religious Beliefs

Luthuli was indeed, as his most recent biographer, Scott Couper, has noted, 'bound by faith'.[5] From his missionary teachers, he learned that Christianity was relevant to the solving of contemporary social problems, and his Christian beliefs encouraged him towards an inclusive and optimistic vision of what was possible in South Africa. Though he grew up a member of the Western-oriented and mission-educated Christian elite known as the *kholwa*, in an essentially rural, relatively sheltered environment, his education enabled him to pursue a middle-class career. At Adams College, with its interracial faculty, Luthuli came into close contact with liberal white educators. His autobiography described how, while he never abandoned his cultural roots and remained proud of his Zulu identity, Luthuli came to champion a vision of a multiracial and democratic South Africa.[6]

It was as an elected chief that Luthuli came to experience what the coming of apartheid meant for the rural community in which he lived. Unlike other chiefs, he was not co-opted by the state, but was instead deposed by the government. He went on to tell South Africa's prime minister Johannes Strijdom in May 1957 – in a letter later made public – that apartheid was 'an attempt by White South Africa to shunt the African off the tried and civilised road by getting him to glorify unduly his tribal past'. For all his criticism of apartheid, however,

4. Nelson Mandela, *Conversations with Myself* (London: Macmillan, 2010), p. 78.
5. Scott Couper, *Albert Luthuli: Bound by Faith* (Scottsville: University of KwaZulu-Natal Press, 2010).
6. Luthuli, *Let My People Go*.

Luthuli remained a patriot, believing that his country was capable of following a more enlightened path. His relative moderation and adherence to non-violence made him an attractive figure to liberals, both black and white. Though Nelson Mandela and others in the ANC were very critical of liberalism, Luthuli enjoyed close relations with the novelist Alan Paton, who was leader of the Liberal Party, while Ebrahim Mahomed, a Muslim South African of Indian origin, who has been described as Luthuli's 'closest friend',[7] was also a member of the Liberal Party.[8] At the same time, Luthuli recognised, pragmatically, that the ANC needed the support even of communists in the struggle against apartheid. He regarded the movement as a broad church, and became its articulate, progressive and moderate president who, as a Zulu in a Xhosa-dominated organisation, stood above its various factions. Mandela remembered 'the Chief' as combining 'an air of humility with deep-seated confidence', and as 'a man of patience and fortitude, who spoke slowly and clearly as though every word was of equal importance'.[9]

Luthuli's modesty and sincerity shine through in his autobiography, which he dictated to his missionary friends Charles and Sheila Hooper in 1961, before news broke of the award of the Nobel Prize. *Let My People Go* cleverly took its title from the biblical reference to what the Lord had said to Moses, the phrase that had been worked into the song widely sung in the American South during the time of the Civil Rights Movement: 'When Israel was in Egypt's land,/ Let My people go!/ Oppressed so hard they could not stand,/ Let My people go!' The refrain ran: 'Go down, Moses,/ Way down in Egypt's land;/ Tell old Pharaoh/ To Let My people go!' (see also Robinson, Chapter 3, and Daniels, Chapter 5, in this volume.) Luthuli's autobiography appeared in 1962, making no mention of the prize, but the award of the prize meant that

7. Couper, *Albert Luthuli*, p. 123.
8. For Paton's song of praise to Luthuli when he was awarded the Nobel Prize, see ibid., p. 131. When Paton spoke at Luthuli's funeral, he was not allowed to quote the ANC leader; Alan Paton, *The Long View* (London: Pall Mall, 1968), p. 265. Privately, Paton complained to Mary Benson, Luthuli's first biographer, of Luthuli's laziness; Peter Alexander (ed.), *Alan Paton: Selected Letters* (Cape Town: Van Riebeeck Society, 2009), p. 307, Paton to Benson, 27 January 1964.
9. Nelson Mandela, *Long Walk to Freedom* (London: Abacus, 1995), p. 165.

his autobiography gained a much wider readership internationally than it otherwise would have. As Luthuli was a 'banned' person, the book could not be sold in South Africa, but some copies circulated underground. An impressive work, it was dedicated, significantly, to 'Mother Africa', to his own mother, and to Nokukhanya, his wife, who was of immense support to him throughout his marriage.[10]

The Award of the Nobel Peace Prize

In 1960 the Nobel Peace Committee decided that none of the nominees that year met the criteria outlined in the will of Alfred Nobel, and awarded no peace prize. The following year, however, the committee, for the first time, explicitly adopted a policy of supporting human rights in awarding the prize,[11] and in October 1961 Luthuli was informed that he had been awarded the Peace Prize for 1960. The 1961 prize went to the Swedish Secretary General of the United Nations, Dag Hammarskjöld, who had been killed in an air crash over Zambia the previous month (see Jonah, Chapter 4 in this volume). Introducing the prizewinners in Oslo on 10 December 1961, Gunnar Jahn, the Norwegian chair of the Nobel Peace Committee, linked the two men and referred to both as fighters for human rights:

> Never has [Luthuli] succumbed to the temptation to use violent means in the struggle for his people. Nothing has shaken him from this firm resolve, so firmly rooted in his conviction that violence and terror must not be employed.... Well might we ask: will the nonwhites of South Africa, by their suffering, their humiliation, and their patience, show the other nations of the world that human rights can be won without violence, by following a road to which we Europeans are committed both intellectually and emotionally, but which we have all too often abandoned? If the nonwhite people of South Africa ever lift themselves from their humiliation without resorting to violence and terror, then it will be above all because of the work of Lutuli, their fearless and incorruptible leader who, thanks to his own high ethical standards, has rallied his

---

10. See Peter Rule, Marilyn Aitken and Jenny van Dyk, *Nokukhanya: Mother of Light* (Braamfontein: Grail, 1993).

11. Kader Asmal, David Chidester and Wilmot James (eds), *South Africa's Nobel Laureates: Peace, Literature, and Science* (Johannesburg: Jonathan Ball, 2004), p. 63.

people in support of this policy, and who throughout his adult life has staked everything and suffered everything without bitterness and without allowing hatred and aggression to replace his abiding love of his fellow men. But if the day should come when the struggle of the nonwhites in South Africa to win their freedom degenerates into bloody slaughter, then Lutuli's voice will be heard no more. But let us remember him then and never forget that his way was unwavering and clear.[12]

Wearing a suit but also a Zulu headdress and an African necklace, to emphasise his origins, Luthuli accepted the award. He began his Nobel speech by paying tribute to his fellow Swedish laureate Dag Hammarskjöld, who had, said Luthuli, sacrificed his life in the quest for peace in Africa. 'The Chief' then told his audience that when the South African minister of interior, Johannes (Jan) de Klerk, had grudgingly agreed to give him a passport to allow him to travel to Oslo, de Klerk had told him that he did not deserve the prize. 'Such is the magic of a peace prize', Luthuli continued in a self-deprecating vein, 'that it has even managed to produce an issue on which I agree with the Government of South Africa. I don't think there are very many issues on which we agree.' Luthuli then noted that he accepted the award not for himself but 'on behalf of the people of South Africa, all the people of South Africa, especially the freedom-loving people [and] for the whole continent of Africa'. He regarded the award 'as recognition of the sacrifice made by many of all races, particularly the African people, who have endured and suffered so much for so long'.[13]

The next day, Luthuli delivered his Nobel lecture at the University of Oslo. Titled 'Africa and Freedom', this is one of the greatest speeches ever made by a South African.[14] After observing that the award was a 'declaration of solidarity with those who fight to widen the area of liberty in my part of the world', he called the prize 'welcome recognition of the role played by the African people during the last fifty years

---

12. www.nobelprize.org/nobel_prizes/peace/laureates/1960/press.html.
13. Luthuli's acceptance speech is available at www.nobelprize.org/nobel_prizes/peace/laureates/1960/lutuli-acceptance.html.
14. The speech was drafted in part by Rusty Bernstein, who records this in his autobiography, *Memory Against Forgetting* (London: Viking, 1999). Bernstein was among those charged in the Rivonia trial for involvement with MK.

to establish, peacefully, a society in which merit and not race would fix the position of the individual in the life of the nation'. He then went on to tell his audience that Africa as a whole was 'a continent in revolution against oppression', with 'people everywhere from north to south of the continent ... reclaiming their land, their right to participate in government, their dignity as men, their nationhood'. The goal was 'a united Africa in which the standards of life and liberty are constantly expanding; in which the ancient legacy of illiteracy and disease is swept aside; in which the dignity of man is rescued from beneath the heels of colonialism which have trampled it'. In South Africa too, said Luthuli, 'the spirit of Africa's militant struggle for liberty, equality, and independence asserts itself'. But it was unforgivable that apartheid was 'utterly indifferent to the suffering of individual persons, who lose their land, their homes, their jobs, in the pursuit of what is surely the most terrible dream in the world', and that the 'golden age of Africa's independence' should also be 'the dark age of South Africa's decline and retrogression, brought about by men who, when revolutionary changes that entrenched fundamental human rights were taking place in Europe ... missed the wind of progressive change'. While methods of struggle may differ from time to time, Luthuli noted that 'the universal human strivings for liberty remain unchanged'. He stressed that 'we, in our situation, have chosen the path of non-violence of our own voli-tion', adding that 'all the strength of progressive leadership in South Africa, all my life and strength, have been given to the pursuance of this method [and] nothing which we have suffered at the hands of the government has turned us from our chosen path of disciplined resistance'.

Knowing that his speech would reach a broad international audience, Luthuli took the opportunity to make the point that the ANC had 'passed up opportunities for an easy demagogic appeal to the natural passions of a people denied freedom and liberty'. Instead, he claimed, the party's vision 'has always been that of a non-racial, democratic South Africa which upholds the rights of all who live in our country to remain there as *full* citizens, with equal rights and responsibilities with all others'. Here, Luthuli was implicitly rejecting the views of the breakaway Pan-Africanist Congress and the 'Africanist' tendency among those within the ANC who had rejected the clause in the Freedom Charter of 1955 affirming that 'South Africa belongs to all who live in it, black and white'. Instead, Luthuli stressed the fact that South Africa was an African country that would be ruled by black Africans. But the ANC itself, in the 1950s, had been a member of the multiracial Congress Alliance, which critics said reproduced the very racial categories of the apartheid state, even as it denounced them. Luthuli knew, of course, that his international audience would appreciate his emphasis on a non-racial vision. The ANC had been sustained, he noted, by the 'magnificent support of the progressive people and governments throughout the world, among whom number the people and government of the country of which I am today a guest; our brothers in Africa, especially in the independent African states; organisations who share the outlook we embrace in countries scattered right across the face of the globe; the United Nations Organisation jointly and some of its member nations singly'. All these had 'reinforced our undying faith in the unassailable rightness and justness of our cause'. But Luthuli went on to tell his audience that South Africans understood that 'our freedom cannot come to us as a gift from abroad. Our freedom we must make ourselves.' Addressing his compatriots as much as his Oslo audience, he added that 'what we need is the courage that rises with danger'.

Luthuli concluded his speech by noting that the new order for which he called would, he hoped, 'stand as a lasting monument to the millions of men and women, to such devoted and distinguished world citizens and fighters for peace as the late Dag Hammarskjöld, who have given their lives that we may live in happiness and peace'.[15] He then sang 'Nkosi Sikelel' iAfrika' (God Bless Africa), the ANC anthem that would, in 1994, be incorporated into the national anthem of a democratic South Africa.

---

15. Luthuli's Nobel lecture of 11 December 1961 is reproduced in Couper, *Albert Luthuli*, pp. 222–34.

After the Nobel Peace Prize

Annoyed by the praise that Luthuli's speech received around the world, and the way he had been received in Oslo, South Africa's apartheid government tightened the bans on him in 1962, the year in which his autobiography appeared. Now nothing that the ANC chieftain said could be reported in South Africa. Another ban, confining him to the immediate vicinity of his home for five years, was issued in May 1964. These restrictions, and his deteriorating health, increasingly marginalised Luthuli within the ANC, but he continued to meet with other ANC leaders in secret. Nelson Mandela, after travelling to a number of African countries and Britain in 1962, returned to Groutville to brief Luthuli on his trip. It was immediately after this meeting that Mandela was arrested[16] (see Boehmer, Chapter 8 in this volume).

Luthuli used the substantial money he received from the Nobel Prize to buy two farms in Swaziland, which he intended to be used by those driven out of South Africa by apartheid.[17] He could never visit the farms himself, but his wife tried to work them; when the farms failed and were sold, the money raised was put into an educational fund based in London for black South Africans.[18] After Luthuli was awarded the Nobel Prize, his contacts with Martin Luther King Jr (see Robinson, Chapter 3, and Daniels, Chapter 5, in this volume), the leading figure in the Civil Rights Movement in the United States, increased. Impressed by the non-violent struggle in South Africa, King had sent Luthuli a copy of his autobiography, *Stride Towards Freedom*, in 1959.[19] In October 1962 the two men issued a joint statement calling for international action against apartheid. Intensified persecution might lead to 'violence and armed rebellion', they declared, and 'large-scale violence would take the form of a racial war', whereas the alternative was to force

---

16. Mandela, *Long Walk to Freedom*, pp. 370–72.
17. Couper says the prize was worth R31,000 in 1961; *Bound by Faith*, p. 140. The suggestion that Luthuli purchased the farms to help MK, and that this indicated his support for the armed struggle, has been refuted by Couper in 'Emasculating Agency: An Unambiguous Assessment of Albert Luthuli's Stance on Violence', *South African Historical Journal* 64(3) (September 2012), pp. 582–3.
18. Raymond Suttner, '"The Road to Freedom is via the Cross": "Just Means" in Chief Albert Luthuli's Life', *South African Historical Journal* 62(4) (2010), pp. 693–715.
19. Martin Luther King Jr, *Stride Towards Freedom: The Montgomery Story* (New York: Harper & Row, 1958).

the government, 'by pressures, both internal and external, to come to terms with the demands of the non-white majority'. Luthuli and King called on 'men of goodwill' to hold meetings and demonstrations on 10 December – which was recognised internationally as Human Rights Day – for economic sanctions and the isolation of South Africa at the United Nations. The facts about what was happening in South Africa should be spread far and wide, they added, until 'an effective international quarantine of apartheid is established'.[20]

None of this could be reported in South Africa, and when the National Union of South African Students (NUSAS) elected Luthuli as honorary president a NUSAS delegation had to meet with him secretly in a field near his Groutville home to tell him the news.[21] In the outside world, Luthuli's fame grew: among the new honours that came his way was being voted rector of Glasgow University in Scotland. In June 1966, US senator Robert Kennedy, having travelled to South Africa to deliver his famous 'Ripple of Hope' speech at the University of Cape Town, visited Luthuli in Groutville. Kennedy reported that Luthuli was one of the most impressive people he had ever met, which brought the restricted leader new attention both in South Africa and globally.[22] But Luthuli was increasingly forgotten about, and in the last years of his life the ANC – now with hardly any presence in the country – was unable to keep lines of communication open between him and its leadership in exile.

Luthuli had experienced a stroke in 1955, after which he suffered from high blood pressure. With age, his hearing and eyesight also became impaired, and this was perhaps a factor in his death. In July 1967, at the age of 69, Luthuli was fatally injured when he was struck by a freight train as he walked on the bridge over the Umvoti river near his home. There were immediately some who blamed the apartheid state for his death and suspected that he had been assassinated,

20. Lewis Baldwin, *Toward the Beloved Community: Martin Luther King Jr. and South Africa* (Cleveland: Pilgrim, 1995); Couper, *Albert Luthuli*, pp. 166, 168–74, 205.
21. John Daniel, a member of the NUSAS delegation, described vividly to me the impression Luthuli made on him, and how awful it was to meet him under such circumstances; interview, 2011.
22. See Larry Shore, 'Ripple of Hope in the Land of Apartheid: Robert F. Kennedy in South Africa, June 4th–9th, 1966', *Safundi* 3(2) (May 2002) (www.safundi.com/issues/3.2/default.asp?nc=).

but no convincing evidence for this claim has ever been produced. On Robben Island, Mandela and his fellow prisoners grieved when they heard of their leader's death. Others, however, who had disliked Luthuli's moderation, inclusiveness and commitment to peaceful means of struggle, continued to view him as a collaborationist, in part for his acceptance of the Nobel Peace Prize.[23]

Luthuli's Relations with Other Nobel Peace Laureates

We have already noted Luthuli's connections with two non–South African Nobel laureates, whom he never had the opportunity to meet: Dag Hammarskjöld, who was posthumously awarded the Peace Prize alongside Luthuli in 1961, and Martin Luther King Jr., who received the prize in 1964. Though King and Luthuli lived in very different contexts, both provided visionary leadership to their people in the struggle against oppression.[24]

Luthuli did meet two later South African Nobel peace laureates. One was the young Frederik Willem de Klerk (see Houston, Chapter 9 in this volume), who had as a student invited Luthuli to speak to the Afrikaner Studentebond at Potchefstroom University. When that university refused to allow the meeting to take place on the campus, de Klerk went ahead with it elsewhere. Though he was to recall this episode in his autobiography, de Klerk emphasised that he was fundamentally opposed to Luthuli's views. Not long after the meeting, it was Frederik's father, South African minister of interior Johannes de Klerk, who said that Luthuli did not deserve the Nobel Prize.[25] While F.W. de Klerk did not mention Luthuli in his Nobel lecture in 1993, Nelson Mandela, who was awarded the Nobel Peace Prize alongside de Klerk, paid tribute in his lecture in 1993 to both Luthuli and Desmond Tutu

23. For this view expressed by Neville Alexander on Robben Island, see Mandela, *Long Walk to Freedom,* p. 523.

24. For a detailed comparison of the two men, see Robert Cook, 'Awake the Beloved Country: A Comparative Perspective on the Visionary Leadership of Martin Luther King and Albert Luthuli', *Safundi* 5(1–2) (2004), pp. 1–19.

25. See F.W. de Klerk, *The Last Trek – A New Beginning: The Autobiography* (London: Pan, 2000).

(see Isaacson, Chapter 7 in this volume), for their peaceful struggles against the evil system of apartheid. When Mandela delivered his Nobel lecture, he was one of Luthuli's successors as president of the ANC, and he had enjoyed close, if not always harmonious, relations with Luthuli until Mandela's arrest in August 1962. Both men had publicly burnt their apartheid passes in March 1960, but Mandela had then led the opposition to Luthuli over the armed struggle in 1961, insisting that the time had come to abandon the path of non-violence.[26] Mandela had by this time become commander-in-chief of the ANC's armed wing, Umkhonto we Sizwe (MK). Luthuli was offended when MK was launched so soon after his Nobel speech, along with flyers boldly stating that non-violence was dead. But, as already noted, Luthuli met with Mandela just before the latter's arrest in August 1962. We do not know what Luthuli's reaction was when he heard that a meeting of the ANC in Lobatsi – in what was then Bechuanaland (now Botswana) in 1962 – had decided that MK, which had been founded as a quite separate organisation, was to be the armed wing of the ANC. He was probably further angered by this news. Nevertheless, when judgment was handed down in the Rivonia trial in 1964, and Mandela and his co-accused were sentenced to life imprisonment, Luthuli issued a statement, as president-general of the ANC, describing them as 'brave men' and calling for their release.[27] When news of Luthuli's death reached Robben Island in 1967, Mandela and his fellow prisoners held a memorial service for him.[28]

Concluding Reflections

The award of the Nobel Peace Prize to Albert Luthuli was a great coup for the ANC, and helped to inspire the anti-apartheid movement both in the Nordic countries and more broadly.[29] South African journalist

---

26. Mandela, *Long Walk to Freedom*, p. 273; Paul Landau, 'The ANC, MK, and the Turn to Violence (1960–1962)', *South African Historical Journal* 64(3) (September 2012), pp. 538–63.
27. Luthuli's Rivonia statement is reported in Couper, *Albert Luthuli*.
28. Mandela, *Long Walk to Freedom*, p. 523.
29. See Tor Sellström, *Sweden and National Liberation in Southern Africa*, vol. 1 (Uppsala: Nordic Africa Institute, 1999), pp. 176ff.

Mary Benson and American academic Edward Callan published bio-
graphical accounts of Luthuli and his work that fed into the growing
international admiration for his role in the South African struggle.[30]
Before he received the Nobel Prize, Luthuli had already called for an
international economic boycott of South Africa. After receiving the
prize, he continued to believe that the international community could
play a decisive role in the defeat of apartheid. It was ironic that the way
that the ANC in exile chose to honour him, immediately on receiving
the news of his death, was to name the MK armed force, which at that
time was about to cross into what is now Zimbabwe, the Luthuli Detachment. The idea was that this force would move through Zimbabwe
and into South Africa itself, but Rhodesian and South African police
soon forced the abandonment of the mission.[31] While the ANC and
the South African Communist Party continued to portray Luthuli as a
militant opponent of apartheid, the head of the South African security
police, General Hendrik van den Bergh, made the ludicrous suggestion
in August 1967, presumably to counter the claims that Luthuli had been
assassinated, that 'the Chief', before he died, had become a collaborator
and had been about to denounce communism and violence and declare
support for what the apartheid state called 'separate development': the
development of so-called Homelands.[32]

While contestations over Luthuli's legacy continued, there were at
first few attempts to honour him. No new edition of his autobiography,
which remained banned in South Africa, appeared, and in the 1970s
and 1980s he became, at least outside what was then the province
of Natal,[33] an almost forgotten figure. As the South African conflict
intensified, and the emphasis fell increasingly on the armed struggle,
Luthuli came to be seen as yesterday's man. Only with the change of

30. Mary Benson, *Chief Albert Lutuli of South Africa* (London: Oxford University Press, 1963);
Edward Callan, *Albert John Luthuli and the South African Race Conflict*, rev. edn (Kalamazoo:
Institute of International and Area Studies, Western Michigan University, 1965).
    31. See, for example, *The Luthuli Detachment*, video (Johannesburg: Qoma Film, c. 2007).
    32. Jabulani Sithole and Sibongiseni Mkhize, 'Truth or Lies? Selective Memories, Imaginings,
and Representations of Chief Albert John Luthuli in Recent Political Discourses', *History and Theory*
39(4) (September 2000), p. 72, drawing on Van den Bergh's press release in *Ilanga*, 12 August 1967.
    33. On the way in which Mangosuthu Buthelezi and Inkatha used Luthuli's name, see Sithole
and Mkhize, 'Truth or Lies?', pp. 75ff.

government in South Africa in 1994, as a result of the negotiated settlement reached between the ANC and the government (see Houston, Chapter 9 in this volume), did this situation really begin to change. The late Kader Asmal, one of the members of South Africa's first democratic government, had from his teenage years viewed Luthuli, whom he had met in Stanger in what was then Natal, as a hero and mentor. After 1994, Asmal, as water affairs and forestry minister in Mandela's cabinet, tried to persuade his colleagues to commemorate appropriately the contributions that Luthuli had made to the struggle against apartheid.[34] The ANC soon renamed the building in Johannesburg that housed its headquarters – which until then had been called Shell House – Luthuli House. Luthuli's picture also appeared in the watermark of all South African passports, while a set of stamps honoured all of South Africa's Nobel laureates, including Luthuli. Major streets were named after him in Durban and Pietermaritzburg. It was not until 2004, however, that then-president Thabo Mbeki launched the Luthuli Legacy Project, and the Luthuli Museum was opened at his home in Groutville.[35]

Fifty years after the award of the Nobel Prize to Albert Luthuli, a new set of postage stamps was issued in his honour, while in central Cape Town an area was named Chief Albert Luthuli Place, close to where he had spoken on the city's Grand Parade in 1959.[36] In the lead-up to the ANC's centenary in January 2012, new controversies emerged, with the ANC president, Jacob Zuma, linking Luthuli directly with MK. This was very strongly criticised as a nationalist myth by Scott Couper, the American historian and biographer of Luthuli.[37] Thanks to such controversies, Luthuli received even more attention. Some now look back to him, along with other early leaders of the ANC, as the source of values to which they wished the present-day ANC, rent as it is by factionalism, would return.[38]

34. See Kader Asmal, *Politics in My Blood: A Memoir* (Johannesburg: Jacana, 2011), ch. 6.
35. Thabo Mbeki's address on that occasion is reproduced in Luthuli, *Let My People Go*, new edn (Cape Town: Tafelberg, 2006), pp. vii–xii.
36. *Sempe*, September–December 2011, p. 22.
37. Scott Couper, 'Irony upon Irony upon Irony: The Mythologizing of Nationalist History', *South African Historical Journal* 63(2) (2011), pp. 339–46; Couper, 'Emasculating Agency'.
38. See, for example, Chris Saunders, 'We Would Do Well to Remember Luthuli's Words of Wisdom and Peace', *Cape Argus*, 10 October 2011.

Bibliography

Alexander, Peter (ed.), *Alan Paton: Selected Letters* (Cape Town: Van Riebeeck Society, 2009).

Asmal, Kader, *Politics in My Blood: A Memoir* (Auckland Park: Jacana, 2011).

Asmal, Kader, David Chidester and Wilmot James (eds), *South Africa's Nobel Laureates: Peace, Literature, and Science* (Johannesburg: Jonathan Ball, 2004).

Baldwin, Lewis, *Toward the Beloved Community: Martin Luther King Jr. and South Africa* (Cleveland: Pilgrim, 1995).

Benson, Mary, *Chief Albert Lutuli of South Africa* (London: Oxford University Press, 1963).

Bernstein, Rusty, *Memory Against Forgetting* (London: Viking, 1999).

Callan, Edward, *Albert John Luthuli and the South African Race Conflict,* rev. edn (Kalamazoo: Institute of International and Area Studies, Western Michigan University, 1965).

Cook, Robert, 'Awake the Beloved Country: A Comparative Perspective on the Visionary Leadership of Martin Luther King and Albert Luthuli', *Safundi* 5(1–2) (2004), pp. 1–19.

Couper, Scott, 'Irony upon Irony upon Irony: The Mythologizing of Nationalist History', *South African Historical Journal* 63(2) (2011), pp. 339–46.

Couper, Scott, 'Emasculating Agency: An Unambiguous Assessment of Albert Luthuli's Stance on Violence', *South African Historical Journal* 64(3) (September 2012).

de Klerk, F.W., *The Last Trek – A New Beginning: The Autobiography* (London: Pan Books, 2000 [1999]).

Gordimer, Nadine, 'Chief Luthuli', *Atlantic Monthly*, April 1959.

King Jr, Martin Luther, *Stride Towards Freedom: The Montgomery Story* (New York: Harper & Row, 1958).

Landau, Paul, 'The ANC, MK, and the Turn to Violence (1960–1962)', *South African Historical Journal* 64(3) (September 2012), pp. 538–63.

Luthuli, Albert, *Let My People Go: An Autobiography* (Johannesburg: Collins, 1962; new edn Cape Town: Tafelberg, 2006).

The Luthuli Detachment, video (Johannesburg: Qoma Film, *c.* 2007).

Mandela, Nelson, *Long Walk to Freedom* (London: Abacus, 1995).

Mandela, Nelson, *Conversations with Myself* (London: Macmillan, 2010).

Paton, Alan, *The Long View* (London: Pall Mall, 1968).

Pillay, Gerald (ed.), *Voices of Liberation*, Volume 1: *Albert Luthuli*, 2nd edn (Cape Town: Human Sciences Research Council Press, 2012).

Rule, Peter, Marilyn Aitken and Jenny van Dyk, *Nokukhanya: Mother of Light* (Braamfontein: Grail, 1993).

Sampson, Anthony, 'The Chief', in *The Treason Cage: The Opposition on Trial in South Africa* (London: Heinemann, 1958).

Saunders, Chris, 'We Would Do Well to Remember Luthuli's Words of Wisdom and Peace', *Cape Argus*, 10 October 2011.

Scott Couper, *Albert Luthuli: Bound by Faith* (Pietermaritzburg: University of KwaZulu-Natal Press, 2010).

Sellström, Tor, *Sweden and National Liberation in Southern Africa*, vol. 1 (Uppsala: Nordic Africa Institute, 1999).

Shore, Larry, 'Ripple of Hope in the Land of Apartheid: Robert F. Kennedy in South Africa, June 4th–9th, 1966', *Safundi* 3(2) (May 2002) (www.safundi.com/issues/3.2/default.asp?nc=).

Sithole, Jabulani, and Sibongiseni Mkhize, 'Truth or Lies? Selective Memories, Imaginings, and Representations of Chief Albert John Luthuli in Recent Political Discourses', *History and Theory* 39(4) (September 2000).

Suttner, Raymond, '"The Road to Freedom is via the Cross": "Just Means" in Chief Albert Luthuli's Life', *South African Historical Journal* 62(4) (2010), pp. 693–715.

SEVEN

DESMOND TUTU:
THE WOUNDED HEALER

MAUREEN ISAACSON

Anglican emeritus archbishop Desmond Mpilo Tutu, who received the
Nobel Peace Prize in 1984 for his role as a unifying figure in South
Africa's non-violent struggle for liberation, remains a 'wounded healer'
in the twenty-first century.[1] For the 'troublesome priest', who carried
the scriptural teachings into the raging battle during the 1980s, was
a prominent catalyst in the healing of the nation, which continues to
lick the wounds of three centuries of oppression. This essay explores
Tutu's role in the delivery of his country from apartheid bondage and
the ensuing healing that he was able to engender in the process, against
the backdrop of his own life.

I begin with a broad introduction to Desmond Mpilo Tutu, setting
down the defining themes of his life. Tutu's role as the 'performer' was
to serve him as the lead actor in South Africa's Truth and Reconciliation Commission (TRC). Also discussed is a comparison of the
careers of South Africa's first two Nobel peace laureates: Chief Albert
Luthuli (1960) (see Saunders, Chapter 6 in this volume) and Tutu
(1984). I further analyse Tutu's introduction to black liberation politics
and non-retributive justice during his tenure as director of the South

---

1. See Maureen Isaacson, 'Wisdom of a Wounded Healer', *Sunday Independent*, 7 December
2008, p. 13.

African Council of Churches' Theological Education Fund (TEF). The essay addresses Tutu's regret over the nomination of the last apartheid president, F.W. de Klerk (see Houston, Chapter 9 in this volume), as Nobel peace laureate alongside Nelson Mandela (see Boehmer, Chapter 8 in this volume), before concluding by assessing Tutu's relationship with South African presidents Nelson Mandela, Thabo Mbeki and Jacob Zuma, and offering lessons for US president Barack Obama (see Mazrui, Chapter 2 in this volume) from Tutu's peacemaking efforts.

The Troublesome Priest

By the time that Desmond Tutu took the podium in Oslo as the guest of the Nobel Peace Committee in December 1984, the black township of Klerksdorp on Johannesburg's West Rand had long since been razed. It was there that Tutu's umbilical cord had been buried after his birth in 1931; he would grapple all of his life with the structural inequality that was his birthright, in the land of 'rolling mountains, singing birds and bright shining stars'.[2] In Tutu's Nobel lecture, he laid out the iniquitous laws of the Land Act of 1913, which granted 87 per cent of the land to the white minority. Its response to peaceful protest was 'intransigence and violence, police dogs, tear gas, detention without trial, exile and even death'.[3] Where was the revulsion of the West?[4]

The dramatic solemnity of the Nobel ceremony in 1984, broken by a bomb scare, was recovered and revitalized with the moving rendition of the current South African national anthem, 'Nkosi Sikilel' iAfrika' (God Bless Africa),[5] by the Tutu family and members of the South African Council of Churches, who had accompanied Tutu to Oslo. Egil Aarvik, chair of the Nobel Peace Committee, rose to the complex emotions of the occasion, apologising for 'the oppressive experience' that apartheid had inflicted, while bestowing on Tutu an award 'with

---

2. Desmond Tutu, 'Nobel Lecture', 11 December 1984, http://nobelprize.org/nobel_prizes/peace/laureates/1984/tutu-lecture.html.
3. Ibid.
4. Ibid.
5. John Allen, *Rabble-Rouser for Peace: The Authorised Biography of Desmond Tutu* (London and Johannesburg: Random House, 2006), p. 183.

a white man's hands'. The 'sorrow' Aarvik expressed 'over the wounds inflicted by injustice and racial hatred' struck home.[6]

Tutu's characterisation of himself as a 'wounded healer' refers to a Jungian conception of a healing process that is made possible in delving into the darkness of the personal story – making whole what has been broken. The quest for wholeness is the defining theme of Tutu's life work, connecting his spiritual search with his search for justice. In his address to an international convention of fund-raisers in 2010, Tutu reportedly recalled that, as the Anglican archbishop of Cape Town, he had been told, 'Don't mix politics with religion' or 'Don't mix politics with sport'. He stood up on his toes and shouted to the fund-raisers, 'Politics mixes with everything!'[7]

Essentially a performer, Tutu played out his career centre stage, on the pulpit and in the streets, in the years leading to his Nobel Prize in 1984 and in the decades that followed. As chair of South Africa's Truth and Reconciliation Commission in 1996, he used his gifts of emotional articulation to inject a spectacular tension into the confrontation with state-sponsored atrocity. The well-publicised Commission hearings over which Tutu presided rendered him the global face of reconcil-iation, a moral beacon. Tutu's presence, with his coaxing, begging and pleading with victims and their families to forgive perpetrators for egregious crimes against humanity, enabled the process and also stole the show.

A slight man, his right hand slightly withered by infantile polio, dressed in his purple cassock, Desmond Tutu cut a sometimes comic figure. A singer, a dancer, a showman even, he drew his props from Christian iconography. The inconsistencies and contradictions intrinsic to all struggles for liberation – both internal and external – manifested in his kinetic relationship with God. Tutu at times raged against his God for permitting the suffering of black people, yet he was inspired by Him to revolt against the perpetrators. He understood that God

---

6. Egil Aarvik, 'The Nobel Peace Prize 1984: Presentation Speech', 8 February 2012, www.nobelprize.org/nobel_prizes/peace/laureates/1984/presentation-speech.html.

7. Joan Flanagan, 'Politics Mixes with Everything!', *Imagine 2050*, http://imagine2050.newcomm.org/tag/desmond-tutu.

required human agency in the transfiguration of the world. 'Join the winning side!' was his war cry. In 1989, decrying the continent's devastating human rights record in Zaire (now the Democratic Republic of the Congo [DRC]), Tutu proclaimed: 'Our God is a God who takes sides. Our God is a God who takes the side of the oppressed, of the poor and the downtrodden. We say to unjust rulers everywhere: Beware! Watch it! Look out in South Africa, look out wherever you may be, unjust ruler. We have no doubt we shall be free.'[8]

A transformative relationship took place at the deepest level. Black theology would heal 'the split in the African soul, imposed by Western theology; it provided a context for the lives of the people it served; it was 'concerned for the whole of the black man, to help him come to terms with his own existence' and to become 'liberated from all kinds of bondage which have dehumanized him'.[9] Black theology further rejected the imposition of Western values dictating a universal and final theology; it was 'a gut level theology',[10] its context related directly to the lives of black people. Similarly, Chief Albert Luthuli, South Africa's and Africa's first Nobel peace laureate, in 1960, had revolted against 'white paternalist Christianity', which 'estranges my people from Christ'.[11]

Tutu's intimate communion with God was to prove a powerful weapon, used to good effect when he famously warned apartheid prime minister John Vorster of 'a point of no return' before 'a bloody denouement' was reached.[12] The warning came a month ahead of the June 1976 uprising in Soweto, and Tutu was aware of the Old Testament's 'strictures against false prophets'. He was able to distinguish between God's voice and his own.[13] Tutu's mission, like that of the prophet

8. Desmond Tutu, 'All That Has Changed Is the Complexion of the Oppressor', extract from a sermon in Mobutu Sese Seko's Zaire (1989), in Desmond Tutu, *The Rainbow People of God: A Spiritual Journey from Apartheid to Freedom*, ed. John Allen (Cape Town: Double Storey, 1994), pp. 154–5.

9. Desmond Mpilo Tutu, 'Why Black?', in *God Is Not a Christian: Speaking Truth in Times of Crisis*, ed. John Allen (London: Rider & Ebury, 2011), p. 139.

10. Quoted in Allen, *Rabble-Rouser for Peace*, p. 139.

11. See Gerald Pillay (ed.), *Voices of Liberation*, Volume 1: *Albert Luthuli*, 2nd edn (Cape Town: Human Sciences Research Council Press, 2012).

12. Desmond Tutu, 'A Growing Nightmarish Fear: An Open Letter to Prime Minister BJ Vorster', 6 May 1976, in Tutu, *The Rainbow People of God*, p. 11.

13. Quoted in Allen, *Rabble-Rouser for Peace*, p. 154.

Moses, was to carry the word of God to his people. Casting oneself as a liberation prophet undoubtedly requires a leap of faith. Tutu's African philosophy translates simplistically as love and acceptance, which create the conditions for the realisation of a shared humanity. These are the working tools of *ubuntu*, translated from isiXhosa as 'a person is a person only through other persons'.[14] This is Tutu's essential message. He traces its origins to the Old Testament's Book of Leviticus, citing the creed of Moses.[15]

Tutu found that after retirement in 2010 he was unable 'to shut up'.[16] He discovered that if he did not speak out against injustice, it was 'as if the word of God burned like a fire in my breast'.[17] He insisted that he was not confrontational by nature, but instead propelled by circumstances into the combative campaign that he was to continue to wage well into his eighties. As chair of the Elders, an independent group of global leaders working for peace,[18] Tutu pursued a wide range of targets, including nuclear proliferation, sexism and child marriage.

In September 2012, Tutu cancelled his commitment to take part in a leadership summit in Johannesburg, refusing to share a platform with former British prime minister Tony Blair. He argued that Blair and former US president George W. Bush should face charges of war crimes for the 2003 invasion of Iraq, conducted without a UN Security Council mandate. Tutu raged against the lopsided world order that allows a

---

14. Desmond Mpilo Tutu, 'Ubuntu: On the Nature of Human Community', in *God Is Not a Christian*, p. 20.

15. Desmond Tutu, 'Oh God, How Long Can We Go On?', speech at Steve Biko's funeral, 25 September 1977, in Tutu, *The Rainbow People of God*, p. 20.

16. Desmond Tutu, foreword to *God Is Not a Christian*, p. xi.

17. Ibid., p. xii.

18. The Elders is a group that works to promote human rights. The idea of founding a group of elders dedicated to solving global problems was introduced by entrepreneur Richard Branson and musician Peter Gabriel. Nelson Mandela, South Africa's first democratic president, with the help of Graça Machel and Tutu, brought the group together and formally launched it in July 2007; Mandela remains an Honorary Elder in 2013. The group was chaired by Tutu for six years until he stepped down in May 2013; he too remains an Honorary Elder. The group is chaired by Kofi Annan, former UN Secretary General and Nobel peace laureate, and includes Mary Robinson, Ireland's first woman president; Graça Machel, Mozambique's first minister of education; Jimmy Carter, former president of the United States and Nobel peace laureate; Fernando Cardoso, former president of Brazil; Gro Harlem Brundtland, first woman prime minister of Norway; Lakhdar Brahimi, former foreign minister of Algeria and UN troubleshooter; Ela Bhatt, pioneer of women's empowerment and grassroots development in India; and Martti Ahtisaari, former president of Finland and Nobel peace laureate. See the group's website at www.theelders.org.

warmonger such as Blair to be unleashed on leadership summits while recommending, for instance, that Zimbabwean leader Robert Mugabe should be tried at The Hague and that al-Qaeda leader Osama bin Laden should be killed. Assessing Tutu's campaign, Nelson Jones in the *New Statesman* astutely probed the nature of his 'peculiar sort of soft power', which he argued 'owes little to any formal position and everything to personality, an image of saintliness and a high media profile'.[19]

Domestic Drama

Tutu's unwavering attraction to the limelight is one of transcendence, and it set the stage for his peacemaking efforts. He characterised his fifty-eight-year marriage to Nomalizo Leah as having been made in heaven. It produced three daughters, two of whom have followed in his footsteps: Naomi, a human rights activist, set up a foundation in her father's name in Connecticut; Mpho, ordained by her father as an Episcopal priest, returned to South Africa in 2011 from the United States to found the Desmond and Leah Tutu Legacy Foundation. The institution seeks to preserve her father's papers, regulate the use of his name, and provide an honest commentary on moral issues. Tutu's son, Trevor, was granted amnesty by the TRC in 1997 for a bomb scare he caused in 1991. The incident received extensive airplay in South Africa.

Although spiritual celebrity opened the doors to the lavish bishoprics and brought Hollywood to his door, Tutu never forgot his origins. The archbishop would look back on his origins, remembering how he had built his own toy cars with discarded boot-polish tins and scraps of wire. Christmas holidays in his grandmother's crowded home in Stirtonville, on the East Rand, with its single water tap shared by three families, were a major highlight. He said that it had never occurred to him that his family was poor.

---

19. Nelson Jones, 'Tony Blair v Desmond Tutu: Who Has More Moral Authority?' *New Statesman* blog, 3 September 2012, www.newstatesman.com/blogs/politics/2012/09/tony-blair-v-desmond-tutu-who-has-more-moral-authority.

Desmond Tutu was born on 7 October 1931 in Mokoateng in South Africa's North West province, to Zachariah Zelilo Tutu, an isiXhosa-speaker, and Aletta Dorothea Marvoetsek Mathlare, a Motswana woman.[20] Tutu, who adopted isiXhosa as his mother tongue, was a child born of diversity; he has celebrated this discovery through a genome project that revealed that his genetic lineage, primarily from the Sotho-Tswana and Nguni language groups, could be traced back to the Khoi San people.[21] This possibility would not have been incorporated into Tutu's world-view in childhood, as his parents struggled financially 'from paycheck to paycheck'. Zachariah supplemented his teacher's salary with extra funds earned as a liquor store 'delivery boy'. For Aletta, with only a primary school education under her belt, domestic work was the only option. She earned 2 shillings a day, 'enough to buy half a pound of sugar, some cornmeal and a serving of the cheapest meat for the evening meal'.[22]

Tutu has written about the unconditional love that shaped him, but was to recall 'the hard tangle of emotions that I bring to the memory of my father's acts of violence' as he tried to forgive himself for refusing to speak to his father before he died.[23] Racist jibes angled at Tutu on the street cut deep, as did the humiliation by whites that he witnessed his father endure, and these wounds would take a lifetime to salve. But in the process Tutu proved indomitable. The Nobel Peace Committee noted that his award renewed recognition of the 'courage and heroism demonstrated by black South Africans in their use of peaceful methods in the struggle against a racist regime'.[24]

Tutu and Luthuli: The Double Act

As earlier mentioned, South Africa's and Africa's first Nobel peace laureate was Chief Albert Luthuli, in 1960. The lives of Luthuli and

---

20. Allen, *Rabble-Rouser for Peace*, p. 10.
21. Gary Styx, 'Archbishop Tutu Gets Sequenced – and Finds a Surprise in His Ancestry', *Scientific American*, February 2010.
22. Quoted in Desmond Mpilo Tutu and Mpho Tutu, 'An Invitation to Wholeness', in *Made for Goodness – and Why This Makes All the Difference*, ed. Douglas C. Abrams (London: Rider, 2010), p. 45.
23. Ibid. p. 151.
24. Tutu, 'Nobel Lecture'.

Tutu have further similarities. Both came to political life perforce, propelled by apartheid's increasing stranglehold on the lives of black people. Both men began their careers as teachers, and both were schooled in the precepts of Christianity.

Luthuli, the president of the African National Congress (ANC) from 1951 to 1967, worked as a lay preacher and incorporated the traditional values he had fostered until the apartheid government deposed him as a chief in 1953. He worked as an adviser to the organised church and, like his successor, cast his net wide, seeking international networks. He was chairman of the South African Board of the Congregationalist Church of America, president of the Natal Mission Conference, and a delegate to the International Missionary Conference in Madras in 1938. In 1948, he spent nine months on a lecture tour of the United States, sponsored by two missionary organisations. Luthuli was an executive member of the Christian Council of South Africa, the forerunner of the South African Council of Churches (SACC) – which Tutu was later to head.[25]

Tutu reached the highest level in the Anglican Church in Southern Africa when he was ordained Archbishop of Cape Town in September 1986. The Bantu Education Act, expunging mathematics and science from the school curriculum for blacks, was passed in 1954, the year after Tutu qualified with a teacher's diploma. In 1958, a career that was to take him to heights unimagined began with his entry into St Peter's Theological College in the Eastern Cape town of Alice. He was ordained a deacon in the Anglican Church in 1960 and then a priest a year later, before becoming Dean of Johannesburg in 1975. Tutu was ordained Bishop of Lesotho a year later, a position that kept him out of the country, something he regretted during the June 1976 Soweto uprising against the enforcement of Afrikaans as the medium of instruction in black schools.[26] This revolt continued Luthuli's earlier

25. 'Nobel Peace Prize Biography: Albert Luthuli', 1960, www.nobelprize.org/nobel_prizes/peace/laureates/1960/lutuli-bio.html.
26. 'Nobel Peace Prize Biography: Desmond Mpilo Tutu', 1984, www.nobelprize.org/nobel_prizes/peace/laureates/1984/tutu-bio.html.

battle against inequality in education, which he fought as secretary, and later as president, of the African Teachers Association.[27]

Both leaders were versed in the language of the grand gesture. Luthuli, in defiance of the egregious apartheid pass laws that made it obligatory for black people to carry 'passbooks' restricting their movements, burned his own pass in public in 1960, and suffered constant restrictions to his freedom of movement.

The Nobel Peace Committee cited Tutu's injunction to a crowd after a township massacre 'not to hate' and to 'choose the peaceful way to freedom'. What could have propelled this man, small of stature and never enormously robust, to go where angels feared to tread? Tutu's successor as Archbishop of Cape Town, Njongongkulu Ndungane, ascribes Tutu's 'almost reckless courage' to a security in his faith. Ndungane recounts events during a visit with Tutu to a Gauteng township: 'We were surrounded by an angry mob of young people who had tied a lad up and were preparing to put a tire around his neck and burn him to death. Somehow, miraculously, Desmond convinced them to release their victim.'[28]

There were other incidents, of increasing intensity. They involved rescuing a suspected informer, or *impimpi*, from the jaws of death on two occasions, both at funerals. On the first occasion, Tutu, with Bishop Simeon Nkoane, hauled a man already doused with petrol away from a crowd and into Nkoane's car. The second incident involved Tutu flinging himself upon the bleeding body of a man about to be 'necklaced' after the funeral of Griffiths Mxenge, the prominent human rights lawyer murdered by the apartheid state. Tutu succeeded in staving off the 'necklacing', with the assistance of his aides, though the mob later burned the man to death.[29]

In an interview in 2008, Tutu told me that he was protected by his 'rhino skin'.[30] This would have been a necessary shield: he was the

---

27. 'Nobel Peace Prize Biography: Albert Luthuli'.
28. Njongonkulu Ndungane, 'Reckless Courage', in Lavinia Crawford-Browne with Piet Meiring (eds), *Tutu As I Know Him: On a Personal Note* (Cape Town: Umuzi, 2006), p. 147.
29. Allister Sparks and Mpho A. Tutu, *Tutu: The Authorized Portrait* (London: Macmillan, 2011), p. 4.
30. See Isaacson, 'Wisdom of a Wounded Healer', p. 13.

target of both the right-wing elements within the Anglican Church and recalcitrant whites outside the church. The 'troublesome priest' was told to stick to the Bible, and leave politics to the politicians.

Tutu's frequently repeated public declaration that he was 'not a politician' and rejection of 'the false dichotomies' that separated the sacred and the secular worked against him in several ways. He articulated many of the ideals of the ANC, although he was never a card-carrying member of any party. However, the apartheid government accused him of promoting the ANC's campaign of violence. Then, his calls for an end to violence angered those committed to fighting fire with fire. Tutu's radical critics found his campaign for sanctions as meek as his call for universal suffrage. He led protest marches and civil disobedience campaigns even when they placed him at risk of imprisonment. The label 'liberal' stuck to the priest.

However, like Luthuli, Tutu was focused on the end-goal. Like Luthuli, he regarded disinvestment as the sole route to South Africa's transformation. Luthuli had campaigned alongside African-American Nobel peace laureate Martin Luther King Jr to isolate South Africa internationally, and noted King's major influence on his own approach to peaceful change (see Robinson, Chapter 3, and Daniels, Chapter 5, in this volume). King, who advocated non-violent civil resistance, recalling Indian politico-spiritual leader Mahatma Gandhi's practice of *satyagraha*, has been described as a 'conservative militant', a description also ascribed to Luthuli. Tutu – the aptly named 'rabble rouser for peace' – can also be described in this way. Nonetheless, the inevitable limits of pacifism became excruciatingly obvious to both South African Nobel peace laureates. Luthuli, as ANC president, never condoned violence, but agreed not to stand in the way of members who, like Nelson Mandela, wished to take up arms. Tutu, in July 1978, as the first black secretary general of the South African Council of Churches, persuaded the ten-yearly Lambeth Conference – attended by the world's Anglican bishops – that the Church should not abandon those fighting a violent struggle.[31]

31. Allen, *Rabble-Rouser for Peace*, p. 174.

Tutu's Nobel acceptance speech attempted to deal with the position of the Church after the African National Congress and the Pan-Africanist Congress (PAC) declared that they had no option but to carry out an armed struggle:

> We in the South African Council of Churches have said we are opposed to all forms of violence – that of a repressive and unjust system, and that of those who seek to overthrow that system. However, we understand those who say they have had to adopt what is a last resort for them. The South African situation is violent already, and the primary violence is that of apartheid.[32]

Luthuli's presidency of the ANC distinguished his life from Tutu's. Although Tutu was harassed by security police, he was also shielded by his high-profile position in the Church. Luthuli is remembered for his humility; Tutu has been accused of hubris, of narcissism, as well as of conservatism. The latter has confronted himself, aware of the danger of self-aggrandisement, the insecurity that propels arrogance, and the need to keep his own ego in check. Tutu has confessed to 'a horrible but human weakness in that I want very much to be loved – this desire to be loved can become an obsession and you can find you are ready to do almost anything to gain the approval of others'.[33]

Accusations of populism levelled against Tutu by South African presidents Nelson Mandela (1994–99) and Thabo Mbeki (1999–2008) did no harm to the prophet's image; his was the podium of truth. Tutu remains an enigmatic figure, describing himself as 'a ventriloquist for causes'. He has said that his ideas were largely inspirational, and that he was not a deep thinker.[34] However, his writings and speeches belie this claim. They also provide links to the sources of his ideas.

---

32. Tutu, 'Nobel Lecture'.
33. Desmond Tutu with Douglas Abrams, 'Seeing with the Eyes of the Heart', in *God Has a Dream: A Vision of Hope for Our Time* (London: Rider, 2004), p. 84.
34. See Allen, *Rabble-Rouser for Peace*.

Restorative Justice and Healing

A lesser-known aspect of Tutu's life is the pan-African odyssey he made as African director of the Theological Education Fund of the South African Council of Churches, a journey that commenced in Bromley in England in 1972 and continued until 1975. John Allen has reconstructed this voyage through Tutu's journals, letters and speeches. Tutu described the experiences in the TEF as 'the most exhilarating and formative years of my life'. They prepared him for his battles against apartheid.[35]

The archbishop's lessons in those years – the failure of post-independence African governments to deal with the inter-ethnic divisions sown by the colonial past, and the need for non-retributive justice – present a model for conflict resolution beyond the continent. Threats of revenge in the aftermath of an attempted coup by the majority Hutu against the ruling minority Tutsi in Rwanda in 1972 persuaded Tutu of the need for restorative justice. In a 1995 address, he urged Rwandans to 'break the cycle of killing' after the 1994 genocide in that country, which resulted in 800,000 deaths, and expressed 'solidarity and participation as an African, as a human being and especially as a Christian'.[36]

Surely Tutu had an idea of what South Africa's future could look like after seeing how little change had been brought by Africa's neocolonial governments. In 1987, South Africa's 'troublesome priest' was elected president of the All Africa Conference of Churches (AACC), and for a decade he worked to achieve an 'African Renaissance' and to support member churches.

Tutu had come a long way from his introduction to theology by Anglican parish priest and anti-apartheid activist Father Trevor Huddleston, whom the archbishop has named as his chief influence. Tutu had earned a Master's degree in theology from King's College London, where his teachers were yet to embrace the concept of liberation

35. Desmond Tutu, address at the Golden Jubilee Ecumenical Theological Education Conference, Neapolis, Greece, 31 May 2008, in *Ministerial Formation*, Jubilee Issue 110, April 2008, p. 9 (http://wocati.org/publication/ministerial-formation-issue-110-april-2008/wppa_open/main/documents/p5/Ministerial_formation/MF_110_April_08.pdf).
36. Allen, *Rabble-Rouser for Peace*, pp. 123–39.

theology. He was subsequently introduced to this theology by Aharon Sapsezian, a Brazilian of Armenian descent, and a colleague at the TEF.

Tutu incorporated black liberation theology into his own teachings because it involved the liberation of both black and white – he was to say throughout his life that those who ravage the humanity of blacks dehumanise themselves in the process. This idea dovetailed neatly with the Black Consciousness philosophy – popularised by Steve Biko, the founder and leader of the Black Consciousness Movement, who was martyred by the apartheid regime in 1977, and at whose funeral Tutu led the obsequies. It was this philosophy that Tutu had embraced at Fort Hare University, where he served as a chaplain.

For Tutu, the forgiveness that was central to non-retributive justice could not be simplified. In this, he was influenced by the writings of German Lutheran pastor Dietrich Bonhoeffer, who described 'cheap grace' as the grace we bestow upon ourselves. Unlike the costly grace Bonhoeffer advocated, cheap grace is the preaching of forgiveness without requiring repentance, baptism without church discipline. Tutu's ideas were incorporated into South Africa's Promotion of National Unity and Reconciliation Act of 1995 (which established the TRC), the outcome of an intensive process involving several key legal and political figures.

The low-intensity civil war in South Africa brought a dramatic escalation in violence in the country, with a consequent increase in the number of human rights violations in the run-up to the country's negotiated transition between 1990 and 1994.[37] During these years, an estimated 14,000 deaths were registered. The ANC and the apartheid government articulated different solutions. Rejecting the ANC's preference for trials for gross violations, the apartheid government stuck to its guns, insisting on a blanket amnesty, including for apartheid's security forces. The compromise was a conditional amnesty predicated on full disclosure and prosecution of only the most egregious crimes.

---

37. 'Period Following Mandela's Release: TRC Excerpts – Political Violence in the Era of Negotiations and Transition', O. Malley Archives, www.nelsonmandela.org/omalley/index.php/site/q/03lv02167/04lv02264/05lv02335/06lv02336/07lv02340.htm; accessed 8 June 2012.

The compromise was spelt out in South Africa's Original Interim Constitution Accord, the epilogue at the end of its Interim Constitution of 1993: 'In order to advance such reconciliation and reconstruction, amnesty shall be granted in respect of acts, omissions and offences associated with political objectives and committed in the course of the conflicts of the past.'[38] Thabo Mbeki, then deputy president of South Africa, said in 1997 that within the ANC the cry was 'catch the bastards and hang them'. But had there been Nuremberg-style trials for members of the apartheid security establishment, South Africa would never have undergone a peaceful change.[39]

While the TRC addressed human rights atrocities committed by both sides, the beneficiaries of apartheid – the whites – and the business community were never brought to account, just as the structural violence of apartheid and its root causes were never addressed. While the TRC became engaged with the national reconciliation project, the politics of redress was compromised by the process.[40]

Tutu became the embodiment of the 'forgiveness' project, while the symbolism of Nelson Mandela holding hands with F.W. de Klerk in 1994 resonated across the world: the picture of a remarkable 'rainbow nation'.[41] Truth commissioners who served under Tutu's chairmanship had varying experiences of his leadership. Some found that the hierarchical nature of the Church was carried down into Tutu's leadership style. Yet Tutu was deeply respected by others. Yasmin Sooka, who served as a truth commissioner and deputy of the Human Rights Violations Committee, recalled Tutu as having been 'a brilliant leader; his moral authority was unequalled in the commission. He had a canny sense of the political moment, and remarkable insight.'[42]

---

38. *Constitution of the Republic of South Africa*, Act 200 (1993), ch. 16, 'National Unity and Reconciliation'.

39. In Jonathan D. Tepperman, 'Truth and Consequences', *Foreign Affairs*, March–April 2002, p. 129.

40. Yasmin Sooka, 'Race and Reconciliation: *E Pluribus Unum*?', in Adekeye Adebajo, Adebayo Adedeji and Chris Landsberg (eds), *South Africa in Africa: The Post-Apartheid Era* (Scottsville: University of KwaZulu-Natal Press, 2007), p. 87.

41. Ibid.

42. Interview with Yasmin Sooka, Johannesburg, 14 February 2013.

Off-Stage: One-on-One

By the time I interviewed Archbishop Desmond Tutu in Johannesburg in December 2008,[43] the failure of white South Africans to make a gesture of apology, and the absence of any form of restitution, had become increasingly distressing to him, amid the increasing inequality ravaging the nation. Tutu reiterated that he was a wounded healer:

> Despite the truth commission having run its course, the nation has not yet healed. There has been no ritual cleansing. Whites need to confront the fact that they benefited from apartheid, to acknowledge it. We are forgetting the power of symbol. At circumcision school, you get new clothes because you are a new person; we may need something like a national day.

A confrontation such as this would make 'the mess' South Africa was in manageable. How naive he had been, Tutu told me, to have imagined the values of the struggle would prevail in this democratic state now consumed by crass materialism. The 'original sin' had not disappeared with the end of apartheid, and Tutu said that he felt 'let down' by the all-pervasive poverty: 'It is abominable that people go to bed hungry – even when we were poor, we would not allow this.'

Moreover, political infighting and slander had led Tutu to consider asking the world's religious leaders to intercede. Things had become so bad in the ruling ANC that Tutu, who had been prevented by apartheid from voting until the age of 63, had threatened to abstain from voting unless the ruling party got its house in order. (Tutu later said in May 2013 that he would not vote for the ruling party again.)

In the hotel room where Tutu was holed up in Johannesburg's leafy and wealthy northern suburb of Sandton, he offered me a cold drink, elevating his legs against thrombosis and relaxing into a conversation that took some pleasantly unexpected turns. 'I have had prostate cancer for several years', he revealed. 'I am taking hormone treatment. Leah [his wife] says that I will soon need to wear a bra!'[44] He continued: 'It

---

43. See Isaacson, 'Wisdom of a Wounded Healer', p. 13.
44. In 1997, and again in 1999 and 2006, Tutu was diagnosed with prostate cancer.

is funny getting old', as if surprised that simple movements required effort. He recalled contracting tuberculosis at age 14: 'Father Trevor Huddleston [the Anglican anti-apartheid priest] believed I would not survive.' Huddleston had visited him weekly for the twenty months during which he was hospitalised.

Throughout the interview, Tutu was at ease, attentive and bright, even though it was clear that he was fighting the need to rest. He has said often that he is essentially shy beneath his public facade, but I had no sense of reticence here. He was companionable, rather, and communicative. I had the sense that he welcomed the discussion about his preoccupations.

The corrosion of respect was a preoccupying theme. He had sustained attacks from the youth, who resented him for endorsing the principles of the Truth Commission, which they believed had glossed over the essential confrontations with the white minority who had reaped apartheid's fruits in the pursuit of forgiveness. They also spoke out against his outspoken criticisms of Jacob Zuma, for whom the ANC Youth League and the Congress of South African Students were lobbying ahead of the April 2009 general election.

At the launch of an exhibition on Nelson Mandela's life at the Apartheid Museum in Johannesburg prior to our 2008 interview, Tutu had repeated a well-used homily: 'My father said, sharpen your argument, don't raise your voice', Tutu admonished, believing the freedom hard-earned by his generation was being squandered. 'We were not born with a silver spoon.'[45]

Now, at the time of our interview, Tutu said he was able to handle the youth, but was still concerned: 'I am worried for them, because in my culture we say that when young people abuse their elders, they will be cursed. When youth lose their reverence for life, for law and for custom, there is a texture to the unease – things don't just disappear.'

This approach is consistent with threats Tutu was later to make that he would pray for the downfall of the ANC, after the government

45. Tutu was speaking at the launch of the photographic exhibition at the Apartheid Museum in Johannesburg on 8 November 2008. The exhibition, *Mandela: Leader, Comrade, Negotiater, Prisoner, Statesman*, was among the tributes paid to Mandela in the year of his ninetieth birthday, on 18 July 2008.

refused entry to the spiritual leader of Tibet, the Dalai Lama – Tutu's close friend – for the second time, in October 2011. It was uncertain what the meaning of such curses and warnings held in context. After all, the Dalai Lama had said he and Tutu shared a similar spiritual approach, and that only their 'creators' were different.

In our 2008 interview in Johannesburg, Tutu said that while he did not believe in the laws of *karma*, 'someone has said that in the world of soul-making, everything we do has consequences … a good deed creates a pathway in your being, that allows you to move smoothly.' The Dalai Lama was recognised as the fourteenth reincarnation of the Buddha of Compassion. I asked Tutu whether he believed in reincarnation.

> No, for Christians, life is not cyclical. It is linear. It has a beginning, middle and an end. For the Buddhists, the purpose is *mokshah*, the liberation from the cycle of being born and reborn. We say you really have this life only. We say each person is your family. Hurting the other is hurting yourself. We saw in South Africa the way those who tortured ended up being dehumanised themselves. I used to say we are concerned not just with black liberation but with white liberation; I said the whites would not be free until we were free.

I wondered aloud how Tutu had dealt with the considerable pain he has witnessed. 'God had this wonderful idea of inventing women and wives. When Chris Hani was shot [in April 1993] I broke down and went into the bedroom and Leah held me to the extent she could, like a baby. She held me in her arms. She's just been extraordinary in her support. Yes, I hurt, but not in the same way as I used to.'

Nonetheless, Tutu continues to grapple with memories of degradation, remembering his first-time flight to Nigeria with the World Council of Churches in the 1970s:

> I noticed that there were only black people in the cockpit and when the plane encountered turbulence mid-air, I worried because there were no white people to save us. I had not realised how brainwashed I was. It just came like that from the depths of my being. We should be finding ways of acknowledging this.

F.W. de Klerk: White Impunity

Tutu's call for a 'white tax' in April 2011 was made in anger. Gone was the jubilant embrace of the 'rainbow nation' of God, Tutu's concept of a union of the previous divided nation. In the absence of tangible changes in the lives of South Africa's black majority, the privileged circumstances of the white minority remained largely unaltered under the new dispensation, while many whites still remained socially unconscious. Tutu was also to regret his nomination of F.W. de Klerk, the National Party leader, as Nobel peace laureate alongside Nelson Mandela in 1992. At the time, he had been so determined in this that even eighteen months later when asked if his nomination still held good, he concurred. Tutu had felt the changes made by de Klerk very directly.

De Klerk, in September 1989, ahead of his inauguration as state president, had lifted the ban on protest marches then in place under the state-of-emergency regulations. A day later, Archbishop Desmond Tutu led a protest march without any police interference. In the following months, de Klerk proceeded to dismantle many aspects of petty apartheid, such as segregated beaches (see Houston, Chapter 9 in this volume).

This nomination was complex at the time. De Klerk's own reservations about Tutu were well known. He was to be disappointed in his respect for the 'wounded healer' when Tutu blamed him for not owning up to apartheid crimes, and when the Tutu-chaired TRC found de Klerk culpable of complicity, which de Klerk felt damaged his reputation. Tutu later noted that if he had known in 1993 what he knew five years later, he would not have nominated de Klerk for the Nobel Peace Prize. He argued that de Klerk had become 'a small man, lacking magnanimity and generosity of spirit'.[46] In an interview in May 2012 with CNN anchor Christiane Amanpour, de Klerk seized the opportunity to defend apartheid. He said he had made a 'profound apology' about the injustices wrought by apartheid in front of the TRC and on other occasions. In response to Amanpour's question as to

---

46. Allen, *Rabble-Rouser for Peace*, p. 364.

whether, in retrospect, de Klerk considered apartheid to be morally repugnant, he said:

> I can only say in a qualified way, in as much as it [apartheid] trampled human rights, it was – and remains – and that I've said also publicly, morally reprehensible. But the concept of … saying that ethnic unities with one culture, with one language, can be happy and can fulfil their democratic aspirations in their own state, that is not repugnant.[47]

This statement rekindled criticisms of Tutu's Truth Commission and its failure to condemn apartheid adequately, although it had demonstrated that it was a crime against humanity. The Commission had put the ANC on the spot too. Many felt that the Truth Commission's conclusion that the liberation movement had committed gross human rights violations in exile was exaggerated and detracted from the enormity of suffering wrought by apartheid. In addition, the post-apartheid government's tardiness in paying reparations to victims of apartheid and its limited definition of these victims underplayed the atrocities of the apartheid government.

When both the National Party and the ANC attempted to obtain a judicial order to prevent the publication of the TRC report, Tutu was furious: 'I did not struggle against a tyranny in order to substitute another. If there is tyranny and an abuse of power, let them know I will fight it.'[48]

Concluding Reflections: No Curtain Call

Desmond Tutu has been preoccupied throughout his life with the ways in which power was abused. His attacks on the apartheid government were extended to South Africa's black leaders. 'Speaking truth to power' placed Tutu at the centre of the national conversation. South Africa's saintly first democratic president, Nelson Mandela, would not be exempt. Before Mandela was jailed in 1964, Tutu and Mandela had

---

47. Samuel Burke, 'Under Fire, South Africa's Former President Repudiates Apartheid', 16 May 2012, http://amanpour.blogs.cnn.com/2012/05/16/under-fire-south-africas-former-president-repudiates-apartheid.

48. Allen, *Rabble-Rouser for Peace*, p. 367.

met only once in the long-distant past, with little connection. But the struggle had brought them together.

In July 1980, Mandela wrote to Tutu from Robben Island: 'Men like you are making an invaluable contribution in feeding that fighting spirit and hope of victory.' For Mandela, 'the will to continue fighting and the hope of victory' remained 'one of the most splendid spiritual weapons in the hands of the oppressed people inside and outside prison.'[49] Tutu learned long after the fact that Mandela and the ANC's exiled president Oliver Tambo were among the exceptions in the ANC leadership who had appreciated his contributions.

Mandela stayed at Tutu's official residence at Bishops Court in Cape Town on the first night of his release from prison in February 1990. Tutu had, in fact, introduced Mandela to the crowds, thus ending his own term as interim political leader. He would return to his role of pastor and keep well out of party politics. Tutu quickly asserted the independence of the Church and his intention to continue the campaign for justice, maintaining critical solidarity with South Africa's pro-democracy forces.[50]

One of Tutu's well-worn Mandela stories centred on the response of 'Madiba' (Mandela's clan name) to Tutu's criticism of the president's gaudy shirts: 'That's pretty thick coming from a man who wears a dress in public!'[51] Tutu had, in fact, told Mandela that his Japanese shirts were not appreciated by mourners at funerals. He attacked Mandela's administration only three months into the new democracy for failing to resolve the R43 billion arms deal conducted on his government's watch, and for allowing parliamentarians increased salaries, thus 'stopping the gravy train just long enough to jump on it'.[52] That is when Mandela called Tutu a 'populist', noting that the archbishop should have spoken to him first before going public. Tutu retorted that he had done so, and accused Mandela of forgetfulness or lying. A few months

49. Ibid., p. 183.
50. Ibid., p. 315.
51. Desmond Tutu, Second Nelson Mandela Annual Lecture Address, Johannesburg, 23 November 2004, www.nelsonmandela.org/news/entry/ the-second-nelson-mandela-annual-lecture-address.
52. Quoted in Allen, *Rabble-Rouser for Peace*, p. 345.

later, in 1995, Mandela appointed Tutu as chair of the TRC.[53] Further
accusations surfaced during Thabo Mbeki's presidency, amid attacks
and counter-attacks. At the 2004 annual Nelson Mandela lecture, Tutu
lashed out at Mbeki's AIDS 'denialism', his 'pontificating decrees',
and his Black Economic Empowerment (BEE) policies that recycled
the privilege of the small elite. Tutu further derided 'the uncritical
sycophantic obsequious conformity' of the ANC's 'voting cattle'.[54] In
our December 2008 interview in Johannesburg, Tutu was still smarting
from Mbeki's counter-attack on him as the 'icon of the white elite'.
However, he spoke out against Mbeki's ousting by the ANC as president
in September 2008.

Mbeki's forced resignation has a backstory. He had sacked Zuma
as deputy president following his alleged implication in a corruption
scandal in 2005. After a high court ruled in April 2009 that the corruption charges had been politically motivated, Tutu was disappointed,
reminding the world that Zuma had condoned the violent behaviour of
his supporters outside the court during a rape trial in 2006.

Shortly before South Africa's 2009 elections, Tutu said: 'In the
year of [Barack] Obama, can you imagine what it is like when you
are walking down the street in New York and they ask you who will
be the next president.… [A]t the present time, I can't pretend to be
looking forward to having him as my president.'[55] Tutu expressed the
hope that there would be no political solution to Zuma's fraud and
corruption prosecution.

But the Nobel laureate was to bow to whatever forces dictated the
apparent moral tectonic shift, one minute praising Zuma's openness and
African style of leadership,[56] the next telling him and his government
that they did not represent him.[57] After Obama's presidential triumph
in 2008, Tutu told the BBC that his election made him want to 'jump
and dance and shout', but he warned that Obama (who had visited

53. Ibid.
54. Tutu, Second Nelson Mandela Annual Lecture Address.
55. 'Tutu Tells It Like It Is', *The Witness*, 2 April 2009.
56. 'Tutu to Retire from Public Life', *Al Jazeera*, 22 July 2012.
57. Nashira Davids, 'Tutu Launches Attack on Zuma about Dalai Lama's Visa', *The Sowetan*, 5 October 2011 (www.sowetanlive.co.za/news/2011/10/05/tutu-launches-attack-on-zuma-about-dalai-lama-s-visa).

Tutu in 2006, when Obama was a US senator) that he 'could easily squander the goodwill that his election generated if he disappoints'. Tutu further wanted Obama to apologise for the US-led invasion of Iraq in 2003 'on behalf of the American people'.[58]

Shortly thereafter, in July 2009, Obama bestowed the Medal of Freedom – his country's highest civilian honour for a non-American – on Tutu, pronouncing him 'the moral conscience of South Africa'.[59] A year later, Tutu warned that reducing America's financial commitments to AIDS programmes could wipe out decades of progress in Africa, following Obama's decision to cut aid to Africa's anti-AIDS battle as well as contributions to the Global Fund to Fight AIDS, Tuberculosis and Malaria.[60] Tutu complained that Obama had added only $366 million to the programme in 2010 – well below the $1 billion per year he had promised to add while on the campaign trail. In comparison, under the George W. Bush administration, about 400,000 more African patients had received treatment every year. Obama's policies would reduce the number of new patients receiving treatment to 320,000. Congratulating Tutu, 'the moral titan and dedicated peacemaker', on his official retirement a few months later, in October 2010, Obama lamented that he would 'miss his insight and his activism', but pledged 'to continue to learn from his example'.[61] But would he really do so?

In his 2009 lecture after receiving the Nobel Peace Prize, Obama claimed to be living testimony to the moral force of non-violence, his award being a direct consequence of the life work of Martin Luther King Jr (see Robinson, Chapter 3, and Daniels, Chapter 5, in this volume). He noted, however, that the world was not yet ready for peaceful solutions to violent situations, and that the soldiers who gave

58. Desmond Tutu, 'Viewpoint: A Word of Caution to Obama', *BBC News*, 19 February 2009 (http://news.bbc.co.uk/2/hi/africa/7897206.stm).

59. 'Remarks by the President at the Medal of Freedom Ceremony', press release, Office of the Press Secretary, White House, Washington DC, 12 August 2009 (www.whitehouse.gov/the_press_office/Remarks-by-the-President-at-the-Medal-of-Freedom-ceremony).

60. Desmond Tutu, 'Obama's Overdue Aids Bill', *New York Times*, 20 July 2010 (www.nytimes.com/2010/07/21/opinion/21tutu.html?_r=0).

61. See Becky Brittain, 'Obama Praises "Moral Titan" Desmond Tutu on His Retirement', CNN International Division online, 7 October 2010, http://edition.cnn.com/2010/POLITICS/10/07/obama.desmond.tutu.retirement/index.html.

their blood for the wars that the USA had fought abroad were 'wagers of peace'.[62]

From his Nobel African ancestor – Tutu – Obama could observe a determined adherence to the path of peace, while understanding its limitations. Also exemplary has been Tutu's consistent and tireless campaign to promote human rights; social, economic and gender justice; an unequivocal defence of same-sex relationships; and condemnation of the oppression of Palestinians by Israel.

Tutu has never said he is perfect. In fact, his God specifically does not demand perfection. To seek in Tutu's life a definitive measure of the man will prove only partially successful. It is enough to acknowledge that, amid all the contradictions and the many personal attacks he has endured over a long career, his focus has remained consistent. Tutu has said that he hurts less than he did before. But the wounds persist.

Bibliography

Aarvik, Egil, 'The Nobel Peace Prize 1984: Presentation Speech', 8 February 2012, www.nobelprize.org/nobel_prizes/peace/laureates/1984/presentation-speech.html.

Al Jazeera, 'Tutu to Retire from Public Life', Al Jazeera, 22 July 2012.

Allen, John, Rabble-Rouser for Peace: The Authorised Biography of Desmond Tutu (London and Johannesburg: Random House, 2006).

Davids, Nashira, 'Tutu Launches Attack on Zuma about Dalai Lama's Visa', The Sowetan, 5 October 2011 (www.sowetanlive.co.za/news/2011/10/05/tutu-launches-attack-on-zuma-about-dalai-lama-s-visa).

Isaacson, Maureen, 'Wisdom of a Wounded Healer', Sunday Independent, 7 December 2008.

Ndungane, Njongonkulu, 'Reckless Courage', in Lavinia Crawford-Browne with Piet Meiring (eds), Tutu As I Know Him: On a Personal Note (Cape Town: Umuzi, 2006).

Nobel Prize, 'Nobel Peace Prize Biography: Albert Luthuli', 1960, www.nobelprize.org/nobel_prizes/peace/laureates/1960/lutuli-bio.html.

Nobel Prize, 'Nobel Peace Prize Biography: Desmond Mpilo Tutu', 1984, www.nobelprize.org/nobel_prizes/peace/laureates/1984/tutu-bio.html.

Obama, Barack, 'Remarks by the President at the Medal of Freedom Ceremony', press release, Office of the Press Secretary, White House, Washington DC, 12 August 2009 (www.whitehouse.gov/the_press_office/Remarks-by-the-President-at-the-Medal-of-Freedom-ceremony).

Obama, Barack, 'Nobel Lecture: "A Just and Lasting Peace"', 10 December 2009, www.nobelprize.org/nobel_prizes/peace/laureates/2009/obama-lecture_en.html.

Pillay, Gerald (ed.), Voices of Liberation, Volume 1: Albert Luthuli, 2nd edn (Cape Town: Human Sciences Research Council Press, 2012).

Sooka, Yasmin, 'Race and Reconciliation: E Pluribus Unum?', in Adekeye Adebajo, Adebayo Adedeji and Chris Landsberg (eds), South Africa in Africa: The Post-Apartheid Era (Scottsville: University of KwaZulu-Natal Press, 2007).

---

62. Barack Obama, 'Nobel Lecture: "A Just and Lasting Peace"', 10 December 2009, www.nobelprize.org/nobel_prizes/peace/laureates/2009/obama-lecture_en.html.

Sparks, Allister, and Mpho A. Tutu, *Tutu: The Authorized Portrait* (London: Macmillan, 2011).

Styx, Gary, 'Archbishop Tutu Gets Sequenced – and Finds a Surprise in His Ancestry', *Scientific American*, February 2010.

Tepperman, Jonathan D., 'Truth and Consequences', *Foreign Affairs*, March–April 2002.

Tutu, Desmond, 'Nobel Lecture', 11 December 1984, http://nobelprize.org/nobel_prizes/peace/laureates/1984/tutu-lecture.html.

Tutu, Desmond, *The Rainbow People of God: A Spiritual Journey from Apartheid to Freedom*, ed. John Allen (Cape Town: Double Storey, 1994).

Tutu, Desmond, with Douglas Abrams, *God Has a Dream: A Vision of Hope for Our Time* (London: Rider, 2004).

Tutu, Desmond, Second Nelson Mandela Annual Lecture Address, Johannesburg, 23 November 2004, www.nelsonmandela.org/news/entry/ the-second-nelson-mandela-annual-lecture-address.

Tutu, Desmond, address at the Golden Jubilee Ecumenical Theological Education Conference, Neapolis, Greece, 31 May 2008, in *Ministerial Formation*, Jubilee Issue 110, April 2008 (http://wocati.org/publication/ministerial-formation-issue-110-april-2008/wppa_open/main/documents/p5/Ministerial_formation/MF_110_April_08.pdf).

Tutu, Desmond, 'Obama's Overdue Aids Bill', *New York Times*, 20 July 2010 (www.nytimes.com/2010/07/21/opinion/21tutu.html?_r=0).

Tutu, Desmond, *God Is Not a Christian: Speaking Truth in Times of Crisis*, ed. John Allen (London: Rider & Ebury, 2011).

Tutu, Desmond, and Mpho Tutu, 'An Invitation to Wholeness', *Made for Goodness – and Why This Makes All the Difference*, ed. Douglas C. Abrams (London: Rider, 2010).

The Witness, 'Tutu Tells It Like It Is', *The Witness*, 2 April 2009.

EIGHT

NELSON MANDELA:
THE ORATORY OF THE BLACK PIMPERNEL

ELLEKE BOEHMER

Among US president Barack Obama's African Nobel ancestors, Nelson Mandela, South Africa's first democratic president following his election in 1994, stands close to the first black American president for the historic impact of his speeches. Like Obama, Mandela is acclaimed for the power of his words in seeking to change the world. If Obama is widely recognised to be a born orator and a gifted rhetorician – though also a highly practised one – Mandela's oratorical performances are known to have been carefully honed and choreographed over decades of training. His speeches have moved law courts, national fortunes and world opinion through the special combination of his magnetism as a leader, his appeal to the great human constants of socio-economic freedom and justice, and the ethical force arising from his life experience and invested in his words.

As African-American author Alice Walker recognised during Obama's 2008 election campaign, the South African president's template could be discerned within the American leader's authoritative and crusading self-representation. In Obama, both the American people and the wider world could recognise a worthy heir to Mandela. It is possible to say that Mandela – as well as Martin Luther King Jr – showed Obama a way to moral power and political authority (see Mazrui, Chapter 2,

Robinson, Chapter 3, and Daniels, Chapter 5, in this volume). Obama stands on the shoulders of both men. In this essay, the dynamics and semantics of this Nobel line of inheritance will be more carefully unravelled, with particular focus, at the end, on Mandela's own Nobel Prize acceptance speech.

Any comparison between Nelson Mandela and Barack Obama must of course recognise that they emerge out of very different historical eras, family backgrounds and national geographies. To begin with, Obama is American, though partly of African (Kenyan) descent; Mandela stems from a minor branch of a Xhosa royal family. Yet because of this very difference, the parallels between the two men in terms of leadership style and approach are the more striking, as are the connections that can be drawn between their political reputations and historical legacies, including the remarkable charisma that unites them. It can justly be said that Mandela and Obama embody that quality of 'individual personality ... set apart from ordinary men' defined by social theorist Max Weber as the charisma of the great leader.[1] Keenly aware from the beginning that their leadership could help found, consolidate and safeguard traditions of democracy in their countries, both men saw, too, that they represented important sources of inspiration and legitimation for their national communities.

In many ways, Nelson Mandela, whose name and face are internationally famous, needs no introduction. He is widely perceived and celebrated as a symbol of social justice, an exemplary figure connoting non-racialism and democracy, a moral giant. At the beginning of the twenty-first century, not long after he stepped down as the first democratic president of South Africa (1994–99), it was said that his face was second only to the golden arches of McDonald's in terms of its international 'name-brand' recognition. When the statue of 'Madiba' (Mandela's clan name) was unveiled in Parliament Square in London in 2007, he was hailed as 'President of the World', and his ninetieth

1. Anthony Giddens, *Capitalism and Modern Social Theory: An Analysis of the Writings of Marx, Durkheim and Max Weber* (Cambridge: Cambridge University Press, 1971), pp. 160–61; Max Weber, *The Theory of Social and Economic Organization*, trans. A.M. Henderson and Talcott Parsons (New York: Free Press, 1947).

birthday celebrations in July 2008 were marked by well-attended concerts in major cities on several continents. Beginning in the 1960s, when Mandela's famous court addresses first drew the world's attention (at his 1962 sabotage trial and the 1964 Rivonia trial), and resuming in 1988 with his televised seventieth 'birthday party' at England's Wembley Stadium (while he was still in prison), Mandela was established by his advisers and supporters as the pre-eminent symbol of the ongoing struggle against exploitation within, but not confined to, South Africa. Indeed, if across the 1970s and 1980s apartheid was internationally seen as a timeless force of iniquity, then 'Madiba' – the figure who led the struggle against that iniquity – was seen to have absorbed something of that iconic timelessness.

From the beginning, too, Mandela's personal charisma was described as palpable and is itself now famous. Many who have met him remark on the charm, the 'Madiba magic', that radiates from him: a combination of his fame, height and good looks (again not unlike Obama), his encyclopedic memory for faces, and a 'something else' that is undefinable. Central to his character, writes his admirer South African Nobel literature laureate Nadine Gordimer, is a 'remove from self-centredness, the capacity to live for others'.[2]

Yet precisely because Mandela is perhaps now better known as a global icon of freedom and justice around the world than for his actual life-story and achievements, it is important to recollect some of the key events that have defined his long career. 'Madiba' is on record as one of the world's longest-detained political prisoners, having endured twenty-seven years of imprisonment on Robben Island, and later in Pollsmoor and Victor Verster prisons. He walked to freedom in February 1990. Before his imprisonment, Mandela was, during the 1950s, president of his movement (and later party) the African National Congress's (ANC) Youth League, one of the leaders of the peaceful ANC-led Defiance Campaign (from 1952), and then, when that was suppressed by the apartheid regime, the underground leader of the newly formed armed

2. Nadine Gordimer, *Living in Hope and History* (London: Bloomsbury, 1990), p. 48.

wing of the ANC, Umkhonto we Sizwe (MK, from 1961). For over four decades, while his country was vilified the world over for its apartheid policies of state-sanctioned racism, Mandela symbolically, and to some extent practically, led the movement of resistance to that injustice. He and then-president of South Africa Frederik Willem de Klerk (see Houston, Chapter 9 in this volume) jointly received the Nobel Peace Prize in 1993. After South Africa's first democratic elections in April 1994, Mandela was inaugurated as president of the country a month later. He served one term as president, graciously handing over power to his deputy, Thabo Mbeki, in 1999.

The Struggle against Apartheid

Although it is often assumed that Nelson Mandela was the chief architect of the new South Africa, and fought an almost single-handed battle for the rights of the black masses, in fact, as he himself repeated many times, South Africa's liberation was effectively struggled for and won while Mandela languished in jail. Already at his 1962 trial, 'Madiba' emphasised: 'I have been only one in a large army of people.'[3] Like Obama, Mandela has always been quick to acknowledge the support of those who sustained his career. As Mandela put it in an interview with African-American television host Oprah Winfrey:

> If there is any significant role that I played it was that of being a vessel through which the struggle was presented to the nation and the world. The struggle had to have a symbol for it to be effective. The great men and women of the struggle chose that I be that symbol.[4]

Although it is true that Mandela's good guidance and charisma represented important sources of inspiration for the making of post-apartheid South Africa, he was right to forswear authorship of the new South African democracy in this way. It was not merely the modesty of the loyal party man that motivated such statements, but his keen insight

---

3. Elleke Boehmer, *Nelson Mandela* (Oxford: Oxford University Press, 2008), p. 3.
4. Ibid., p. 172.

into the business of politics as well. With Mandela, it is manifestly the case that his leadership alone cannot explain the historical development in South Africa from apartheid to freedom. Inner radiance alone cannot account for why his icon should loom so large in the world's imagination.

The true picture – the real-life 'Madiba magic' – is more complicated than the story of individual specialness suggests, even though that radiance remains an important ingredient. Mandela's leadership is based in a quality of character certainly, but this is combined with other key traits, not least his fine talents for negotiation and arbitration, his insights into his political opponents, and his career-long proximity to several outstanding colleagues and friends, themselves astute political minds, particularly Oliver Tambo, Walter Sisulu and Ahmed Kathrada. Then there is Mandela's talent as a performer – his facility for finding the words and the attire to draw out, appeal to and convince an audience. As his previously quoted comment to Oprah Winfrey suggests, Mandela has always been acutely aware of, and able to mould, his own iconicity. He is able to play to the way in which the unfolding of his life can be seen to underpin South Africa's long road to freedom, just as Obama's presidential triumph in 2008 can be viewed as representing the fulfilment of Martin Luther King's dream – as Obama himself signalled in his acceptance and inaugural speeches as president of the United States in 2008 and 2009. Both Mandela and Obama were trained as lawyers, and share a keen sense of the powers of verbal advocacy and defence.

In any memoir involving Mandela – the ANC's most famous leader – the key note that is repeatedly struck relates to his chameleon-like talent for donning different guises, his theatrical flair for costume and gesture, and his shrewd awareness of the power of his own image. Across his career, as he played such diverse and varied roles as counsellor, lawyer, showman, guerrilla leader and statesman, he allowed himself to be widely photographed in these guises. He delighted in acting the shape-shifter, assuming a range of contrasting 'masks' and convincing others of their authenticity. On the run in 1961–62, before his long imprisonment, he positively thrived in the costumes that his

life-in-hiding necessitated, as well as in the sense of theatre and risk
of exposure involved in wearing them. It was for good reason that he
was called the 'Black Pimpernel', after the protagonist of Baroness
Emmuska Orczy's well-loved 1905 novel *The Scarlet Pimpernel*, an
aristocratic English master of ingenious disguises who was active at the
time of the French Terror of 1792.[5] Mandela is said not to have resented
the appellation. It appealed to his sense of himself as able to establish
rapport with a variety of different audiences – 'with Muslims in the
Cape ... sugar-workers in Natal ... factory workers in Port Elizabeth',
as he writes in his 1995 autobiography *Long Walk to Freedom*.[6] It appealed also to Mandela's desire for mastery of any situation in which
he might find himself.

Up until 1990, for an exiled movement in need of messianic leadership,
as the ANC was, Nelson Mandela perfectly fitted the bill and indeed
was happy to style his image so as to advance the nationalist cause. It is
this factor that accounts for the choreographed quality that any account
of his life and self-presentation inevitably carries: his performances
were composed with a remarkable degree of self-knowledge. Mandela
was never unaware of the power of making a physical statement, of the
efficacy whether in public or private of masks, of how his life might
be read as a model for African upward mobility and political success.
Even on the 1994 presidential campaign trail, when his reputation was
relatively secure, 'Madiba' was famous for addressing several People's
Forums in a single day, while changing clothes as needed to suit his
different audiences (a woolly jumper for a talk to older people, an open
shirt for a village crowd). As fellow ANC activist Raymond Mhlaba once
remarked, Mandela was groomed from the late 1950s to be the internal
ANC leader (the counterpart to Oliver Tambo in exile), and 'he himself
of course conducted himself to attain that status'.[7]

But Mandela's mastery of performance, though often taken as a
given, is rarely analysed in any depth. Until recently, this was probably

5. Baroness Emmuska Orczy, *The Scarlet Pimpernel* (London: Hutchinson, 1905).
6. Nelson Mandela, *Long Walk to Freedom* (New York: Little, Brown, 1994), ch. 40.
7. Boehmer, *Nelson Mandela*, pp. 64–5.

due to the association of such theatricality with charges of change-ability. Yet Mandela's capacity for working his image as if it were itself an expression of his politics tells us a great deal – and not only about his shrewd ability to manipulate his own myth. It also reflects on his proverbial dynamism: how he transformed his style of activism into a credo for action. It relays his understanding, which he shares with the Indian political-spiritual leader Mahatma Gandhi (who lived in South Africa for twenty-one years until 1914), and more recently again with Barack Obama, that method and medium are central to politics, that principle is most effectively conveyed through display. Political success, to a great extent, means transmitting a more humanly convincing message than does one's rival, and Mandela shows that he keenly embraces this precept.

Mandela's awareness of his iconic status can appear cynical, almost cunningly post-modern, and seems to cut across his otherwise appar-ently genuine asseverations of modesty. At the time, however, his astute manipulations of his image could most accurately have been described as expedient. He saw, as did the first prime minister of independent India, Jawaharlal Nehru, that it was important to stand as an 'idealized personification' of the ideals and ambitions of his people: he understood that embattled anti-colonial nationalist movements require compelling and unifying images.[8] A reader of Nehru's life-writing, Mandela, in his own autobiography fifty years later, constructed his life on the assumption that the national leader's narrative is indeed interlocked with the nation's story. In the case of South Africa, this was the story of anti-apartheid resistance. In Mandela's view, the leader, the first democratic president-to-be, *embodies* the nation. Significantly, during his later years in office, 'Madiba' often came across in ways that sug-gested a self entirely bound up in a public mask, as his co-biographer Richard Stengel in fact commented.[9]

But Mandela's talent for performance and styling his body language was always accompanied by finely pitched and modulated speeches.

---

8. Jawaharlal Nehru, *An Autobiography* (London: Bodley Head, 1942), p. 253.
9. Anthony Sampson, *Mandela: The Authorized Biography* (London: HarperCollins, 1999), p. 498.

In fact, his performances are so deeply plaited with his spoken words and rhetorical stance that the one is hardly conceivable without the other. What more might be said about the first black South African president's winning way with words?

Mandela's big speeches under apartheid tended to track, generate and justify significant changes or new initiatives in the liberation struggle. Post-1990, his talks and speeches again marked important occasions and were used to declaim and to persuade, as well as to castigate and cajole. Yet no matter how many different objectives these verbal performances may have had, virtually all were notable once again both for their quality as performances and for their performativeness. Mandela was always particularly talented at using a speech to call a certain historical moment or mode of political awareness into being. For example, in his famous statement from the dock at the end of the Rivonia trial in April 1964, as Mandela declared the ANC to be implacably opposed to racialism in all its manifestations, he thereby powerfully committed his movement, in the eyes of the world, to resisting white and black domination. That is to say, he launched the South African struggle internationally under a non-racial banner. And also at his trial in 1962, Mandela had chosen, after consultation, to represent himself from the dock, rightly thinking that the direct form of address this afforded him would create an ideal opportunity for broadcasting the political vision of the already-banned ANC.

Several of Mandela's most famous early speeches were in their different ways preoccupied with explaining the ANC's graduated turn to armed resistance, both to the movement as a whole and more widely. A particularly vivid example is his 'A Land Ruled by the Gun' speech, delivered at one of the 1962 precursor meetings to the founding of the Organisation of African Unity (OAU). In this speech, Mandela uncompromisingly transmitted the ANC's new militant message to Africa, that there were only two choices left facing South Africa: to submit or to fight.[10] But Mandela's speech from the dock in April 1964

---

10. Francis Meli, *South Africa Belongs to Us: A History of the ANC* (Harare: Zimbabwe Press, 1988). See also Nelson Mandela, 'I Am Prepared to Die', *In His Own Words: From Freedom to the*

at the end of the Rivonia trial was also illuminating regarding his views on militancy and democracy. Realising how important the forum of this particular trial was (the outcome of which could have been the death sentence), Mandela had decided to forfeit the debating forum provided by the witness box, and to present directly from the dock, while at the same time playing upon the heroic image that his time underground had created. As a lawyer himself, Mandela was more aware than most that the space of the court could be used as a political theatre. It was a place unconstrained like no other in the country by the discriminatory restrictions imposed on the black South African majority.

In his carefully modulated 1964 statement, oscillating between personal history and political vision, Mandela began strategically by invoking the influence upon his political beliefs of his African background, in particular of the egalitarian structures of pre-colonial African society. Though he was familiar with the liberation writings of African nationalist leaders such as Ghana's Kwame Nkrumah, and of the widely influential Trinidadian pan-Africanist George Padmore, 'Madiba' always remained an African nationalist with a specifically South African focus. As in his 1962 court speech at his trial for sabotage, Mandela made it clear from the dock two years later that he saw himself as indebted first and foremost to indigenous, not imported, traditions of resistance struggle, even where African models were being transmitted back to the continent through the diaspora. 'Madiba' walked his audience step by step through his beloved ANC's history and the turn to armed violence, and spoke of the 'wars fought by our ancestors in defence of the fatherland' as having inspired him with the hope 'to serve my people and make my own humble contribution to their freedom struggle'.[11] Nearly fifty years later, Obama would cite surprisingly similar black and civil rights influences in November 2008, most prominently Martin Luther King Jr.[12]

Future (London: Little, Brown, 2003), p. 33.

11. Mandela, 'I Am Prepared to Die'.

12. Barack Obama, *Celebrating Change: Key Speeches* (Rockville MD: Arc Manor, 2008), pp. 105–16.

Mandela moved on, at his 1964 trial, to draw attention to the apartheid government's intransigence: despite peaceful protest, the 'rights of Africans [had become] less instead of becoming greater'. Once again strategically, he was concerned to underline the ANC's and even MK's distance from the South African Communist Party, though he did not disavow that connections between the groups existed, on the grounds of common cause and expediency. Socialist redistribution, he said, was to be recommended to allow 'our people' to 'catch up' with the advanced nations. He declared himself an admirer of the Westminster parliamentary system.[13]

Throughout the 1964 speech, Mandela finely balanced his different allegiances – to tradition and modernity, to nationalism and communism, to the West and Africa. He showed himself to be conscious that each measured word not only delivered an exposé of the injustices that black South Africans were suffering, but also, even more powerfully, dramatised the black commitment to justice in contrast with the 'banditry' of white law – in writer Bloke Modisane's memorable description.[14] Mandela was keenly aware of the urgent need to bear authoritative witness to black integrity and capability here and now, within South Africa. The French philosopher Jacques Derrida memorably evoked Mandela's invocation of the pure spirit of the law in a 1986 essay.[15] Appealing over the heads of his judges – representatives of a debased law – Mandela stood for a higher justice, Derrida noted. '[Setting] himself against the code within the code', Mandela became the ultimate expression of the rationalist legal traditions associated with the Enlightenment, as in April 1964 he certainly positioned himself as being. Finally, 'Madiba' rounded off what is still counted as his most powerful speech with that poised, now-famous statement abjuring racial exclusivity, causing a sigh of acclaim to sweep through the court – and then swiftly to ripple around the world through reports in the international news media.

13. Mandela, *In His Own Words*.
14. Boehmer, *Nelson Mandela*, p. 132.
15. Jacques Derrida and Mustafa Tlili (eds), *For Nelson Mandela* (New York: Seaver, 1986).

The March to Freedom

In contrast with his major speeches before his long incarceration beginning in 1963, Mandela's speech from Cape Town city hall on 11 February 1990 – the day of his release – was perceived by many to be overly formal and formulaic, and hence disappointing. His expressed determination to progress the fight for freedom on every front, however, reassured the ANC leadership abroad, which was precisely what the speech had been intended to do. The entire speech in fact operated as something of a long-winded salutation to the ANC's many supporting constituencies. By and by, however, the newly emerged leader began to evolve in a softer, more reassuring light as his new message took hold. In meeting after meeting, as he traversed the country to promote the new path to negotiation and 'talks about talks', Mandela rejected bitterness, praised the integrity of his opponents, acted in deliberately self-effacing ways, and yet, again strategically, seemed always to defer to 'the people's will'. The catalyst of the democratic future had been released back into his 'beloved country' – as he patriotically called it – and he was clearly determined to win it over to the new phase of struggle that he had chosen.

Contrasting sharply with that somewhat predictable first speech following his release from prison four years earlier, Mandela's inaugural speech as South Africa's first democratic president on 10 May 1994, before the Union Buildings in Pretoria (now Tshwane), more than made up for its somewhat formulaic qualities, both qua speech and qua performance. 'Never, never and never again', Mandela urged, 'shall it be that this beautiful land will again experience the oppression of one by another.... Let freedom reign.'[16] These words, which are now often cited as the catchphrase for his entire achievement, are once again strongly declarative and performative. In lines that the Irish poet Seamus Heaney wrote for *The Cure at Troy*, his translation of Sophocles, at the time of hearing of Mandela's release, 'hope' and

---

16. Mandela, 'Inauguration as President', in *In His Own Words*, p. 70.

'history' – for the moment at least – appeared to rhyme, to have been summoned into harmonious formation.[17]

No account of Mandela the rhetorician can be complete without giving some attention to the sometimes curious immobility of his verbal performances: of how the strained, affectless tones that marked his early attempts at public speaking continued, though with some modification, across his entire political career. This stiffness characterised not merely his speeches, but also some of the polemical articles he wrote as a young man in the 1950s, and his political-pedagogical statements in prison. How did this seemingly formal, unmoving language coordinate with the versatility of his statesmanlike behaviour? In asking this question, we take into account the fact that Mandela is manifestly, as a politician, the child of a more formal era: the 1950s. His whole demeanour has been described as 'Edwardian', gentlemanly, a little straight-backed and withheld – features that appear to mark his 1993 Nobel acceptance speech as well.

Rhetoric – according to the classic definition – is fundamental to persuasion, as is good delivery to a successful performance. For Mandela, however, persuasion clearly depended in part on the projection of leader-like authority through somewhat predictable or mechanical forms of address. Revealingly, in a poem titled 'Tamed', written in response to Mandela's February 1990 'Release' speech, Tatamkhulu Afrika, a writer born in Egypt and brought up in South Africa and Namibia, evocatively described Mandela both as a godhead raised on an 'alienating pedestal, piled for your pinioning', and as a mere old man, manipulated by historical forces, fed 'stolidly' with words 'as into a machine'.[18] Across the years, as this implies, Mandela's sartorial language often worked with as eloquent and persuasive an effect as did his formal speeches, though with his stolidity and reliability at the same time underpinning his gentlemanly and chiefly demeanour.

---

17. Seamus Heaney, *The Cure at Troy* (Derry: Field Day, 1990), pp. 80–81.
18. Tatamkhulu Afrika, 'Tamed', in Leon de Kock and Ian Tromp (eds), *The Heart in Exile: South African Poetry in English* (Johannesburg: Penguin, 1996). See also Leon de Kock and Ian Tromp, 'South African Poetry in English', *ARIEL: A Review of International English Literature* 27(1) (1996), p. 113.

Rather than being a master of post-apartheid rhetoric, as the critic Philippe Joseph Salazar suggests, Mandela could instead be said to have deployed the rhetoric of post-apartheid mastery, both before and after 1990.[19] This is most apparent from that same February 1990 speech, which was drafted together with Cyril Ramaphosa and Trevor Manuel. At this time of the re-emergence of the leader-in-waiting, the chief concern of the speech-writing troika was evidently to assert collective leadership and dispel suspicions regarding Mandela's possible collaboration with the enemy – hence the disappointment of some listeners. Similar litanies of acknowledgement marked other speeches at the time. (Interestingly, though 'Madiba' worked with several different speech-writers during his career, the formal quality of his language remained a constant and so, presumably, a preference.)

It is indicative that Mandela was always a more impressive speaker in court than out of it. The advocate's bench and the dock granted him a certain licence as a crowd-pleaser, and it was here where he learned to mould his formal tones to fit the smooth modulations of a legal argument. Elsewhere, motivated by a strong sense of responsibility to his people, he consistently avoided appearing to be a demagogue. To encourage support, it was important to him to use a pared-down, generalist language, the verbs straightforward and workmanlike, the nouns often abstract – invoking freedom and democracy – but unadorned. In all cases – from the dock and from the podium – Mandela's reasoned, stage-by-stage progressions and set phrases were designed to control the expression of subjective emotion.

Other than on those relatively rare occasions where his anger at an abuse of power was expressed as exhortation, Mandela's was a public discourse from which the affect had been extracted. We were not to know how Mandela the man, the human being, felt. For one as dedicated as he was to achieving consensus through the assertion of agreed-upon principles, it made no sense to amplify or overqualify his words. Combining repetitive, starkly polarised binaries (dark/light,

19. Philippe Joseph Salazar, *An African Athens: Rhetoric and the Shaping of Democracy in South Africa* (Hillsdale NJ: Lawrence Erlbaum, 2002).

life/death, African people/white government), as in the statement from
the dock, with the predictable imagery of extensive battles, long walks
and slow upward climbs (made safe by endorsements from William
Shakespeare and Jawaharlal Nehru), the clichés he so preferred were
first and foremost a means of insisting upon concord.

The Nobel Speech

As this background implies, Nelson Mandela's 1993 Nobel Peace Prize
acceptance speech in Oslo is in many ways highly characteristic –
vintage Mandela, in fact.[20] The remarks are relatively short and to the
point, though referring throughout to the great ideals behind which
he has always rallied: justice, respect for human rights, democracy.
Throughout, too, partial though still recognisable references are made,
even if in passing, to the great core texts to which he has repeatedly had
moral and rhetorical recourse. These include, most prominently, the
Bible and the works of Shakespeare. So Mandela depicts disgrace as an
experience of being spat upon, as Jesus Christ is in the New Testament,
and he refers to reaping the rewards of freedom, and the coming of a
new earth in which South Africa's children will live like 'children of
paradise', both once again biblical references. As for Shakespeare, the
idea of taking the tide at its flood, as in *Hamlet*, also harks back to the
quotation from *Measure for Measure* he had cited in the 1964 Rivonia
speech. 'Madiba' also makes reference to certain important African
and pan-African precursors, in particular Martiniquan writer Frantz
Fanon, in the 'wretched of the earth' phrase, and to Martin Luther
King Jr's 'dream' being more precious than 'diamonds or silver or gold'.
Another part-allusion to King is the almost ritualistic self-effacement at
the beginning of the Nobel speech, where Mandela speaks of himself
for the hundredth time as 'nothing more than a representative of the
millions of our people who dared to rise up against a social system

---

20. Nelson Mandela's 1993 Nobel Peace Prize acceptance speech is available at www.nobelprize.
org/nobel_prizes/peace/laureates/1993/mandela-lecture. See also Mandela, 'Nobel Peace Prize', in
In His Own Words.

whose very essence is war'. This is, as we have seen, classic Mandela-esque self-denial.

But where the Nobel speech becomes a particularly interesting con-tribution in itself, rather than by analogy, is in Mandela's invocation throughout of South Africa as poised at a promising though also still dangerous tipping point between the past and the future, where certain rewards long worked for have yet to be fully secured. Repeatedly his words look to the past yet also anticipate the future; his tenses keep oscillating between the two modes. To grasp the significance of this, it is crucial to realise that Mandela was making the speech in 1993, before the historic democratic elections the following year, when South Africa was gripped by a moment of change, tumult and possibility. Many areas were still riven by the community violence believed to be fomented by a mysterious 'third force' – a force that, he was convinced, had links to the apartheid government (see Houston, Chapter 9 in this volume). At this stage, Mandela was not yet president, not yet the official leader: he could not yet formally exert his authority to calm the situation. Moreover, in invoking such a moment in, as it were, charting and tracking the uncertain present in his speech, 'Madiba' could not have been unaware of his friend and fellow Nobel laureate Nadine Gordimer's hugely important and well-known diagnosis of the South African situation in the final years of apartheid as a condition of interregnum, as in her 1983 novel *July's People*.[21] For Gordimer, 'interregnum' – a term she borrowed from Italian Marxist intellectual Antonio Gramsci – signified a time in which an old world was dying, yet the new one could not yet be born.

But Mandela's allusion to a present state of interregnum in his 1993 Nobel Peace Prize speech was, as ever, strategic as well as rhetorical. It urged, in effect, both a pessimism of the intellect and an optimism of the will. The state the country was in and the fine balance on which it was poised gave him occasion to urge his people to a greater moral watchfulness – something Barack Obama, too, often does, and did in

---

21. Nadine Gordimer, *July's People* (New York: Viking, 1981).

his own Nobel Peace Prize acceptance speech in 2009[22] (see Robinson, Chapter 3 in this volume.) In speaking in this way, it is also worth remarking that Mandela made no distinction between his people. It was to a united country that he addressed his exhortatory – though, as ever, performative – remarks at the end of his Nobel speech, as if as a rehearsal for May 1994: 'Let freedom reign. Let a new age dawn.' Here was the president-in-waiting announcing himself both to the world and to his strife-torn country as a man proceeding with caution, yet filled with hope.

Concluding Reflections

Nelson Mandela and Barack Obama emerge out of very different strands of social, cultural and national history. This means that, at one level, the links in terms of leadership qualities and oratorical ability that draw them together seem merely superficial. Yet, as this essay has sought to demonstrate, both national leaders tap into legacies of African and African diaspora speech-making and performance to the extent that invites a comparative analysis of their rhetorical skills as well as of their charisma and leadership abilities.

While generally sticking to their political principles, Nelson Mandela and Barack Obama are both in essence bridge-builders, forging links between communities, and persuading people to find areas of agreement that might draw them together. In these efforts of bridge-building, both leaders have also been well served by their way with words and their special gift of moulding image and shaping rhythm to match their nation's best dreams for the future, all the while balancing strong caution with passionate hope.

---

22. Barack Obama's 2009 Nobel Peach Prize acceptance speech is available at www.nobelprize.org/nobel_prizes/peace/laureates/2009/obama-lecture_en.

Bibliography

Afrika, Tatamkhulu, 'Tamed', in Leon de Kock and Ian Tromp (eds), *The Heart in Exile: South African Poetry in English* (Johannesburg: Penguin, 1996).

Boehmer, Elleke, *Nelson Mandela* (Oxford: Oxford University Press, 2008).

de Kock, Leon, and Ian Tromp, 'South African Poetry in English', *ARIEL: A Review of International English Literature* 27(1) (1996).

Derrida, Jacques, and Mustafa Tlili (eds), *For Nelson Mandela* (New York: Seaver, 1986).

Giddens, Anthony, *Capitalism and Modern Social Theory: An Analysis of the Writings of Marx, Durkheim and Max Weber* (Cambridge: Cambridge University Press, 1971).

Gordimer, Nadine, *July's People* (New York: Viking, 1981).

Gordimer, Nadine, *Living in Hope and History* (London: Bloomsbury, 1990).

Heaney, Seamus, *The Cure at Troy* (Derry: Field Day, 1990).

Mandela, Nelson, 1993 Nobel Peace Prize acceptance speech, www.nobelprize.org/nobel_prizes/peace/laureates/1993/mandela-lecture.

Mandela, Nelson, *Long Walk to Freedom* (New York: Little, Brown, 1994).

Mandela, Nelson, *In His Own Words: From Freedom to the Future* (London: Little, Brown, 2003).

Meli, Francis, *South Africa Belongs to Us: A History of the ANC* (Harare: Zimbabwe Press, 1988).

Nehru, Jawaharlal, *An Autobiography* (London: Bodley Head, 1942).

Obama, Barack, *Celebrating Change: Key Speeches* (Rockville MD: Arc Manor, 2008).

Obama, Barack, 2009 Nobel Peach Prize acceptance speech, www.nobelprize.org/nobel_prizes/peace/laureates/2009/obama-lecture_en.

Orczy, Baroness Emmuska, *The Scarlet Pimpernel* (London: Hutchinson, 1905).

Salazar, Philippe Joseph, *An African Athens: Rhetoric and the Shaping of Democracy in South Africa* (Hillsdale NJ: Lawrence Erlbaum, 2002).

Sampson, Anthony, *Mandela: The Authorized Biography* (London: HarperCollins, 1999).

Weber, Max, *The Theory of Social and Economic Organization,* trans. A.M. Henderson and Talcott Parsons (New York: Free Press, 1947).

NINE

FREDERIK WILLEM DE KLERK:
THE PRAGMATIC PEACEMAKER

GREGORY F. HOUSTON

The 1993 Nobel Peace Prize was jointly awarded to two South Africans, Nelson Rolihlahla Mandela and Frederik Willem de Klerk, for 'their work for the peaceful termination of the apartheid regime, and for laying the foundations for a new democratic South Africa'.[1] In the biography for de Klerk on the Nobel Prize website it is stated that

> in his first speech after assuming the party leadership, he called for a nonracist South Africa and for negotiations about the country's future. He lifted the ban on the African National Congress (ANC) and released Nelson Mandela. He brought apartheid to an end and opened the way for the drafting of a new Constitution for the country based on the principle of 'one person, one vote'.[2]

There are thus two broad reasons that the Nobel Peace Prize was awarded to de Klerk: the central role he played in liberalising the political situation and creating an environment for negotiations, and the necessary steps he took through negotiations to bring an end to apartheid and usher in a democratic South Africa.

1. 'The Nobel Peace Prize 1993', http://nobelprize.org/nobel_prizes/peace/laureates/1993.
2. Tore Frängsmyr (ed.), *Les Prix Nobel: The Nobel Prizes 1993* (Stockholm: Nobel Foundation, 1994) (http://nobelprize.org/nobel_prizes/peace/laureates/1993/klerk).

De Klerk is the only African of European descent to have been awarded the Nobel Peace Prize. What is significant about this award is that at the time he received it he was the leader of the National Party (NP), which had entrenched white minority rule through its policy of apartheid. This was a policy that denied political rights to the majority of South Africa's population, while entrenching the separation of the races through a wide variety of laws, including the Population Registration Act of 1950, which provided for classification of all South Africans into one of four racial groups (African, Asian, 'coloured' [mixed race] and white); the Group Areas Act of 1950, which provided for separate residential areas for the four races; the Prohibition of Mixed Marriages Act of 1949, which prohibited marriages between people from different racial groups; the Immorality Act of 1950, which made it a criminal offence for people from different racial groups to engage in sexual relations; the Separate Amenities Act of 1950, which provided for separate beaches, toilets, buses, train compartments and park benches for South Africa's different race groups; and legislation such as the Bantu Authorities Act of 1951 and Promotion of Bantu Self-Government Act of 1959, which provided for separate 'homelands' for the eight government-designated black South African ethnic groups.

Liberalising the Political Situation and Creating an Environment for Negotiations

The historic speech that F.W. de Klerk made as the last apartheid leader in the South African parliament on 2 February 1990 opened the way for negotiations when the ban was lifted on a number of political organisations and the release of political prisoners was announced. De Klerk also declared his willingness to enter into negotiations with the unbanned political organisations to draft a new constitution under which all South Africans would enjoy equal rights.[3]

---

3. Allister Sparks, *Tomorrow Is Another Country: The Inside Story of South Africa's Negotiated Revolution* (Sandton: Struik, 1994), p. 9.

However, in a 1999 book review titled 'Getting Away with Murder and a Nobel Prize', Leon Kamin argued that de Klerk did not deserve a Nobel Peace Prize for unbanning political organisations and releasing Mandela, because he had been forced to take both actions. According to this view,

> By the time of de Klerk's celebrated speech in February 1990, the ANC's armed struggle and the militant mass action of young blacks had made South Africa ungovernable. South Africa had become a pariah state. The effective worldwide campaign for sanctions was reducing the economy to a shambles. The prospects for a racial bloodbath increased daily. For white South Africans to survive, an accommodation with South African blacks was essential.[4]

Many scholars have echoed this view. To these internal reasons for an 'accommodation with South African blacks', they have often added international developments such as the collapse of Communism in the Soviet Union and, prior to that, the increasing cooperation between Mikhail Gorbachev's Soviet Union and Western powers to resolve regional conflicts in places such as Namibia, Angola and Mozambique. Such critics have thus argued that de Klerk took these actions to 'bring an end to apartheid before he was forced to'.[5] However, in order to understand both the significance of the announcements made that day and the challenges de Klerk faced in reaching the decision to introduce such extensive reforms, it is important to go back at least a year.

De Klerk faced several challenges in the period immediately prior to his 2 February 1990 speech. The first was becoming the leader of the National Party and president of apartheid South Africa. The obstacle here was his hard-line predecessor, P.W. Botha. De Klerk noted in 2003 that 'almost right up to the end of [Botha's] reign, [the] dichotomy that we need to negotiate, but we won't negotiate at all, was the main stumbling block towards the negotiation route being developed at an

---

4. Leon J. Kamin, 'Review: Getting Away with Murder and a Nobel Prize', *Journal of Blacks in Higher Education* 24 (Summer 1999), p. 134.
5. See Alex Callinicos, 'South Africa: End of Apartheid and After', *Economic and Political Weekly* 29 (1994), p. 2358.

earlier stage.'[6] A few months earlier, Botha had considered stepping down from the leadership of the National Party and of the country. About four months before the annual party congress in 1988, the finance minister, Barend du Plessis, had a private meeting with Botha at the Union Buildings in Pretoria, the seat of South Africa's government. Du Plessis recalled that Botha wanted to know if it was time for him to leave office. Botha also wanted du Plessis to find out who would be most likely to replace him. At a subsequent meeting, du Plessis advised Botha to resign at the forthcoming party congress, which would also mark his tenth anniversary as party leader. The finance minister further informed Botha that F.W. de Klerk would be chosen to replace him. Botha rejected du Plessis's advice that he resign: 'I can't go now. Africa will be chaos.'[7]

In part, this statement must be understood in the context of negotiations on South Africa's involvement in Angola and Namibia at the time. By June 1988, Mikhail Gorbachev and Ronald Reagan had reached agreement at a summit in Moscow on the processes that would lead to the independence of Namibia. Negotiations earlier that year had centred on reaching an agreement on Angola, with the South Africans stating that they would withdraw into Namibia if Russian and Cuban forces also agreed to withdraw from Angola. There was no mention of Namibian independence. However, the agreement reached in Moscow paved the way for discussions about Namibia's future. In December 1988, the foreign ministers of South Africa, Cuba and Angola signed the New York Accord, which paved the way both for Namibian independence and for the withdrawal of foreign troops from Angola.[8] The impending independence of Namibia left South Africa as the last outpost of white minority rule, and Botha felt that he still had

---

6. Interview with Frederick W. de Klerk conducted by Gregory Houston and Chris Saunders, Cape Town, 10 February 2003, South African Democracy Education Trust Oral History Project (hereafter SOHP).
    7. Interview with Barend du Plessis conducted by Bernard Magubane and Gregory Houston, Kosmos, 7 November 2001, SOHP.
    8. For more detail about the process that led to Namibia's independence, see Brian Wood, 'Preventing the Vacuum: Determinants of the Namibia Settlement', *Journal of Southern African Studies* 17(4) (December 1991), pp. 742–9.

a role to play in maintaining white rule on the continent.[9] However, in January 1989, P.W. Botha suffered a stroke; two weeks later his resignation as leader of the National Party was announced in a letter to its parliamentary caucus.[10] Botha was to continue in office as state president. The first step in his removal was reached when de Klerk was elected leader of the National Party by its parliamentary caucus in February 1989.

Botha's resignation as party leader and de Klerk's election to the post led to another challenge for the latter: overcoming his own tendency to be conservative. De Klerk has maintained in a number of forums and on several occasions that he had become an enlightened (*verligte*, or liberal) member of the National Party some time before he became its leader. For example, as he stated in an interview in February 2003: 'I was in a sense, before I became a Member of Parliament – this is the ... last few years of the sixties – quite actively involved already in the debate, the growing debate which there was that we must change.'[11] He claimed that it was from this stage that he became part of the reformist or *verligte* faction of the National Party, and that it was his pragmatism that had led to the mistaken perception that he was conservative.

However, many party insiders and outside observers knew de Klerk to be a conservative politician who had been 'utterly consistent on the cornerstones of NP policy'.[12] His conservatism is borne out by his actions in government as well as his family background. De Klerk's family had a long history of involvement in Afrikaner nationalist politics, beginning with his great-grandfather, who had served in the South African Senate immediately after the establishment of the Union of South Africa in 1910. His father was a senator who became a minister in the South African government, while his uncle, Hans Strijdom, served as prime minister in the National Party government between

9. Interview with P.W. Botha conducted by Gregory Houston, Daan Prinsloo and Elsa Kruger, George, 28 November 2005, SOHP.
10. F.W. de Klerk, *The Last Trek – A New Beginning: The Autobiography* (London: Pan Books, 2000 [1999]), pp. 130–31.
11. Interview with de Klerk, SOHP. See also de Klerk, *The Last Trek*, pp. 43–4.
12. Hennie Kotze and Deon Geldenhuys, 'Damascus Road', *Leadership* 9 (1990), p. 14, cited in Betty Glad, 'Passing the Baton: Transformational Political Leadership from Gorbachev to Yeltsin – From de Klerk to Mandela', *Political Psychology* 17(1) (March 1996), p. 3.

1953 and 1958.[13] Thus, when de Klerk became active in politics, he was carrying on a family tradition that had its roots in the role it had played in erecting the edifice of Afrikaner nationalist politics and the system of apartheid.

It is thus no surprise that many of de Klerk's actions, beginning in 1972 as a member of parliament and, starting in 1978, in a number of cabinet positions, were aimed at the entrenchment of apartheid. As noted in his biography on the Nobel Prize website: 'As Minister of National Education, F.W. de Klerk was a supporter of segregated universities, and as a leader of the National Party in Transvaal, he was not known to advocate reform.'[14] Nelson Mandela's biographer, Anthony Sampson, observed that de Klerk had resisted many of Botha's reforms.[15] According to former colleagues in the National Party, change was forced on de Klerk. 'Pik' Botha, the long-serving foreign minister of apartheid South Africa, recalled attending the meeting of the parliamentary caucus that elected de Klerk as leader of the National Party in February 1989: '[De Klerk] defeated Barend du Plessis by a few votes, 4 or 6, no more. And if some of the NP members who were not in the caucus that day [had been] there, Barend could have won.'[16] Du Plessis added that 'a few that would have voted for me were not there, and three of them apologized to me afterwards for having voted in the final round for F.W. [de Klerk] instead of for me, because in the meantime they had realised that they had voted against me for the wrong reason.'[17]

'Pik' Botha maintained that the caucus was divided along ideological lines, with the conservative (*verkrampe*) parliamentarians voting for de Klerk and the 'liberals' voting for du Plessis. He added that 'Barend got up and made a speech, and said to F.W.: "You'll have to make a quantum leap, and when you have made it you will find me there.

---

13. De Klerk, *The Last Trek*, pp. 10–11.
14. Frängsmyr, *Les Prix Nobel*.
15. Anthony Sampson, *Mandela: The Authorized Biography* (London: HarperCollins, 1999), p. 386.
16. Interview with 'Pik' Botha conducted by Sifiso Ndlovu and Bernard Magubane, Johannesburg, 18 September 2001, SOHP. The votes were actually 69 for de Klerk and 61 for du Plessis.
17. Interview with du Plessis, SOHP.

Make it and you'll find me there.'" The consequence, according to 'Pik' Botha, was that de Klerk

> saw the writing on the wall that day in the caucus; that almost half his party did not want him. And he saw clearly he'd better move, and move fast or everything is lost. All my colleagues … will tell you that it is to some extent inexplicable that this arch conservative who was against any major change suddenly became the leader who was eventually amenable. Let me give him that credit. It assisted us to enter into a peaceful new future. For that I give him credit. For that I'm pleased, and for that I respect him.[18]

Once F.W. de Klerk assumed leadership of the party, he stepped up the pace of reform to such an extent that one of the 'liberal' cabinet ministers later noted that 'we are all having to run as fast as we can just to keep up with him'.[19] Shortly after his election as party leader in February 1989, de Klerk called for a new constitution, hinting that it would have to include further concessions to the black majority.[20] Among the early steps was the agreement reached in June 1989 by the National Party's Federal Council, under de Klerk's leadership, to a five-year plan to reform apartheid that included bringing an end to discrimination and introducing a democratic constitution. This was to be followed by a meeting between de Klerk and Zambian president Kenneth Kaunda later that year to discuss the proposed reforms. As state president, P.W. Botha objected to the pace of the proposed reforms, and opposed any plan to hold discussions with Kaunda.[21]

Botha's resistance to the reform process led to the decision of the leadership of the National Party at a meeting on 12 August 1989 to remove him as state president. At a cabinet meeting held two days later, Botha was informed that the party leadership wanted him to take sick

18. Interview with 'Pik' Botha, 18 September 2001, SOHP. De Klerk noted that the voting pattern was a message that many members of the caucus wanted 'to move quickly ahead with reform'; de Klerk, *The Last Trek*, p. 134. David Welsh supports the view that the liberals who voted for du Plessis would not have allowed de Klerk to postpone serious reform as P.W. Botha had done; David Welsh, 'F.W. de Klerk and Constitutional Change', *Issue: A Journal of Opinion* 18(2) (Summer 1990), p. 7.
19. Robert Schrire, *Adapt or Die: The End of White Politics in South Africa* (New York: Ford Foundation and Foreign Policy Association, 1991), p. 131, cited in Glad, 'Passing the Baton', p. 6.
20. Betty Glad and Robert Blanton, 'F.W. de Klerk and Nelson Mandela: A Study in Cooperative Transformational Leadership', *Presidential Studies Quarterly* 27(3) (Summer 1997), p. 567.
21. De Klerk, *The Last Trek*, pp. 141–3.

leave until the general elections scheduled for September 1989. An acting president would be appointed in his place. Botha rejected the proposal. He informed the cabinet that he would resign instead.[22] He announced his resignation to the nation in a televised broadcast that evening, and de Klerk was appointed acting president the following day. In national elections in September 1989, de Klerk was confirmed as state president for a five-year term. He was to initiate a number of reforms before the end of the year.

On 12 September 1989, just prior to his inauguration as state president, de Klerk lifted the ban on protest marches that was then in place under the 'state of emergency' regulations.[23] A day later, Nobel peace laureate and Anglican archbishop of Cape Town Desmond Tutu (see Isaacson, Chapter 7 in this volume), led a protest march without any police interference. In the following months, de Klerk proceeded to dismantle many aspects of 'petty apartheid', such as segregated beaches, parks, lavatories and restaurants. Another step in the reform process was taken when he released a number of high-profile political prisoners, including those who had been imprisoned with Nelson Mandela after the treason trial concluded in 1964. In October 1989, after twenty-six years in prison, Walter Sisulu, Ahmed Kathrada, Andrew Mlangeni, Elias Motsoaledi, Raymond Mhlaba and Wilton Mkwayi were released, along with Oscar Mpetha and Japhta Masemola. Anthony Sampson credited the secret negotiations going on between Mandela and government representatives at the time for this breakthrough.[24]

De Klerk also dismantled the National Security Management System, the 'brain centre' of an elaborate national security network, in an apparent effort to curb the 'securocrats' who had dominated policymaking in this area during the Botha administration. Included here was his assertion that the State Security Council (SSC), the organ at the apex of the national security system, would be confined to its statutory role as an advisory body.[25] The political office-bearers of the Council were

22. Ibid., pp. 142–7.
23. Ibid., p. 159.
24. Sampson, *Mandela*, p. 395.
25. Welsh, 'F.W. de Klerk and Constitutional Change', p. 6.

constituted as a separate cabinet committee for security affairs, and its decisions had to be submitted to the full cabinet for final approval.[26] As de Klerk stated:

> And one of the first things I did when I became President was to return to Cabinet government: to reduce the Security Council to just a Cabinet Committee to break down this tremendous securocrat system which was built up and to say Cabinet must know all the facts, and Cabinet is the policy-making body, deciding on policy and monitoring implementation of policy.[27]

The steps that de Klerk took to create the conditions for negotiations by unbanning political organisations and releasing political prisoners were in sharp contrast to his predecessor's resistance to negotiations. De Klerk could have continued with the path of mass repression taken by P.W. Botha. As Sampson put it, de Klerk 'was still in command of a formidable military machine, police force and intelligence system; and he had no intention of giving way to a black majority unless he was compelled to'.[28] According to Betty Glad and Robert Blanton, de Klerk felt that he could have clung to power for five to ten years without reform. But he also noted that it was 'a way toward destruction'.[29] The route he took, as a number of scholars have pointed out, was courageous.[30]

However, the path de Klerk had embarked upon seemed to have been in line with the thinking among prominent Afrikaners at the time. A study conducted in 1988 among the Afrikaner elite concluded that there had been a loss in confidence in the apartheid government's ability to govern in the interests of the white community by securing national borders against the liberation movements, maintaining general law and order, protecting the socio-economic interests of the population, and ensuring the interests of whites in particular. Close to one-third

26. Deon Geldenhuys, 'The Head of Government and South Africa's Foreign Relations', in Robert Schrire (ed.), *Malan to de Klerk: Leadership in the Apartheid State* (London: Hurst, 1994), p. 289.
27. Interview with de Klerk, SOHP.
28. Sampson, *Mandela*, p. 422.
29. Glad and Blanton, 'F. W. de Klerk and Nelson Mandela', p. 585 n17.
30. Helinna Ayalew, 'Political Leadership in the Transformation of Societies: F.W. de Klerk and Pim Fortuyn in the Multicultural Project', *Macalester International* 25(6), 2010, p. 6 (http://digitalcommons.macalester.edu/macintl/vol25/iss1/6).

of prominent Afrikaners found apartheid to be a serious threat to their security, while nearly 50 per cent regarded apartheid as somewhat threatening to their security. The study also found that the Afrikaner elite did not believe that majority rule would destroy the South African economy. They felt that the effects of black rule on the economy would be both negative and positive. However, the Afrikaner elite expected government and politics to degenerate to what they believed to be 'typical' of black-ruled countries elsewhere in Africa, including a decrease in government efficiency and democracy, and an increase in government corruption and communist influence. Nevertheless, nearly 90 per cent of the Afrikaner elite believed that global acceptance of South Africa would increase with the end of apartheid rule. Finally, the study concluded that there was a strong belief among prominent Afrikaners that the policy of apartheid had failed.[31]

Negotiating the End of Apartheid

The second broad reason that de Klerk was awarded the Nobel Peace Prize was the role he played in the negotiation process that led to the ending of apartheid and the holding of the first democratic election in South Africa in April 1994. Immediately after the February 1990 speech (after which Nelson Mandela was released), de Klerk embarked on a number of reforms. Membership of the National Party was opened up to all races, the Separate Amenities Act and other 'petty apartheid' laws were repealed, and the Land Acts of 1913 and 1936 and the Population Registration Act of 1950 were abolished. The negotiation process was begun very soon after the release of Mandela on 11 February 1990. Ten days later, a number of leading ANC figures in exile, including Jacob Zuma and Penuel Maduna, were smuggled into the country to begin preparations with representatives of the apartheid regime for talks

---

31. Kate Manzo and Pat McGowan, 'Afrikaner Fears and the Politics of Despair: Understanding Change in South Africa', *International Studies Quarterly* 36(1) (March 1992), pp. 1–24. The study was based on the results of a detailed questionnaire sent in July and August 1988 to a carefully selected sample of 843 Afrikaner elites in politics, the civil service, public- and private-sector business, the Dutch Reformed Churches, universities, and the print and electronic media.

between government officials and an ANC delegation led by Mandela, which were to be held on 11 April 1990 in Cape Town.[32] The talks were intended to discuss obstacles to the negotiation process.

However, on 26 March 1990, police fired on marching protestors in Sebokeng township in southern Gauteng, killing eight people and injuring hundreds. This was followed by an announcement five days later that the ANC had decided not to hold talks with the South African government, scheduled for April 1990, due to the Sebokeng killings. On 5 April, at an informal meeting in Cape Town, de Klerk and Mandela agreed that formal talks between the government and the ANC would be held from 2 to 4 May 1990. On 27 April, the first senior members of the ANC, including Thabo Mbeki, Joe Slovo, Aziz Pahad, Joe Nhanhla, Joe Modise, Alfred Nzo, Ruth Mompati and Steve Tshwete, returned to South Africa after more than a quarter of a century in exile. The subsequent meeting between the government and the ANC in Cape Town led to the 'Groote Schuur Minute', which was primarily concerned with creating conditions for the release of political prisoners and the return of exiled members of the liberation movements.

Among the main challenges that de Klerk faced after the unbanning of political organisations and Mandela's release was how to strike a balance between negotiating with the ANC to bring an end to apartheid and maintaining the support base of the National Party, particularly the conservatives. The reforms de Klerk had embarked upon and the beginning of negotiations were alarming to conservative supporters of the National Party, as well as to the white right wing. Among conservative white South Africans, these two acts were tantamount to treason. On 26 May 1990, a short while after the Groote Schuur talks, more than 60,000 pro-apartheid whites participated in a rally against de Klerk's reforms.[33] Opposition to the path taken by de Klerk among white South Africans was also registered when the National Party candidate lost the Potchefstroom mayoral election to a Conservative Party candidate

---

32. Interview with Mathews Phosa conducted by Lesetja Marepo, Nelspruit, 30 January 2004, SOHP.
33. Glad and Blanton, 'F.W. de Klerk and Nelson Mandela', p. 571.

in February 1992, despite de Klerk having actively campaigned for the
candidate. The Conservative Party immediately demanded a national
election. Apartheid's last leader took a major risk when he called for a
whites-only referendum to seek approval for his reforms.

De Klerk believed that the referendum was necessary to test white
support for the reform process. However, in the September 1989 election campaign, and again in the February 1992 by-election campaign,
the National Party promised white voters that it would submit any
new constitution arising from negotiations for their approval. This was
reversed in the referendum campaign, with the National Party making
clear that if de Klerk were given a mandate to continue with the reform
process, it would not submit a new constitution to the white electorate
for approval.[34] De Klerk promised to resign if support was not provided
for his reforms in the referendum. In the end, he received a mandate for
reform from 68.6 per cent of whites who participated in the referendum
in March 1992.[35] De Klerk later noted in a 2003 interview: 'I took a
tremendous risk.' The Nobel peace laureate must thus also be credited
for some of the political risks he took to ensure that the reform process
continued. As de Klerk observed in the same interview, the outcome
of the referendum 'liberated me from constantly having to worry about
the conservative element because I now had even clearer guidelines,
which we spelt out in that referendum. And as long as I stayed within
it I was within my mandate.'[36]

The meeting at Groote Schuur in Cape Town on 4 May 1990 was followed by another in Pretoria three months later that led to the 'Pretoria
Minute', in which the ANC agreed to suspend its armed struggle, and
the National Party-led government agreed to release political prisoners
and indemnify exiles for political offences. However, it was becoming
increasingly apparent that the greatest threat in the transition period
was the ongoing political violence, which in 1990 was still concentrated
in present-day KwaZulu-Natal province. A low-intensity 'civil war' was

34. Marina Ottaway, 'The March 1992 Referendum', in Helen Kitchen and J. Coleman Kitchen
(eds), *South Africa: Twelve Perspectives on the Transition* (London: Praeger, 1994), pp. 124–5.
35. Glad and Blanton, 'F.W. de Klerk and Nelson Mandela', p. 570.
36. Interview with de Klerk, SOHP.

being waged between ANC-aligned organisations and Inkatha, the Zulu cultural movement led by Chief Mangosuthu Buthelezi, which had begun in earnest in August 1985. From that time until the unbanning of the ANC in 1990, thousands of people were killed, maimed and injured, and driven from their homes in the course of this internecine violence. In 1989 alone, according to official figures, 1,279 people were killed in incidents of political violence in what was then Natal province.[37] Ample evidence has been provided to show that the apartheid security forces not only intervened in the conflict on the side of Inkatha, but also deliberately aggravated the crisis.

During the course of the negotiations, Mandela and de Klerk established a relationship – at times antagonistic and at other times conciliatory – that played an important role in the successful transformation of the country from apartheid to democracy.[38] However, political violence was to emerge as one of the two main issues in the four years of negotiations (1990–94) that brought into question Mandela's tribute to de Klerk on the day of his release from prison as 'a man of integrity'. Mandela's frequent public outbursts at de Klerk during the negotiation process were partially motivated by his belief that the latter was fuelling the political violence, even as he professed to talk peace.[39]

The Sebokeng massacre in March 1990 marked the shift of the violence to South Africa's industrial heartland of Johannesburg and the Vaal Triangle. Another attack on Sebokeng residents in which thirty-two people were killed occurred on 22 July 1990 after an Inkatha rally. The ANC had received information about the planned rally two days before it was to take place, and had written to the minister of law and order, Adriaan Vlok, requesting that the rally be cancelled because of the volatile climate. This was not done, and Inkatha went ahead with its rally. Mandela confronted de Klerk over the failure to protect the residents of Sebokeng township two days after the killings. De Klerk responded that police reinforcements had been sent to Sebokeng, but

37. Carole Cooper et al., *Race Relations Survey, 1989/90* (Johannesburg: South African Institute of Race Relations, 1990), p. 250.
38. See Glad, 'Passing the Baton', p. 2.
39. See Sampson, *Mandela*, pp. 474–5.

noted that this had been done a day after the massacre. To make matters worse, a month later the government changed the 'Zulu code' in Natal province to allow only Zulus to carry dangerous weapons such as spears, knobkerries and pangas (machetes) to political rallies.[40]

Following another attack on Sebokeng residents in September 1990, the violence spread elsewhere, and included random attacks on commuters at train stations in Johannesburg. In March 1991, forty-five people died during attacks on residents of Alexandra carried out by members of Inkatha. Victims provided affidavits to the ANC of police collusion with Inkatha in the attacks. This was followed by an Inkatha rally in Alexandra the same month, which the police allowed to proceed despite the violence that had been raging in the township for nine days. Later in March 1991, police fired on an ANC demonstration in Daveyton, near Johannesburg, killing twelve people.[41] According to Johannes Rantete, ANC suspicions of the existence of a 'third force' were fuelled by the sophisticated and high-level secrecy behind the attacks, as well as their indiscriminate nature in shifting to commuter trains, shebeens (taverns), funerals and other centres where people gathered in large numbers.[42] According to de Klerk, however, the only evidence he had about security force complicity in the political violence was the findings of the Harms Commission, which had been presented to him in November 1990. The Harms Commission reported that revelations of death squad activities undertaken by the South African police, made by two former policemen, Dirk Coetzee and Almond Nofomela, in late 1989 and early 1990, were false. The commission did find, however, that the Civil Cooperation Bureau (CCB), a secret South African Defence Force (SADF) front organisation, had been involved in bombings and attempted murders.[43]

In April 1991 the ANC issued an ultimatum to the de Klerk government that it would withdraw from the discussions for the proposed

40. David Ottaway, *Chained Together* (New York: Times Books, 1993), p. 127.
41. Ibid., p. 130.
42. Johannes Mutshutshu Rantete, 'Facing the Challenges of Transition: A Critical Analysis of the African National Congress in the 1990s', M.A. dissertation, University of the Witwatersrand, 1994, p. 103.
43. De Klerk, *The Last Trek*, p. 203.

all-party conference to negotiate the end of apartheid if a number of
its demands were not met by May 1991. These demands included the
banning of dangerous weapons in public places; the dismissal of the
ministers of law and order, and defence; the dismantling of all special
counter-insurgency units; the phasing out of hostels; and the appointment of an independent commission of inquiry to investigate complaints
of misconduct by the police and other security forces. Although the
government did not meet the demands by the date set, and although the
ministers (Adriaan Vlok, law and order; and Magnus Malan, defence)
were not dismissed, the government acceded to the banning of dangerous weapons such as pangas, bush knives and axes (but refused to
include 'traditional weapons' such as shields, sticks, knobkerries and
spears), and agreed to the appointment of the Goldstone Commission to
investigate security force involvement in fomenting political violence.[44]

In July 1991, however, evidence of continued police support for
Inkatha was revealed in what became known as the 'Inkathagate'
scandal. This included security forces providing funds to Inkatha for
its rallies and other activities. De Klerk claimed to have had no knowledge of these activities. But his denials of security force involvement
in a 'third force' became less and less convincing.[45] Vlok and Malan
were removed from their positions and shuffled to other portfolios in
the cabinet later that month – not in response to ANC pressure or
acknowledgement of their complicity in 'third force' activities, according to de Klerk, but for other reasons.[46]

The violence continued unabated. On 8 September 1991, twenty-
three members of Inkatha were killed by unknown gunmen in an
attack on an Inkatha march. Inkatha members retaliated, and, in the
days that followed, indiscriminate attacks on people in buses, taxis
and trains resulted in the deaths of about a hundred people.[47] The
violence continued into the next year, with Inkatha members attacking
residents in Alexandra township in March 1992, while the Boipatong

44. Rantete, 'Facing the Challenges of Transition', p. 103.
45. Sparks, *Tomorrow Is Another Country*, pp. 154–5.
46. De Klerk, *The Last Trek*, p. 203.
47. Ottaway, *Chained Together*, p. 166.

massacre in June 1992 resulted in the death of forty-six people at the hands of Inkatha members in one night. The ANC withdrew from all-party negotiations under way at the time in protest against de Klerk's reluctance to take the steps it was demanding to quell the violence.

The Goldstone Commission, which reported in 1992 and 1993, found damning evidence of the existence of a 'third force'. The first revelation, made in November 1992, was the discovery of the headquarters of a secret branch of military intelligence, the Directorate of Covert Collection (DCC), and evidence that it was conducting propaganda activities against Umkhonto we Sizwe (MK), the military wing of the ANC. However, it was only in March 1994 that the Commission reported on the involvement of elements of the security police in what de Klerk described as 'a silent war against the leaders and activities of the ANC and its allies'. Most important, a unit based at Vakplaas had been involved since 1989 in fomenting violence, including the organisation of train and hostel violence and the channelling of arms to senior members of Inkatha for use against the ANC.[48] It took almost four years and close to 4,000 deaths to acquire the evidence that supported what black victims of the violence and the ANC had known for years.

In his 1999 review of de Klerk's autobiography, Leon Kamin questioned de Klerk's honesty when he claimed to have had no knowledge of criminal activities undertaken by members of the security forces.[49] Allister Sparks also pointed out that most black South Africans felt that de Klerk had been behind the violence, largely because they could not believe that a regime that had been so successful in the past in tracking down members of the liberation movements was now incapable of arresting anyone in connection with the violence.[50] But, as Mark Gevisser noted, de Klerk's complicity in the political violence remains a mystery. He was found culpable of complicity by the Desmond Tutu-chaired Truth and Reconciliation Commission (TRC), which had been established by the democratic government to investigate human

48. De Klerk, *The Last Trek*, pp. 316–17.
49. Kamin, 'Review: Getting Away with Murder and a Nobel Prize', pp. 132–4.
50. Sparks, *Tomorrow Is Another Country*, p. 153.

rights abuses during the apartheid era (see Isaacson, Chapter 7 in this volume). However, the TRC was prevented by a judicial order from including this finding in its final report.[51]

The second main issue that brought de Klerk's integrity into question was his (and the National Party government's) recalcitrance on many issues during the negotiation process. This, together with his apparent reluctance to deal with political violence, led to the increasing deterioration of his relationship with Mandela. Disagreements here included the failure of the government to stick to accords reached in the 'Pretoria Minute', as well as the different approaches of the ANC and the government to transitional mechanisms.

In the first place, the ANC consistently complained that the government was dragging its feet in implementing agreements to expedite the return of political exiles and to release political prisoners. A working group had been established under the 'Groote Schuur Minute'; on 21 May 1990 it set out the definition of political offences in the South African situation.[52] At the joint meeting between the ANC and the government at the presidency in Pretoria in August 1990, both sides accepted the recommendations of the working group. Target dates were set for the phased release of political prisoners beginning in September 1990, and for the granting of indemnities by October 1990. A working group was established and instructed to draw up a plan for the release of ANC political prisoners and the granting of indemnity to exiles. The process of granting indemnity to specific categories of persons was to be completed no later than December 1990, while the process of granting indemnity to individuals was to be completed by April 1991.[53] However, in October 1990 the ANC announced that it was postponing its national conference, set for December 1990, to June 1991, due to the slow pace of efforts to secure the return of more than 20,000 exiles and the release of some 3,000 political prisoners.

---

51. Mark Gevisser, 'Strange Bedfellows: Mandela, de Klerk, and the New South Africa', *Foreign Affairs* 79(1) (January/February 2000).
52. Report of the Working Group established under Paragraph 1 of the Groote Schuur Minute, www.anc.org.za.
53. Pretoria Minute, 6 August 1990, www.anc.org.za.

The April 1991 deadline for the release of all political prisoners and the return of exiles passed while hundreds were still in prison and thousands still abroad. Among the key problems that emerged with regard to the release of political prisoners was disagreement between the ANC and the government on the definition of 'political prisoner', and therefore who should be given amnesty and released from prison. This gave rise to endless delays in the process of releasing political prisoners, as each 'crime' had to be assessed on a case-by-case basis to determine that it had been 'politically motivated'. It would take almost two years before agreement was finally reached on all politically motivated crimes.[54]

De Klerk states that he found the ANC's demand 'for the unconditional release of its followers that it regarded as political prisoners' very difficult to accept. By September 1992, the government had released all those prisoners that it felt had met the definition of 'political prisoner'. This excluded all those prisoners who had committed acts that included 'the gratuitous murder of civilians and other crimes with a high degree of premeditation and violence'.[55] The number of such prisoners was about 300, all of whom were sitting on death row. A planned summit of the two main parties in the negotiations set for September 1992 was preceded by bilateral meetings between negotiators from both sides. These reached agreement on all issues except the release of political prisoners. This had the potential to be a major stumbling block in the negotiation process. However, Mandela discussed the issue with de Klerk several times over the phone, demanding that he agree to the release of all political prisoners on death row at the same time if he wanted the summit to proceed.[56] De Klerk eventually agreed to release them all, and this was included in the 'Record of Understanding' that emerged from the summit in September 1992.

The National Party-led government's delaying tactics over the release of political prisoners was mirrored in its conduct over the return of

---

54. Ottaway, *Chained Together*, p. 108.
55. De Klerk, *The Last Trek*, p. 250.
56. Sparks, *Tomorrow Is Another Country*, p. 183.

political exiles. Indemnity from arrest and prosecution for carrying out politically motivated crimes had to be granted to 20,000 political exiles. Most were seeking, at the very least, indemnity for leaving the country without a valid travel document. Jackie Selebi, who oversaw the process of obtaining indemnity for political exiles on behalf of the ANC, identified a number of obstacles that the government had created in this process.[57] The most significant was the requirement imposed by Pretoria that political exiles seeking indemnity complete a questionnaire detailing all the acts for which they were seeking exemption. Another major problem with the process, according to Selebi, was foot-dragging on the part of individuals in the Justice Department who were responsible for the granting of indemnity. They would take a long time to reach a decision on individual indemnity applications. Finally, officials of the Department of Home Affairs delayed providing the necessary travel documents to individuals who had been granted indemnity. Of course, de Klerk would be blamed for these delaying tactics by the ANC because of his failure to take steps to accelerate the process.

While the ANC, from the outset, called for the establishment of an inclusive interim government to oversee the transition process and a Constituent Assembly to draft a new constitution,[58] the National Party wanted agreement on a constitution to be negotiated while it held on to the reins of political power. De Klerk based his hopes on a power-sharing system that would not lead to majority rule, telling Western diplomats that he could not be expected to 'negotiate myself out of power'.[59] The basis of power-sharing was the protection of Afrikaner rights in a non-racial democracy. A House of Representatives would be elected by universal franchise, while a Senate would be made up of representatives of all parties above a certain threshold of support, with the body having to reach decisions by consensus. The executive would be made up of an all-party 'collegiate' cabinet with a rotating

57. Interview with Jackie Selebe (sic) conducted by Padraig O'Malley, 19 December 1990, O'Malley Archives, www.nelsonmandela.org.za.
58. Rantete, 'Facing the Challenges of Transition', p. 142.
59. Sparks, *Tomorrow Is Another Country*, p. 14.

presidency that would also have to reach decisions by consensus. Thus a white minority could veto decisions made in both the legislative and executive branches of government.[60] De Klerk was still hoping to hold on to some of the vestiges of the apartheid system.

The ANC's demand for a Constituent Assembly to draft a new constitution while an interim government oversaw the process, and the National Party-led government's demand that a convention of all existing political organisations draft the constitution, held up the negotiation process for nearly two years. De Klerk realised that the National Party and its allies would be in the minority in a Constituent Assembly elected through a one-person, one-vote system, while the ANC was opposed to an all-party convention that would bring in puppet 'homeland' and other parties that had no popular support. A compromise was reached when the ANC agreed that an 'all-party congress' should be held to negotiate the route to a Constituent Assembly. The assembly would draft the final constitution, but, as a sop to the National Party, the all-party congress would draft an interim constitution that would include a set of binding principles, including the requirement of special majorities on certain issues.[61] Thus, nearly two years after the release of Nelson Mandela, negotiations began in December 1991 in the Convention for a Democratic South Africa (CODESA) at the World Trade Centre near Johannesburg.

Five months later, when CODESA II began in May 1992, the negotiating parties were still deadlocked on one core issue: the percentage of the majority vote that would be required in the Constituent Assembly to pass key points in the constitution. All parties had been expected to sign the agreements reached during the previous five months of this session. However, a week before the opening of CODESA II, de Klerk introduced a new proposal: he insisted on a three-quarters majority vote for the adoption of all important sections of the constitution. De Klerk was still insisting on a constitutional model that would give veto power to 'minorities'. Despite this setback, agreement was reached

60. Ibid., p. 13.
61. Ibid., pp. 128-9.

that the negotiations could proceed. However, just over a month after negotiations resumed the Boipatong massacre occurred, and the ANC withdrew from the negotiation process.[62]

From CODESA II to the Nobel Peace Prize

The Nobel Peace Prize is awarded in acknowledgement of a laureate's prior actions. For many black South Africans, the joint awarding of the prize to de Klerk and Mandela was both shocking and insulting. In their view de Klerk had done very little to deserve the award, and he had done much to make it difficult for them to understand why he was being granted the prize.[63] However, the Nobel Peace Prize is often awarded to encourage or discourage future actions. The joint awarding of the prize to Mandela and de Klerk suggested that the latter reason was a significant factor. In the case of de Klerk, it was designed to encourage further actions that would lead to a successful conclusion of the negotiation process and to discourage those actions that would disrupt the process.

But what happened between 1992 and 1994 to support this viewpoint? The Nobel Peace Prize winners for 1993 were informed that they would receive the prize on 15 October 1993. Three months earlier, Mandela and de Klerk had been jointly presented with the Philadelphia Liberty Medal by US president Bill Clinton for their 'enormous courage, integrity, forbearance, sense of justice and devotion to freedom and consensus for the common good'.[64] The eyes of the world were firmly focused on South Africa, and there were many different ways to encourage the process of dismantling apartheid. One of these was to reward the key players for progress in the process.

In June 1992 the talks at CODESA II broke down in the aftermath of the massacre in the black township of Boipatong. The ANC had for

62. Sampson, *Mandela*, pp. 460–61.
63. Note the remark made by Winnie Mandela that it 'was an insult to give it to him jointly with his jailor', cited in Sampson, *Mandela*, p. 474. See also Mamphela Ramphele, *Laying Ghosts to Rest: Dilemmas of the Transformation in South Africa* (Cape Town: Tafelberg, 2008), p. 63.
64. '1993 Liberty Medal Recipients', www.constitutioncenter.org.

some time been insisting that the National Party-led government take responsibility for resolving the violence in the country, while accusing de Klerk's administration of complicity in fomenting the clashes. The ANC embarked on a campaign of non-violent 'mass action' (mainly street protests and labour strikes) to force concessions from the de Klerk government. The campaign was aimed at the introduction of an all-party interim government to oversee the transition to a post-apartheid era.[65] In the process, however, militants in the ANC had been given scope by the Tripartite Alliance – the ANC, the South African Communist Party (SACP) and the Congress of South African Trade Unions (COSATU) – to take action. The result was the Bisho massacre in September 1992, during which 'homeland' soldiers fired on some of the 70,000 ANC supporters who entered a stadium near Bisho, the capital of the 'independent' Ciskei homeland, during a protest march. Twenty-eight people were killed.

The massacre was a turning point in the negotiations. Private meetings between key negotiators from both parties led to an agreement on a summit to be held on 26 September 1992 at the World Trade Centre. The 'Record of Understanding' that emerged from this meeting included de Klerk's acceptance of an elected Constituent Assembly to draft and adopt a new constitution, and to serve as a transitional parliament. The parties also agreed to resume negotiations. Bilateral meetings between the ANC and the government resumed in December 1992. In February 1993, both parties announced that they had reached agreement on a number of issues. There would be a five-year transitional period during which a multi-party cabinet, government and parliament would share power after a general election to be held in early 1994. Each party would be represented in a transitional Government of National Unity (GNU) on the basis of the number of votes it had garnered in the country's first democratic election. Parties that had gained at least 5 per cent of the vote would have the right to be included in the transitional government.

---

65. James Hamill, 'South Africa: From CODESA to Leipzig?', *World Today* 49(1) (January 1993), pp. 12–14.

In the interim, a transitional executive council representing all parties would oversee preparations for the polls.

This agreement was formalised at negotiations in CODESA III, which began in March 1993. Both Mandela and de Klerk were lauded the world over for this achievement. Seven months later, the two men were informed that they were to be awarded the Nobel Peace Prize for that year. There was no turning back in the negotiation process from then on, because de Klerk was now recognised the world over as a 'man of peace'.

The Post-Apartheid Era

After South Africa's first democratic elections took place on 27 April 1994, F.W. de Klerk entered the post-apartheid government as one of the country's two deputy presidents (the other being Thabo Mbeki) under the leadership of his fellow Nobel laureate Nelson Mandela. De Klerk's own recollection is that early in the history of the Government of National Unity he had misgivings because President Mandela had allocated cabinet portfolios without consulting him. This was a shocking act for de Klerk, because the interim constitution required the president to consult with the deputy presidents both on the division of portfolios between political parties and on the people who would be appointed to the various portfolios. This slight was, according to de Klerk, 'a foretaste of the many difficulties' the National Party would encounter with the ANC in the GNU.[66]

However, de Klerk has rather fond memories of his first year in the Government of National Unity, especially the respect shown to him by both ANC and Inkatha cabinet ministers at meetings he chaired, the good relationship he established with Thabo Mbeki, and the progress the cabinet made in reaching common approaches to a number of critical issues. But the 'political honeymoon' was marred by Mandela's unwillingness to allow de Klerk to represent the country on trips

---

66. De Klerk, *The Last Trek*, p. 342. See also Sampson, *Mandela*, p. 507.

abroad, and the increase in differences on policy issues between ANC and National Party members of the cabinet.[67]

According to Sampson, Mandela continued to distrust de Klerk because he had felt profoundly betrayed by the latter's 'connivance with the third force'. Matters came to a head in January 1995 when Mandela discovered that de Klerk had secretly granted indemnity from prosecution for crimes carried out during the apartheid years to 3,500 policemen. Mandela attacked de Klerk on this issue during a cabinet meeting in the same month. De Klerk responded by saying that he would have to reconsider his participation in the government. However, de Klerk's colleagues convinced him to stay on.[68] In de Klerk's recollection of events, the new constitution that had been drawn up by 1996, after an elaborate nationwide consultation process, provided the impetus that led to his departure from the GNU. He argued that the constitution did not make provision for power-sharing and therefore participation of the National Party in the cabinet. Thus, a month after the adoption of the new constitution, in May 1996, the National Party withdrew from the GNU.[69] The departure of the 'Nats' from the government led to the withdrawal of a number of people from the party, and de Klerk retired from national politics in August 1997.[70] In 2000 he established the F.W. de Klerk Foundation, which aims to uphold the South African Constitution and the national accord; to work for harmonious relations in multicultural societies; to promote the peaceful and negotiated resolution of disputes; and to mobilise resources for disabled and underprivileged children.

Concluding Reflections

F.W. de Klerk had the opportunity to meet the two South Africans who had been awarded the Nobel Peace Prize prior to himself and Mandela. As a student leader in the 1950s, he was behind an initiative

---

67. De Klerk, *The Last Trek*, p. 342.
68. Sampson, *Mandela*, p. 511. See also de Klerk, *The Last Trek*, pp. 349-50.
69. De Klerk, *The Last Trek*, pp. 358-62.
70. Ibid., p. 364.

to invite Chief Albert Luthuli, president of the ANC and future Nobel
Peace Prize winner, to address students at Potchefstroom University
(see Saunders, Chapter 6 in this volume). Luthuli impressed de Klerk,
but Afrikaner youth remained unconvinced by his argument that there
should be universal franchise for all South Africans in an undivided
country.[71] Instead, de Klerk claims to have taken inspiration at the time
from Hendrik Verwoerd – widely regarded as the intellectual architect
of the doctrine of apartheid – whom he saw as a 'theoretician of the
vision for the future'. Verwoerd's policy of separate development and
independent homelands for Africans would have, in de Klerk's view,
resulted in a country in which his Afrikaner group would also have
achieved 'self-determination'. This would have been 'the culmination
of the Afrikaners' liberation struggle against colonialism'.[72] De Klerk
also 'had considerable respect for' the other previous Nobel Peace Prize
winner, Archbishop Desmond Tutu, who 'had proved his integrity
and independence on a number of occasions'. However, de Klerk had
some reservations about Tutu, because 'much of his own career had,
after all, been dedicated to opposing' the apartheid government[73] (see
Isaacson, Chapter 7 in this volume).

In the period after 1993 – when de Klerk was awarded the Nobel
Peace Prize – and the country's first democratic elections, in 1994,
South Africans had mixed feelings about the appropriateness of awarding de Klerk the prize. In the view of the millions of black people and
the much smaller number of white people who had been the victims
of the apartheid system, he did not deserve the prize. This sentiment
was shared by a large number of conservative whites, who felt that
de Klerk had given 'their country' away to black South Africans. On
the other hand, many white South Africans who had realised that
apartheid was no longer workable felt that de Klerk deserved the award
because he had secured their future in a democratic South Africa. Many
black South Africans, in particular some sections of the 'coloured'

---

71. Ibid., p. 31.
72. Interview with de Klerk, SOHP.
73. De Klerk, *The Last Trek*, p. 370.

(mixed race) community, also felt that de Klerk deserved the award, because he was *the* person who had brought about the end of apartheid. Indeed, as Mark Gevisser noted, de Klerk asked again and again in his autobiography why he had been 'so vilified when he voluntarily gave up his power and birthright for the sake of justice'.[74] Perhaps from the latter statement can be drawn one of the most appropriate lessons of the work of the Nobel laureate reviewed here: that humanity places great value on those who make sacrifices in the cause of the fight for justice. Acknowledging a leader who gave up his illegitimate power can serve as encouragement to future leaders in similar situations to take the same step.

However, de Klerk defended the apartheid system – in particular its policy of separate development in the form of the 'homelands' – in an interview with CNN's Christiane Amanpour in May 2012. He stated that he would not apologise for 'the original concept of seeking to bring justice to all South Africans through the concept of nation states' (essentially creating two separate states, one black and one white).[75] This predictably sparked outrage in South Africa and across the world.

Bibliography

Ayalew, Helinna, 'Political Leadership in the Transformation of Societies: F.W. de Klerk and Pim Fortuyn in the Multicultural Project', *Macalester International* 25(6) (2010) (http://digitalcommons.macalester.edu/macintl/vol25/iss1/6).

Callinicos, Alex, 'South Africa: End of Apartheid and After', *Economic and Political Weekly* 29 (1994).

Cooper, Carole, et al., *Race Relations Survey, 1989/90* (Johannesburg: South African Institute of Race Relations, 1990).

de Klerk, F.W., *The Last Trek – A New Beginning: The Autobiography* (London: Pan Books, 2000 [1999]).

Frängsmyr, Tore (ed.), *Les Prix Nobel: The Nobel Prizes 1993* (Stockholm: Nobel Foundation, 1994), http://nobelprize.org/nobel_prizes/peace/laureates/1993/klerk.

Geldenhuys, Deon, 'The Head of Government and South Africa's Foreign Relations', in Robert Schrire (ed.), *Malan to de Klerk: Leadership in the Apartheid State* (London: Hurst, 1994).

Glad, Betty, and Robert Blanton, 'F. W. de Klerk and Nelson Mandela: A Study in Cooperative Transformational Leadership', *Presidential Studies Quarterly* 27(3) (Summer 1997).

Hamill, James, 'South Africa: From CODESA to Leipzig?' *World Today* 49(1) (January 1993).

---

74. Gevisser, 'Strange Bedfellows'.
75. F.W. de Klerk interview with Christiane Amanpour, May 2012 (see http://edition.cnn.com).

Kamin, Leon J., 'Review: Getting Away with Murder and a Nobel Prize', *Journal of Blacks in Higher Education* 24 (Summer 1999).

Kotze, Hennie, and Deon Geldenhuys, 'Damascus Road', *Leadership* 9 (1990),

Manzo, Kate, and Pat McGowan, 'Afrikaner Fears and the Politics of Despair: Understanding Change in South Africa', *International Studies Quarterly* 36(1) (March 1992), pp. 1–24.

Nobel Prize, 'The Nobel Peace Prize 1993', http://nobelprize.org/nobel_prizes/peace/laureates/1993.

Ottaway, David, *Chained Together* (New York: Times Books, 1993).

Ottaway, Marina, 'The March 1992 Referendum', in Helen Kitchen and J. Coleman Kitchen (eds), *South Africa: Twelve Perspectives on the Transition* (London: Praeger, 1994).

Ramphele, Mamphela, *Laying Ghosts to Rest: Dilemmas of the Transformation in South Africa* (Cape Town: Tafelberg, 2008).

Rantete, Johannes Mutshutshu, 'Facing the Challenges of Transition: A Critical Analysis of the African National Congress in the 1990s', M.A. dissertation, University of the Witwatersrand, 1994.

Sampson, Anthony, *Mandela: The Authorized Biography* (London: HarperCollins, 1999).

Schrire, Robert, *Adapt or Die: The End of White Politics in South Africa* (New York: Ford Foundation and Foreign Policy Association, 1991).

Sparks, Allister, *Tomorrow Is Another Country: The Inside Story of South Africa's Negotiated Revolution* (Sandton: Struik, 1994).

Welsh, David, 'F.W. de Klerk and Constitutional Change', *Issue: A Journal of Opinion* 18(2) (Summer 1990).

Wood, Brian, 'Preventing the Vacuum: Determinants of the Namibia Settlement', *Journal of Southern African Studies* 17(4) (December 1991), pp. 742–9.

PART FOUR

THE TWO EGYPTIANS

TEN

ANWAR SADAT:
THE TRAGIC PEACEMAKER

BOUTROS BOUTROS-GHALI

On 27 October 1978 the Nobel Peace Committee announced that the Peace Prize for that year would be awarded jointly to President Anwar Sadat of Egypt and Menachem Begin of Israel, for their contributions to peace in the Middle East.[1] When Aase Lionaes, the Norwegian chair of the committee, addressed the assembled guests at the award ceremony on 10 December 1978 he noted that it was the first time that the committee had 'considered it apposite to award the Peace Prize to statesmen from the troubled and sadly devastated Middle East', adding that 'never has the Peace Prize expressed a greater or more audacious hope – a hope of peace for the people of Egypt, for the people of Israel, and for all the peoples of the strife-torn and war-ravaged Middle East'. The chair went on to acknowledge that, though the prize was being awarded jointly, it was Sadat who had 'cut the Gordian knot at a single stroke' by seizing the initiative in making peace with Israel.[2]

---

1. This chapter draws from Boutros Boutros-Ghali, *Egypt's Road to Jerusalem: A Diplomat's Story of the Struggle for Peace in the Middle East* (New York: Random House, 1997); and Daniel Pipes, 'Interview with Boutros Boutros-Ghali', *Middle East Quarterly* 4(3) (September 1997), with additional material provided by Chris Saunders, emeritus professor at the University of Cape Town (UCT), and Dawn Nagar, researcher at the Centre for Conflict Resolution (CCR) in Cape Town.
2. Boutros-Ghali, *Egypt's Road to Jerusalem*, pp. 11–12.

The Road to Jerusalem

Anwar Sadat was born to a peasant family, one of thirteen children of a father who became a government clerk. He spent his early years in a small village on the banks of the famous River Nile.[3] After the family moved to Cairo, he entered the Royal Military Academy, where he met Gamal Abdel Nasser and other military officers who shared his wish to oust the British from Egypt. Sadat was imprisoned for working against the British, then helped Nasser in the military *coup d'état* that forced King Farouk to abdicate in 1952. When Nasser died in 1970, Sadat took over as Egypt's president. Three years later, Sadat launched Egyptian troops across the Suez Canal into the Sinai Peninsula. Though he failed in this attempt to regain the territory that Egypt had lost to Israel in the 1967 war, the Egyptians fought bravely and Sadat emerged from the war – in the eyes of his people – as a victor. But other Arab countries would not give Sadat the means to rebuild the Egyptian military forces, and the Soviet Union refused to supply him with the weapons that would have made those forces a credible threat to Israel.

I was Sadat's chief foreign policy aide at the time of the major shift in policy that led to his being awarded the Nobel Peace Prize. I had first met him in October 1954 at an event marking United Nations Day, but had then had no dealings with him for twenty-three years, until October 1977. I was suddenly summoned to leave my thirty-year academic career at Cairo University and requested to join Sadat's Council of Ministers. I did not know at the time that he was about to take the steps that would lead to his being awarded the Peace Prize a year later. In choosing me as an adviser in 1977, Sadat had apparently been influenced by articles I had published in the preceding years in the daily newspaper *Al-Ahram* and the quarterly *As-Siyasa ad-Dawliya* that had explored the possibility of Egypt making peace with Israel. Tel Aviv had argued that its Arab enemies would not negotiate directly with it, so Sadat decided to call its bluff. He also realised that the Geneva conference process, which had begun in 1973 under the auspices of

---

3. Anwar el-Sadat, *In Search of Identity: An Autobiography* (London: Collins, 1978), p. 9.

the United Nations, with the United States and the Soviet Union as co-chairs, was getting nowhere.

In November 1977, Sadat addressed Egypt's People's Assembly, in the presence of Yasser Arafat, the leader of the Palestine Liberation Organisation (PLO). In the course of his speech, he said:

> I am ready to travel to the ends of the earth if this will in any way protect an Egyptian boy, soldier, or officer from being killed or wounded. I say that I am ready for sure to go to the ends of the earth. I am ready to go to their country, even to the Knesset itself and talk with them.[4]

At the time, no one anticipated that this mention of going to the Knesset would lead to a visit to Jerusalem ten days later. When Sadat told his aides of his intention to go to Jerusalem to break the diplomatic deadlock over the Middle East, they opposed this, and his prepared text contained no reference to the holy city. Both Egypt's foreign minister, Ismail Fahmi, and its minister of state for foreign affairs, Muhammad Riyad, resigned in protest. I was then asked to accompany Sadat to Israel, where he said prayers at the Al-Aqsa Mosque and addressed the Knesset in Arabic. He called Jerusalem 'the City of Peace' and noted: 'Today we have a good chance for peace, an opportunity that cannot be repeated, if we are really serious in the quest for peace. If we throw or fritter away this chance, the curse of mankind and the curse of history will befall the one who plots against it.'[5] Though the Israelis were disappointed by a number of aspects of the speech, a private session after the speech between Sadat and the dovish Israeli minister of defence Ezer Weizman marked the beginning of negotiations between the two countries.

Then began a tortuous and exhausting process that led eventually to the signing of a peace agreement in March 1979 between Egypt and Israel which provided for the return of Sinai to Egypt. When Begin, the Israeli prime minister, made a return visit to Cairo, which happened to coincide with Sadat's fifty-ninth birthday, he told Sadat that Israel now recognised Egypt's sovereignty over the whole Sinai peninsula.

---

4. Boutros-Ghali, *Egypt's Road to Jerusalem*, p. 12.
5. Sadat's speech to the Knesset is available at http://sadat.umd.edu/archives/speeches/AADI%20Sadat%20Speech%20to%20Knesset%2011.20.77.pdf.

I was opposed to such bilateral talks, fearing that they would lead to a separate peace between the two countries that would exclude the issue of the Palestinians and not help produce a comprehensive Middle East peace. Though Sadat initially insisted that Israel must withdraw from all the lands it had occupied in June 1967 – as the United Nations Security Council had demanded in Resolution 242 of November that year – and allow the Palestinians to exercise their right to self-determination, in the end Sadat gave way on this issue and allowed the linkage between Israel withdrawing from Sinai and a solution for the Palestinian issue to fade away.

A highly intelligent man who had the makings of a brilliant orator, Sadat was obsessed with the idea that securing a peace with Israel was the only way to prevent another war in the region. He thought that the Arab states would never be able to defeat Israel so long as Tel Aviv continued to enjoy the backing of the United States. He believed that the initiative he had taken – of opening the door to negotiations with Israel – had given the Egyptians new pride and self-confidence. Sadat's main concern was with Egypt itself rather than the Arab world as a whole. Widely read, despite a reputation for never having time to read, Sadat admired Western culture and tradition and did not share Nasser's deep anti-colonial and anti-Western sentiments. He was ready to ally himself and his country with the United States and others who regarded communism as their enemy. Whereas Nasser had come to power at a time of confrontation with the former colonial powers, Sadat ruled Egypt at a time when reconciliation with these powers seemed possible. Nasser's heir therefore had no problems with forging closer ties with Washington.

Sadat's dramatic and historic visit to Jerusalem in 1977 and his engagement with Israel aroused much opposition in the Arab world, within the Organisation of African Unity (OAU) and among members of the Non-Aligned Movement (NAM). I had to try to mend fences and minimise the fallout from this initiative, while Sadat considered the opposition to what he was doing irrelevant to his purpose. He seemed not to be unduly concerned about Egypt being diplomatically isolated in the Third World. His opponents said that he had betrayed the Arab cause by giving the return of Sinai to Egypt priority over the issue of the Palestinians. However, for Sadat, Egypt came first and he began to scorn the rest of the Arab world and the African states that opposed him. He reasoned that they had achieved nothing in their confrontation with Israel. He was, in contrast, securing tangible benefits from engaging with Tel Aviv. For Sadat, the recovery of land was more important than any diplomatic difficulties that might result from his initiative. He argued that, while he expected Egypt's political isolation to end eventually, the land regained 'was ours forever'.

While Sadat's strategy was to regain Sinai first, others feared that this first step would be the last, and that Israel would make no more concessions and remain dominant in the Middle East. Sadat's critics demanded that the Israeli withdrawal from Sinai be linked to withdrawal from the West Bank and the Gaza Strip, and perhaps the Golan Heights as well, as part of the comprehensive, just and durable peace for which the United Nations Security Council had called in Resolution 338 of October 1973. What right had Sadat to negotiate on the Palestinian issue, anyway, his critics asked, without the involvement of the PLO, which was the chief organisation representing the people directly affected?

I had to engage in a flurry of diplomatic activity to try to respond to the criticisms of Sadat's initiative in Arab and African countries. The OAU summit in the Sudanese capital of Khartoum in July 1978 was a crucial test. Sadat seemed almost uninterested in the outcome, and once he had spoken at the meeting he decided to leave. I was annoyed at his cavalier attitude. Though a number of African countries continued to support Egypt, the more radical, rejectionist and Marxist countries – especially Algeria, Libya and Angola – united against Cairo and pushed to isolate Egypt from the Arab world. I flew to the then Yugoslav capital of Belgrade the same month to prevent Egypt from being ostracised at the ministerial conference for non-aligned nations. Later, at the meeting of the Non-Aligned Movement in Havana, Cuba, in 1979, I called Sadat an authentic revolutionary who had 'faced the enemy in his own house'. I noted that he had gone to Jerusalem to liberate Palestine from Israeli imperialism and to liberate the Arab lands from military occupation. My remarks did not, however, persuade those who, like Angolan foreign minister Paulo Jorge, remained adamant that, by going to Israel and recognising it as a state, Sadat had betrayed the PLO in particular and the Third World in general.

It was the United States, with its strategic interests in the Middle East, that took the lead in helping to push Israel and Egypt towards an agreement. President Jimmy Carter (who would himself be awarded the Nobel Peace Prize belatedly in 2002), who had adopted a slightly more critical stance towards Israel after coming to office in January 1977, called Sadat and Begin to meet at Camp David, the US presidential retreat outside Washington DC, in 1978 in order to produce an agreement for a peace treaty between Tel Aviv and Cairo. With Carter as mediator, applying pressure on both men, the two governments concluded a framework agreement on 17 September 1978. Carter had said that if they were unable to reach an agreement his career would be at an end, while Sadat linked failure at Camp David to the failure of his peace initiative as a whole. The Egyptian leader could not afford to have his visit to Jerusalem the previous year now seen as a mistake. The new popularity he had gained among the Egyptian people as a 'Hero of Peace' would be forfeited, and his radical opponents would be vindicated. Sadat knew too that Egypt did not pose a credible military threat to Israel. The Americans told him that whatever he agreed to at Camp David would eventually lead to further Israeli concessions, and he may have believed them.

A two-part agreement was reached at Camp David. The first provided for a staged withdrawal by Israel from the Sinai, the second for 'autonomy' – the meaning of which was never made clear, though in later negotiations the Israelis insisted that it implied no reduction in their presence in Gaza and the West Bank. Six weeks after the signing of the framework agreement at Camp David, the award of the Nobel Peace Prize was announced. The Nobel Peace Committee said that in awarding the prize to Sadat and Begin, it wished 'not only to honour actions already performed in the service of peace, but also to encourage further efforts to work out practical solutions which can give reality to those hopes of lasting peace'.[6]

The Nobel Peace Prize and Its Aftermath

Menachem Begin travelled to Oslo to accept the Nobel Peace Prize in December 1978, but Anwar Sadat did not, after the Egyptians had called off a further negotiating session with the Israelis. Sadat probably felt that he should have been the sole recipient of the prize. (Nelson Mandela was said to have had a similar reaction to being jointly awarded the Peace Prize alongside Frederik Willem de Klerk; see Boehmer, Chapter 8, and Houston, Chapter 9, in this volume.) An Egyptian representative, Sayed Marei, accepted the prize on Sadat's behalf on 10 December 1978, reading a speech in which Sadat noted that he accepted the prize in the name of his people:

> The decision of the Nobel Prize Committee to bestow upon me the Peace Award has been received by the people of Egypt not only as an honour, but also as a confirmation of the universal recognition of our relentless efforts to achieve peace in an area in which God has chosen to bring to mankind, through Moses, Jesus and Mohamed, His message of wisdom and light.

He referred to the first recorded peace treaty, 3,000 years earlier, between the Egyptians and the Hittites, before noting:

> The peace process comprises a beginning and steps towards an end. In reaching this end the process must achieve its projected goal. That goal is to bring security to the peoples of the area, and the Palestinians in particular, restoring to them all their right to a life of liberty and dignity. We are moving steadily towards this goal for all the peoples of the region. This is what I stand for. This is the letter and the spirit of Camp David.... [P]eace is a dynamic construction to which all should contribute, each adding a new brick. It goes far beyond a formal agreement or treaty, it transcends a word here or there. That is why it requires politicians who enjoy vision and imagination and who, beyond the present,

---

6. This speech was delivered by Aase Lionaes, chairman of the Nobel Peace Committee, in Oslo on 10 December 1978; see www.nobelprize.org/nobel_prizes/peace/laureates/1978/press.html.

look towards the future. It is with this conviction, deeply rooted in our history and our faith, that the people of Egypt have embarked upon a major effort to achieve peace in the Middle East, an area of paramount importance to the whole world. We will spare no effort, we will not tire or despair, we will not lose faith, and we are confident that, in the end, our aim will be achieved.[7]

Sadat chose to give the money he received from the Peace Prize to develop the village close to the Nile – Mit Abdul-Kum – in which he had grown up. The award of the Nobel Peace Prize encouraged Sadat and Begin to continue with, and complete, the peace process they had embarked upon. The treaty between Egypt and Israel was finally signed on 26 March 1979. It provided for the normalisation of relations between the two countries and for trade and cultural exchanges, for Israel's step-by-step withdrawal from the Sinai peninsula by 1982, and for further negotiations on Palestinian 'autonomy' – a concept that the West Bank Palestinians were quick to reject as meaningless. But the insertion of an international force between Egypt and Israel meant that Cairo would, in future, pose no threat to Tel Aviv. The United Nations was to provide forces and observers to supervise the implementation of the return of Sinai to Egyptian sovereignty. But the Soviet Union vetoed a UN Security Council resolution setting up such a force, and Tel Aviv demanded guarantees that Egyptian oil would continue to flow from wells in the Sinai to Israel. Much diplomatic activity had to be undertaken to try to make the Camp David Accords work. Cairo won support in Latin America for sending troops from countries in that region as part of a peacekeeping force to be deployed in the Sinai. By September 1981, Israel was satisfied with a multinational force to be made up of troops from the United States, Fiji, Colombia and Uruguay. But negotiations over the force continued after Sadat's assassination in 1981, since Washington also wanted European participation in the mission. It was not until March 1982 that the Multilateral Force and

7. 'The Nobel Peace Prize 1978: Anwar al-Sadat Nobel Lecture', 10 December, www.nobelprize.org/nobel_prizes/peace/laureates/1978/al-sadat-lecture.html.

Observers (MFO) was deployed. It was never replaced by a United Nations force.

The signing of the peace treaty in 1979 infuriated Sadat's opponents, who feared that it would mean, in effect, an alliance between Israel and Egypt, with the backing of the United States, to dominate the Middle East. At the OAU summit in the Liberian capital of Monrovia in July 1979, Sadat was outraged when the Nigerian head of state General Olusegun Obasanjo characterised the 1973 war not as a real war but as 'a concoction and a conspiracy'. In a highly emotional speech to the OAU Assembly of Heads of State, the Egyptian leader replied that he had lost his younger brother in that war. While the summit's focus then turned elsewhere, and Cairo escaped further censure, pressure built up, diplomatic ties with Egypt were severed, and the Arab League's headquarters was transferred from Cairo to Tunis in 1979. For his part, Sadat continued to despise those who opposed his peace treaty with Israel and he felt that their opposition to it would soon collapse. He had shut down the consulates of the Soviet Union and Eastern European countries in Egypt, and strengthened his anti-communist stance following the Soviet invasion of Afghanistan in 1979. Sadat did not object when Begin called the PLO a 'tool of international communism', for he was more concerned with communism than with his status in the Arab and African worlds. He refused to meet with Angolan president Agostinho Neto at the Monrovia OAU summit in 1979, for example, because he regarded Neto as a communist, and he opposed efforts by his own foreign ministry to have the Egyptian ambassador sent back to his post in Moscow.

Sadat's schizophrenic behaviour on occasion placed me in a vulnerable, if not dangerous and awkward, position. He agreed that it was important for Egypt to build solid relations with Ethiopia, from which 85 per cent of the Nile waters originate, and to get Addis Ababa to guarantee their continued flow. In 1981, Sadat asked me to visit Ethiopia to take a message to its leader, Mengistu Haile Mariam, to try to secure his support at a forthcoming OAU summit in Nairobi. As we flew over the Aswan High Dam, I thought about how this project could help draw Egypt and Sudan together to conquer the desert. But when our plane was flying over Addis Ababa, it was refused permission to land. After almost running out of fuel, the plane was allowed to land, but our delegation was then refused a meeting with Mengistu. The reason later became clear: a few hours before our delegation was due to arrive in Addis Ababa, Sadat had issued a statement to the press criticising Mengistu as corrupt, and threatening him with military intervention if he dared touch the waters of the Nile. A furious Mengistu had given instructions that the plane should not be allowed to land. As Sadat never mentioned the incident to me, I never found out whether he had forgotten that he had sent me to see Mengistu.

After the award of the Nobel Peace Prize and the conclusion of the peace treaty in 1979, Sadat grew closer to Begin, with whom he had another summit in January 1980. I observed then that the peace treaty with Israel would remain a hollow shell unless the Palestinian problem was resolved. Sadat continued to make concessions to Israel, and did not denounce the Israelis whenever Palestinian homes were destroyed and their lands confiscated. At my suggestion, Sadat met with the Israeli Labour Party in November 1980, a day after Ronald Reagan's election as president of the United States. On that occasion, Sadat insisted that the Palestinians would join in the peace process in the course of 1981. Then, in July 1981, Israeli fighter jets struck at Palestinian targets in Lebanon and killed more than 300 people in Beirut. Some critics argued that Israel's aggression had been made possible by Egypt's separate peace with Tel Aviv. Sadat, however, argued that, despite such events, he would continue to try to make the peace process with Israel work. In August 1981, Begin and Reagan signed an agreement that inaugurated the Multinational Force and Observers for Sinai, and a month later a new United States–Israeli strategic cooperation agreement was reached that included joint military manoeuvres. It was now clear that Israel would make no more concessions. There would not even be another separate peace with Syria on the Golan Heights. While Egypt's 'normalisation' with Israel proceeded apace, no progress was achieved in the talks on 'autonomy' for the Palestinians.

From the moment that Sadat announced that he was to travel to Israel, many anticipated that he might be assassinated. He was called a traitor, someone who had betrayed his country and sold out to 'imperialism' and 'Zionism'. He was said to have stabbed the Palestinian people in the back, and was derided as a dictator. The latter charge was unjust, though he certainly enjoyed demonstrating his power, and saw himself as the boss. Sadat had no patience for details and left decisions about them to his lieutenants, which gave him the autonomy to overturn or bypass them at the last minute. He took harsh measures against Egypt's Muslim extremists, who were inspired by the 1979 Iranian Revolution. In 1981, over 1,500 opponents of the regime were rounded up and imprisoned, and mosques were seized from militant preachers. Sadat's opponents never forgave him for this. Above all, they could not forgive him for his having made a separate peace with Israel.

On 6 October 1981, before the return of Sinai to Egypt was complete, Sadat was assassinated by radical Egyptian soldiers as he stood on a podium inspecting his troops. This, ironically, occurred during a military parade held to commemorate and celebrate the day on which Egyptian forces had broken through Israel's Bar-Lev line on the Sinai front in 1973. Some saw what they called Sadat's 'execution' by Islamic fundamentalists as a just reward for 'dictatorship, Camp David, poverty and the continued absence of progress'.[8] Others regarded Sadat as a martyr for peace.

Concluding Reflections

Though the 1978 Nobel Peace Prize was awarded jointly to Sadat and Begin, it was Sadat who was the visionary who had begun the process that led to the Camp David Accords by coming up with the idea that he should travel to Jerusalem – the heart of the country that, until that point, had been seen as the enemy. His initiative, which so dramatically reversed previous policy, was a courageous one, both personally

8. Ghali Shoukri, *Portrait of a President, 1971–1981* (London: Zed Books, 1981), p. iv.

and politically, though it led eventually to his martyrdom. The peace treaty that Sadat signed with Israel in 1979 held, relations with Egypt were normalised, and, the year after his assassination, the Israeli withdrawal from Sinai was completed. Israel has not subsequently sought to reclaim the Sinai from Egypt, despite its unhappiness with events in recent years on the Egypt–Gaza border. Sadat's concern to regain Sinai has therefore been vindicated, even though in working to achieve this goal he let all else become secondary.

Sadat's peace initiative meant that he moved Egypt decisively into the American camp. He cancelled the treaties that Egypt had with Moscow, and expelled the Soviet ambassador from Cairo. While he was doing all this, his dependence on American aid increased, especially as the other Arab countries now refused to provide him with any funding. Sadat seems to have felt that Egypt could become a new American-backed regional hegemon, reducing Israel's importance in Washington's eyes. In the event, while the United States was never to supply Cairo with weaponry that would pose any threat to Israel, and while Tel Aviv remained fundamentally important to American policy in the Middle East, Egypt was to become the second largest recipient of American aid after Israel (about $1.5 billion a year by 2013). This realignment did bring Egypt peace and the end of Israeli occupation, at the cost of accepting a new form of Western influence in Egyptian affairs. Some have subsequently claimed that this made Egypt virtually a client state of the United States.

Sadat's apparent indifference to the Palestinian issue reflected his conviction that the Israel–Egypt treaty should come first, and that the Palestinian issue could not be dealt with simultaneously. It is impossible to know for certain, of course, what would have happened in the Middle East had Sadat not been assassinated. Nevertheless, Israel benefited from signing a separate peace with Egypt that split the Arab world and cost Cairo much support in Africa, without achieving anything for the Palestinians. The peace that Sadat signed with Israel did not lead to a comprehensive Middle East peace. Perhaps there was never any possibility that it could, given Israel's intransigence on the Palestinian issue and its insistence on Jerusalem remaining united under Israeli sovereignty. Sadat was a realist as well as a visionary, and in the end he accepted the limits of what he could achieve. Another Nobel peace laureate, Nelson Mandela, after becoming president of South Africa, was again to call for a comprehensive Middle East peace and to denounce the unilateral actions of the United States in the region (see Boehmer, Chapter 8 in this volume.) Despite Mandela's call, and despite the award of the Nobel Peace Prize to Sadat two decades earlier, the goal of a comprehensive peace in the Middle East remains as elusive as ever.

Bibliography

Boutros-Ghali, Boutros, *Egypt's Road to Jerusalem: A Diplomat's Story of the Struggle for Peace in the Middle East* (New York: Random House, 1997).

Lionaes, Aase, chairman of the Nobel Peace Committee, speech, Oslo, 10 December 1978 (www. nobelprize.org/nobel_prizes/peace/laureates/1978/press.html).

Pipes, Daniel, 'Interview with Boutros Boutros-Ghali', *Middle East Quarterly* 4(3) (September 1997).

el-Sadat, Anwar, speech to the Knesset, Jerusalem, 20 November 1977, http://sadat.umd.edu/ archives/speeches/AADI%20Sadat%20Speech%20to%20Knesset%2011.20.77.pdf.

el-Sadat, Anwar, *In Search of Identity: An Autobiography* (London: Collins, 1978).

el-Sadat, Anwar, 'The Nobel Peace Prize 1978: Anwar al-Sadat Nobel Lecture', 10 December, www. nobelprize.org/nobel_prizes/peace/laureates/1978/al-sadat-lecture.html.

Shoukri, Ghali, *Portrait of a President, 1971–1981* (London: Zed Books, 1981).

ELEVEN

MOHAMED ELBARADEI: THE ROCKET MAN

MORAD ABOU-SABÉ

The 2005 award of the Nobel Peace Prize to Mohamed ElBaradei, the Egyptian director general of the UN's International Atomic Energy Agency (IAEA), was a testament to the importance of nuclear disarmament and nuclear non-proliferation for the Nobel Peace Committee in Oslo. This award followed three previous prizes that acknowledged their recipients' efforts to free the world of nuclear weapons and the potential for nuclear war.

The first of these Peace Prizes was awarded in 1975 to Russian national Andrei Sakharov for his struggle for human rights, disarmament and cooperation between all nations to achieve these goals.[1] The second prize, in 1985, was awarded to International Physicians for the Prevention of Nuclear War in recognition of the group's work on the creation of an 'authoritative information system' and for 'creating an awareness of the catastrophic consequences of atomic warfare'. In the Nobel Peace Committee's statement for the award, it noted that the group's work had contributed to an increase in the pressure of public opposition to the proliferation of atomic weapons, as well as to a redefining of the budgetary priorities of countries, with greater attention afforded to health and

---

1. 'The Nobel Peace Prize 1975', www.nobelprize.org/nobel_prizes/peace/laureates/1975.

other humanitarian issues.[2] The third prize, in 1995, was awarded to the Joseph Rotblat Pugwash Conferences on Sciences and World Affairs for their efforts to reduce the importance of nuclear arms in international politics. It was hoped that in the longer term this work would result in the eventual elimination of nuclear weapons.[3]

Mohamed ElBaradei's Nobel Peace Prize, in 2005, was awarded not only for his relentless efforts in support of nuclear disarmament and nuclear non-proliferation, but also for his campaigning against nuclear holocaust and for world peace. In addition to ElBaradei, the Nobel Peace Prize of 2005 was awarded to the International Atomic Energy Agency, which he headed, for its role in fighting for world peace against all odds and sometimes against the interests of powerful countries, in particular the United States.

The distinction given to both ElBaradei and the IAEA exemplifies the important role that each played, as well as the contributions that both ultimately made to world peace. The timing of the award made an especially emphatic statement on the American invasion of Iraq in 2003, which had not been sanctioned by the UN Security Council and was widely considered to have been illegitimate. Despite ElBaradei's efforts to prevent the Iraq War, the decision of the US administration, under George W. Bush, to invade the country had already been made.[4] Bush's 'pre-emptive strike' against Iraq was made in spite of the IAEA's inability to find weapons of mass destruction in the country, which the invasion also failed to uncover. The drumbeat of war was so deafening that sane voices could no longer be heard.

Why Was ElBaradei Awarded the Nobel Prize?

Mohamed ElBaradei's winning of the Nobel Peace Prize did not come from a particular discovery he had made or from a special declaration that his IAEA had issued. The award came as a result of a lifelong

---

2. 'The Nobel Peace Prize 1985', www.nobelprize.org/nobel_prizes/peace/laureates/1985.
3. 'The Nobel Peace Prize 1995', www.nobelprize.org/nobel_prizes/peace/laureates/1995.
4. Bob Woodward, *Bush at War* (New York: Simon & Schuster, 2002).

system of personal beliefs that not only helped ElBaradei in his professional career, but also led to his rise to the leadership of the IAEA.
ElBaradei was born into a religious, middle-class, Muslim family in
Dokki, Egypt. In this small suburb of Cairo, at the time, middle-class
family traditions were characterised by honesty, humility and persever-
ance. His early experience growing up in this conservative, religious
environment set the basic characteristics that were to guide ElBaradei
throughout his life. He was born to a distinguished lineage of lawyers:
his father served as the head of the Egyptian Bar Association, while
his grandfather had been a member of the Egyptian High Court. Both
men instilled in Mohamed a deep devotion to public service and a
sense of *noblesse oblige*. However, the similarity in personality of these
three men did not stop at their career choices. All three shared a deep
concern for the rights of all citizens, the need to support the vulnerable
in society, and to stand up collectively for the rights of all. As with
his father, Mustafa ElBaradei, who had stood up against Gamal Abdel
Nasser's military regime during the 1950s, Mohamed was throughout
his career a staunch advocate of the rule of law. Following the example
modelled by his father, Mohamed embraced a consistently fair-minded
outlook in his respect for others.

During his tenure at the IAEA, between 1997 and 2009, ElBaradei was widely praised for his objectivity and his determined efforts
through the agency's dedicated monitoring programmes to prevent
nuclear proliferation. In his 2010 book *The Age of Deception: Nuclear
Diplomacy in Treacherous Times*,[5] ElBaradei described the many
examples of the difficult international dealings he had to balance to
ensure that all governments that the IAEA dealt with – both large and
small – were treated equally.

ElBaradei's career in international affairs started at the time of
his graduation from Cairo University's law school in 1964. He later
obtained a doctorate in law from New York University. His first appointment was at the Egyptian Ministry of Foreign Affairs, where he

---

5. Mohamed ElBaradei, *The Age of Deception: Nuclear Diplomacy in Treacherous Times* (New
York: Holt, 2010).

served in the country's mission to the United Nations, both in New York and in Geneva. From the age of 22, ElBaradei was thus destined to have a long and exceptional career in international relations. At the Egyptian mission to the UN he was quickly recognised for his thorough and diplomatic approaches to problem-solving, as well as his attention to detail and meticulousness.

While serving at the Egyptian mission to the UN, ElBaradei was in charge of legal and political matters. He was also responsible for arms control issues, and was subsequently appointed as a special assistant to Egypt's foreign minister, Ismail Fahmy (1974–78). In 1980, ElBaradei became a senior fellow at the UN Institute for Training and Research (UNITAR), administering its international law programmes. Subsequently in 1984, he became a senior staff member at the IAEA, a position that brought him close to the leadership of the organisation. In 1997 the Egyptian diplomat was appointed to his first term as director general of the IAEA, a position he held until his retirement in 2009.

ElBaradei's Contributions before the Nobel Prize

During his leadership of the IAEA, ElBaradei was credited with introducing new and tightly controlled monitoring protocols.[6] Under his leadership as director general, the IAEA played important roles at a time in the agency's history that was marked by serious international crises and conflicts. Through ElBaradei's efforts and skilful negotiations, and more importantly his sincere desire to rid the world of all nuclear weapons, he was able to maintain both his objectivity and transparency.

ElBaradei's work at the IAEA was not without criticism and opposition. As a Muslim director general from an Afro-Arab country – Egypt – his decisions regarding Iraq's weapons of mass destruction and Iran's nuclear weapons programme were often criticised by the United States as an effort at 'concealing evidence' that would have incriminated Baghdad and Tehran. John Bolton, the combative US permanent

---

6. Paul Kerr, 'IAEA Board Seeks Strengthened Safeguards', *Arms Control Today* 35(6) (July–August 2005) (www.armscontrol.org/print/1847).

representative to the United Nations between 2005 and 2006, scathingly criticised ElBaradei in his 2007 book about the IAEA's role regarding Iran's alleged nuclear weapons programme.[7] Bolton accused ElBaradei of hampering his efforts to bring the Iran case to the UN Security Council.[8] After one of ElBaradei's visits to Tehran, the Egyptian was told that he needed to be more circumspect about his knowledge of Iran's nuclear activities. However, the independent-minded ElBaradei often ignored Bolton's warnings, leading the American diplomat to complain: 'He [ElBaradei] was a career international bureaucrat from Egypt, first elected to head the IAEA in 1997, who made excuses for Iran the entire time I was in the Bush administration.'[9] Such remarks exemplify the difficult working relationship ElBaradei had with the Bush administration, which reached its nadir during the run-up to the US invasion of Iraq in 2003. Such condescending statements by Bolton were not out of character for this neoconservative who was well known for his outspoken and harsh commentaries and anti-UN positions.[10] For ElBaradei, the United Nations was an organisation that represented the whole world and whose goal was to protect the rights of all states, irrespective of how powerful or weak they were. ElBaradei was consistent in his approach in attempting to prevent the 'pre-emptive strike' on Iraq by the United States and Britain in 2003. He also continually sought to use diplomatic means to bring Iran into compliance with the demands of the IAEA and the UN Security Council to allow open inspections of its nuclear facilities.

These approaches enabled the IAEA, under ElBaradei's leadership, to control nuclear proliferation successfully, to tighten the regulations that controlled the distribution of nuclear materials, and to ensure their use for peaceful purposes. These were the systems that helped the Egyptian director general to build the IAEA and its staff into the agency that shared the Nobel Peace Prize with him. As with the

7. John Bolton, *Surrender Is Not an Option: Defending America at the United Nations and Abroad* (New York: Threshold, 2007), p. 137.
8. Ibid.
9. Ibid.
10. Adam Zagorin, 'John Bolton: The Angriest Neocon', *Time*, November 2007.

IAEA's work, ElBaradei's positions on international issues often put him at odds with the UN's great powers. His independence and loyalty to the goals of the agency made his tenure particularly difficult. The IAEA had been conducting its functions by seeking to balance the need to ensure transparency with the indispensability of maintaining the integrity of its decisions. This was especially difficult when the IAEA's role required bringing major powers into compliance with its charter and into line with its objectives.

ElBaradei's directorship coincided with a period when many serious international conflicts were taking place. During his first term and just before he was to be reappointed for his second term of office, the terrorist attacks of 11 September 2001 took place in New York and Washington DC, presenting a challenge that the agency clearly had not anticipated. The attacks also introduced a new dimension to the IAEA's tasks. The possibility of nuclear materials falling into the hands of terrorists and extremist groups became a clear and present danger. As if that were not enough, the run-up to the invasion of Iraq that followed these events quickly took centre stage, and the IAEA became a central player in this political drama.

The threat of Iraq's nuclear capabilities was the debate that preceded the US invasion in 2003. The Bush administration maintained that Iraq possessed or was developing weapons of mass destruction, or both, which could pose a threat not only to America's national security, but also to the security of the world at large. The hysteria that ensued from this debate showed how intent Washington was on invading Iraq. There were popular demonstrations and anti-war protests across the USA and around the world. In February 2003, the anti-war protests were estimated to have involved up to 10 million people in as many as sixty countries around the globe.

In the meantime, ElBaradei and the IAEA were hard at work painstakingly inspecting Iraq's weapons programmes. The IAEA disagreed strongly with the stance of the Bush administration. Conflicting testimonies before the UN Security Council between US representatives – including, most notoriously, US secretary of state Colin Powell – and

IAEA representatives, only deepened the acrimony. ElBaradei repeatedly questioned the American stance and persistently requested a three-month period to give a final determination on the issue of the weapons of mass destruction.[11] Powell later described his UN speech as a lasting 'blot' on his political record.[12]

In stark contrast, ElBaradei testified at the UN Security Council that documents which purported to demonstrate that Iraqi leader Saddam Hussein had sought to buy uranium from Niger were false.[13] In his testimony to the Security Council in March 2003, ElBaradei refuted Powell's assertions that Iraq had acquired weapons of mass destruction. He later described the American invasion of Iraq as a 'glaring example of how, in many cases, the use of force exacerbates the problem rather than [solves] it'. ElBaradei further stated that 'we learned, from Iraq, that an inspection takes time, that we should be patient, that an inspection can, in fact, work'. He concluded that he had 'been validated' in arguing consistently that Saddam Hussein had not revived his nuclear programme.[14] Nuclear, biological and chemical weapons searches had been thoroughly conducted in every conceivable corner of Iraq by the IAEA and the UN Monitoring, Verification, and Inspection Commission (UNMOVIC), to no avail. There were no weapons of mass destruction to be found anywhere in Iraq.

The Nobel Speech

In his Nobel lecture in December 2005, Mohamed ElBaradei presented a detailed analysis of the problems confronting the world. He argued that, since the end of the Cold War, the global landscape had changed fundamentally, as had the tools for managing conflicts. ElBaradei narrated a simple story that defined his passion for human rights, equality among nations, and the responsibilities that the powerful nations

11. ElBaradei, *The Age of Deception*, p. 48.
12. Steven R. Weisman, 'Powell Calls His U.N. Speech a Lasting Blot on His Record', *New York Times*, 9 September 2005.
13. See ElBaradei, *The Age of Deception*.
14. Colum Lynch and Dafna Linzer, 'U.N. Nuclear Agency Chief Urges Iran to Suspend Activities', *Washington Post*, 2 November 2004, p. A14.

should have towards the weaker ones. He defined his understanding of the world's inequalities among peoples and nations in terms of 'the haves and have-nots', and emphasised the responsibilities of all to the 'human family':

> My sister-in-law works for a group that supports orphanages in Cairo. She and her colleagues take care of children left behind by circumstances beyond their control. They feed these children, clothe them and teach them to read.... At the International Atomic Energy Agency, my colleagues and I work to keep nuclear materials out of the reach of extremist groups. We inspect nuclear facilities all over the world, to be sure that peaceful nuclear activities are not being used as a cloak for weapons programmes.... My sister-in-law and I are working towards the same goal, through different paths: the security of the human family.[15]

Throughout the lecture, ElBaradei expressed strong convictions about the need to rid the world of nuclear weapons. He talked about the 'myth of nuclear deterrence' in a world in which the norms of conflict resolution had changed. Reflecting on the ever-expanding inequity in the distribution of global resources and the inequity in the utilisation of these resources, ElBaradei argued that 'in today's world, especially since the end of the Cold War, conflicts have become without borders, whether it is evidenced by the prevailing terrorism, poverty and hunger, armed conflicts, organized crime or the continuing race for nuclear power by countries currently without it'. He noted that these 'new' realities had changed the global landscape to such an extent that conflict could no longer be dealt with by creating new divisions; rather, they must now be confronted through diplomacy and dialogue.

After the Nobel Prize

In January 2011 the Egyptian people, led by their youth, organised and executed a popular revolution that toppled the three-decade dictatorship of Hosni Mubarak (1981–2011). A new chapter in Mohamed ElBaradei's career started after his return to Egypt in 2010. It is important

---

15. Mohamed ElBaradei Nobel Lecture, 10 December 2005, www.nobelprize.org/nobel_prizes/peace/laureates/2005/elbaradei-lecture-en.html.

to understand how much Egypt had changed during his absence. The country has grown enormously in population, reaching 83 million people, a sixfold increase from Egypt's population of 14 million in the 1960s, when ElBaradei left Cairo for the UN.

Egypt's economy had disintegrated, with unemployment reaching 22 per cent by some estimates. The country's ever-expanding gap between rich and poor, its antiquated education system, an illiteracy rate of over 40 per cent, and its much reduced diplomatic stature had all but sidelined Egypt – once the political and cultural centre of the Arab world – not only internationally but also regionally. This decline accelerated rapidly under the three decades of the Mubarak dictatorship. The economic disparity between the rich and the poor grew to such an extent that by 2008 some 43 per cent of Egyptians were living on less than two dollars a day.[16]

Before moving to Egypt, ElBaradei had given a lecture at the Kennedy School of Government at Harvard University in 2010. During the speech, he had jokingly talked about what his next move would be following his departure from the IAEA: 'I guess I'll now be looking for a job.'[17] It was no accident that ElBaradei's equally challenging new job took him back to his homeland. He had long yearned to make Egypt a free and democratic society.

ElBaradei's guide for the transformation of Egypt was his inner moral compass and a lifetime spent in Europe and the United States. The impact of his long experience abroad came from living in countries where freedom and the rule of law were taken for granted. In these countries, unlike in Egypt, equal opportunity was the norm, and citizens could hold their governments accountable and peaceably replace them through elections. It was this mindset that ElBaradei took back with him to Egypt, and it was these values and freedoms that he sought to bring to the Egyptian people.

---

16. See Samir Radwan, *Employment and Unemployment in Egypt: Conventional Problems, Unconventional Remedies*, Working Paper no. 70 (Cairo: Egyptian Centre for Economic Studies, August 2002); World Bank, *Global Development Finance*, vol. 1 (Washington DC: World Bank, 2008), p. 143.

17. Mohamed ElBaradei, 'Corliss Lamont Lecture', Kennedy School of Government, Harvard University, 27 April 2010.

Upon his return to his homeland, ElBaradei quickly formed the National Association for Change (NAC) as a political interest group. At its first meeting, held at his home in Cairo, in February 2010, ElBaradei gathered about thirty of the country's political elite, including a number of political scientists. The group was described as a 'broad opposition coalition pushing for pro-democracy constitutional reforms in Egypt'. It was distinctly characterised as a 'coalition' and not a political party, to differentiate it from the failed 'opposition parties' that had made no impact on the Mubarak government for decades.

ElBaradei's return to Egypt created a problem for the Mubarak regime. Recognising his high profile and distinguished career, especially as a Nobel peace laureate, the government realised that it could not mistreat him, at least not overtly. Throughout 2010, ElBaradei subtly criticised the Mubarak regime, while demanding political reform and democracy for the people. His call for 'change' was his primary message, especially in his interaction with the youth of Egypt. Young people, yearning for an opportunity and a leader, saw in ElBaradei an inspirational figure. At the same time, the NAC needed young volunteers who could spread its message and expand the organisation's reach throughout the country.

Focusing on democratic reforms, ElBaradei and the NAC started a petition campaign to suspend the 'emergency law' that had been instituted following the assasination of Egypt's former leader Anwar Sadat in October 1981 (see Boutros-Ghali, Chapter 10 in this volume). ElBaradei initiated a campaign to collect a million signatures to force the government to suspend the draconian law. It was abundantly clear – both inside and outside Egypt – that this law was mainly being used to suppress the people's rights of assembly, free speech and equal opportunity, as well as their right to dignity, all under the hands of Egypt's repressive security forces. The NAC pushed to overturn the law and also insisted on institutionalising the right of every Egyptian to run for the presidency, without the arbitrary restrictions that had been introduced into the Egyptian Constitution in 1971. In making such demands, ElBaradei was directly confronting Mubarak's autocracy. In response, the regime undertook a full-blown smear campaign, ridiculing ElBaradei and labelling him 'an agent of the West' who had lived his entire adult life outside Egypt and was thus out of touch with the concerns of ordinary citizens.

The NAC received much attention during 2010 with its nationwide campaign to collect a million signatures. Its seven-point programme of reforms to ensure free and fair elections gathered momentum among the Egyptian people, especially the youth. The reform programme sought to (1) ensure judicial oversight over the election process; (2) allow local and international civil society groups to monitor elections; (3) permit equal access to the media for all candidates, particularly during presidential elections; (4) give Egyptians living abroad the right to vote at Egyptian embassies and consulates; (5) ensure the right of all citizens to run for the presidency without arbitrary restrictions; (6) limit the president's tenure to two terms; and (7) conduct voting by using the national identification card rather than a special voter registration card. All seven reforms have now been instituted under Egypt's new political system following the elections of June 2012, in which Mohamed Morsi, a moderate Islamist and US-trained engineer, was elected president.

ElBaradei put forth his vision for a post-Mubarak Egypt in a *Financial Times* article in February 2011:

> Every morning for the past week I have awoken with the same thought:
> I have witnessed a miracle; we have toppled a dictator. Then I consider
> the steps that lie ahead, and think, with renewed determination: we have
> sowed the seeds for a new Egypt, but it is not enough; we must nurture
> and grow the plant.... Egypt's awakening has spread hope across the
> Arab world. The courage shown by the Libyan people risking everything
> for their freedom is only the latest incredible example. But to realise
> this vision of Egypt's 'Second Republic' – a democracy rooted in social
> justice, equal opportunity, respect for human rights and other universal
> values – is an enormous, complex undertaking. Egypt under Hosni
> Mubarak had deteriorated to the status of a failed state. We must wipe
> the slate clean and start again.[18]

18. Mohamed ElBaradei, 'My Vision For the Next Phase of Egypt's Revolution', *Financial Times*, 22 February 2011.

Even after ElBaradei announced that he would run for the presidency of Egypt in 2012, his mistrust of the country's Supreme Military Council (SCAF) was a continuing constraint. Unsure of the SCAF's intentions for the country, he was extremely apprehensive that the Council could derail the 'revolution'. The military's delaying tactics, its lack of transparency and its unwillingness to provide a clear road map of where it was taking the country were all evidence for ElBaradei that Egypt's military brass had no interest in leading the 'revolution' to its democratic end. ElBaradei repeatedly offered to forgo his run for the presidency if he were given the opportunity to work in a civilian transitional presidential council. Convinced that he needed to establish the inalienable rights of all Egyptians, and guarantee that these rights could not be violated by any future government, ElBaradei put forth an eleven-point 'Bill of Rights' in June 2011 that would supersede the constitution.[19] This plan became the basis of many constitutional declarations that were proposed by other political parties and culminated in a central document called the Al-Azhar Declaration, which was adopted by all parties that same month.[20]

This was essentially the last significant contribution that ElBaradei made to the Egyptian 'revolution'. Following subsequent attempts to participate in the presidential election of 2012, he withdrew from the race on the grounds that he could not participate in polls while Egypt lacked a constitution that defined the responsibilities of the presidency.[21] ElBaradei's withdrawal from the presidential race essentially ended his high-profile political role. Following a military coup in Egypt that toppled the elected government of Mohamed Morsi in July 2013, ElBaradei was appointed vice president in July 2013, but resigned in protest a month later.

19. Heba Saleh, 'ElBaradei to Launch Bill of Rights for Egypt', *Financial Times*, 19 June 2011.
20. Noha El-Hennawy, 'Al Azhar Declaration, a New Leap into Politics', *Egypt Independent,* 30 June 2011.
21. Heba Afifi, 'ElBaradei's Withdrawal from the Presidential Race Raises Hopes for Revolutionary Change', *Egypt Independent,* 15 January 2012.

Concluding Reflections

Mohamed ElBaradei has always fought for the weak and the poor, internationally as well as domestically in Egypt. Fairness and transparency have been his watchwords. His lifelong preoccupation with the rule of law will remain his enduring legacy. But many influential people have misread ElBaradei's openness and even-handed approach as misguided, ever since his return to Egypt in 2010. Despite his experience, intellect, sound political instincts, and sincere desire to steer his country to genuine democracy, ElBaradei lacked the charisma required to wholly reinvent Egyptian politics. Yet the country and its youth have much to be grateful for, as the 'rocket man' played a major role in catalysing Egypt's democratic transformation.

Bibliography

Afifi, Heba, 'ElBaradei's Withdrawal from the Presidential Race Raises Hopes for Revolutionary Change', *Egypt Independent*, 15 January 2012.

Bolton, John, *Surrender Is Not an Option: Defending America at the United Nations and Abroad* (New York: Threshold, 2007).

El-Hennawy, Noha, 'Al Azhar Declaration, a New Leap into Politics', *Egypt Independent*, 30 June 2011.

ElBaradei, Mohamed, Nobel Lecture, 10 December 2005, www.nobelprize.org/nobel_prizes/peace/laureates/2005/elbaradei-lecture-en.html.

ElBaradei, Mohamed, *The Age of Deception: Nuclear Diplomacy in Treacherous Times* (New York: Holt, 2010).

ElBaradei, Mohamed, 'Corliss Lamont Lecture', Kennedy School of Government, Harvard University, 27 April 2010.

ElBaradei, Mohamed, 'My Vision For the Next Phase of Egypt's Revolution', *Financial Times*, 22 February 2011.

Kerr, Paul, 'IAEA Board Seeks Strengthened Safeguards', *Arms Control Today* 35(6) (July–August 2005) (www.armscontrol.org/print/1847).

Lynch, Colum, and Dafna Linzer, 'U.N. Nuclear Agency Chief Urges Iran to Suspend Activities', *Washington Post*, 2 November 2004.

Nobel Prize, 'The Nobel Peace Prize 1975', www.nobelprize.org/nobel_prizes/peace/laureates/1975.

Nobel Prize, 'The Nobel Peace Prize 1985', www.nobelprize.org/nobel_prizes/peace/laureates/1985.

Nobel Prize, 'The Nobel Peace Prize 1995', www.nobelprize.org/nobel_prizes/peace/laureates/1995.

Perry, Tom, 'ElBaradei Launches a New Political Party in Egypt', Reuters (Cairo), 29 April 2012.

Radwan, Samir, *Employment and Unemployment in Egypt: Conventional Problems, Unconventional Remedies*, Working Paper no. 70 (Cairo: Egyptian Centre for Economic Studies, August 2002).

Saleh, Heba, 'ElBaradei to Launch Bill of Rights for Egypt', *Financial Times*, 19 June 2011.

Weisman, Steven R., 'Powell Calls His U.N. Speech a Lasting Blot on His Record', *New York Times*, 9 September 2005.

Woodward, Bob, *Bush at War* (New York: Simon & Schuster, 2002).

World Bank, *Global Development Finance*, vol. 1 (Washington DC: World Bank, 2008).

Zagorin, Adam, 'John Bolton: The Angriest Neocon', *Time*, November 2007.

PART FIVE

THE KENYAN AND THE GHANAIAN

TWELVE

WANGARI MAATHAI:
THE EARTH MOTHER

JANICE GOLDING

'Earth Mother' Wangari Muta Maathai (1940–2011), environmental activist and diplomat, women's rights supporter, and pro-democracy advocate from Kenya, was the first woman from Africa to be honoured with the Nobel Peace Prize. She received the prize for 'her contribution to sustainable development that embraces democracy, human rights and women's rights'.[1] Maathai was also the first individual to receive the Nobel Peace Prize, awarded in 2004, for a life's work of steadfast protection of the natural environment. Of the ninety-seven individuals awarded the Nobel Peace Prize before Maathai in 2004, only twelve were women.[2] The presentation speech by Ole Danbolt Mjøs, chair of the Nobel Peace Committee, described Maathai's efforts in a particularly poignant manner:

> Peace on earth depends on our ability to secure our living environment. Maathai stands at the front of the fight to promote ecologically viable social, economic and cultural development in Kenya and in Africa. She has taken a holistic approach to sustainable development that embraces democracy, human rights and women's rights in particular. She thinks globally and acts locally.[3]

1. 'The Nobel Peace Prize 2004: Award Ceremony Speech', www.nobelprize.org/nobel_prizes/peace/laureates/2004/presentation-speech.html.
2. See Judith Hicks Stiehm, *Champions for Peace: Women Winners of the Nobel Peace Prize* (Lanham MD: Rowman & Littlefield, 2006).
3. 'The Nobel Peace Prize 2004: Award Ceremony Speech'.

Africa's Earth Mother was laid to rest in Nairobi on 26 September 2011 at the age of 71, having succumbed to ovarian cancer. The landscape of her life was expansive and productive. With great energy and vision for more than forty years she demonstrated many times over that fighting environmental injustices captures the essence of democracy.[4] In drawing inspiration from nature and dedicating her life to helping the poorest of the poor, she is widely considered to have been the world's first icon of sustainable development. As one of Africa's most charismatic and loved female leaders, Maathai taught and inspired hundreds of thousands of people to improve their quality of life by protecting the natural environment. She is remembered as a humble and compassionate traditionalist with the determination and strength of character of a lion.

The Evolution of an Environmental Activist

Wangari Maathai started her career as an academic. She was appointed associate professor and served as chair of the Department of Veterinary Anatomy at the University of Nairobi in 1977. She was the first woman in East Africa to occupy these academic positions. Prior to these achievements, at the age of 31, she was also the first woman from East Africa to obtain a doctorate. Maathai was active in Kenya's National Council of Women between 1976 and 1987, and served as its chair between 1981 and 1987 – a busy period that shaped the course of her life's work. In 1976, she founded a community-based tree-planting organisation, the Green Belt Movement. This organisation, which worked with women's groups in Kenya, became the mother body for her environmental peace-building efforts.[5]

Maathai actively lobbied to protect the environment, human rights and democracy, and stridently fought government corruption. She made strategic use of platforms for building transnational relationships.

4. Wangari Maathai, *Unbowed: A Memoir* (New York: Knopf, 2006). See also Judith Hicks Stiehm, 'Wangari Muta Maathai: Kenya's "Green Doctor"', in Stiehm, *Champions for Peace*, pp. 201–17.
5. Wangari Maathai, *The Green Belt Movement: Sharing the Approach and the Experience* (New York: Lantern, 2004).

She addressed the United Nations on several occasions and served on commissions associated with civil society groups and non-governmental organisations (NGOs). Maathai and her Green Belt Movement were honoured with numerous prestigious awards that brought international attention to their efforts.[6] As far back as 1987, the Green Belt Movement was recognised by the United Nations Environment Programme (UNEP)[7] through its 'Global 500 Roll of Honour'.[8] Maathai was thus a pioneer of the global environmental movement at a time when there was not that much awareness about these issues.

Environmental conflict – from political confrontation to violent struggle – is produced through resistance to certain forms of governance and acts of power. Maathai's persistent agitations for environmental justice and social equality were driven by illegal developments on public land or in ecologically fragile territories on which people depended for their well-being and incomes. She also fought against 'big men' elites and those in high office in post-colonial Kenya who forcibly displaced poor communities from public land.

Between 1978 and 2002, during the tumultuous years of Daniel arap Moi's dictatorship in Kenya, the Green Belt Movement led campaigns that aimed to narrow power divides. These ranged from excursions to tree nurseries and tree-planting ceremonies, to mass rallies. These campaigns sometimes ended up with the protestors being beaten and even killed by the police. Moi labelled Maathai 'a mad woman' and declared her a serious threat to the stability of Kenya. Throughout those years, Maathai endured ethnic prejudice (she was Kikuyu, the most populous ethnic group in Kenya), repressive patriarchy, jail sentences, police brutality and living in hiding.[9]

By mobilising activism against Kenya's history of domination and dispossession of its natural resources,[10] Maathai provided a bold and

---

6. See the Green Belt Movement website, http://greenbeltmovement.org/w.php?id=47.
7. See, for example, Aseghedech Ghirmazion, 'The UN Environment Programme', in Adekeye Adebajo (ed.), *From Global Apartheid to Global Village: Africa and the United Nations* (Scottsville: University of KwaZulu-Natal Press, 2009), pp. 515–39.
8. UNEP Global 500 Award, www.global500.org.
9. It must have come at a great surprise to Maathai when, in 1990, Daniel arap Moi was listed on UNEP's 'Global 500 Roll of Honour' for 'planting trees and erecting gabions'.
10. See, for example, William Beinart, 'African History and Environmental History', *African*

independent voice for peace and justice. She took up the challenge of changing this history. She worked to include the excluded in social and political life, and inspired people to take up the reins of self-sufficiency in order to reap the rewards of hard work and commitment.

There was a stellar rise in global awareness of environmental concerns in the decade preceding 2004. International NGOs such as the World Conservation Monitoring Centre (WCMC), the International Union for the Conservation of Nature (IUCN), the World Resources Institute (WRI) and the World Wildlife Fund (WWF), among many others, released reports that created waves of alarm. Termed the 'sixth wave of extinction', the accelerating rate at which species and natural ecosystems were being lost due to human activities was unprecedented in the history of the planet.[11] Enabled by the boom in Internet, satellite television and other forms of communication, environmental crises from remote locations in the developing world riveted public attention: large tracts of forest ecosystems were still intact but steadily dwindling; bushmeat hunting and trade had reached critical levels; illegal logging of forests by multinational companies was being sanctioned by governments; 'land-grabbing' from local communities by governments colluding with businesses was rampant; and erosion of cultural heritage and indigenous environmental knowledge systems continued apace.[12] That conflicts arising from poverty, mismanagement and corruption greatly impacted the environment had become evident.

Maathai introduced a new understanding of the drivers of environmental conflict. Her work became widely appreciated for enriching a global understanding about how disaffection and humiliations associated with environmental inequalities triggered confrontational misunderstandings, social rage and mass violence. This provided

---

Affairs 99 (2000), pp. 269–302.

11. John Anderson, *Towards Gondwana Alive: Promoting Biodiversity and Stemming the Sixth Extinction* (Tshwane: National Botanical Institute, 2001).

12. See, for example, Brian Groombridge, *Global Biodiversity: Status of the Earth's Living Resources* (London: Chapman & Hall, 1992); Jeffrey McNeely, *Coping with Change: People, Forests, and Biodiversity* (Geneva: International Union for Conservation of Nature, 1994); World Resources Institute, *World Resources 2000–2001: People and Ecosystems – The Fraying Web of Life* (Washington DC: WRI, 2000).

diagnoses for civil paths to democracy and governance accountability.[13] The awarding of the Nobel Peace Prize to Maathai credited her for constructing a conciliatory approach to environmentalism by using peace activism and civic education to resolve environmental problems and, more importantly, for placing environmental issues at the top of the global development agenda. The prize thus marked a major, global transition in the understanding that environmental protection can be a path to peace-building. Resolving environmental conflicts such as those relating to community rights of ownership and accessibility to land, water and biodiversity resources was finally being widely recognised as a fundamental prerequisite for democracy and peace. However, the award had been long overdue. Twenty years before being awarded the Nobel Peace Prize, Maathai was honoured with the Right Livelihood Award in 1984 'for converting the Kenyan ecological debate into mass action for reforestation'.[14] This award, founded by Swedish parliamentarian and writer Jacob von Uexküll and often referred to as the 'alternative Nobel Peace Prize', was visionary in its recognition of the relationship between peace, environmental protection and human rights.

Sowing the Seeds: Genesis of the Journey

Wangari Maathai's inspiration was deeply embedded in her memories of pre-independence Kenya and the landscape surrounding her child-hood home near the town of Nyeri. She has often said that the person she most admired was her mother, who encouraged her to attend missionary school during an era when it was frowned upon for Kenyan girls to do so.

Maathai was a beneficiary of American benevolence. As one of around 300 Africans selected in 1959 for scholarships from the prestigious Joseph P. Kennedy Junior Foundation, she rode this wave of academic opportunity that initiated the 'Kennedy Airlift' (or 'Airlift

---

13. See, for example, Commonwealth Commission on Respect and Understanding, *Civil Paths to Peace* (London: Commonwealth Secretariat, 2007).
14. Right Livelihood Award, www.rightlivelihood.org/maathai.html.

Africa') and shaped her destiny to global success. She spent six years in the United States pursuing university education during the height of the American Civil Rights Movement. In 1960, she enrolled at Mount St. Scholastica College (now Benedictine College) in Kansas, where she received her Bachelor of Science degree in 1964 (biology major, with minors in chemistry and German), after which she took up graduate studies at the University of Pittsburgh, where she received a Master's degree in biology. The latter studies were funded by the Africa–America Institute. At the time, Martin Luther King Jr had just received the 1964 Nobel Peace Prize, one year after his 'I Have a Dream' speech (see Robinson, Chapter 3, and Daniels, Chapter 5, in this volume). Maathai, in her early twenties and a devoted student and Catholic, did not, however, participate in the Black Renaissance protest meetings or marches that flared up across America.

The late 1970s marked a turning point for Maathai, as her time in the United States had shaped her political consciousness. On returning to a recently independent Kenya in 1966 as a newly single mother with three young children, Maathai was overwhelmed by the frustration, destitution and injustice in her country. She took to heart the realisation that these problems were associated with similar changes she too had experienced during her rural childhood. Her memories were of pristine landscapes that had been tamed by the colonial British rulers and subjected to their own imperial needs. Natural woodlands had been converted to cash crops such as tea and coffee, a practice that continued after Kenya's independence in the form of political favours exchanged for land bribes.

The catalyst for the formation of the Green Belt Movement was Maathai's empathy for rural women who had begun to complain about a lack of clean water, the depletion of tree and firewood stocks, and changing rainfall patterns. The decline in soil productivity and drying of rivers had resulted in insufficient food production and impoverishment. Maathai's commitment to the environmental cause was ignited by empowering women to become financially self-sufficient. These early experiences provided impetus for her extensive tree-planting projects.

In addition, a series of global environmental policy events, led primarily by the United Nations over a forty-year period, gradually built an ideological platform for environmental peace-building. The earliest and most notable of these can be traced to the Conference on the Human Environment (also known as the Stockholm Conference), hosted in 1972 by the UN General Assembly at the initiative of the Swedish government.[15] In recognising the ecological importance of forests, the Stockholm Conference had made recommendations to monitor, protect and manage forest ecosystems as natural assets.

A more pronounced and strategic approach to environmental governance came about after 1983, from the UN Brundtland Commission, named after its chair Gro Harlem Brundtland, a doctor and diplomat who served three terms as prime minister of Norway (1981, 1986–89, 1990–96). The Commission discussed the social, economic and political dimensions of environmental management and governance, introducing a shift from narrow species-based concerns for nature (*saving species and ecosystems*) to broader but still well-defined objectives and solutions for protecting the environment.[16]

The Brundtland Commission's 1987 report, *Our Common Future*, was groundbreaking in that it put forth the concept of sustainable development: 'Sustainable development is development that meets the needs of the present without compromising the ability of future generations to meet their own needs.'[17] This concept became the engine of the environmental movement in subsequent years. It heralded the emergence of a concerted global response, in particular an increasingly sophisticated governance response, to the requirements for, and expectations of, sustainable development.

The global community's renewed commitment to, and aspiration for, sustainable development took place at the UN Conference on Environment and Development (popularly called the Earth Summit), which was held in Rio de Janeiro in 1992. Here the Convention on

---

15. Stockholm Conference, www.unep.org/Documents.Multilingual/Default.asp?documentid=97.
16. Brundtland Commission, www.un-documents.net/wced-ocf.htm (General Assembly Resolution 42/187, 1987).
17. Gro Harlem Brundtland, *Our Common Future* (Oxford: Oxford University Press, 1987).

Biological Diversity was opened for signature.[18] The Convention's three key aims were to conserve biological diversity, to ensure sustainable use and development of the environment, and to bring about fair and equitable sharing of benefits.

Maathai was witness to this dynamic epoch of environmental governance. She attended the Earth Summit in Rio in 1992. Her addresses to UN delegates on behalf of an international NGO coalition raised her international profile, bolstered the Green Belt Movement's activities and provided inspiration to align its work to the UN's sustainable development agenda.

Not Merely a Tree Gardener: Maathai's Essential Contribution

Poverty is often associated with multidimensional social, cultural and political aspects of economic deprivation. It strips personal power. Unemployed and low-income people, referred to in such denigrating terms as 'the bottom billion', are frequently portrayed as abstractions of development projects. This 'curse' of poverty, as British economist Paul Collier called it, dehumanises the poor as they struggle to eke out a decent livelihood in developing countries.[19]

Maathai understood that the gap between rich and poor could not be reduced unless people's relationship with the state was changed. She recognised that restoring and affirming self-worth, which is typically negated by abject poverty, would be necessary to improve the lives of the masses. The excluded and marginalised would need to develop a personal sense of citizenship in order to unlock the potential for change that resided within them.

By working to protect the environment and to plant trees, Maathai provided opportunities for ordinary people to claim their dignity by becoming self-reliant. Her approach was to advocate that poor people be recognised as under-engaged citizens who possess untapped

18. Convention on Biological Diversity, www.cbd.int/convention.
19. Paul Collier, *The Bottom Billion: Why the Poorest Countries Are Failing and What Can Be Done About It* (Oxford: Oxford University Press, 2007).

reservoirs of innovation from which society could draw, and not be seen as powerless subjects without 'know-how' and at the mercy of the patronage of others. Maathai's key role, therefore, was to serve as an agent of change – a leader of sustainable development and a builder of peace and democracy.

After the 1992 Earth Summit, vast resources and mechanisms were put in place to mobilise the Convention on Biological Diversity and the sustainable development agenda. In Western countries, this enabled environmental 'radicals' and protestors from the 1970s and 1980s to establish a professionalised form of nature-based social activism rooted in the UN's sustainable development agenda. Many entered political office or influential NGOs. Unlike Maathai, however, many lost touch with the needs and aspirations of local communities with whom they were working. Few noted the gaps between the actual and perceived impacts of their work on the lives of ordinary people. Amid the quest of others to translate the concept of sustainable development into practical activities, Maathai had long been practising this approach herself. She remained one of a handful of seasoned activists who continued to work in the 'trenches' and to get soil under her nails.

The Green Belt Movement grew rapidly. By 1980, just four years after the movement had been founded, almost 600 tree nurseries involving as many as 3,000 women had been built. By that time, some 2,000 green public areas with about 1,000 seedlings each had also been established, and more than 15,000 farmers had planted woodlots on their farms. By 2004, over 30 million trees had been planted across Africa through the Green Belt Movement's influence. Through its modus operandi of simplicity and old-fashioned naturalism, the movement developed a pan-African mandate, which became widely adopted in several African countries by the late 1980s. In the process, farming techniques and knowledge were also transferred to local communities.

The Green Belt Movement further provided civic education about the link between degradation of the environment and development, and encouraged women to create jobs by preventing soil loss, retarding desertification and reducing the loss of biodiversity. As a result of the more stable natural environment that was created by tree planting, women were able to grow and sell crops, support the needs of their family and release themselves from the enslavement of poverty.

Maathai's other contribution, less recognised but equally important, was bringing to light what ecologist and writer Robert Pyle described as the 'extinction of experience'.[20] This phenomenon refers to social disaffection and apathy to nature. One of the greatest causes of the environmental crisis is the state of personal alienation from nature in which many people live. Nigerian author Ben Okri captured the spirit of the 'extinction of experience' with remarkable pathos in his celebrated work of literary fiction *The Famished Road*, for which he won the Booker Prize in 1991.[21] The dialogue between the spirit-child, Azaro and Madame Koto illustrates Azaro's imaginative empathy for the annihilation of nature and its influence on his identity. Azaro imagines himself first becoming a tree and part of the forest. Then, to preserve his identity and *sense of place*, he imagines himself turning into a road:

> 'Then I will become a tree', I said.
> 'Then they will cut you down because of a road.'
> 'Then I will turn into the road.'
> 'Cars will ride on you, cows will shit on you, people will perform
>   sacrifices on your face.'
> 'And I will cry at night. And then people will remember the forest.'[22]

Thus, Maathai's corpus of work demonstrated that the majority of poor rural people in societies throughout the world have retained a distinct dependence on nature, unlike their faster-paced urban counterparts. While the wisdom associated with traditional environmental knowledge and indigenous identities is often sneered at in contemporary society, Maathai commanded great admiration for retaining the *old ways* of doing things. Examples were evident in how seeds were selected and planted, the methods of cultivating and tending to seedlings, and harvesting techniques. The Kenyan environmentalist rarely relied on

---

20. Richard Pyle, *The Thunder Tree: Lessons from an Urban Wildland* (New York: Lyons, 1998).
21. Ben Okri, *The Famished Road* (London: Jonathan Cape, 1991).
22. Ibid., p. 219.

Western scientific advice or textbooks, preferring instead the trial-and-error methods of cultivating tree seedlings in nurseries and transplanting them to unlock people's spiritual connectedness to nature.

The environmental impacts of Maathai's work are multiple and have resulted in tangible benefits. Reforestation improves Planet Earth's green lungs because forests function as carbon sinks of greenhouse gases, thereby helping to inhibit the effects of climate change.[23] The Green Belt Movement's tree-planting projects curbed soil erosion in critical watersheds. Thousands of acres of biodiversity-rich indigenous forest and woodland were rehabilitated and safeguarded. Stocks of wood for fire-making, fencing and building were better managed, both for the rural people and for the urban poor.

Wishing to contribute more purposefully to nation-building by infusing holistic and socially responsible principles into governance challenges in Kenya, Maathai was encouraged to enter the political arena and work towards uniting opposition parties in her country. She ran unsuccessfully for the Kenyan parliament and presidency in 1997. Maathai again campaigned for parliament in the 2002 Kenyan elections. In 2003, after Moi had stepped down after twenty-four years in office, she won a parliamentary seat by a 98 per cent margin in her rural constituency. She was subsequently appointed assistant minister of Kenya's Ministry of Environment and Natural Resources in the government of President Mwai Kibaki.

Changing the Climate for Women and the Planet

Maathai's position in parliament was short-lived. The prestige associated with the Nobel Peace Prize attracted envy and disfavour among fellow parliamentarians and rivals. Amid ballot-box controversy, she was voted out of national office in the 2007 primary elections. Apocalyptic fears fuelled by climate change, particularly concerning food and water security, and the race for technological intelligence,

---

23. See, for example, Gordon Bonan, 'Forests and Climate Change: Forcings, Feedbacks, and the Climate Benefits of Forests', *Science* 320 (2008), pp. 1444-9.

appear to have shaped Maathai's post-Nobel work. Her intention was to help reduce greenhouse gas emissions by actively promoting forest protection and tree planting, as well as by lobbying governments to undertake concerted efforts to combat the effects of climate change.

In 2005, Maathai was elected the first president of the African Union's (AU) Economic, Social and Cultural Council (ECOSOCC), which was charged with promoting interaction between the AU's leaders and civil society.[24] She sought to place climate change on the AU's agenda, and called on African heads of state to reduce the vulnerability of their countries to this phenomenon by equipping them with knowledge, skills and jobs to adopt sustainable technologies. As Maathai pointed out in a press release on the eve of the AU Summit in Malabo, Equatorial Guinea, in June 2011:

> Many of our countries have experienced decades of environmental mismanagement or outright neglect. Indeed, some governments – including my own – have facilitated the plunder of the forests, the degradation of the land and unsustainable agricultural practices. Many communities in Africa are already threatened by the negative impacts of climate change. Children in Africa are dying from malnutrition as women struggle to farm on land that is less and less productive. People on coastlines are losing their homes as the seas consume the coastlines.[25]

Maathai argued that climate change presented a serious threat to Africa, with the poorest people likely to be hardest hit.[26] (The AU honoured her by posthumously recognising her life's work in January 2012.[27]) Maathai was appointed by the African Development Bank as the 'Goodwill Ambassador of the Congo Forest Basin' in 2005.[28] She noted that 'the Congo rainforest should not be seen just as a national

24. See, for example, Charles Mutasa, 'A Critical Appraisal of the African Union–ECOSOCC Civil Society Interface', in John Akokpari, Angela Ndinga-Muvumba and Tim Murithi (eds), *The African Union and Its Institutions* (Johannesburg: Jacana, 2008), pp. 291–306.

25. Media release preceding the African Union Summit, Malabo, Equatorial Guinea, 29 June 2011, http://nobelwomensinitiative.org/2011/06/media-release-wangari-maathai-calls-on-au-leaders-to-take-action-on-climate-change.

26. Camilla Toulman, *Climate Change in Africa* (London: Zed Books, 2009).

27. African Union, Assembly of the Union, Eighteenth Ordinary Session, Addis Ababa, 29–30 January 2012, Decision Recognising the Life and Work of Wangari Muta Maathai, Doc. Assembly/AU/14(XVIII) Add.6.

28. Funds totalling more than US$200 million were provided by the Norwegian and British governments for the Congo Basin Fund, which was managed by the African Development Bank.

or regional resource, but rather as a global treasure that acts as the Earth's lung and one of its greatest hopes for the mitigation of global warming and climate change.'[29] Beginning in 2006, Maathai was an active patron of the UN's 'Plant for the Planet: Billion Tree Campaign', which today has a presence in 170 countries. As of September 2012, more than 12.6 billion trees have been planted under this project.[30]

Maathai's campaign activities on behalf of the UN climate change process were launched when she was inaugurated as a UN 'Messenger of Peace' in 2009. At the fifteenth Conference of Parties convened by the UN Framework Convention on Climate Change (UNFCCC), also called COP15, which was hosted in the Danish capital of Copenhagen in 2009, the Kenyan environmentalist called on world leaders to commit resources to support African countries in addressing the destructive impacts of climate change. Principally obstructed by the position of the United States (which refused to commit to carbon emission targets because developing countries are exempted from setting targets), expectations for a breakthrough deal at COP15 to bind countries into further climate change agreements were dashed. Fewer than thirty countries agreed to an accord. Undeterred, Maathai put shoulder to the wheel on behalf of the UN's calls to action, including becoming an advocate of its new Reducing Emissions from Deforestation and Degradation in Developing Countries Programme (UN-REDD).

Maathai also sought to elevate the influence of female leadership and to garner support for women's rights, first through the Green Belt Movement and later through various international platforms. She was a founding member of the Nobel Women's Initiative, along with female Nobel peace laureates Shirin Ebadi (2003, Iran), Jody Williams (1997, United States), Rigoberta Menchú Tum (1992, Guatemala) and Betty Williams and Mairead Corrigan Maguire (Northern Ireland, jointly 1976).[31] Until her death in September 2011, Maathai continued to be

29. Wangari Maathai, 'State of the Congo Basin', in *The Challenge for Africa: A New Vision* (London: Heinemann, 2009), pp. 260-73.
30. United Nations, 'Plant for the Planet: Billion Tree Campaign', 17 September 2012, www.unep.org/billiontreecampaign.
31. Nobel Women's Initiative, www.nobelwomensinitiative.org.

active in Kenya and on the world stage – particularly through the United Nations – and was still being honoured with awards of lifetime achievement and honorary doctorates from universities across the globe.

Apostles and Disciples of Peace

Wangari Maathai had several significant interactions with other Nobel peace laureates, the most notable being Al Gore, who was awarded the Nobel Peace Prize in 2007, jointly with the UN Intergovernmental Panel on the Convention for Climate Change (IPCCC). Maathai met Gore (then still an American senator and an ardent and charismatic Green campaigner) when he visited the Green Belt Movement's headquarters and field sites in Kenya in 1990. Together, they planted a *Podocarpus* tree (African yellow wood). Gore subsequently recounted his positive impressions about the Green Belt Movement in his 1992 bestseller *Earth in the Balance*.[32]

In 1992, two years after their meeting in Kenya and the year that Gore was elected US vice president in the Bill Clinton administration (1993–2000), Maathai called on the US Senate Foreign Relations Committee to intervene against criminal charges from the Kenyan government that prevented her from travelling to the Earth Summit that year. Eight senators, including Gore, asked the Moi regime to substantiate the charges against her. By then, Maathai was already well known internationally for her pro-democracy campaign. The charges were dropped, and she was able to attend the Earth Summit, where she held a much publicised press conference with Gore and another Nobel peace laureate, Tibetan spiritual leader the Dalai Lama (awarded the Peace Prize in 1989).

Maathai continued to work tirelessly with Gore in lobbying powerful donors to protect the world's forest expanses in order to reverse the damaging effects of climate change. They lobbied the US Senate, as well as the UN General Assembly, NGOs and others to invest in forest

---

32. Al Gore, *Earth in the Balance: Ecology and the Human Spirit* (Boston: Houghton Mifflin, 1992).

conservation projects that could significantly reduce deforestation and in turn mitigate the negative effects of climate change.

Maathai's meeting with US president Barack Obama took place in the same way as that with Gore. In 2006, Obama, then a US senator on a pre-election tour, paid his first official visit to Kenya. Maathai and Obama held a public tree-planting ceremony at Uhuru Park in the Kenyan capital of Nairobi: the same site where Maathai had held a successful mass protest rally some fifteen years earlier against the proposed Kenya Times Media Trust Complex development on public land. Uhuru Park's Freedom Corner became synonymous with Maathai's struggle for democracy and environmental conservation in Kenya. It was in this park that hunger strikes, violent skirmishes and unlawful arrests involving security forces armed with live ammunition had occurred on several occasions. At the 2006 tree-planting ceremony, which Obama's family also attended, the US senator deplored President George W. Bush's refusal to join the UN Framework Convention on Climate Change. Later, Maathai, together with Muhammad Yunus, who was honoured with the Nobel Peace Prize in 2007 for his banking social entrepreneurship schemes for the poor in Bangladesh, strongly endorsed Obama as a candidate for the Nobel Peace Prize in 2009, referring to him in their media campaign as the 'leader of the free world' (on Obama, see Mazrui, Chapter 2, and Robinson, Chapter 3, in this volume).

During her brief parliamentary tenure, Maathai worked with another prominent Nobel peace laureate, former UN Secretary General Kofi Annan of Ghana, who was awarded the Peace Prize in 2001 (see Mikell, Chapter 13 in this volume). Years earlier, she had served on Annan's advisory board on disarmament, which had condemned the 1998 violence at Karura Forest, an ecologically spectacular area just 20 kilometres from the centre of Nairobi. The upheaval, which killed more than 200 people, was the result of opposition to the juggernaut of proposed luxury developments in which government officials reportedly held personal business interests. Large groups of concerned citizens, members of the UN Environment Programme and the Kenya Human Rights Commission, as well as parliamentarians, journalists and affiliates of the Green Belt Movement, confronted thugs hired by the developers. Maathai was severely beaten until she lost consciousness. When Annan was appointed by the African Union as its chief mediator to facilitate a power-sharing election deal in Kenya between Raila Odinga and Mwai Kibaki in 2007, Maathai worked with Annan on national pro-democracy efforts. Brutal clashes had erupted throughout Kenya in the aftermath of the 2007 polls, resulting in thirty days of violence during which more than 1,220 people were killed, 3,500 were injured and 350,000 were displaced.[33]

In the run-up to the fifteenth Conference of Parties convened by the UN Framework Convention on Climate Change in Copenhagen in 2009, Maathai and South Africa's Archbishop Desmond Tutu (Nobel peace laureate in 1984; see Isaacson, Chapter 7 in this volume) came out in strong support of Annan's 'Time for Climate Justice' campaign. As a means to help break the deadlock in the COP15 negotiations, Maathai addressed the UN General Assembly, urging the United States to persuade wealthier industrialised countries to reward developing countries for conserving and augmenting their remaining forest cover. Tutu and Maathai appealed to Africa to have its voice heard, and argued that because the continent had emitted an almost negligible amount of carbon compared to wealthier countries, support from these African countries for climate change projects was required. Maathai and Tutu lobbied for concrete actions that aimed to pressure Western countries and China to accelerate support to the countries most vulnerable to climate change. Nobel peace laureates Maathai, Gore, Annan and Tutu thus joined forces to further drive the global climate change agenda.

Ecce Africana:[34] The World Turns to Africa?

There is little doubt that Maathai's African descent is relevant to her Nobel Peace Prize award. Her contributions to the peace movement

33. The Hague Justice Portal, 'The Situation in Kenya', March 2010, www.haguejusticeportal.net/index.php?id=11604.
34. Latin: 'look, Africa'.

were especially significant in the decade following the tragic public execution of Ken Saro-Wiwa and eight of his fellow environmental activists by General Sani Abacha's military dictatorship in Nigeria in November 1995. As the founder of the Movement for the Survival of Ogoni People (MOSOP), Saro-Wiwa had fought against Anglo-Dutch company Shell's exploitation of oil, which had turned Nigeria's Niger Delta region into an environmental wasteland and impoverished the Ogoni people.[35] Though South Africa was often able to exercise its influence on the continent, even the pleas of its president, Nobel peace laureate Nelson Mandela, could not convince Abacha to grant clemency for the activists[36] (on Mandela, see Boehmer, Chapter 8 in this volume).

Of great concern to Africa, too, was the global conversion of unculti-vated territory into agricultural land, reflected in the loss of total forest area and increased exploitation of remaining forests around the world, but of highest prevalence in Africa.[37] The continent's overreliance on its natural capital for economic growth and to provide basic human welfare (firewood, food, medicines and shelter, and ecosystem services such as water and productive soil) motivated an attempt by global forces to secure Africa's natural heritage as an asset base for raw materials. The appetite of foreign markets for biological resources from Africa, such as indigenous timber and bio-patent rights for herbal pharmaceutical products, was steadily increasing.

Critical of the international community's apathy towards Africa, Maathai was a much-needed voice of hope for the continent.[38] Hers was a voice that was recognisable to the United Nations and other influential global institutions long before she received the Nobel Peace Prize in 2004, all the more so because Africa has had so few female icons and role models. The vast majority of African women today still remain undereducated and subject to patriarchal norms that inhibit them from

35. Ken Saro-Wiwa, *Genocide in Nigeria: The Ogoni Tragedy* (London: Saros International, 1992). See also Ike Okonta and Oronto Douglas, *Where Vultures Feast: Shell, Human Rights, and Oil in the Niger Delta* (San Francisco: Sierra Club, 2001).

36. See, for example, Adekeye Adebajo, Adebayo Adedeji and Chris Landsberg (eds), *South Africa in Africa: The Post-Apartheid Era* (Scottsville: University of KwaZulu-Natal Press, 2007).

37. United Nations Environment Programme, *Global Environment Outlook: Past, Present, and Future Perspectives* (London: Earthscan, 2002).

38. Wangari Maathai, *The Challenge for Africa: A New Vision* (London: Heinemann, 2009).

reaching their full potential. As the first African woman to be awarded
the Nobel Peace Prize, Maathai inspired Africans, especially its young
women, to liberate themselves from fear and silence. Similar to the other
two female African Nobel peace laureates (Liberia's Ellen Johnson Sirleaf
and Leymah Gbowee were awarded the prize in 2011; see Adebajo,
Chapter 14, and Daniel, Chapter 15, in this volume), Maathai, through
her social activism, provoked significant changes to entrenched social
inequalities and injustices. Her focus was on inadequate access to natural
resources as she rejuvenated environmental activism around the world.

Concluding Reflections

At the highly charged UN World Summit on Sustainable Development, held in the South African megalopolis of Johannesburg in 2002,
Britain's secretary of international development Clare Short denounced
environmentalism by suggesting that it was an elitist 'greenie' concern of
the privileged classes and therefore of less priority than poverty eradication. This statement caused considerable consternation among the
environmental NGOs and civil society groups in attendance. The suggestion that environmentalism and poverty eradication were somehow
in contradiction with each other was comprehensively debunked by
Maathai, who demonstrated through her life's work that poverty and
environmental degradation are not mutually independent phenomena.
Each drives the other. The cycle of poverty – from unemployment and
hopelessness to illness and malnutrition – can only be broken when the
natural environment is managed in a responsible manner. A widespread
belief among many environmentalists from developing countries, like
Maathai, was the idea that the protection of nature requires an overall
recasting of society's norms and values, as well as economic structures.

Maathai's work further brings to light the inconsistent relationship
that many environmentalists have with science. The hazards posed to
the climate by greenhouse gas emissions are rarely questioned today.
But, unlike the science behind climate change, the equally compelling
science behind genetically modified organisms (GMOs) is often given

a lot less credence. Maathai was an advocate of planting indigenous and genetically unaltered tree species, and was resolutely opposed to genetically modified organisms. She adopted the UN's 'precautionary principle' stance (from the UN Cartagena Protocol on Biosafety of the Convention on Biological Diversity of 2000), which called for more research into the potential environmental impacts associated with GMOs and clarification on corporate monopolies arising from biotechnological patent rights.[39] Maathai blamed Christianity, a theology to which she herself subscribed, for the commercialisation of nature. Since founding the Green Belt Movement in 1976, she had consistently warned that fast-growing commercial trees, such as eucalyptus (originally from Australia), were causing rivers in parts of Africa to dry up and water tables to recede. In fact, one of the Kikuyu names for eucalyptus is *munyua maai*, which means 'drinker of water'. Maathai was strongly opposed to the Kenyan government's provision to farmers of several million cuttings of genetically modified eucalyptus that had been imported from South Africa.[40]

Ideological differences existed between Maathai and Norman Borlaug, who won the Nobel Peace Prize in 1970 for 'improving crop management practices that transformed food production in much of the developing world'.[41] Borlaug, who died in 2009 at the age of 91, was a biotechnological pioneer in the global fight against hunger and malnutrition. The American reasoned that poor farmers in developing countries could be guaranteed sustainable incomes, which in turn would reduce pressure to convert large swathes of nature into agricultural landscapes.[42] There is a growing demand from farmers for genetically modified organisms. Compared to indigenous species, crop yields of GMOs are purported to be higher, more drought-resistant and less prone to insect predation, which in turn results in higher

---

39. Cartagena Protocol on Biosafety, http://bch.cbd.int/protocol.
40. Chris Lang, 'Kenya: Biotechnology, Eucalyptus but No GM Trees', *World Rainforest Movement Bulletin* 88 (2004) (www.wrm.org.uy/bulletin/88/viewpoint.html).
41. 'The Nobel Peace Prize 1970: Award Ceremony Speech', www.nobelprize.org/nobel_prizes/peace/laureates/1970/press.html.
42. Leon Hesser, *The Man Who Fed the World: Nobel Peace Prize Laureate Norman Borlaug and His Battle to End World Hunger* (Dallas TX: Durban, 2006).

and more secure forms of income.[43] African countries are fearful that allowing corporations to sell patented seeds will lead to a new form of neo-colonialism, while others are of the opinion that these debates are being controlled by the rich North. It had been hoped that Maathai would use her considerable stature to influence these debates in a world where food crises are compounded by changing climate patterns.

The UN Framework Convention on Climate Change hosted its first Conference of Parties (COP1) in the German capital Berlin in 1995, where the Berlin Mandate was passed to define solutions to climate change.[44] The conference agreed to the Kyoto Protocol at COP3 in 1997. The Protocol binds the wealthiest, most polluting countries to set clear targets for reductions in carbon emissions. As of 2013, the carbon-intensive Group of Eight (G8) economies (including the United States, Canada and Russia) have yet to commit to carbon reduction targets, reflecting the enduring stumbling block in the Kyoto Protocol negotiations associated with the phrase 'common but differentiated responsibilities'.[45]

Maathai's 2004 Nobel Peace Prize award marked the 120th anniversary of an important historical event: German chancellor Otto von Bismarck's Conference of Berlin, held in 1884–85, which brought together fourteen mostly European countries that set the rules for the subsequent partition of Africa.[46] The legacy of Berlin left by the 'Scramble for Africa' has left the continent in disarray. This imperialism has some parallels with the rigorous, multilateral approach to climate change solutions that arose from the UN's COP1 Berlin Mandate. The discontent stems from the fact that a single global body (the United Nations) has exercised rigorous control of the climate change agenda and exerted influence on national sovereignties. The world

43. See, for example, Robert Paarlberg, *Starved for Science: How Biotechnology Is Being Kept Out of Africa* (Cambridge MA: Harvard University Press, 2009).

44. UNFCCC documentation, http://unfccc.int/documentation/items/2643.php.

45. See the Berlin Mandate's Article 3: 'The Parties should protect the climate system for the benefit of present and future generations of humankind, on the basis of equity and in accordance with their common but differentiated responsibilities and respective capabilities.' United Nations Framework Convention on Climate Change, *Report of the Conference of the Parties on Its First Session*, Berlin, 6 June 1995.

46. Adekeye Adebajo, *The Curse of Berlin: Africa After the Cold War* (London: Hurst, 2010).

body has steered the direction of climate change science (published in successive reports of the IPCCC), provoked alarmism in the guise of raising awareness (principally the Stern Review of 2007),[47] facilitated international treaties such as the Kyoto Protocol of 1997, put in place and promoted a carbon-trading concept, and monitored and regulated carbon emissions.

The 'curse' of the Berlin mandate is becoming evident. Many analysts have pronounced the UN's multilateral approach to be dead. If it is, then the UN's climate change efforts represent the greatest process failure in the history of the organisation. Wangari Maathai and other Nobel peace laureates who supported this cause would have been greatly disillusioned. The seeds sown by Maathai have germinated. Whether they can still take root remains to be seen.

Maathai was a distinguished environmentalist. As one of Africa's most powerful female leaders and ambassadors, she is unrivalled on the continent for the decisiveness and consistency of her contributions to the global environmental movement. She demonstrated that self-sufficiency and resourcefulness provide the only gateway to global sustainability. When we behave in a humane way and respect our natural heritage – even through simple actions such as planting trees – we can sustain the cultural and moral ties that bind us together as human beings responsible for future generations. For these insights and her tireless efforts, the world has many reasons to be grateful to Africa's 'Earth Mother'.

Bibliography

Adebajo, Adekeye, *The Curse of Berlin: Africa After the Cold War* (London: Hurst, 2010).

Adebajo, Adekeye, Adebayo Adedeji and Chris Landsberg (eds), *South Africa in Africa: The Post-Apartheid Era* (Scottsville: University of KwaZulu-Natal Press, 2007).

Anderson, John, *Towards Gondwana Alive: Promoting Biodiversity and Stemming the Sixth Extinction* (Tshwane: National Botanical Institute, 2001).

Beinart, William, 'African History and Environmental History', *African Affairs* 99 (2000), pp. 269–302.

Bonan, Gordon, 'Forests and Climate Change: Forcings, Feedbacks, and the Climate Benefits of Forests', *Science* 320 (2008), pp. 1444–9.

---

47. Nicholas Stern, *The Economics of Climate Change: The Stern Review* (Cambridge: Cambridge University Press, 2007).

Brundtland, Gro Harlem, *Our Common Future* (Oxford: Oxford University Press, 1987).

Collier, Paul, *The Bottom Billion: Why the Poorest Countries Are Failing and What Can Be Done About It* (Oxford: Oxford University Press, 2007).

Commonwealth Commission on Respect and Understanding, *Civil Paths to Peace* (London: Commonwealth Secretariat, 2007).

Ghirmazion, Aseghedech, 'The UN Environment Programme', in Adekeye Adebajo (ed.), *From Global Apartheid to Global Village: Africa and the United Nations* (Scottsville: University of KwaZulu-Natal Press, 2009), pp. 515–39.

Gore, Al, *Earth in the Balance: Ecology and the Human Spirit* (Boston MA: Houghton Mifflin, 1992).

Groombridge, Brian, *Global Biodiversity: Status of the Earth's Living Resources* (London: Chapman & Hall, 1992).

Hesser, Leon, *The Man Who Fed the World: Nobel Peace Prize Laureate Norman Borlaug and His Battle to End World Hunger* (Dallas TX: Durban, 2006)

Lang, Chris, 'Kenya: Biotechnology, Eucalyptus but No GM Trees', *World Rainforest Movement Bulletin* 88 (2004) (www.wrm.org.uy/bulletin/88/viewpoint.html).

Maathai, Wangari, *The Green Belt Movement: Sharing the Approach and the Experience* (New York: Lantern, 2004).

Maathai, Wangari, *Unbowed: A Memoir* (New York: Knopf, 2006).

Maathai, Wangari, *The Challenge for Africa: A New Vision* (London: Heinemann, 2009).

McNeely, Jeffrey, *Coping with Change: People, Forests, and Biodiversity* (Geneva: International Union for Conservation of Nature, 1994).

Mutasa, Charles, 'A Critical Appraisal of the African Union–ECOSOCC Civil Society Interface', in John Akokpari, Angela Ndinga-Muvumba and Tim Murithi (eds), *The African Union and Its Institutions* (Johannesburg: Jacana, 2008), pp. 291–306.

Nobel Prize, 'The Nobel Peace Prize 1970: Award Ceremony Speech', www.nobelprize.org/nobel_prizes/peace/laureates/1970/press.html.

Nobel Prize, 'The Nobel Peace Prize 2004: Award Ceremony Speech', www.nobelprize.org/nobel_prizes/peace/laureates/2004/presentation-speech.html.

Okonta, Ike, and Oronto Douglas, *Where Vultures Feast: Shell, Human Rights, and Oil in the Niger Delta* (San Francisco: Sierra Club, 2001).

Okri, Ben, *The Famished Road* (London: Jonathan Cape, 1991).

Paarlberg, Robert, *Starved for Science: How Biotechnology Is Being Kept Out of Africa* (Cambridge MA: Harvard University Press, 2009).

Richard Pyle, *The Thunder Tree: Lessons from an Urban Wildland* (New York: Lyons, 1998).

Saro-Wiwa, Ken, *Genocide in Nigeria: The Ogoni Tragedy* (London: Saros International, 1992).

Stern, Nicholas, *The Economics of Climate Change: The Stern Review* (Cambridge: Cambridge University Press, 2007).

Stiehm, Judith Hicks, *Champions for Peace: Women Winners of the Nobel Peace Prize* (Lanham MD: Rowman & Littlefield, 2006).

Toulmin, Camilla, *Climate Change in Africa* (London: Zed Books, 2009).

United Nations Environment Programme, *Global Environment Outlook: Past, Present and Future Perspectives* (London: Earthscan, 2002).

United Nations Framework Convention on Climate Change, *Report of the Conference of the Parties on Its First Session*, Berlin, 6 June 1995.

World Resources Institute, *World Resources 2000–2001: People and Ecosystems – The Fraying Web of Life* (Washington DC: WRI, 2000).

THIRTEEN

KOFI ANNAN:
THE SOFT-SPOKEN PROPHET

GWENDOLYN MIKELL

Kofi Annan was born in Ghana on 8 April 1938, the son of a chief and governor of Ashanti province. He attended a Methodist school and the University of Science and Technology in Kumasi before going abroad to study at the Graduate Institute of International Studies in Geneva and at Macalester College in Minnesota; he received a Master's degree in management at the Massachusetts Institute of Technology in 1972. He returned to Ghana in 1974 to head his country's national tourist development company for two years, before returning to a career at the United Nations.[1]

In 2001, Kofi Annan, the seventh UN Secretary General (the second to come from Africa, after Egypt's Boutros Boutros-Ghali, who held the office between 1992 and 1996), won the Nobel Peace Prize along with the United Nations itself. As the Nobel Peace Committee noted:

> The only one of the UN's previous six Secretaries-General who can be compared to Annan in personal force and historical importance is Dag Hammarskjöld, the organisation's second Secretary-General and the recipient of the Nobel Peace Prize in 1961. For Kofi Annan, Dag Hammarskjöld has been a model. In his Hammarskjöld Memorial Lecture in September this year (2001), Annan said, 'There can be no better rule

1. See Kofi Annan, *Interventions: A Life in War and Peace* (New York: Penguin, 2012).

of thumb for a Secretary-General, as he approaches each new challenge or crisis, than to ask himself, "how would Hammarskjöld have handled this?"[2]

Few would have predicted this accolade in 1997, when Kofi Annan became UN Secretary General due to Western unease with Africa insisting on a second term for an African secretary general, and because of the widespread unease among African leaders who felt that they had no choice but to nominate Annan – the only African candidate who could pass muster with the Americans. Annan's predecessor, Boutros Boutros-Ghali, who had creative ideas on the UN's role in conflict management, as demonstrated by his 1992 *An Agenda for Peace*, and on how to address the world's development challenges, as evidenced by his 1993 *An Agenda for Development*,[3] had numerous clashes with the Americans on Bosnia, Somalia, Rwanda, Libya and the Middle East. So it was not a surprise when the US administration of Bill Clinton (1993–2000) refused to grant Boutros-Ghali a second term (the other fourteen Security Council members agreed to extend the Egyptian's tenure by another five years). In contrast, Kofi Annan entered office with considerable Western support. Despite some initial public reticence due to the long shadow of the Rwandan genocide of 1994 that followed him (Annan had been UN Undersecretary General for Peacekeeping under Boutros-Ghali at the time of the massacre of 800,000 people, and was criticised for a lacklustre response), Annan proved himself to be quite successful – eloquent and visionary, and creative and sensitive to promoting human rights in places where conflict and war had denied them.

Further distinctions surfaced rather quickly in that Kofi Annan began to be acknowledged through his actions as the Secretary General who brought Africa into greater synergy with UN norms and expectations.[4] His initiatives made the world body's then 192 (now 193) member states, and indeed the world, think more deeply about the causes of

---

2. 'Award Ceremony Speech', presented by Gunnar Berge, chairman of the Nobel Peace Committee, Oslo, 10 December 2001. See also Sten Ask and Anna Mark-Jungkvist (eds), *The Adventure of Peace: Dag Hammarskjöld and the Future of the UN* (New York: Palgrave Macmillan, 2005).

3. Boutros Boutros-Ghali, *Unvanquished: A U.S.–U.N. Saga* (New York: Random House, 1999).

4. Author interview with Ambassador Ibrahim Gambari, New York, 18 December 2007.

conflict, and work in a more deliberate fashion to plant post-conflict seeds for socio-economic development. Annan must also be credited with setting out an African agenda for change that would help move the continent towards stemming some of its endemic conflicts, insisting on guaranteeing human rights within a democratic framework, and integrating development and poverty reduction into post-conflict humanitarian interventions. His initiatives met with varying degrees of success, perhaps yielding the greatest results in terms of human rights and conflict resolution in Africa – initiatives that lay closer to the original mission of the UN at its founding in 1945. Thus Annan's initiatives provided a partial answer to African leaders who questioned his loyalty to the continent.

Interesting lessons can be gleaned from the way the world perceived Annan, as represented by his 2001 Nobel Peace Prize, and how his African colleagues viewed him over his two terms as UN Secretary General. Few would deny that his initiatives helped to integrate the actions of the disparate UN agencies and representatives, and thereby strengthen a fractured global institution. Most of the professional staff within the UN Secretariat in New York grew to appreciate him for his commitment to them and the institution, despite the UN Staff Union's criticisms of senior management in November 2004 for its alleged lack of transparency and mismanagement.[5] However, few outside the UN could agree on whether Annan's initiatives actually moderated the extensive power that the world body exercised over the developing world, especially in Africa.

Publications on Kofi Annan's tenure at the UN have been extensive.[6] However, recent research on Annan's legacy for Africa reveals several dichotomies: between the views of African leaders as opposed to perspectives of African laypersons and civil society activists; between American officials and government representatives as opposed to

5. Todd Conner and Catherine Donaldson-Evans, 'U.N. Staff: No Confidence in Top Leaders', Fox News, 14 November 2004.
6. Stanley Meisler, *Kofi Annan: A Man of Peace in a World of War* (Hoboken NJ: Wiley, 2007); James Traub, *The Best Intentions: Kofi Annan and the UN in the Era of American World Power* (New York: Farrar, Straus & Giroux, 2006).

representatives of other Western countries and international organisations; and between UN officials and staff as opposed to Africans who worked at the UN and its component agencies. These assessments overlap in a kaleidoscopic fashion, but they also point to the controversies that swirled around the UN Secretary General as a result of what Chinmaya Gharekhan and Brian Frederking described as clashing national security interests within the five veto-wielding permanent members of the UN Security Council (P5) – the United States, Russia, China, France and Britain[7] – and between the rich North and the global South.[8] Nevertheless, history has been very kind to Annan in acknowledging that his initiatives helped to move the UN into a new era, and into new sets of 'human-focused' responsibilities that reinforced the peace missions that had formerly dominated the organisation's agenda in Africa.

In retrospect, it is clear that the Nobel Peace Committee was prescient in 2001, in that appreciation for Annan's Africa legacy grows ever larger and stronger nearly a decade after the end of his tenure at the UN in 2006. His leadership within Africa had a heavy emphasis on 'good governance', in a way that would become more pronounced even after he left office in December 2006. This extended to working with other African leaders on a 'Panel of the Wise'; helping negotiate a settlement to the Kenyan electoral crisis in 2007–08; playing a role in establishing the Mo Ibrahim prize celebrating former African presidents whose governance strategies reflected the values of transparency, democracy and a commitment to enhancing the welfare of their citizens; championing peer review as a process to promote democratic governance in Africa; advocating global assistance to countries in restoring agriculture in Africa; and pushing for greater attention to meeting the UN's Millennium Development Goals (MDGs) of poverty alleviation and the

7. Gharekhan concludes his analysis of the UN Security Council with the observation that justice and equity are not the basis on which the members promote a settlement. He argues that members of both the Security Council and the General Assembly 'are guided solely by considerations of national interests of the countries they represent'. See Chinmaya R. Gharekhan, *The Horseshoe Table: An Inside View of the UN Security Council* (New Delhi: Longman, 2006), p. 310. See also Brian Frederking, *The U.S. and the Security Council: Collective Security Since the Cold War* (New York: Routledge, 2007), pp. 1–4.

8. Adekeye Adebajo, *The Curse of Berlin: Africa After the Cold War* (London: Hurst, 2010).

empowerment of women. Annan was able to act on his convictions more decisively after leaving the position of UN Secretary General in 2006 because – as he himself noted – he no longer had the world's great powers looking over his shoulder.

The Route to the Nobel Peace Prize

Kofi Annan's extensive thirty-year experience in the UN Secretariat and system was the key to his success as Secretary General. It was a delight in his accomplishments and appreciation of his promise that led the Nobel Peace Committee to award him and the UN the prize in 2001. While acknowledging that the veto power and the ideological differences of the permanent five members of the UN Security Council often made it difficult for the world body to act in the interests of peace, the committee commended Annan and the UN 'for their work for a better organised and a more peaceful world'.[9] It congratulated him on 'revitalising' the UN, re-establishing internal morale, and acting on his personal principles of concern for the interests of individuals facing human rights abuses, and for his activism in the struggle against the scourge of HIV/AIDS.[10] With these words, the Nobel committee also announced its approval of Annan's defence of multilateralism as the core principle in global governance, and support for his activist approach to the role of the UN Secretary General despite American irritation under the George W. Bush administration (2001–08) that he was 'more general, than secretary'.[11]

Kofi Annan had come up through the ranks, having worked at the UN Secretariat in Geneva and at its headquarters in New York in human resource management and budget and finance, and also as Undersecretary General for Peacekeeping. In addition, he held special assignments such as his appointment as assistant secretary general

9. 'The Nobel Peace Prize 2001: Presentation Speech', www.nobelprize.org/nobel_prizes/peace/laureates/2001/presentation-speech.html.
10. 'A Call to Action' (presented at the Abuja Summit on HIV/AIDS), June 2001, www.un.org/ecosocdev/geninfo/afrec/vol15no1/151aids6.htm.
11. Simon Chesterman (ed.), *Secretary or General? The UN Secretary General in World Politics* (Cambridge: Cambridge University Press, 2007), pp. 13–66.

in the Office of Programme Planning, Budget and Finance when the UN negotiated the sale of Iraq's oil for humanitarian relief (1990–92), and as Boutros-Ghali's personal representative in Bosnia (1995–96). Annan had a reputation for getting things done quietly, and for cultivating goodwill among Western member states and the UN staff and leadership.

When he took office as UN Secretary General in January 1997, Kofi Annan inherited from Boutros-Ghali an institution that was suffering a financial crisis mirroring the dynamics of the world economy, the consequences of the earlier American withdrawal from payment of dues amounting to about $1.3 billion, and the failure of the institution's leadership to reflect the diverse post-Cold War era instead of the world of 1945.[12] The UN was also facing new challenges in addressing pervasive conflicts, international crime and the sheer volume of victims needing humanitarian assistance. Although Boutros-Ghali had put forth brilliant and unique proposals for greater involvement by the group of seven industrialised countries, the G7 – later the G8 – in the 'global South', he was viewed by the P5 (and especially by the US permanent representative to the UN, Madeleine Albright) as elitist, pompous, bureaucratic, confrontational, ineffective and distant.[13] In contrast, the Nobel Peace Committee's citation in 2001 noted that Annan had 'brought new life to the organisation' and had 'risen to new challenges such as HIV/AIDS and international terrorism'.[14]

Kofi Annan was well thought of by European diplomats (who had come to know him well in Geneva), and by the Americans, who saw him as a valuable ally. Institutional reform became his top priority.[15] He thus focused on three key issues: using financial resources efficiently and effectively in order to deliver humanitarian assistance, undertake peacekeeping and promote human rights worldwide; promoting transparency,

---

12. Brian Urquhart, *A Life in War and Peace* (New York: Harper & Row, 1987). See also Adebajo, *The Curse of Berlin*, p. 59.
13. Madeleine Albright, *Madame Secretary: A Memoir* (New York: Miramax, 2003), pp. 151–8, 185–6.
14. 'Press Release: Nobel Peace Prize 2001', www.nobelprize.org/nobel_prizes/peace/laureates/2001/press.html.
15. *United Nations Year in Review, 1997*, PAL Video no. 081.

accountability and 'good governance' in carrying out the wishes of UN member states; and creating an environment in which maximum productivity and creativity were expected of those pursuing the UN's goals and missions. His 1998 report *The Causes of Conflict and the Promotion of Durable Peace and Sustainable Development in Africa*[16] sought to craft a new agenda for the multilateral institutions that had emerged from the 1944 Bretton Woods conference – the World Bank and the International Monetary Fund (IMF) – and identified economic injustices as causal factors in initiating and prolonging armed conflicts.

Institutional reform was also the top priority of the P5, especially the Americans, who, having castigated Boutros-Ghali following the death of eighteen American soldiers during a UN peacekeeping mission in Somalia in 1993, had then backed the nomination of Annan for the position of UN Secretary General. For the African Group at the UN, the best organisational reform would have been that which gave Africa two veto-wielding permanent seats (to add to its three rotating seats) on the Security Council, and reduced the 'European neo-colonialism' in UN thinking, processes and operations.[17] Nelson Mandela and many other Africans had backed Boutros-Ghali for a second term. However, faced with the inevitable, the African Group reluctantly put forward a number of candidates to replace Boutros-Ghali.[18] With strong American support, Annan garnered the most votes.

Over his two terms as UN Secretary General, from 1997 and 2006, Annan became acutely conscious of the fact that, while he had the support of the then 192-member UN General Assembly, the collaboration of some of the P5 members on important security issues in the Middle East often left much to be desired. Essentially, enthusiastic

---

16. Kofi Annan, *The Causes of Conflict and the Promotion of Durable Peace and Sustainable Development in Africa*, Report of UN Secretary General, 16 April 1998, www.un.org/ecosocdev/geninfo/afrec/sgreport/index.html.

17. Brian Urquhart, *Decolonization and World Peace* (Austin: University of Texas Press, 1988), pp. 1–25.

18. Chief among the candidates suggested by the OAU and African Group were Amara Essy of Côte d'Ivoire, Ahmedou Ould-Abdallah of Mauritania, Olara Otunnu of Uganda, Lakhdar Brahimi of Algeria and Salim Ahmed Salim of Tanzania. Salim had angered the US with his support for mainland China to replace Taiwan on the UN Security Council in 1971, and France objected to his lack of fluency in French. Kofi Annan eventually won the votes of the P5 in the Security Council.

American support for Israel clashed with the UN's long-held approval of a 'two-state' solution. While Annan was careful not to wade too far into the murky waters of the Middle East, throughout his first term he dealt with the UN Observer Forces in Lebanon, as well as successive resolutions from the Arab League about Israel and Syria. When the second World Conference Against Racism was held in the South African port city of Durban in August–September 2001, Annan identified Israeli suppression of Palestinians and American resistance to reparations for slavery as reasons for the failure of the conference. Blame was, however, also laid at Kofi Annan's door for the conference's failure. Comprehensive support from the P5 was greater during Annan's first term (1997–2001) than during his second (2002–06), because of the more explosive issues that he engaged with after the terrorist attack on New York and Washington DC in September 2011.

'The Responsibility to Protect'

Kofi Annan brought with him to the position of UN Secretary General a wealth of experience dealing with the P5 as well as with African regional organisations on peace and security issues. As UN Undersecretary General for Peacekeeping operations under Boutros-Ghali, Annan had been challenged to help keep the peace in difficult places, and he earned his stripes in some of these. From these tough experiences was born a greater appreciation of what victims of violence suffered, and a greater determination that the UN would prevail in its bid to reach peace agreements to end global conflicts. Although critics have tended to focus on Annan's response to the 1994 Rwandan crisis, the other dramatic crises that also held his attention were the impending agreement on a newly demarcated border between Iraq and Kuwait, and the horrific human rights abuses in the former Yugoslavia – genocide, rape and mutilation – primarily perpetrated on Bosnian Muslims by Bosnian Serbs between 1992 and 1995.

The UN Investigative Commission for the former Yugoslavia, led by Egyptian-American Cherif Bassouni, in 1994, was pessimistic that,

given the deliberate separation of Serbian military leaders and opera-
tional units during the atrocities, the perpetrators would be brought to
justice in the foreseeable future.[19] The BBC hastened to point out the
difficulties that Annan faced in 'serving two masters', as mediator as
well as top diplomat at the UN. That difficulty, however, temporarily
lessened as Washington selectively re-engaged with the UN during
the Clinton administration, from 1993 to 2000. The signing of the
Dayton Accords in 1995 brought an end to the war in Bosnia, and the
Europeans appreciated the UN's role in supporting the United States,
Britain and France during the conflict.[20] Thus, Annan was praised
for having kept peace among P5 members during the later phases of
the Yugoslavian crises, and for having created increased human rights
protections out of the tragedy of massacres in Rwanda and Kosovo.
Nevertheless, he was criticised for allowing Western governments –
especially the United States – to transgress the UN Charter through
unilateral military action in Kosovo in 1999, and for having proclaimed
'peace through war'.[21]

The pain of Rwanda weighed heavily on Annan, and it appeared to
motivate his advocacy of human rights protections. As the Nobel Peace
Committee commented: 'The massacres in Rwanda taught us all, and
not least Annan, that the world does not necessarily get any better if
one refrains from intervening.'[22] He had chafed about constraints from
P5 members that he felt had prevented him from sending an effective peace mission into Rwanda in April 1994, most of which flowed
from the eighteen American deaths in Somalia six months earlier. He
resented the fact that the shadow of the genocide fell on him, when
Boutros-Ghali's Indian personal pepresentative to the Security Council,
Chinmaya Gharekhan,[23] had the sole power to communicate with the
P5. He was also angered by the fact that the Americans had opposed

19. Paul Lewis, 'Word for Word/The Balkan War-Crimes Report; If There Ever Were a Nuremburg for the Former Yugoslavia', *New York Times*, 12 June 1994.
20. Mark Devenport, 'Kofi Annan's Delicate Balance', *BBC News*, 13 April 1999.
21. Andre Gunder Frank, 'On Kofi Annan and the Peace Prize', 13 October 2001, www.rrojasdatabank.info/agfrank/annan_prize.html.
22. 'The Nobel Peace Prize 2001: Presentation Speech'.
23. See Gharekhan, *The Horseshoe Table*.

or delayed immediate action in Rwanda, and prevented discussions in the UN Security Council. Annan complained about the visceral anger that African leaders felt regarding what they described as 'abandoning responsibility for the Rwandan genocide'.[24] Whether responsibility rested with the Americans, with the P5, with Boutros-Ghali or with Annan as head of the UN peacekeeping department would be hotly debated over the coming years.[25] Annan felt an obligation to put things right, and he was aggressive in supporting the *Responsibility to Protect* report, issued in 2001. That report presented the arguments and stated the emergent agreement that neither humanitarian intervention nor the protection of human rights should ever again be held hostage by state sovereignty or the absence of 'international will' and 'civic courage', as had been the case in Rwanda in 1994.[26]

Annan was delighted with his role in the successful negotiation of the 1998 Rome Statute, which, when signed into force in 2002, laid the basis for the creation of the International Criminal Court (ICC). The Nobel Peace Committee applauded Annan for the creation of the human rights tribunals for Rwanda and Yugoslavia, as well as for the ICC initiative, which was ratified despite the opposition of the United States, Israel and Sudan.[27] Annan applied consistent pressure and provided constant support for these institutions to deal with war crimes and crimes against humanity. He was putting in place a means of enforcement for the idea that 'sovereign power is responsible for the welfare of its citizens',[28] and that when this failed, ordinary citizens and the global community, through the UN, should hold that sovereign power to account.

The Nobel Peace Committee recognised that in the post–Cold War era, American insistence on unilateral approaches to conflicts and to

24. Author interview with Kofi Annan, Villa Rigot, Geneva, 25 April 2008.
25. Roméo Dellaire, *Shake Hands with the Devil: The Failure of Humanity in Rwanda* (London: Arrow, 2004).
26. International Commission on Intervention and State Sovereignty, *The Responsibility to Protect*, 2001, http://responsibilitytoprotect.org/ICISS%20Report.pdf.
27. John Bolton, *Surrender Is Not an Option: Defending America at the United Nations and Abroad* (New York: Simon & Schuster, 2007), pp. 85–7, 349.
28. Francis Deng, 'The Evolution of the Idea of "Sovereignty as Responsibility"', in Adekeye Adebajo (ed.), *From Global Apartheid to Global Village: Africa and the United Nations* (Scottsville: University of KwaZulu-Natal Press, 2009), pp. 191–213.

transnational terrorist networks frequently brought Washington into conflict with the UN, which instead promoted multilateral approaches. The committee commended Annan on his role in dealing with the repercussions of the Gulf War of 1991, the status of East Timor (which won its independence in 2002 after a UN-supervised referendum), the war in the Democratic Republic of the Congo since 1996, the continuing disputes in the Middle East, and the post-September 2001 role of the UN in fighting international terrorism.

Annan had an unshakable faith in the United Nations, and he was willing to go anywhere in search of dialogue, if that would enable the world body to bring about peace. The Americans were pleasantly surprised but not convinced by the memorandum of understanding that Annan secured with Iraqi autocrat Saddam Hussein, in February 1998, indicating agreement to International Atomic Energy Agency (IAEA) inspections.

Restoring Human Rights and Dignity in Post-Conflict Situations

Annan was often labelled a 'norm entrepreneur'[29] – a Secretary General who used the 'bully pulpit', offered him under Article 99 of the UN Charter, to create ways of empowering individuals to make claims for protection; who gave civil society a new language of human rights to use against intransigent states; and who sought to hold nations to higher standards of responsibility for the protection of their citizens.[30] He was impatient with theoretical 'intellectualism', and preferred instead to focus on how to draw out strategies to resolve problems that confronted him. However, Annan always had staff working with him who enquired more deeply into disciplinary, legalistic and economic traditions, and helped him to operationalise his goals. This creativity extended to the ties between peace and economics that were inherent in Annan's 1998

---

29. Ian Johnstone, 'The Secretary General as Norm Entrepreneur', in Chesterman, *Secretary or General?*, pp. 123–38.
30. United Nations, *We the Peoples: The Role of the UN in the 21st Century,* 3 April 2000, www. un.org/Pubs/whatsnew/e00136.htm.

Causes of Conflict report,[31] which laid the basis for his later work on post-conflict capacity-building. His yearly reports to the UN General Assembly laid out new concepts, and forged new links between UN agencies, requiring them to coordinate their activities more than ever before, in order to increase their effectiveness.

Annan strengthened the focus on socio-economic justice, poverty alleviation through the Millennium Development Goals, and protection of vulnerable women and children after conflicts.[32] Notably, in Sierra Leone and Liberia after the end of civil wars by 2002 and 2003 respectively, women's organisations acted as significant partners to the UN and bilateral donors in disarmament, demobilisation and re-education and training programmes for girl victims and child soldiers. The MDGs cemented Kofi Annan's identity as a central norm entrepreneur in global development thinking.[33]

Annan gave considerable encouragement to women's empowerment in the UN's activities, perhaps because of his consciousness of the important roles that women had played in resolving some of the conflicts in countries such as Liberia and Sierra Leone during the decade of the 1990s. The greater involvement of women non-governmental organisation (NGO) representatives in the workshops and deliberations of the UN after 1997 also increased support for women's empowerment in peace and conflict resolution processes. The identification of rape as an instrument of war, the emergence of greater respect for women's rights, and pressure for the prosecution of perpetrators of violence against women and girls were all manifestations of the work of the UN Development Fund for Women (UNIFEM, now UN Women), the UN World Conferences on Women, and the greater presence of women in UN activities, in African politics, and in peacekeeping and peace-building initiatives.[34] The number of women in senior UN positions,

31. Annan, *The Causes of Conflict*.
32. Kofi Annan, *In Larger Freedom: Toward Security, Development, and Human Rights for All*, September 2005, www.un.org/largerfreedom.
33. United Nations, *Road Map Toward the Implementation of the United Nations Millennium Declaration*, 6 September 2001, www.un.org/documents/ga/docs/56/a56326.pdf. See also United Nations, *Implementation of the United Nations Millennium Declaration*, 27 August 2004, www.un.org/millenniumgoals/sgreport2004.pdf?OpenElement.
34. UN Security Council Resolution 1325 of 2000 called for the equal involvement of women in

however, remained embarrassingly low during Annan's tenure, a trend that continues as of 2013.

Some of the problems of humanitarian intervention – 'donor fatigue', inadequate resources to sustain refugee populations, and tensions with communities near refugee camps – did not easily disappear. However, the new dialogues that Annan set in motion, between state and regional representatives, and between NGO administrators and personnel in refugee camps, produced some results. As Western generosity declined, UN agencies found strategies to encourage African states to integrate long-term refugees, pursue a 'go and see, come back and tell' strategy that encouraged refugees to return home, and assist the repatriation of refugees to their home countries. For example, the Lukole camps in north-western Tanzania, where refugees from Rwanda and Burundi had been located since 1971 and 1994 respectively, have been largely emptied as refugees returned home.[35]

In 2006, Annan's last year in office, two new and important institutions grew out of the UN's emphasis on human rights and peace and security under his tenure. The UN Peacebuilding Commission's work in Burundi, Sierra Leone and the Central African Republic, while initially celebrated, also triggered criticisms about use of resources, and lack of capacity-building for the African Union. The UN Human Rights Council was the logical evolution of the UN's declarations of protections for the individual as enshrined in the 1948 Universal Declaration of Human Rights, the 1966 International Covenant on Civil and Political Rights and the 1976 International Covenant on Economic, Social and Cultural Rights – collectively referred to as the 'International Bill of Human Rights'.[36]

---

security, peace and conflict resolution activities at the national as well as the global level. See also Gwendolyn Mikell, Jeanne Maddox Toungara and Vivian Lowery-Derryck, *The Empowerment of African Women: Strategies and Recommendations* (London: Department for International Development, 2008).

35. In 2007, in conducting research for the Kofi Annan Legacy for Africa project, I visited two of the Lukoli camps in Tanzania where these problems existed; this provided documentary proof of severe dietary inadequacies among camp inhabitants, though the Tanzanian government was working to resolve the refugee issues.

36. See, for example, Cameron Jacobs and Jody Kollapen, 'The UN Human Rights Council: New Wine in Old Bottles?' in Adebajo, *From Global Apartheid to Global Village*, p. 125.

Annan's Socio-Economic Development Efforts

Race was not discussed as an issue for Kofi Annan's Western supporters, although it was perceived as a triumph and a source of pride
for many ordinary Africans, African Americans and blacks around
the world. Initially, among the political and economic elites in Africa,
Annan faced unfavourable comparisons to the intellectually accomplished and assertive Boutros-Ghali. Perhaps because of Rwanda, and
because of his time spent in Europe, initially many African leaders
perceived Annan as less committed to resolving African conflicts than
Boutros-Ghali,[37] and he was regarded by some as more loyal to the
West than to Africa. Some African heads of state were known to scoff
that since Annan had never been a president or a minister on his own
continent, nor held any elected position there, he had no authority
to claim knowledge of how to govern an African state.[38] However,
these critics underestimated Annan. His family background of chiefly
responsibilities in Ghana and his familiarity with the requirements of
leadership gave him a quiet assurance. Annan had been disillusioned
with African governance as a result of his two-year experience in Ghana
between 1974 and 1976 during the military rule of Colonel Ignatius
Acheampong; his concerns about peace, conflict resolution and 'good
governance' probably stemmed from this period.

During Annan's first term (1997–2001), as the Organisation of
African Unity was transforming into the African Union (inaugurated
in 2002), he was presented with a unique opportunity to forge a new
relationship with African leaders. Annan went to several of the African
Union summits, where he spoke in exceptionally blunt language to
African leaders about democracy and the rule of law, as well as about
transparency and 'good governance'. He strengthened the role of the
UN Economic Commission for Africa (UNECA) by empowering its
executive secretary and his compatriot K.Y. Amoako, who had been
inherited from Boutros-Ghali's administration. Amoako had Annan's

---

37. Adekeye Adebajo, 'The Role of the Secretary-General', in Adebajo, *From Global Apartheid
to Global Village*, pp. 87–106.
38. Author interview with Gambari, New York, 18 December 2007.

support to forge new economic relationships between Africa and the West.

Convinced that the time was ripe to pursue socio-economic justice through capacity-building in economic governance, Annan encouraged Amoako to provide leadership in this important area. In the 'big-table talks' in Europe, Amoako and African and Western finance ministers exchanged ideas about finance and development, and on how to monitor and use public resources for the greater good of Africa's 800 million citizens.[39] There are disagreements about whether Amoako and his colleagues from the UN and Bretton Woods institutions (the World Bank and the IMF) originated the strategies of the New Partnership for Africa's Development (NEPAD) in 2001, or whether the competing South African and Senegalese strategies were the founding force for the initiative. Amoako often ran into difficulties in his UNECA office in Addis Ababa, where his political influence in Africa was dwarfed by that of the African Union, and where Kofi Annan could do little to reinforce his authority.

Yet no one doubted Annan's support for transparency, efficiency and accountability in African state processes to promote economic development. Mark Malloch-Brown, administrator of the UN Development Programme (UNDP) and later Deputy UN Secretary General under Annan between April and December 2006, remarked that 'the most striking achievement of Kofi Annan even beyond his peacekeeping in Africa was to completely reverse both the direction and trend in aid to Africa but also the UN's capacity for being a major part of that.'[40]

The Aftermath of the Nobel Peace Prize

For Kofi Annan, the period after winning the Nobel Peace Prize in 2001 was much more difficult than the pre-Nobel period, because of the shift in perceptions of national interests among the P5 members after 11 September 2001. Although the political honeymoon was effectively over,

39. Author interview with K.Y. Amoako, Alexandria, Virginia, 8 February 2007.
40. Author interview with Mark Malloch-Brown, House of Lords, London, 22 February 2008.

Annan accomplished much between 2001 and 2006: decisive support for the Millennium Development Goals; work towards the creation of the Global Fund for HIV/AIDS, malaria, tuberculosis and other diseases through public–private partnerships outside of UN structures; and the continued promotion of women's rights and equality, especially through Security Council Resolution 1325 of 2000 on the post-conflict needs of women and girls.

Annan faced continuous pressure from the Americans, who wanted to know whether he 'was with them in fighting terrorism'. The George W. Bush White House was angered by the extensive conversations between US secretary of state Colin Powell and Annan over nuclear weapons materials in Iraq, because they felt that Annan was second-guessing American national interests. They were also angered by Annan's insistence on multilateralism, given the 2002 Bush doctrine of 'pre-emptive diplomacy'.

In September 2009, in response to a question about the most difficult decision he had had to make while serving as UN Secretary General, Kofi Annan responded:

> I think perhaps one of the most difficult issues that the UN dealt with when I was SG [Secretary General] was the discussions and decision regarding the Iraq War, what the organisation's decision should be, and how I as SG should act. I had no doubt that going to war was wrong ... and I made it clear to the leaders I was in touch with and also publicly made a statement. But the member states were divided, and when the member states are divided, including on the Security Council, the SG has a special role. He has to try to manage and steer things in a way that does not lead to a serious and permanent rupture within the Security Council.[41]

It is instructive to assess Annan's African support during this difficult post-Nobel Prize period. It is difficult to say whether the American invasion of Iraq in 2003 without a UN Security Council mandate, and the crisis that followed, transformed how African officials viewed Annan. But it is clear that African leaders had greater sympathy for

---

41. 'Kofi Annan on His Most Difficult Moment as Secretary General', speech at Saint Xavier University, 21 September 2009, www.youtube.com/watch?v=6kgVdkyueXs.

the Ghanaian after the Iraq War and the bombing of the UN building in Baghdad in August 2003. They admired the way he opposed
heavy-handed American unilaterialism, especially US efforts to gain
UN Security Council support for what most considered an illegitimate
war in Iraq. They also knew that Annan felt personal responsibility
for the death of the Brazilian UN special representative in Iraq, Sergio
Vieira de Mello,[42] a close friend of Annan. De Mello had gone to Iraq
at the request of Washington and Annan, so it was an emotional blow
to him to see de Mello die in the bombing in Baghdad.

Staff within the UN Secretariat could see that this challenge to its
mission and relevance shook Annan to the core, leaving him depressed
and disoriented for several months.[43] However, times were changing. More Africans understood the limitations on the role of the UN
Secretary General, and many praised the inauguration of the Kofi
Annan Peacekeeping Centre in Accra in 2004.[44] They were proud of
this Ghanaian whose activism was transforming the quality of life in
many places on the continent.

After 2004, Annan faced heightened American criticisms and a
relentless Republican Party campaign to destroy him politically with
charges of corruption over the Iraq oil-for-food programme, and inadequate reform of the UN. Between 2003 and 2004, Annan was likely
grieving over the loss of colleagues and the damage done to the UN's
credibility. However, he mobilized the P5 to take on the massacres in
Sudan's Darfur region of an estimated 200,000 people by 2003, and
helped lay the basis for the peacekeeping force that became the United
Nations–African Union Hybrid Mission in Darfur (UNAMID) in 2007.

Some of Annan's most irritating challenges came from John Bolton,
the abrasive neoconservative who held a recess appointment as US
permanent representative to the UN from August 2005 to December
2006. Bolton took a special joy in trying to harass or intimidate senior

---

42. See, for example, Samantha Power, *Chasing the Flame: Sergio Vieira de Mello and the Fight
to Save the World* (New York: Penguin, 2008).
43. Author interview with Gillian Sorenson, UN Foundation, New York City, 23 May 2008.
44. 'Secretary General Praises Ghana's "Steadfast", 40-Year Commitment to UN Peacekeeping, in Message to Inauguration of the Kofi Annan Peacekeeping Centre in Accra', UN Information
Centre, 27 January 2004.

African-American officials, such as the US secretary of state Colin Powell and the former US permanent representative to the UN Edward J. Perkins. He came to the UN with a mission of advancing the 'revolution of reform'[45] advocated in US secretary of state Condoleezza Rice's 2005 address to the UN General Assembly. Bolton subjected every major UN process, conversation and document to incessant scrutiny and criticism. The African Group at the UN noted that he had already been a severe critic of the UN before he became America's permanent representative, and he was now a strong critic of Annan's focus on African conflict situations. Bolton was anxious to see the UN's focus shift away from Africa, and wondered aloud and in his 2007 book about whether Annan's departure could accomplish this.[46] Some speculated that Bolton's appointment was designed to punish Annan, and perhaps to pressure him to resign.

However, Annan did not resign as UN Secretary General, and strategic support was offered to him by many, including UNDP administrator Malloch-Brown. Important political support was also offered by the former British minister for international development Clare Short, who went public with charges that Annan was being spied on in the run-up to the Iraq War, and waged a media battle on his behalf.[47] Short had worked closely with Kofi Annan and K.Y. Amoako on development issues. In a 2008 interview, she characterised the impact of these assaults on Annan and the UN as having left both diminished. She felt that Annan had made Africa proud in a way second only to South Africa's Nelson Mandela.

Winning the Nobel Peace Prize in 2001 helped to restore Annan's credibility with Africans, which had been badly damaged over the Rwandan crisis of 1994 and the denial of a second term to Boutros-Ghali in 1996. Much had changed since January 1997: the creation of the African Union and NEPAD in 2002; new standards for transparency in budgeting and finance within African governments; the creation

45. Bolton, *Surrender Is Not an Option*, p. 222.
46. Ibid., p. 343.
47. 'UK Spied on UN's Kofi Annan', *BBC News*, 26 February 2004.

of the Pan-African Parliament in 2004; new approaches to dealing with civil society and NGOs;[48] as well as support by key African leaders and Western governments for the 2003 African Peer Review Mechanism for promoting 'good governance' and accountability.[49] Despite isolated criticisms, African leaders gained greater appreciation of Annan's independence by watching how he handled the lead-up to the Iraq War. While they felt that the war had made it more difficult for Annan to carry out an African agenda, their solidarity with him strengthened.

Concluding Reflections

Annan took as role models a number of previous Nobel Peace Prize laureates of African descent. He greatly admired Nelson Mandela and interacted closely with five of the African and African-American Nobel peace laureates over the course of his long career at the UN: the three South Africans – Desmond Tutu, Nelson Mandela and Frederik Willem de Klerk – because of his work on Southern Africa at the UN (see Isaacson, Chapter 7; Boehmer, Chapter 8; and Houston, Chapter 9, in this volume); Kenya's Wangari Maathai, due to her environmental and human rights work during his tenure as Secretary General (see Golding, Chapter 12 in this volume); and Egypt's Mohamed ElBaradei, whose work with the IAEA from 1997 to 2006 Annan respected, and with whom Annan closely collaborated (see Abou-Sabé, Chapter 11 in this volume).

We can draw four important lessons from Kofi Annan's experience as UN Secretary General. First is the importance of being earnest – of having a vision of how the Secretary General can lead a significant global institution like the United Nations. That vision was manifest in the numerous initiatives that Annan put forward over his decade in office, and it was what motivated diplomats and NGO staff around

48. *The United Nations and Civil Society: The Role of NGOs,* proceedings of the thirtieth United Nations Issues Conference (New York: Stanley Foundation, 1999).

49. Adebayo Adedeji, 'NEPAD's African Peer Review Mechanism: Progress and Prospects', in John Akokpari, Angela Ndinga-Muvumba and Tim Murithi (eds), *The African Union and Its Institutions* (Johannesburg: Jacana, 2008), pp. 241–69.

the world to come to his assistance. If the UN and its agencies are to play a central role in global governance, they will need to become focal points for those with imagination, vision and determination.

Second is the struggle between multilateralism – which is at the core of the UN's mission – and unilateralism, which is an ongoing tendency among some of its powerful members. Kofi Annan tried to stress the importance of multilateralism, often with great difficulty, especially as global terrorism and 'pre-emptive strikes' dominated the thinking of the United States and other major powers. It is essential to put the emphasis back on multilateralism, and to guarantee that justice is seen to be done by all UN member states.

Third is the continuation of racism, which still manifests itself within the dynamics of the UN. Frequently, this phenomenon is visible in Western sensitivity and resentment when non-white but powerful representatives are determined to engage each other in dialogue to find justice outcomes, rather than to use the power politics of their national status. This can also take a religious form, with tensions often surfacing when Western Christian representatives appear to go out of their way to examine justice concerns voiced by people of the Islamic faith. Yet the UN will only be strengthened by ideas from peoples of all backgrounds, and by genuinely integrating people from all parts of the world into international society.

The final lesson is the difficulty of securing commitments of financial and other resources that are necessary to make peacekeeping missions in Africa successful. In addition to 'donor fatigue', Annan found that there was resistance to investing more resources in areas of 'darker' populations, and greater willingness to invest them in parts of the Western world.

Annan's experience shows us the value of remaining committed to our vision of how to make a unique contribution to humanity. But we have only just begun to examine the fullness of his experience, and to extract lessons from it. In an interview I conducted with Kofi Annan in Geneva in 2008, after the success of his negotiations in Kenya, he spoke eloquently and passionately about his UN career:

I was pleased that by the time I had left the UN, I had got the member states to the summit of 2005 to accept that you need to build the UN and societies on three pillars: peace and security, economic and social development, and respect for human rights and the rule of law.... that you cannot have security without development and you cannot have development without security, and unless these two are rooted in the rule of law and human rights, the situation cannot be sustained and the state cannot expect to be stable and prosperous in the longer term. So that brought all the things I was trying to do together.[50]

The publication of Kofi Annan's memoir *Interventions: A Life in War and Peace* in 2012 provides another source of verification of his commitment to the United Nations as an institution, with his frank criticisms of its actions offered in the hope of sustaining UN legitimacy. Equally important is that the memoir provides Annan's own admission that 'working for the UN was the best way to serve my country and my continent', and that doing so gave him a unique position from which to help advance African leadership and peacemaking.[51] On the book jacket, Indian Nobel economics laureate Amartya Sen describes Annan as 'a great global leader of our time', and as 'such a force for good in the troubled world in which we live'. Nobel peace laureate Kofi Annan acted for ten years as a soft-spoken prophet of African peacemaking, socio-economic justice, and efforts to achieve global norms of governance.

Bibliography

Adedeji, Adebayo, 'NEPAD's African Peer Review Mechanism: Progress and Prospects', in John Akokpari, Angela Ndinga-Muvumba and Tim Murithi (eds), *The African Union and Its Institutions* (Johannesburg: Jacana, 2008), pp. 241–69.

Adebajo, Adekeye, 'The Role of the Secretary-General', in Adekeye Adebajo (ed.), *From Global Apartheid to Global Village: Africa and the United Nations* (Scottsville: University of KwaZulu-Natal Press, 2009), pp. 87–106.

Adebajo, Adekeye, *The Curse of Berlin: Africa After the Cold War* (London: Hurst, 2010).

Albright, Madeleine, *Madame Secretary: A Memoir* (New York: Miramax, 2003).

Annan, Kofi, *The Causes of Conflict and the Promotion of Durable Peace and Sustainable Development in Africa*, Report of UN Secretary General, 16 April 1998, www.un.org/ecosocdev/geninfo/afrec/sgreport/index.html.

Annan, Kofi, *In Larger Freedom: Toward Security, Development, and Human Rights for All*, September 2005, www.un.org/largerfreedom.

---

50. Author interview with Annan.
51. See Annan, *Interventions*, pp. 27, 167–213.

Annan, Kofi, *Interventions: A Life in War and Peace* (New York: Penguin, 2012).
Ask, Sten, and Anna Mark-Jungkvist (eds), *The Adventure of Peace: Dag Hammarskjöld and the Future of the UN* (New York: Palgrave Macmillan, 2005).
Bolton, John, *Surrender Is Not an Option: Defending America at the United Nations and Abroad* (New York: Simon & Schuster, 2007).
Boutros-Ghali, Boutros, *Unvanquished: A U.S.–U.N. Saga* (New York: Random House, 1999).
Chesterman, Simon (ed.), *Secretary or General? The UN Secretary General in World Politics* (Cambridge: Cambridge University Press, 2007).
Dellaire, Roméo, *Shake Hands with the Devil: The Failure of Humanity in Rwanda* (London: Arrow, 2004).
Deng, Francis, 'The Evolution of the Idea of "Sovereignty as Responsibility"', in Adekeye Adebajo (ed.), *From Global Apartheid to Global Village: Africa and the United Nations* (Scottsville: University of KwaZulu-Natal Press, 2009), pp. 191–213.
Frederking, Brian, *The U.S. and the Security Council: Collective Security Since the Cold War* (New York: Routledge, 2007).
Gharekhan, Chinmaya R., *The Horseshoe Table: An Inside View of the UN Security Council* (New Delhi: Longman, 2006).
Gunder Frank, Andre, 'On Kofi Annan and the Peace Prize', 13 October 2001, www.rrojasdatabank.info/agfrank/annan_prize.html.
International Commission on Intervention and State Sovereignty, *The Responsibility to Protect*, 2001, http://responsibilitytoprotect.org/ICISS%20Report.pdf.
Jacobs, Cameron, and Jody Kollapen, 'The UN Human Rights Council: New Wine in Old Bottles?' in Adebajo, *From Global Apartheid to Global Village*.
Johnstone, Ian, 'The Secretary General as Norm Entrepreneur', in Simon Chesterman (ed.), *Secretary or General? The UN Secretary General in World Politics* (Cambridge: Cambridge University Press, 2007), pp. 123–38.
Lewis, Paul, 'Word for Word/The Balkan War-Crimes Report; If There Ever Were a Nuremburg for the Former Yugoslavia', *New York Times*, 12 June 1994.
Meisler, Stanley, *Kofi Annan: A Man of Peace in a World of War* (Hoboken NJ: Wiley, 2007).
Mikell, Gwendolyn, Jeanne Maddox Toungara and Vivian Lowery-Derryck, *The Empowerment of African Women: Strategies and Recommendations* (London: Department for International Development, 2008).
Nobel Prize, 'Award Ceremony Speech', presented by Gunnar Berge, chairman of the Nobel Peace Committee, Oslo, 10 December 2001.
Nobel Prize, 'The Nobel Peace Prize 2001: Presentation Speech', www.nobelprize.org/nobel_prizes/peace/laureates/2001/presentation-speech.html.
Power, Samantha, *Chasing the Flame: Sergio Vieira de Mello and the Fight to Save the World* (New York: Penguin, 2008).
Traub, James, *The Best Intentions: Kofi Annan and the UN in the Era of American World Power* (New York: Farrar, Straus & Giroux, 2006).
United Nations, *The United Nations and Civil Society: The Role of NGOs*, proceedings of the thirtieth United Nations Issues Conference (New York: Stanley Foundation, 1999).
United Nations, *We the Peoples: The Role of the UN in the 21st Century*, 3 April 2000, www.un.org/Pubs/whatsnew/e00136.htm.
United Nations, *Road Map Toward the Implementation of the United Nations Millennium Declaration*, 6 September 2001, www.un.org/documents/ga/docs/56/a56326.pdf.
United Nations, 'Secretary General Praises Ghana's "Steadfast", 40-Year Commitment to UN Peacekeeping, in Message to Inauguration of the Kofi Annan Peacekeeping Centre in Accra', UN Information Centre, 27 January 2004.
United Nations, *Implementation of the United Nations Millennium Declaration*, 27 August 2004, www.un.org/millenniumgoals/sgreport2004.pdf?OpenElement.
Urquhart, Brian, *A Life in War and Peace* (New York: Harper & Row, 1987).
Urquhart, Brian, *Decolonization and World Peace* (Austin: University of Texas Press, 1988).

PART SIX

THE TWO LIBERIANS

FOURTEEN

ELLEN JOHNSON SIRLEAF:
THE IRON LADY

ADEKEYE ADEBAJO

Two Liberian women won the Nobel Peace Prize in 2011: President Ellen Johnson Sirleaf and civil society's Leymah Gbowee (Yemeni activist Tawakul Karman also shared the award). Sirleaf's winning of the prize for championing women's rights was announced in October 2011. The granting of the award four days before a presidential election was, however, one of the most controversial acts in the history of the prize. One could scarcely imagine the prize being awarded to a sitting American or European leader less than a week before such an important election. The prize also exposed the huge gulf between international perceptions of Liberia's 'Iron Lady' and the more critical view that many Liberians and West Africans had of her based on her past political record and six years in power.[1]

Sirleaf's main opponent in the presidential election, Winston Tubman, argued that she did not deserve the Nobel Peace Prize, describing her as a 'warmonger'. In the first round of polling during the October 2011 election, the Liberian president won 43.9 per cent of the vote compared to Tubman's 32.7 per cent. A run-off was therefore required a month later. In a reckless act of political immaturity, Tubman

1. The author would like to thank Kaye Whiteman, Ken Barlow and Bahru Zewde for insightful comments on an earlier version of this essay.

claimed – without producing much credible evidence – that the first round of voting had been rigged in favour of Sirleaf, and called on his supporters to boycott the second round. Violence erupted in Monrovia, resulting in two deaths and accusations of curbs on media freedom. Sirleaf was thus the sole candidate in the second round, and won the election unopposed. The 38 per cent turnout in the second round was in stark contrast to the first round's 72 per cent, meaning that the president's legitimacy was likely to remain a perennial source of questioning in a second six-year term. The fact that Sirleaf's Unity Party still lacked a majority of seats in the House and the Senate after legislative elections was also likely to further weaken her ability to rule effectively. Liberia's 4 million citizens pondered the aftermath of this difficult election.

The life and times of Ellen Johnson Sirleaf, who became Africa's first elected female head of state in November 2005, seem a particularly appropriate subject of study. One of Africa's most accomplished technocrats, Sirleaf has been able to attract foreign investment to her beleaguered country and annul its external debt. In July 2008, she was invited to deliver the sixth Nelson Mandela lecture in Johannesburg, where she eulogised her fellow Nobel peace laureate and praised Mandela's successor, Thabo Mbeki, for his vision of an 'African Renaissance'.[2]

This essay begins by assessing Ellen Johnson Sirleaf's formative experiences and her resulting career as an international and domestic economic technocrat. It next examines her controversial support for Charles Taylor's war efforts at the start of Liberia's civil conflict in 1990, as well as her 'fatal attraction' to the United States. The chapter then turns to an analysis of Sirleaf's often imperious presidency, and briefly examines her Nobel Peace Prize speech in December 2011, before concluding with an assessment of her post-Nobel presidency.

---

2. Ellen Johnson Sirleaf, 'Behold the New Africa', speech at the Sixth Nelson Mandela Annual Lecture, Johannesburg, 12 July 2008.

Formative Experiences[3]

Ellen Johnson Sirleaf was born in Monrovia on 29 October 1938. The title of her 2009 autobiography – *This Child Will Be Great* – is taken from an old man's (a family friend) prophecy: modesty is certainly not one of Sirleaf's qualities. Recounting her childhood, Sirleaf writes of her Gola father, who was raised in an America-Liberian household, ended up as a legislator, but then suffered the tragedy of being crippled and unable to walk. Sirleaf's mother, whose father was a German trader who abandoned his family, was also raised in an America-Liberian family. Sirleaf refers incessantly in her autobiography to individuals from 'settler' families, contrasting these with what she describes as a 'largely docile, uneducated population of young natives' who would later become 'radicalized'. The America-Liberians were a group of freed American slaves who founded the republic of Liberia in 1847 and systematically oppressed and marginalised the indigenous population, while mimicking the culture of their homeland. This corrupt oligarchy ruled Liberia for 133 years until power was seized from them in 1980 in a bloody *coup d'état* led by a semi-literate master-sergeant, Samuel Doe.[4]

Sirleaf attended elite schools. She was a tomboy who enjoyed sports. Her fellow pupils teased her mercilessly, calling her 'Red Pumpkin' due to the light colour of her skin. This led to a defensiveness about her identity, which is evident throughout her 2009 memoir. At the young age of 17 she married James Sirleaf, whose mother was from a prominent America-Liberian family. She had four sons with him. Ellen Johnson Sirleaf studied economics and accounting at the College of West Africa in Monrovia between 1948 and 1955, before working as a bookkeeping assistant to an accountant. She accompanied her husband to study abroad in the United States in 1961, taking advantage of the opportunity to study at Madison Business College. Sirleaf writes of her guilt at having left her sons with family members as she travelled the world;

---

3. The information in this section is largely from Ellen Johnson Sirleaf, *This Child Will Be Great: Memoirs of a Remarkable Life by Africa's First Woman President* (New York: HarperCollins, 2009).

4. See, for example, Gus Liebenow, *The Evolution of Privilege* (Ithaca NY: Cornell University Press, 1969); Amos Sawyer, *The Emergence of Autocracy in Liberia: Tragedy and Challenge* (San Francisco: ICS, 1992).

however, her relationship with her children, despite the lingering strain
on this bond, receives notably little attention in her autobiography,
with some reviewers complaining about a lack of emotional as opposed
to historical content.[5] Sirleaf had a close relationship with her devout
Christian mother and writes touchingly about her. She, however, makes
the rather odd comment in her autobiography that her mother 'was
very fair and did not much look like an African': a narrow definition
of Africanness that again suggests serious identity issues.

Sirleaf left her husband when he became increasingly abusive. The
unflattering picture she paints of him in her autobiography is of a
philandering, jealous, ill-tempered alcoholic. She admits to having had
an affair with an unnamed 'good friend' that lasted until his death, but
she never remarried. Sirleaf joined Liberia's finance ministry, where she
enjoyed a meteoric rise, particularly after obtaining a Master's degree in
public administration from Harvard University in 1971. During her two
years in Massachusetts she learned a great deal about her country while
devouring the vast literature in the institution's well-stocked libraries.
Despite being a civil servant, Sirleaf famously criticised government
corruption at a conference on Liberia in the USA in 1969, though
she lazily describes the twenty-seven-year autocratic rule of William
Tubman (1944–71) in oxymoronic terms as a 'benevolent dictatorship'.
She was deputy minister of finance between 1972 and 1973 under the
successor regime of William Tolbert. Sirleaf used a graduation speech
in 1972 to criticise the Americo-Liberian settler class – of which she
was a de facto member – for its political and cultural hegemony over
indigenous Liberians, warning of increasing socio-political tensions.
This lack of judgement was repeated several times in Sirleaf's career.
It might have been more sensible either to have made private criticisms
to push for reform from inside the system, or to have resigned from
the government and go public. Her attempts to identify with rural
women – based seemingly on sporadic visits to her parents' ancestral
village as a child – are not wholly convincing.

---

5. See, for example, Erin Aubry Kaplan, 'Iron Lady', *Ms.*, May 2009.

The International and Domestic Technocrat[6]

Increasingly sidelined in the William Tolbert administration, Sirleaf joined the World Bank in 1973, travelling to East Africa as well as to Latin America and the Caribbean, and thus greatly expanding her horizons. She showed a consistently impressive determination to succeed, to master her brief and improve herself; her capacity for hard work was beyond doubt. Though in her autobiography she criticised the arrogance of World Bank officials in dealing with leaders of developing countries, she showed less courage in speaking out against the patronising of the Third World in this international setting than she had in her own domestic environment. Sirleaf returned home to the finance ministry in 1975. In another astonishing lack of judgement, she stamped 'BULLSHIT' on the query of a British contractor to the ministry, acccording to a story that appeared in the *Financial Times*, embarrassing the government.

Sirleaf was made finance minister in August 1979, eight months before the Doe coup. Inexplicably, she agreed to work – as president of the Liberian Bank for Development and Investment – for a military regime that had killed thirteen senior officials (including six of her former cabinet colleagues) as well as the president she had served. She curiously described her relationship with Doe as at first 'complex but workable' before souring.[7] Sirleaf again criticised the regime she served, this time during a lecture in the USA in November 1980, before returning to the World Bank. In a telling exchange during a meeting, she sided with the World Bank president Robert McNamara after criticisms by renowned Kenyan academic Ali Mazrui that the American was portraying himself as Africa's saviour.

Sirleaf became the first African female vice president of Citibank in 1981, based in Kenya but travelling across Africa. She clearly revelled in the 'good life', living in a 'big home' in Nairobi's 'Beverly Hills' with

6. The information in this section is largely derived from Sirleaf, *This Child Will Be Grea*

7. On the Doe regime, see, for example, Gus Liebenow, *Liberia: The Quest for Democracy* (Bloomington: Indiana University Press, 1987); Amos Sawyer, *Effective Immediately: Dictatorship in Liberia, 1980–1986 – A Personal Perspective* (Bremen: Liberia Working Group, 1987).

a 'chauffeured car [and] domestic servants'.[8] She employs the royal 'we' throughout her autobiography to describe herself. During visits to Liberia, Sirleaf continued to pay 'courtesy calls' on the autocratic Samuel Doe, whom she says 'had a lot of affection for me and even trusted me'. In another loss of judgement, Sirleaf joined a political party while working at Citibank, though she later acknowledged that she should have resigned first. When she was trying to win a party nomination for presidential elections in Liberia in 1997, she repeated this mistake: she had to be pushed by her employer to resign as head of the United Nations Development Programme's (UNDP) Regional Bureau for Africa after reports emerged in the media that she was running for office.

In another critical speech in the USA in 1984, Sirleaf referred to the Doe regime as 'idiots' (a term she never used to describe the country's Americo-Liberian rulers). Predictably, this landed her in detention on her return to Liberia, as an insecure Doe became increasingly paranoid. She was sentenced to ten years' hard labour. Following international pressure, she was released. She won a seat in the Liberian Senate in 1985 (having resigned from Citibank the same year), which she refused to take up in protest at the fraudulent American-backed election that had led to Doe staying in power. Following a failed coup attempt in the same year, Sirleaf was jailed again. Her unwavering faith and indomitable courage, which earned her the nickname 'Iron Lady of Liberia', were clearly evident during these trials and tribulations. After she was released from prison, she resumed giving advice to Doe, submitting a policy memo to him. After her passport was seized, she escaped abroad. She worked for Equator Bank in the USA, travelling often to Asia. In 1992, Sirleaf became director of the UN Development Programme's Regional Bureau for Africa. In 1997 she resigned the post to run for president of Liberia.

8. See Sirleaf, *This Child Will Be Great*.

Supporting Charles Taylor and Uncle Sam[9]

In the biggest misjudgement of her career (one that clearly still haunts her), Sirleaf helped raise $10,000 to support Charles Taylor's National Patriotic Front of Liberia (NPFL) rebel movement, which had launched a military incursion to oust Doe in December 1989 (Taylor later claimed that Sirleaf had been the international coordinator of his movement between 1986 and 1994).[10] She then went to visit the warlord in his bush hideout in 1990. As a civil war was destroying Liberia at huge human cost (an estimated 250,000 people were killed by 1997), Sirleaf flippantly told a BBC reporter that if Taylor destroyed Monrovia, it would be rebuilt and champagne would be drunk. She later described these words as one of the most 'stupid' public statements she ever made.

Sirleaf criticised historical American economic exploitation of Liberia, but yet was widely perceived, during her presidency, as seeking to remain close to Washington. Even her 2009 autobiography often seems to be aimed, in terms of its language and subject matter, at an American audience. Sirleaf has frequently reflected the naive view of the Liberian settler elite that the USA is 'our great father, our patron saint. It will never let us suffer.' After the outbreak of the Liberian civil war (1989–1997), she had called for American intervention, which never arrived, and criticised the Economic Community of West African States [ECOWAS] Ceasefire Monitoring Group (ECOMOG), arguing – without any evidence and contrary to all military logic – that the force could have ended the fighting in Liberia much earlier. Her portrayal of ECOMOG is rather unflattering considering the incredible sacrifices involved – over 500 fatalities – during seven years of lonely peacekeeping that saved many Liberian lives.[11] Peacekeepers from two leading ECOWAS states, Nigeria and Ghana, would ironically later form the

---

9. The information in this section is largely derived from Sirleaf, *This Child Will Be Great*.
10. See also Economist Intelligence Unit, 'Country Report: Liberia', September 2009, p. 13.
11. For accounts of Liberia's civil war, see Adekeye Adebajo, *Liberia's Civil War: Nigeria, ECOMOG, and Regional Security in West Africa* (Boulder CO: Lynne Rienner, 2002); Alhaji M. S. Bah and Festus Aboagye (eds), *A Tortuous Road to Peace: The Dynamics of Regional, UN, and International Humanitarian Interventions in Liberia* (Tshwane: Institute for Security Studies, 2005); Karl Magyar and Earl Conteh-Morgan (eds), *Peacekeeping in Africa: ECOMOG in Liberia* (London: Macmillan, 1998).

backbone of a UN mission that protected Sirleaf's presidency for nearly a decade.[12]

Even after Liberia's civil war restarted in 1999, continuing until 2003, Sirleaf was still flying to Washington DC to lobby for a more activist role in resolving the conflict. As president, she was frank about having bowed to American pressure to push for Charles Taylor to be handed over from Nigerian exile in June 2006 to stand trial in The Hague for alleged war crimes committed in Sierra Leone. However, Sirleaf admitted that she would have preferred to focus on other pressing domestic priorities rather than disturbing her country's fragile peace by acceding to this request. As most African governments were vociferously opposing the presence of a US military Africa Command (AFRICOM) on their territory, Sirleaf again displayed her 'fatal attraction' to Uncle Sam. Exceptionally, she called for the command to be located in her country, seeing this as an 'opportunity to get what we can'.[13] Sirleaf, again opportunistically and short-sightedly, placed greater faith in Pax Americana – in the form of US arms – than in Liberian institutions.

The Imperious Presidency

While campaigning against Charles Taylor in the 1997 presidential election, Sirleaf was seen as elitist and out of touch with the concerns of ordinary Liberians. This election resulted in a crushing defeat: she won only 9.5 per cent of the vote, with Taylor triumphant in a landslide 75 per cent victory. Liberians overwhelming voted for peace, judging the former warlord's victory as their best guarantee of future stability. Sirleaf did not accept the defeat gracefully, telling former US president Jimmy Carter before the poll that the election would have to be rigged in order for Taylor to win. In a further sign of pettiness, Sirleaf refused to take Taylor's telephone call after his victory, and failed to attend his presidential inauguration.

---

12. See, for example, Adekeye Adebajo, *UN Peacekeeping in Africa: From the Suez Crisis to the Sudan Conflicts* (Boulder CO: Lynne Rienner, 2011), pp. 139–70.
13. Quoted in 'Graft Never Really Went Away', *Africa Confidential*, 3 October 2008, p. 10.

Charles Taylor's autocratic presidency lasted only until 2003, when he went into exile in Nigeria as rebels closed in on Monrovia. He was arrested in 2006 and taken to The Hague for trial by the Special Court for Sierra Leone. Taylor was sentenced to fifty years in jail in May 2012 for allegedly aiding and abetting murder, sexual abuse and exploiting child soldiers in Sierra Leone between 1996 and 2002. He was appealing the decision as of 2013.

Once Taylor had left Liberia, a period of transition ensued between 2003 and 2005. The fact that Sirleaf could muster only 20 per cent of the vote in the first round of presidential elections in October and November 2005 (coming in second to former football superstar George Weah, who won 28 per cent) suggested that Liberians were still unsure about her, although she went on to poll some 60 per cent of the vote in the second round. Sirleaf described her eventual victory as representing the 'rebirth of a nation', later noting that the country was lucky to have the opportunity to consolidate its democracy 'largely because of my own extensive contacts', and suggesting she had been born with leadership qualities.

The 2007 documentary *Iron Ladies of Liberia* charted the first year of Sirleaf's presidency, highlighting the role of some of the five female ministers — finance, commerce, justice, youth and sports, and gender – as well as that of a female police commissioner. The documentary starts with the president preparing for her inauguration in 2006 in traditional African dress and headgear (tied in an eccentric fashion) before making her speech. The action-oriented 'Iron Lady' is then shown attempting to get the wheels of government turning again: she goes to the passport office to harass an official for keeping money in the office rather than depositing it in a bank; she urges her finance minister to sack incompetent civil servants and to replace them with young university graduates; she marches with the police commissioner to clear a crowded market; she calls on the justice minister to release a demonstrator arrested for protesting without a permit; she expresses impatience to the country's international donors on the slow pace of delivery of funds; she hosts then-Chinese president Hu Jintao on a state visit to Monrovia; she meets with then-US president George W. Bush in the White House, where she pushes for debt cancellation; she promotes reconciliation with Liberia's political leaders; she browbeats managers at the Firestone rubber plantation to treat their workers more decently; and she courageously calms a street protest of ex-combatants seeking payment of their entitlements. All this sometimes resembles a system of one-woman rule in which the president tries to direct everything that happens in the country without proper delegation. She describes herself as the 'Mother of the Nation', but 'Ma Ellen' is sometimes too maternalistic in her approach, making her appear at times more like a hectoring headmistress than the president of a country.

The documentary shows Sirleaf able to connect well with ordinary people, speaking in the local vernacular. In contrast, she uses somewhat threatening language in a speech to Liberia's cantankerous legislators, suggesting that her opponents were continuing to 'plot' against her government, and not respecting the will of the people. One of Sirleaf's greatest fears, which comes across clearly in the documentary, is that unemployed youth will be recruited by warlords to restart the country's civil war. The spectre of Charles Taylor (on trial in The Hague at the time) casts a long shadow over Sirleaf's presidency. The documentary nevertheless also reveals some lighter moments: one shows the president exercising on a treadmill in the executive mansion, looking somewhat grandmotherly; in another she dances with a large crowd in a stadium after securing an annulment of the country's $391 million American debt. Sirleaf talks touchingly about the loneliness of power, wistfully expressing a desire to be able to do her own shopping, not take phone calls or receive visitors, and to curl up and read a book. The burden of power on her broad shoulders, as well as her intelligence, determination, energy and domineering ruthlessness, emerge clearly in this insightful documentary.

Many of Sirleaf's critics, however, are disparaging about her some-what messianic approach to leadership. In July 2009, Liberia's Truth and Reconciliation Commission (notwithstanding a vocal dissenting minority) recommended barring Sirleaf – along with forty-nine others

– from holding public office for thirty years due to her support for Charles Taylor at the start of the Liberian civil war. Although Liberia's Supreme Court subsequently declared this recommendation to be unconstitutional in January 2011, Sirleaf's allies sought to demonise and discredit the Commission, thereby threatening the country's fragile process of reconciliation.

Under Sirleaf's leadership, however, Liberia has made progress in its post-conflict reconstruction efforts. By 2010, the country's external debt of $5.8 billion had been largely written off thanks to her incredible energy and prodigious networking. Furthermore, an estimated $16 billion in direct foreign investment had also flowed in by this time, involving a sensible diversification of investors, with the Chinese a particularly significant new presence. Some infrastructure had been repaired. An inherited budget of $80 million had quadrupled. Some 500 'ghost workers' had been purged from ministerial payrolls by 2006, saving about $3 million a year.[14] The International Monetary Fund noted that all of the government's monetary and fiscal targets had been met by December 2010.

As noted earlier, one of Sirleaf's perennial fears has been that unem-ployed youth will be recruited by warlords to restart the country's civil war, which raged for eleven years until 2003 (1989–97, 1999–2003). The 8,000-strong UN Mission in Liberia (UNMIL) continued to guarantee security in the country amid continuing ethnic and religious tensions and a weak police force. But clearly the international presence would not remain indefinitely. Instability across the border in Côte d'Ivoire also continued to be a serious concern following post-election violence in Liberia's neighbouring country in 2011. Liberian mercenaries were involved in this conflict, which spilled 160,000 Ivorian refugees into Liberia. Guinea also remained politically unstable (with 3,000 refugees spilling into Liberia by 2011), even as Sierra Leone continued its fragile

---

14. Economist Intelligence Unit, 'Country Profile: Liberia', January–December 2007, p. 10. See also 'With a Little Help from Her Friends', *The Economist*, 21 August 2008 (www.economist.com).

recovery from a decade of civil war.[15] Liberia was thus located at the epicentre of a volatile Mano River basin.

The problems inherited by Sirleaf's administration clearly overwhelmed even her own incredible determination to succeed. Former combatants were not being provided with jobs quickly enough, leading to instability and crime. In a devastating blow, Sirleaf's American 'godfather' criticised her government's continued failure to tackle corruption in a 2010 US State Department report.[16] Even more detrimental to Sirleaf's declared 'zero-tolerance' approach to corruption, Berlin-based Transparency International, in its Global Corruption Barometre (which measures the general public's views about corruption and government efforts to tackle it), named Liberia the most corrupt country in the world in December 2010.[17] Sirleaf had to fire her information minister Lawrence Bropleh in 2008, as well as her internal affairs minister Ambulai Johnson in 2010, following reports of corruption. The fact that her brother was the internal affairs minister for four years before being dismissed for graft, and her son was a presidential adviser, also replicated the nepotism she had earlier criticised in the Tolbert administration.

With no legislative majority to work with, Sirleaf admitted that she could not afford to alienate this branch of government through an anti-corruption crusade if she wanted to pass crucial legislation. Damaging reports of the government bribing lawmakers have thus been persistent. The president's criticisms and firing of the combative auditor-general John Morlu (who completed forty audits and criticised the president for not taking action against corrupt officials fingered in these reports), by 2011, and the smear campaign run against him by Sirleaf's associates in the local media, again revealed a ruthlessness that contradicted her rhetorical attacks on the 'debilitating cancer of corruption'.[18] Leaked email revelations in 2007 that Sirleaf's former

---

15. United Nations, *Twenty Third Progress Report of the Secretary-General on the United Nations Mission in Liberia*, 5 August 2011, S/2011/497, p. 4.
16. Economist Intelligence Unit, 'Country Report: Liberia', June 2011, p. 15.
17. 'Hold Your Breath', *The Economist*, 10 September 2011 (www.economist.com).
18. See Economist Intelligence Unit, 'Country Report: Liberia', June 2011, p. 15.

public works minister Willis Knuckles had solicited kickbacks, to-gether with the implication of her brother-in-law, Estrada Bernard, in this scandal, caused further embarrassment, as Sirleaf herself publicly admitted.[19] The sacking of House Speaker Edwin Snowe – Taylor's son-in-law, who had been a thorn in the president's side – in 2007, following embezzlement charges, further revealed a selective tackling of corruption. Sirleaf dragged her feet before acting against her own associates, like Harry Greaves Jr, who was also accused of corruption.[20] She continued to defend her finance minister Augustine Ngafuan, and later appointed him foreign minister. Ngafuan had been criticised by the General Auditing Commission for the disappearance of $1 million from the 2007–08 budget.[21] Sirleaf would later admit that she had not realised how deep-rooted and pervasive corruption was in Liberian society,[22] suggesting a somewhat naive and out-of-touch president who had perhaps spent too much time in exile. The president did, however, take some steps to improve governance by dismissing Philip Banks, the justice minister, and Beatrice Munah Sieh, the inspector-general of the national police, by 2009.[23]

The Nobel Speech

In a brief respite from her domestic travails, Ellen Johnson Sirleaf travelled to Oslo in December 2011 to deliver her Nobel Peace Prize speech, titled 'A Voice for Freedom'. She began by noting that she was speaking 'on behalf of all the women of Liberia, the women of Africa, and women everywhere in the world who have struggled for peace, justice, and equality'. She honoured the memory of Wangari Maathai, the late Kenyan environmental activist and first African female Nobel peace laureate (see Golding, Chapter 12 in this volume.) She then praised her fellow Liberian peace laureate Leymah Gbowee,

---

19. 'Graft Never Really Went Away', pp. 10–11.
20. 'Rumours and Plots', *Africa Confidential*, 3 August 2007, p. 8.
21. 'Musical Chairs in Monrovia', *Africa Confidential*, 19 November 2010, p. 9.
22. 'Another Round for Africa's Iron Lady', *The Economist*, 20 May 2010 (www.economist.com).
23. Economist Intelligence Unit, 'Country Report: Liberia', September 2009, pp. 13–14.

who was also present in Oslo: 'Leymah, you are a peacemaker. You had the courage to mobilize the women of Liberia to take back their country.' Sirleaf went on to acknowledge the values that her parents and grandmothers had inculcated in her. She stressed the importance of access to quality education; condemned violence against women in civil wars, from the Democratic Republic of the Congo (DRC) to Liberia; criticised human trafficking as well as the under-reporting of crimes against women and lack of legal protection for victims; bemoaned the underfunding of education for girls; and urged women and men across the globe to fight violence and injustice, and to promote democracy, freedom and peace. Near the end of her speech, Sirleaf quoted fellow Nobel peace laureate Martin Luther King Jr, the martyred African-American civil rights leader: 'The arc of the moral universe is long but it bends toward justice' (see Robinson, Chapter 3, and Daniels, Chapter 5, in this volume). Though her speech was eloquent and well crafted, it disingenuously described the recent flawed presidential election in Liberia as having consolidated the country's transformation into a 'stable, democratic nation'.[24]

Concluding Reflections: The Post-Nobel Era

Following her controversial election victory in November 2011, Ellen Johnson Sirleaf faced a youth protest just before Christmas. She argued that her first presidential term had been about laying a solid foundation and that her second term would now be about 'delivery time'. In her inauguration speech in January 2012, Sirleaf identified four key challenges: youth unemployment, inadequate education, insecurity, and the need for national reconciliation. She also vigorously promoted 'Liberia Vision 2030', a long-term political and economic transformation agenda for the country. Sirleaf still lacked a parliamentary majority. The fact that former allies of Charles Taylor, such as Lewis G. Browne (Taylor's former foreign minister) and Blamo Nelson (Taylor's former cabinet

---

24. This paragraph is based on Ellen Johnson Sirleaf, 'A Voice for Freedom', Nobel lecture, Oslo, 10 December 2011 (www.nobelprize.org).

director), were brought into her government demonstrated the rank opportunism of Liberia's political class.

Sirleaf ruffled more feathers when she appointed three of her sons and her nephew to important government posts in February 2012. Robert Sirleaf was appointed chair of the National Oil Company of Liberia (Nocal); Charles Sirleaf became deputy governor of the Central Bank of Liberia (he was temporarily suspended by his mother for failing to declare his personal assets); Fumba Sirleaf retained his post as national security minister; while Sirleaf's nephew, Varney Sirleaf, was made deputy minister for administration in the powerful Ministry of Internal Affairs. Sirleaf's older sister, Jennie Bernard, and her disgraced husband, Estrada Bernard, were also part of an inner circle of advisers.[25] In response to widespread charges of nepotism, Sirleaf brazenly sought to defend the indefensible by arguing that she had appointed her three sons based on 'talent', 'competence' and 'integrity'.[26] The implication was that these traits were somehow genetically and strongly inherited in her family, but lacking in much of the rest of the Liberian population.

Sirleaf's fellow Nobel peace laureate Leymah Gbowee dropped a political bombshell in October 2012 when she resigned as head of Liberia's Peace and Reconciliation Commission, citing presidential nepotism and a widening socio-economic gap between rich and poor. Gbowee specifically called for Robert Sirleaf to step down as chair of Nocal. As she ruefully noted: 'I've been through a process of really thinking and reflecting and saying to myself "you're as bad as being an accomplice for things that are happening in the country if you don't speak up".' Gbowee went on to complain that 'development in a land of hungry, angry people is nothing'.[27] In typically brutal fashion, the thin-skinned government's attack-dogs accused Gbowee of having misused funds under her commission (see Daniel, Chapter 15 in this volume). Sirleaf herself – who had praised Gbowee's peacemaking

25. 'Keeping It in the Family', *Africa Confidential*, 13 April 2012, p. 4.
26. Cited in Mark Tran, 'Liberia's Johnson Sirleaf Defiant over Nepotism and Corruption Claims', *Guardian*, 1 November 2012 (www.theguardian.com).
27. 'Liberia Laureate Gbowee Chides Sirleaf on Corruption', *BBC News Africa*, 8 October 2012.

efforts in her Nobel speech just ten months earlier – now patronisingly dismissed her fellow Nobel laureate as being too young to know what Liberia had endured to achieve peace.[28] This despite Gbowee's efforts to mobilise Liberian women to bring peace to the country before 2003, while Sirleaf lived abroad in comfortable exile.

The West African subregion in which Liberia was attempting to consolidate its post-conflict gains remained unstable in 2013. Ivorian militias loyal to the deposed president Laurent Gbagbo had reportedly set up camps in Liberia's Grand Gedeh County,[29] even as more than 64,000 Ivorian refugees remained in Liberia in February 2013.[30] In response, Sirleaf launched Operation Restore Hope (the same name as the botched US intervention in Somalia in 1992–94), deploying troops to, and closing the border with, Côte d'Ivoire while sending Ivorian suspects home. The Liberian and Ivorian armies then agreed to conduct joint border patrols after a meeting between the presidents of the two countries in October 2012.

Sirleaf's government continued to rely heavily on the UN Mission in Liberia (which accounted for some 50 per cent of Liberia's imports) to provide security.[31] However, UNMIL was set to be reduced from nearly 7,000 peacekeepers in February 2013 to fewer than 4,000 by 2015. Despite the fact that 100,000 of Liberia's former combatants had been disarmed, there were continuing concerns that the lack of alternative livelihoods could result in a return to instability.[32] Soldiers frequently deserted due to poor accommodation, among other problems, and training and recruitment continued to be substandard. The Liberian National Police also continued to be plagued by corruption and incompetence, while crime remained high, particularly in Monrovia.[33] Armed robberies continued, and incidents of labour unrest were reported in 2012 in Margibi, Bomy, Maryland and Grand Bassa counties. There was

28. Cited in Tran, 'Liberia's Johnson Sirleaf Defiant'.
29. Economist Intelligence Unit, 'ViewsWire Liberia', 6 March 2013; 'Liberia/Côte d'Ivoire', *Africa Confidential*, 22 June 2012, p. 12.
30. United Nations, *Twenty Fifth Progress Report of the Secretary-General on the United Nations Mission in Liberia*, 28 February 2013, S/2013/124, p. 5.
31. Economist Intelligence Unit, 'ViewsWire Liberia'.
32. Ibid.
33. 'Not Out of the Woods', *Africa Confidential*, 7 September 2012, p. 9.

also public unrest in Monrovia in September and October 2012, with hundreds of teachers and students protesting against the non-payment of educators' salaries.[34]

There were some positive signs, however, as remittances from Liberians in the diaspora reached an estimated $360 million in 2011 (some 31 per cent of the country's gross domestic product).[35] The steel multinational ArcelorMittal was exporting Liberian iron ore by 2012, while $19 billion of foreign direct investment was pledged, largely to the mining sector and agribusiness.[36] The country also discovered offshore oil, though its commercial viability remained uncertain and it would take at least five years to come on stream.

Foreign investment was not without controversy, however. A government-commissioned report by international auditors revealed that as of 2013, only two out of sixty-eight resource contracts worth a total of $8 billion had been properly awarded.[37] There were also accusations of Sirleaf 'selling' the country to foreign investors, as well as continuing reports of corruption in the timber sector (resulting in the government temporarily suspending large logging operations). Some 40 per cent of Liberia's forest (and a quarter of its land) was reported to have been awarded to timber companies between 2010 and 2011, sometimes through the abuse of permits, while 600,000 hectares of land had reportedly been pledged to plantation companies.[38] Local communities in western Liberia and elsewhere protested against the government's granting of long-term licences to foreign companies without proper consultation on what they saw as communal land. For example, an estimated 150,000 people were directly affected by the plans of Malaysian firm Sime Darby to develop palm oil plantations.[39]

34. United Nations, *Twenty Fifth Progress Report*, p. 3.
35. Liz Ford, 'Liberia Urged to Invest Remittances, Not Just Spend Them on Everyday Needs', *Guardian*, 30 January 2013 (www.theguardian.com).
36. Xan Rice, 'Unease over the Speed of Change', *Financial Times*, 14 September 2012, 'Special Report: Doing Business in Liberia', p. 1.
37. Afua Hirsch, 'Liberia Natural Resources Deals Not Compliant with Law, Find Auditors', *Guardian*, 8 May 2013 (www.theguardian.com).
38. Rice, 'Unease over the Speed of Change', p. 1.
39. Tran, 'Liberia's Johnson Sirleaf Defiant'.

In Liberia's historically rubber and mining-dominated economy, unemployment stood at 95 per cent five years into Sirleaf's presidency (only 100,000 people out of a work force of 2.7 million were employed), while foreign aid of $425 million exceeded the country's $370 million annual budget. Some 64 per cent of the population were living below the poverty line, while 60 per cent were under the age of 35.[40] Despite claims that Sirleaf had provided Monrovia with electricity (for example, in the 2007 documentary *Iron Ladies of Liberia*), electricity capacity in the city in fact stood at 23 megawatts in May 2013 compared to a pre-war level of 412 megawatts.[41] Only 2 to 3 per cent of the population were actually connected to the national electricity grid,[42] while no more than 5 per cent of the country's road network was paved.[43]

The fact that many of the socio-economic problems and the corruption that Sirleaf has criticised throughout her career have continued under her own presidency suggests that there are complex structural issues at play in efforts to generate the development resources that Liberia needs in order to establish an efficient civil service and political system and reduce the scourge of corruption. The slow pace of change has made Liberians wary of Sirleaf's lofty rhetoric. The controversial election of 2011 has also made it difficult for the president to reconcile and reconstruct her fragile nation. Sirleaf broke an earlier promise to serve only a single term, thus spurning the example of her professed hero and fellow Nobel laureate Nelson Mandela. The ennobling of Liberia's 'Iron Lady' by the Oslo-based Nobel Peace Committee must rank as one of the most controversial choices in the history of the award.

---

40. 'A Low-Key Second Term', *Africa Confidential*, 3 February 2012, p. 9.
41. Economist Intelligence Unit, 'ViewsWire Liberia'.
42. Xan Rice, 'Nation Remains Largely in the Dark After Sunset', *Financial Times*, 14 September 2012, 'Special Report: Doing Business in Liberia', p. 2.
43. Tamasin Ford, 'Growing Pains', *Africa Report* 42 (July 2012), p. 49.

Bibliography

Adebajo, Adekeye, *Liberia's Civil War: Nigeria, ECOMOG, and Regional Security in West Africa* (Boulder CO: Lynne Rienner, 2002).

Adebajo, Adekeye, *UN Peacekeeping in Africa: From the Suez Crisis to the Sudan Conflicts* (Boulder CO: Lynne Rienner, 2011).

Africa Confidential, 'Rumours and Plots', *Africa Confidential*, 3 August 2007.

Africa Confidential, 'Musical Chairs in Monrovia', *Africa Confidential*, 19 November 2010.

Africa Confidential, 'A Low-Key Second Term', *Africa Confidential*, 3 February 2012, p. 9.

Africa Confidential, 'Keeping It in the Family', *Africa Confidential*, 13 April 2012.

Africa Confidential, 'Liberia/Côte d'Ivoire', *Africa Confidential*, 22 June 2012, p. 12.

Africa Confidential, 'Not Out of the Woods', *Africa Confidential*, 7 September 2012.

Bah, Alhaji M.S., and Festus Aboagye (eds), *A Tortuous Road to Peace: The Dynamics of Regional, UN, and International Humanitarian Interventions in Liberia* (Tshwane: Institute for Security Studies, 2005).

The Economist, 'Another Round for Africa's Iron Lady', *The Economist*, 20 May 2010 (www.economist.com).

The Economist, 'Hold Your Breath', *The Economist*, 10 September 2011 (www.economist.com).

Economist Intelligence Unit, 'Country Profile: Liberia', January–December 2007.

Economist Intelligence Unit, 'Country Report: Liberia', June 2011. Economist Intelligence Unit, 'Country Report: Liberia', September 2009.

Economist Intelligence Unit, 'ViewsWire Liberia', 6 March 2013.

Ford, Liz, 'Liberia Urged to Invest Remittances, Not Just Spend Them on Everyday Needs', *Guardian*, 30 January 2013 (www.theguardian.com).

Ford, Tamasin, 'Growing Pains', *Africa Report* 42 (July 2012).

Hirsch, Afua, 'Liberia Natural Resources Deals Not Compliant with Law, Find Auditors', *Guardian*, 8 May 2013 (www.theguardian.com).

Kaplan, Erin Aubry, 'Iron Lady', *Ms.,* May 2009.

Liebenow, Gus, *Liberia: The Quest for a Democracy* (Bloomington: Indiana University Press, 1987).

Liebenow, Gus, *The Evolution of Privilege* (Ithaca NY: Cornell University Press, 1969).

Magyar, Karl, and Earl Conteh-Morgan (eds), *Peacekeeping in Africa: ECOMOG in Liberia* (London: Macmillan, 1998).

Rice, Xan, 'Nation Remains Largely in the Dark After Sunset', *Financial Times*, 14 September 2012, 'Special Report: Doing Business in Liberia'.

Rice, Xan, 'Unease over the Speed of Change', *Financial Times*, 14 September 2012.

Sawyer, Amos, *Effective Immediately: Dictatorship in Liberia, 1980–1986 – A Personal Perspective* (Bremen: Liberia Working Group, 1987).

Sawyer, Amos, *The Emergence of Autocracy in Liberia: Tragedy and Challenge* (San Francisco: ICS, 1992).

Sirleaf, Ellen Johnson, 'Behold the New Africa', speech at the Sixth Nelson Mandela Annual Lecture, Johannesburg, 12 July 2008.

Sirleaf, Ellen Johnson, *This Child Will Be Great: Memoirs of a Remarkable Life by Africa's First Woman President* (New York: HarperCollins, 2009).

Sirleaf, Ellen Johnson, 'A Voice for Freedom', Nobel lecture, Oslo, 10 December 2011, www.nobelprize.org.

Tran, Mark, 'Liberia's Johnson Sirleaf Defiant over Nepotism and Corruption Claims', *Guardian*, 1 November 2012 (www.theguardian.com).

United Nations, *Twenty Fifth Progress Report of the Secretary-General on the United Nations Mission in Liberia*, 28 February 2013, S/2013/124.

United Nations, *Twenty Third Progress Report of the Secretary-General on the United Nations Mission in Liberia,* 5 August 2011, S/2011/497.

FIFTEEN

LEYMAH GBOWEE:
THE PRAYERFUL PEACE WARRIOR

ROSALINE DANIEL

The fourth of five daughters, Leymah Roberta Gbowee comes from a close-knit indigenous Kpelle family of modest means from Bong county in central Liberia.[1] Both of her parents, despite growing up poor, worked hard and were able to send their daughters to some of the best private schools in Monrovia. Family was important to Leymah Gbowee, who in her 2011 memoir, *Mighty Be Our Powers*, describes the community where she grew up as one 'built on togetherness and sharing'. There was always 'someone with less', and the Gbowee home in Monrovia was full of extended family members who had come from the village to work for the family in return for a place to stay.[2]

Gbowee describes a 'clean and modern' Monrovia prior to the civil war (which started in 1989), boasting the most sophisticated medical facility in West Africa, the John F. Kennedy Medical Centre. The Nobel Peace laureate of 2011 (with Ellen Johnson Sirleaf and Tawakul Karman) was due to study biology and chemistry at university when, in December 1989, Charles Taylor and a group of armed rebels known as the National Patriotic Front of Liberia (NPFL) entered northern

---

1. I thank Antonia Porter and Zanele Khumalo, project officers at the Centre for Conflict Resolution (CCR) in Cape Town, South Africa, for useful comments on the first draft of this essay.
2. Leymah Gbowee and Carol Mithers, *Mighty Be Our Powers: How Sisterhood, Prayer, and Sex Changed a Nation at War – A Memoir* (New York: Beast, 2011), pp. 5, 10.

Liberia from Côte d'Ivoire. The war would last until Taylor was elected president of Liberia in 1997. It restarted in 1999 and ended with Taylor's exile to Nigeria in 2003.[3] Coming from an indigenous family, Gbowee did not have the means, as many of Liberia's elite did, to flee to countries such as the United States, although she was able during the course of the war to move her children to Ghana.

In traditional Liberian society, male infidelity and power over women in the home have been the norm. It was not until Gbowee started work as a social worker in 1994 as part of a United Nations Children's Fund (UNICEF) project, providing training in trauma-healing and reconciliation, that she was able to put a name to the domestic violence she was experiencing at the hands of her partner, whom she had met at the age of 19. Ironically, the main reason she signed up for the UNICEF programme was to escape from the abusive relationship with the father of her two children at the time.

Gbowee experienced a range of emotions over the course of the Liberian civil war, which ravaged her country from 1989 to 2003. First there was anger: in her 2001 memoir she tells of her indignation at having had to take responsibility and make important decisions (a notion alien to her at the time) for her family as well as her parents' friends who had fled their homes and come to stay with her family after the rebels took over their communities. Then there was fear: the realisation of her mortality and the uncertainty of life, when at 17 years old she was faced for the first time with the real possibility of succumbing to the death that surrounded her as government and rebel soldiers indiscriminately killed and raped at will amid the smell of the growing number of dead bodies in the streets of Monrovia. Fear was followed by bitterness and apathy, and the perception of the pointlessness of pursuing an education when a bullet was all it would take to undo it. Eventually, this anger and fear culminated in peaceful activism

---

3. Comfort Ero, 'UN Peacekeeping in West Africa', in Adekeye Adebajo (ed.), *From Global Apartheid to Global Village: Africa and the United Nations* (Scottsville: University of KwaZulu-Natal Press, 2009), p. 286.

after Gbowee responded to a dream she had in April 2002 in which
she heard a voice telling her: 'Gather the women to pray for peace!'[4]

The seeds of hope were first planted in the early 1990s, when
Gbowee worked as a social worker with female refugees from Sierra
Leone who were living in Monrovia. Despite the horrors of war that
these women had experienced, they lacked any bitterness and spoke
only of the future, when they would return home and rebuild their
country. Their fortitude made Gbowee realise that the war in Liberia
was a national and political issue that transcended the personal tragedy
she had endured.[5] She eventually went on to mobilise the 'Mass Action
for Peace' campaign, involving women from all social and religious
divides, to take a stand for peace by staging a sit-in near the fish market
in Monrovia on 14 April 2003. According to Gbowee, this was the first
time in Liberia's history that Muslim and Christian women had publicly
engaged in this sort of collective activism. The women remained in the
market under the burning sun and pouring rain in an effort to make
Charles Taylor listen to their cries for an end to the war. They were
eventually granted an audience with the president, on 23 April 2003.

Fighting Gender Norms

Leymah Gbowee's most important struggle, for which she won the
Nobel Peace Prize in 2011, was for gender equality through Liberia's
women's movement.[6] There is a notion that young men fight wars to
protect the vulnerable, which includes women, who are often unable to
protect themselves effectively, particularly in times of conflict. However,
the reality is that it is frequently the so-called protector who poses
the greatest threat to women, thereby destroying the stereotypical
relationship between protector and protected. Liberia's eleven-year
civil war was particularly brutal and had a major impact on women.

---

4. This paragraph is based on Gbowee and Mithers, *Mighty Be Our Powers*, pp. 20, 24, 122.

5. Ibid., p. 53.

6. On gender theory, see Charlotte Hooper, 'Masculinist Practices and Gender Politics: The Operation of Multiple Masculinities in International Relations', in Marysia Zalewski and Jane Papart (eds), *The 'Man' Question in International Relations* (Boulder CO: Westview Press, 1998), pp. 18, 29.

Gbowee recalls incidents of combatants inserting knives into women's genitals, of boys telling women they would come back to rape them, and of combatants cutting open the bellies of pregnant women to verify the winner of a bet to guess the sex of these women's unborn children. And yet women were not just victims in this conflict; they also took part in the violence, through enlistment in the rebel forces or coercion.[7]

But women experience war differently than do men, because they, along with their children, are often disproportionately affected as part of the civilian population. Contemporary warfare is no longer confined to the battlefield, but also takes place in local communities where women and children live, forcing them to flee their homes. War exacerbates the inequalities that exist between men and women; it makes victims of women and children, who suffer economically, physically and emotionally, and women are largely excluded from peace-building and peacekeeping processes.[8] Military conflict creates refugees, and the Liberian conflict, which raged from 1989 to 2003, left an estimated 500,000 to 600,000 people living in refugee camps and claimed about 250,000 lives.[9]

Leymah Gbowee's example has shown that women play a crucial role in promoting peace and simply holding life together during conflicts, through religious activities such as prayer, fasting and vigils, as well as through social action, which may include protests and distributing aid. Yet often there is little media coverage of such activities. During the Liberian conflict, women sometimes sought to provide security for their local communities by offering themselves to be gang-raped in

7. This paragraph is based on Gbowee and Mithers, *Mighty Be Our Powers*, p. 130; Leymah Gbowee and the Women of Liberia, 'Acceptance Speech', John F. Kennedy Presidential Library and Museum, 18 May 2009, www.jfklibrary.org/Events-and-Awards/Profile-in-Courage-Award/Award-Recipients/Leymah-Gbowee-and-the-Women-of-Liberia-2009.aspx?t=3; and Ecoma Alaga, 'Security Sector Reform and the Women's Peace Activism Nexus in Liberia', in 'Funmi Olonisakin and Awino Okech (eds), *Women and Security Governance in Africa* (Cape Town: Pambazuka, 2011), p. 72.
8. Cited in Elizabeth Otitodun and Antonia Porter, 'Gender and Peace-Building', in Chris Saunders, Gwinyayi A. Dzinesa and Dawn Nagar (eds), *Region-Building in Southern Africa: Progress, Problems, and Prospects* (London: Zed Books, 2012), p. 107.
9. Neill Wright, Enda Savage and Vicky Tennant, 'Real-Time Evaluation of UNHCR's IDP Operation in Liberia', United Nations High Commissioner for Refugees Policy Development and Evaluation Service and IDP Advisory Team, 2007, p. 7, www.unhcr.org/cgi-bin/texis/vtx/home/opendocPD-FViewer.html?docid=46a4ae082&query=Meeting%20the%20Rights%20and%20Protection%20Needs%20of%20Refugee%20Children:%20An%20Independent%20Evaluation%20of%20the%20Impact%20of%20UNHCR%27s%20Activities; Gbowee and Mithers, *Mighty Be Our Powers*, p. 167.

order to spare the same fate occurring to their children and community members. They also sometimes sought to protect themselves from being raped by enlisting as rebel soldiers.[10] The American film-maker Abigail Disney, who made the award-winning documentary *Pray the Devil Back to Hell*, which follows Leymah Gbowee's activism in 2008, attests to this invisible nature of women in war. During an interview about the film, Disney recounted the difficulty she experienced in finding footage of the meeting between the women's peace movement and Charles Taylor in April 2003, because convention had branded the women as unimportant due to their gender, class and lack of education. This despite the fact that women have 'untapped power' and can serve as important early-warning systems prior to conflict, as they are able to recognise activities in their local communities that may cause conflict to erupt.[11]

Although Gbowee became one of many Liberian women who suffered infidelity and physical abuse at the hands of their partners, she also came into contact, through her social work, with men who did not subscribe to the traditional gender roles laid down by Liberian society. One such man was Reverend Bartholomew Bioh Colley, a Lutheran minister involved in trauma-healing and reconciliation, who was ready to give Gbowee a chance to prove herself because 'most African women never have the opportunity to work with a man who's open to whatever they want to do'.[12] Gbowee tells of many instances in the Liberian countryside during her work in trauma-healing when she was the only female trainer and was often treated as a mere helper to her male counterparts. The women were also often relegated to the

10. This narrative on the many roles that women had to play during the conflict is based on Gbowee and Mithers, *Mighty Be Our Powers*, p. 92; and Leymah Roberta Gbowee, 'Gender Equality, Empowerment of Women, and Post-Conflict Development', International Expert Panel on Implementing the Internationally Agreed Goals and Commitments in Regard to Gender Equality and Empowerment of Women, United Nations Commission on the Status of Women, 54th session, New York, 1–12 March 2010, p. 3 (www.un.org/womenwatch/daw/beijing15/ipanel_ECOSOC_AMR/Leymah%20Gbowee.pdf).

11. *Pray the Devil Back to Hell* documents Gbowee's fight, alongside other women in Liberia, to bring an end to the civil war. See also Leymah Gbowee and Abigail Disney's interview with Lynn Sherr on the Public Broadcasting Service programme *Bill Moyers Journal*, 19 June 2009 (http://video.pbs.org/video/1157137218); Gbowee, 'Gender Equality', p. 2.

12. Gbowee and Mithers, *Mighty Be Our Powers*, p. 88.

kitchen to cook for the trainers. She consistently challenged the norm that women, although predominantly the victims of war and conflict, are expected to remain invisible in the background while men negotiate peace.[13]

The Inter-Faith Struggle, 2002–03

Originally established in Accra, Ghana, in 2001, the Women in Peace-building Network (WIPNET), comprising women from several West African countries, launched its Liberia office in Monrovia in July 2002, with Gbowee as coordinator. For her, WIPNET represented a consolidation of all that she had learned and assimilated during her years working in trauma-healing and studying for her associate degree in social work at Mother Patern College of Health Sciences in Monrovia. By now, Gbowee had come to the conclusion that with emotional healing comes the full realisation of the extent of one's strength, and only then can this strength be channelled into political action to bring about peace.[14]

The women's movement in Liberia, comprising the Mano River Union Women's Peace Network (MARWOPNET) and the Liberia Women Initiative (LWI), was already well-established – a cause of initial tension between these groups and WIPNET. Indeed, the LWI had been working to end the war since as early as 1994, when it had staged a campaign of protests and strikes in Monrovia. MARWOPNET and the LWI, however, comprised women from educated backgrounds primarily. This, for Gbowee, limited their ultimate effectiveness, as they did not embrace women from all sectors of society.

Gbowee felt restless and unable to help within the peace movement in Liberia until the dream she had in April 2002 urging her to gather Liberia's women for prayer. This led to the creation of the Christian Women's Peace Initiative (CWI), which concentrated first on a weekly prayer meeting at St Peter's chapel in Monrovia. Out of this movement

---

13. This paragraph is based on ibid., pp. 88, 100.
14. Ibid., p. 114.

came the Peace Outreach Project, in July 2002, during which, for three days over a six-month period, representatives of WIPNET urged women in mosques, markets and churches to join the campaign to end the war. In December 2002 a Christian–Muslim women's alliance was born, and by April 2003 Gbowee had resigned from the UNICEF trauma-healing and reconciliation programme to concentrate full-time on WIPNET.

The women of WIPNET started by issuing a public statement – published in a local paper and aired on a radio station – condemning violence and calling for peace. Although Charles Taylor had banned street marches, the women arranged a gathering at Monrovia city hall on 11 April 2003 in which they all wore white, representing peace and unity. They called for an immediate and unconditional ceasefire by all warring factions, for peace talks to be held, and for an international peacekeeping force to be deployed to Liberia. Gbowee's 'Mass Action for Peace' campaign, which included women from all faiths and walks of life, began on 14 April in the field near the fish market, chosen for its central location. The Monrovia sit-in was replicated in other parts of the country, with fifteen such sit-ins eventually taking place in nine different counties in Liberia. The women also picketed in various parts of the capital with placards that read: 'We want peace, no more war!'

The women's peace movement centred on people and the positive impact they can have on bringing an end to war. Their struggle for peace in Liberia lasted for three years, and involved sit-ins, peaceful demonstrations and community awareness initiatives. The women in white served as a constant reminder of the suffering of ordinary Liberians, and many ordinary citizens responded positively to this campaign. Monrovia's bus drivers, for example, let the women in white travel for free to the field, and the partners and families of these women would remind them about meetings. Donations were received mostly from churches, but also from soldiers, warlords, passers-by and international donors, as well as secretly from high-level businesspeople and government officials. The movement drew international media attention, primarily from the BBC, with Gbowee acting as the main spokesperson in conducting radio, television and newspaper interviews. The women also staged a 'sex strike', designed to persuade their partners to join in the struggle to end the war, but this had more success in the rural areas than in the cities. The strike went on intermittently for only a few months and was of little practical effect, but it did serve to draw more media attention to the women's struggle for peace.[15]

The 2003 CPA Sit-In and Mobilising
Women for the 2005 Election

The Liberian women's movement played an important role in pressuring representatives of the warring factions to attend internationally sanctioned peace talks in Accra, Ghana, which began in June 2003. Seven women from various organisations within the women's peace network went to the talks in Ghana and were able to mobilise Liberian women refugees as well as others in that country, 200 of whom staged a sit-in at the entrance to the conference hall.[16] Gbowee and her colleagues were able to tug at the moral heartstrings of the hardened warlords, who were forced to question their roles in the conflict rather than see their 'mothers' strip naked out of sheer desperation at the need to do something to bring peace to Liberia. Gbowee was also able to appeal to the sensitivities of former Nigerian head of state General Abdulsalam Abubakar (1998–99), the principal mediator, who in turn was able to appeal to the humanity of the warlords when he told them that 'real men don't kill their people'.[17] Gbowee's activism was completely non-violent, in the vein of Mahatma Gandhi and Nobel peace laureate Martin Luther King Jr (see Robinson, Chapter 3, and Daniels, Chapter 5, in this volume), both of whose work she had read.

The Liberian civil war finally ended with the signing of the Comprehensive Peace Agreement (CPA) in Accra in August 2003, following peace talks. Gbowee, however, continued her peace activism through

---

15. Ibid., pp. 146–7.
16. Leymah Gbowee, 'Effecting Change', *IDS Bulletin* 40(2) (2009), p. 51.
17. Gbowee and Disney interview with Sherr.

consultative meetings with women in Liberia to educate them on the
CPA and to monitor its implementation. The women's movement also
contributed to the first phase of the disarmament, demobilisation and
reintegration (DDR) process undertaken by the United Nations Mission
in Liberia (UNMIL) in 2003, as well as the second phase in 2004, in
which the UN partnered with WIPNET, which was instrumental in
encouraging former combatants to surrender their arms. In addition,
Gbowee and her colleagues encouraged women to vote, promoted voter
awareness, and educated women in the voting process so that they
no longer felt marginalised but were now active stakeholders in the
political future of their country. During the 2011 presidential election
in Liberia, Gbowee was instrumental in organising election monitors
from nine West African countries – a first in Liberia's history.[18] The
large turnout of women in the 2005 election – about 51 per cent – speaks
to their dedication and contribution to peace-building efforts after the
end of the civil war. In the 2005 election, Ellen Johnson Sirleaf became
Liberia's first elected female leader. With the end of the war, and the
beginning of post-conflict reconstruction, the seeds of hope that had
been planted in Gbowee's mind by refugees from Sierra Leone, whom
she had encountered in Liberia in 1994, were now bearing fruit.

Leymah Gbowee and fellow Nobel peace laureate Ellen Johnson
Sirleaf first met at the Accra peace talks in June 2003. Gbowee had initially been ambivalent about Sirleaf's involvement with Charles Taylor
at the beginning of Liberia's civil war (see Adebajo, Chapter 14 in this
volume), but she eventually campaigned for Sirleaf in the second round
of voting, as she believed that a government run by her would promote
and support women's rights. It is safe to say that the Liberian women's
network, with Gbowee as its face, paved the way for Sirleaf to become
modern Africa's first democratically elected female president in 2005.
Sirleaf acknowledged this in an interview in December 2011, when she
noted that 'I owe my success to them, those women who were in the

18. Eliza Griswold, 'Firebrand for Peace: Liberia's Brutal Civil War Made a Fearless Leader out
of Leymah Gbowee', *Daily Beast*, 26 September 2011 (www.thedailybeast.com/newsweek/2011/09/18/
firebrand-for-peace.html).

sun and the rain', and observed that Gbowee's work had 'led them to believe that it was time for a woman to head the nation'.[19]

From Social Worker to Peacebuilder

Gbowee continues to use the 2008 documentary *Pray the Devil Back to Hell* to galvanise other women the world over to keep working for peace, for the respect of universal human rights, and for socio-economic justice. Hers is a story that has transcended geographical and ethnic boundaries, mobilising women in Peru, Bosnia, Afghanistan, Iraq and Egypt, among other countries, to recognise the parallels in their situations and to think about what can be done to make a change in their lives today. Gbowee's work in Liberia and the West African subregion undoubtedly contributed to her Nobel Peace Prize award, which recognised those 'who were there long before the world's media was there reporting'.[20]

Leymah Gbowee's peace activism is testament to the importance of including women and other local actors in peace and post-conflict reconstruction processes. Indeed, as Ecoma Alaga noted, the grassroots-based strategy of the women's peace movement in Liberia demonstrated the necessity of including women in building peace and security in conflict and post-conflict societies, both at the policy and decision-making level as well as at the grassroots level, as enshrined in UN Security Council Resolution 1325 of 2000 on women, peace and security.[21] Certainly, the UN's initial failure to include local actors and women's groups in the Liberian DDR process was against the spirit of the resolution.[22]

As executive director of the Ghana-based Women Peace and Security Network Africa (WIPSEN–A), an organisation established in May

---

19. 'Interview with the 2011 Nobel Peace Prize Laureates', 9 December 2011, www.nobelprize.org/mediaplayer/index.php?id=1761.

20. Cited in Alan Cowell, Laura Kasinof and Adam Nossiter, 'Nobel Peace Prize Awarded to Three Activist Women', *New York Times*, 7 October 2011 (www.nytimes.com/2011/10/08/world/nobel-peace-prize-johnson-sirleaf-gbowee-karman.html?_r=1&pagewanted=all).

21. See Centre for Conflict Resolution, *Women and Peacebuilding in Africa*, policy report (Cape Town, 27–28 October 2005), www.ccr.org.za.

22. This paragraph is based on Alaga, 'Security Sector Reform', pp. 73, 83.

2006 that seeks to empower African women to participate in fostering human security, sustainable peace and development, Leymah Gbowee remained active throughout West Africa. She continues to believe that what women were able to achieve in Liberia can be replicated in other countries. (Gbowee announced her intention to step down as head of WIPSEN–A in December 2012 due to an increasingly busy schedule of commitments.) She is also founder and president of the Gbowee Peace Foundation Africa, which was launched in February 2012 to provide scholarships for young women to study in Liberia and abroad, among other initiatives. Gbowee sees her role as working with women from communities all over the world – not just in Africa – in order to improve their lives and provide them with opportunities equal to those of men. She believes that Liberia can serve as an example and aspiration for women throughout Africa, echoing the statement by the Nobel Peace Committee that 'we cannot achieve democracy and lasting peace in the world unless women acquire the same opportunities as men to influence developments at all levels of society'.[23]

The Nobel Prize and Speech

From among a record 241 nominations of individuals and organisations, Leymah Gbowee, along with Liberian president Ellen Johnson Sirleaf and Tawakkul Karman, a pro-democracy campaigner from Yemen, was awarded the Nobel Peace Prize in October 2011. In citing Gbowee's work, the Nobel Peace Committee acknowledged how it had 'inspired many women to engage in a non-violent struggle against war and violence and for women's rights', and noted that 'it was very important that Gbowee managed to unite women with quite different religious and ethnic backgrounds'.[24]

In her Nobel Prize speech, Gbowee hailed women throughout the world who continue to fight for peace, equality, social justice and inclusion in political decision-making. She cited the example of Martin

---

23. 'Presentation Speech by Thorbjørn Jagland', www.nobelprize.org/nobel_prizes/peace/laure-ates/2011/presentation-speech.html.
24. Ibid.

Luther King Jr, who advocated only peaceful means to combat violence, and highlighted the plight of the women of the Democratic Republic of the Congo, Uganda, Afghanistan and Zimbabwe who are fighting against sexual violence and war. Gbowee described the Liberian women's peace movement as 'the conscience of the ones who had lost their consciences' and spoke of the 'moral duty' that they had to safeguard the future of their country.[25] She also recognised that the women's struggle for peace in Liberia had been a collaborative effort, comprising many different kinds of women who, because they had lost so much already, had nothing more to lose, and therefore refused to be intimidated by warlords and their guns.

Gbowee further noted the solidarity that all women across the globe share, regardless of country of origin, because they are so often the victims of sexual abuse and exploitation. She observed that women who have been raped and abused in war are often excluded from post-conflict decision-making processes. She cautioned that their absence from such processes can lead to the passing of laws and implementation of policies that not only ignore abuses against women, but can also lead to a failure to implement policies and laws designed to protect women and engage them in peace-building processes. For Gbowee, the Nobel Peace Prize honoured not just women, but all humanity, and represented a call for leaders everywhere to embrace women's rights as human rights and to strive to work towards implementing policies and processes that include women.

Gbowee's African ancestry was not particularly relevant to the award. Of greater relevance was the fact that the three Nobel Peace Prize recipients in 2011 were all women, and indeed the first women to win the Nobel Peace Prize since Kenya's Wangari Maathai in 2004 (see Golding, Chapter 12 in this volume). Up until 2011, the Nobel Peace Committee had honoured only twelve women in its 110-year history.[26] The 2011 Peace Prize, above all, recognised the leadership

---

25. 'The Nobel Peace Prize 2011', www.nobelprize.org/nobel_prizes/peace/laureates/ 2011/ gbowee-lecture_en.html.
26. Judith Hicks Stiehm, *Champions for Peace: Women Winners of the Nobel Peace Prize* (Lanham MD: Rowman & Littlefield, 2006).

role of women in working for peace and security throughout the world, speaking directly to the need for change in certain parts of the world, as well as for a commitment to activism and governance through non-violence.[27] Thorbjørn Jagland, the Norwegian chair of the Nobel Peace Committee, described the award as an 'important siren call for women the world over'. Since the award, Gbowee has continued in her quest to voice the desire of women to participate in political decision-making for conflict prevention at all levels of society and to ensure that issues pertaining to human security and socio-economic development are effectively addressed. In addition, Gbowee continues to fight to empower women to overcome their frequent marginalisation due to a lack of political will to include them in peace and security issues.

An important lesson that can be drawn from Gbowee's work for Africa and the world at large is that women must not be excluded from peace and security processes in conflict and post-conflict environ-ments. They can bring about change and do not have to sit on the sidelines or fulfil gender-stereotyped roles assigned to them by societal norms. Another lesson to be derived from her peace activism is that durable peace does not just imply an end to conflict, but also involves a sustained effort to change post-conflict societies by bringing an end to the physical and structural violence that exists, and by promoting socio-economic justice.

After international peacekeepers arrived in Monrovia and Charles Taylor left for exile in Nigeria in August 2003, Liberian women contin-ued their efforts to ensure sustained peace in their country, recognising that peace is a process and not just an event. Part of this process meant being patient while the UN initially ignored their advice to bring in local actors to assist in disarming former combatants – displaying what could be perceived as a kind of arrogance based on the premiss that only it possessed expertise in rebuilding conflict-torn societies.[28] The

27. Michel Martin, 'Women's Rights Pioneers Win Nobel Peace Prize', Nation-al Public Radio, *Tell Me More,* 7 October 2011 (www.npr.org/2011/10/07/141152981/womens-rights-pioneers-win-nobel-peace-prize).
28. See, for example, Comfort Ero, 'Peacebuilding Through Statebuilding in West Africa? The Cases of Sierra Leone and Liberia', in Devon Curtis and Gwinyayi A. Dzinesa (eds), *Peacebuilding, Power, and Politics in Africa* (Athens: Ohio University Press, 2012).

women of WIPNET understood the cultural context of the Liberian situation, and were thus able to appeal successfully to the humanity of former combatants. The UN, on the other hand, was essentially an outsider coming in with a 'cookie-cutter' solution as to how a traumatised nation should heal following a destructive conflict. Indeed, the UN Development Programme (UNDP) was eventually forced to call on Gbowee for help in setting up a registration campaign specifically targeting Liberian women who were not aware of the fact that they had to register in order to vote in the 2005 presidential election. This campaign resulted in a spectacular rise of registered women voters, from 15 to 51 per cent, by the time of the election. The process continued, with Liberian women promoting democracy and lasting peace during the election, in which they campaigned actively for Ellen Johnson Sirleaf, who, as noted earlier, became the first female elected president of an African nation in 2006.[29]

As the coordinator of WIPNET, Gbowee was its spokesperson. There appears to have been resentment on the part of some of her WIPNET colleagues and among the wider Liberian women's movement at the spotlight that Gbowee enjoyed as a result of her work with the movement. In her memoir, the prayerful peace warrior described how some of her colleagues felt that she had used the protest to become famous by engaging in self-promotion in her regular interviews with media outlets such as the BBC. Some in WIPNET also resented the way in which Gbowee had abruptly resigned after the 2005 election and moved to Ghana. For some women in the LWI and MARWOPNET, peace did not simply occur over the course of a few months. They considered Mary Brownell (who had founded both groups) – and not Gbowee – as the main personality who had laid the groundwork for peace as far back as 1992, and therefore as the woman who should have received the Nobel Peace Prize. Some even believed that Gbowee was 'riding the coat-tails of the women's movement'.[30] While she never gave

---

29. This paragraph is based on Gbowee and Mithers, *Mighty Be Our Powers*, pp. 171, 183.
30. These views were expressed to me in a confidential interview in Johannesburg, South Africa, in September 2012, with Liberian women who participated in the peace struggle.

herself sole credit for the successes of the Liberian women's movement in her memoir – describing herself as the strategist and coordinator – the Nobel Peace Committee, by bestowing the prize on Gbowee, had singled out just one individual in a whole women's movement. It is possible that the documentary *Pray the Devil Back to Hell* as well as Gbowee's determination and drive made her more visible than her colleagues, resulting in a nomination for her as an individual, rather than for the women's network as an organisation.

Concluding Reflections

Women's peace activism has undoubtedly altered the political landscape in Liberia, opening up opportunities for the participation of women in peace-building and governance, and resulting in the election of a female president in 2006. Despite this, the role of women in the peace process and in post-conflict reconstruction, while of immense importance, has not had a direct influence on reforms in Liberia's political and security landscape. Security-sector institutions that had emerged as a result of reforms in Liberia have yet to draw any significant benefit from lessons learned from the engagement of women in the country's broader peace and security processes. Furthermore, because the women's peace network did not have a long-term plan in place, the gains of the 'Mass Action for Peace' campaign have not been maximised to bring about lasting change to Liberia's political and social landscape.[31]

While the adoption of UN resolutions, such as 1325 of 2000 on women, peace and security, and 1820 of 2008 on strengthening the protection of women from sexual violence, are laudable, the resources and political will to implement them have often been lacking in countries like Liberia, where there remains a culture of impunity coupled with a weak justice system that has failed consistently to prosecute perpetrators of violence against women. Under Sirleaf's presidency since 2006, a law that criminalises rape – with life imprisonment for conviction of child

---

31. This paragraph is based on Alaga, 'Security Sector Reform', pp. 75, 82.

and gang rape – has been passed, and a special 'rape court' for victims of the crime now exists.[32] In spite of these developments, however, rape and gender violence remain commonplace in Liberia, where women are still viewed as the property of men and violence against them is still ubiquitous. In 2011 in Liberia, nine out of every ten rape victims treated by Médecins sans Frontières were under 18 years old, with almost half of them under the age of 12. There is also a stigma attached to being raped, and so many prefer to use the informal or traditional justice system, involving mediation by community members or village elders, instead of the formal criminal justice channels.[33]

Although the 2011 presidential election again produced a female president – a second term for Ellen Johnson Sirleaf – who has given women key positions in the executive branch, with women heading the ministries of commerce and industry, education, gender and development, justice and labour, the majority of female candidates vying for legislative positions lost against their male counterparts, with female lawmakers comprising 13 per cent of the legislature after the 2011 election compared to 18 per cent in 2006. Proposed policies such as a gender equity bill that would mandate 30 per cent female representation in government had yet to be passed into law in June 2013. Success is unlikely given the low percentage of women in the legislative branch and the patriarchal nature of Liberian society.[34] Despite the achievements of both Gbowee and Sirleaf, women's empowerment in Liberia seems to have reached only a minority of the population. In addition, Liberia is still faced with numerous challenges, including high unemployment and crime, inadequate rehabilitation of former child soldiers into society, gender-based violence, corruption and a poor education system.

Leymah Gbowee was appointed head of the national Peace and Reconciliation Commission, established by Sirleaf in November 2011.

32. Cited in Lauren Harrison, 'Gender Inequality, Human Rights, and Poverty in Liberia: An Assessment and Proposed Path Forward', http://agirlandagoal.files.wordpress.com/2012/05/liberia-final-paper_lauren-harrison_vf.pdf.

33. Fran Blandy, 'Liberia's Women Still Stalked by Rape', *Mail and Guardian*, 24 November 2011 (http://mg.co.za/article/2011-11-24-liberia-women-still-stalked-by-rape).

34. Wade Williams, 'Slamming the Girl Power: What Went Wrong for Liberia's Women at the 2011 Polls?', 23 November 2011, www.newnarratives.org/featured/slamming-the-girl-power-what-went-wrong-for-liberias-women-at-the-2011-polls.

In this position she sought to promote dialogue following the contested election the previous month. However, Gbowee resigned from this post in August 2012, citing the lack of urgency by the Sirleaf administration in fighting nepotism and corruption, as well as her need to focus on the Gbowee Peace Foundation. Accusations by the Sirleaf administration that Gbowee had misused funds in her capacity as head of the Peace and Reconciliation Commission meant that what Gbowee had previously called 'this first African female president solidarity' among Liberia's fellow peace laureates – who had hitherto enjoyed a strong mentor–mentee relationship – was now over in the most dramatic and public manner.[35]

As a peace activist, Leymah Gbowee has worked to promote development and the rights of women and girls in Liberia, using her expertise in trauma-healing and reconciliation to help usher in peace to her war-torn nation. Her grassroots strategy was both people-centred and context-specific, and paved the way for the first elected female president in Africa in 2006. Since receiving her Peace Prize in 2011, Gbowee has continued her work in promoting the influence of women in Africa and around the world, and in seeking to make the voice of women heard. While not enough time has passed to assess the full impact of her work on peace and reconciliation in Liberia, Gbowee's Nobel Prize-winning effort to promote the non-violent struggle for the safety of women and for their right to full participation in peace-building is indeed a worthy legacy.

---

35. This paragraph is based on Abigail Pesta, 'A Nobel Smackdown in Liberia: Leymah Gbowee vs. Ellen Johnson Sirleaf', *Daily Beast*, 10 October 2012, www.thedailybeast.com/articles/2012/10/10/a-nobel-smackdown-in-liberia-leymah-gbowee-vs-ellen-johnson-sirleaf.html; and Dyujah Bestman, 'Leymah Gbowee Speaks on Resignation', *The News*, 13 December 2012, http://thenewslib.com/news/1059-leymah-gbowee-speaks-on-resignation.

Bibliography

Alaga, Ecoma, 'Security Sector Reform and the Women's Peace Activism Nexus in Liberia', in 'Funmi Olonisakin and Awino Okech (eds), *Women and Security Governance in Africa* (Cape Town: Pambazuka, 2011).

Bestman, Dyujah, 'Leymah Gbowee Speaks on Resignation', *The News*, 13 December 2012 (http://thenewslib.com/news/1059-leymah-gbowee-speaks-on-resignation).

Blandy, Fran, 'Liberia's Women Still Stalked by Rape', *Mail and Guardian*, 24 November 2011 (http://mg.co.za/article/2011-11-24-liberia-women-still-stalked-by-rape).

Centre for Conflict Resolution, *Women and Peacebuilding in Africa*, policy report, Cape Town, 27–28 October 2005 (www.ccr.org.za).

Cowell, Alan, Laura Kasinof and Adam Nossiter, 'Nobel Peace Prize Awarded to Three Activist Women', *New York Times*, 7 October 2011 (www.nytimes.com/2011/10/08/world/nobel-peace-prize-johnson-sirleaf-gbowee-karman.html?_r=1&pagewanted=all).

Ero, Comfort, 'UN Peacekeeping in West Africa', in Adekeye Adebajo (ed.), *From Global Apartheid to Global Village: Africa and the United Nations* (Scottsville: University of KwaZulu-Natal Press, 2009).

Ero, Comfort, 'Peacebuilding Through Statebuilding in West Africa? The Cases of Sierra Leone and Liberia', in Devon Curtis and Gwinyayi A. Dzinesa (eds), *Peacebuilding, Power, and Politics in Africa* (Athens: Ohio University Press, 2012).

Gbowee, Leymah, 'Effecting Change', *IDS Bulletin* 40(2) (2009).

Gbowee, Leymah, 'Gender Equality, Empowerment of Women, and Post-Conflict Development', International Expert Panel on Implementing the Internationally Agreed Goals and Commitments in Regard to Gender Equality and Empowerment of Women, United Nations Commission on the Status of Women, 54th session, New York, 1–12 March 2010 (www.un.org/womenwatch/daw/beijing15/ipanel_ECOSOC_AMR/Leymah%20Gbowee.pdf).

Gbowee, Leymah, and Carol Mithers, *Mighty Be Our Powers: How Sisterhood, Prayer, and Sex Changed a Nation at War – A Memoir* (New York: Beast, 2011).

Gbowee, Leymah, and the Women of Liberia, 'Acceptance Speech', John F. Kennedy Presidential Library and Museum, 18 May 2009, www.jfklibrary.org/Events-and-Awards/Profile-in-Courage-Award/Award-Recipients/Leymah-Gbowee-and-the-Women-of-Liberia-2009.aspx?t=3.

Griswold, Eliza, 'Firebrand for Peace: Liberia's Brutal Civil War Made a Fearless Leader out of Leymah Gbowee', *Daily Beast*, 26 September 2011 (www.thedailybeast.com/newsweek/2011/09/18/firebrand-for-peace.html).

Harrison, Lauren, 'Gender Inequality, Human Rights, and Poverty in Liberia: An Assessment and Proposed Path Forward', http://agirlandagoal.files.wordpress.com/2012/05/liberia-final-paper_lauren-harrison_vf.pdf.

Hooper, Charlotte, 'Masculinist Practices and Gender Politics: The Operation of Multiple Masculinities in International Relations', in Marysia Zalewski and Jane Papart (eds), *The 'Man' Question in International Relations* (Boulder CO: Westview Press, 1998).

Nobel Prize, 'Presentation Speech by Thorbjørn Jagland', www.nobelprize.org/nobel_prizes/peace/laureates/2011/presentation-speech.html.

Nobel Prize, 'The Nobel Peace Prize 2011', www.nobelprize.org/nobel_prizes/peace/laureates/2011/gbowee-lecture_en.html.

Otitodun, Elizabeth, and Antonia Porter, 'Gender and Peace-Building', in Chris Saunders, Gwinyayi A. Dzinesa and Dawn Nagar (eds), *Region-Building in Southern Africa: Progress, Problems, and Prospects* (London: Zed Books, 2012).

Pesta, Abigail, 'A Nobel Smackdown in Liberia: Leymah Gbowee vs. Ellen Johnson Sirleaf', *Daily Beast*, 10 October 2012, www.thedailybeast.com/articles/2012/10/10/a-nobel-smackdown-in-liberia-leymah-gbowee-vs-ellen-johnson-sirleaf.html.

Stiehm, Judith Hicks, *Champions for Peace: Women Winners of the Nobel Peace Prize* (Lanham MD: Rowman & Littlefield, 2006).

ABOUT THE CONTRIBUTORS

Morad Abou-Sabé received his Bachelor's degree from Alexandria University in Egypt, his Master's from the University of California, Berkeley, and his doctorate from Pittsburgh University, before joining Rutgers University in New Jersey in 1968, where he remains an emeritus professor. Abou-Sabé has published numerous research articles in scientific journals in his field of molecular genetics, in addition to two books: *Microbial Genetics* and *Cyclic Nucleotides and the Regulation of Cell Growth*.

Adekeye Adebajo has been executive director of the Centre for Conflict Resolution in Cape Town, South Africa, since 2003. He obtained his doctorate from Oxford University, where he studied as a Rhodes Scholar. He has served on United Nations missions in South Africa, Western Sahara and Iraq. Dr Adebajo is the author of four books: *Building Peace in West Africa*; *Liberia's Civil War*; *The Curse of Berlin: Africa After the Cold War*; and *UN Peacekeeping in Africa: From the Suez Crisis to the Sudan Conflicts*. He is editor or co-editor of seven books, on managing global conflicts, the United Nations, the European Union, West African security, and South Africa's and Nigeria's foreign policies in Africa.

Elleke Boehmer is Professor of World Literature in English at the University of Oxford, and Governing Body Fellow at Wolfson College. Internationally renowned for her research in post-colonial theory and the literature of empire, Professor Boehmer currently works on questions of migration, identity and resistance in both colonial and post-colonial literature (sub-Saharan Africa and South Asia). She has published over eighteen books, including four novels; her best-selling biography of Nelson Mandela has been translated into Arabic, Portuguese and Thai. She obtained her doctorate from Oxford University, where she studied as a Rhodes Scholar.

Boutros Boutros-Ghali served as the sixth Secretary General of the United Nations between 1992 and 1996. During his term of office he mounted more peacekeeping operations than in the UN's previous forty years, and convened international conferences such as the Earth Summit in Rio de Janeiro, the Population Conference in Cairo, and the Conference on Women in Beijing. Before his tenure as UN Secretary General, Boutros-Ghali served as Egypt's minister of state for foreign affairs under Nobel peace laureate Anwar Sadat, playing a major role in the Arab–Israeli Camp David peace accords. Boutros-Ghali taught at Cairo University for twenty-eight years. He obtained his doctorate from the Sorbonne in France. He is the author of *Egypt's Road to Jerusalem: A Diplomat's Story of the Struggle for Peace in the Middle East* and *Unvanquished: A US–UN Saga.*

Rosaline Daniel is a senior project officer at the Centre for Conflict Resolution in Cape Town, South Africa. She holds Master's degrees from the University of Westminster and from Strayer University in the United States. Her interests include conflict resolution, gender and peace-building, international organisations, the global arms trade and Russia's foreign policy.

Lee A. Daniels is a journalist who has worked for the *Washington Post* and the *New York Times*, among other US media organisations. He is also a former editor of the National Urban League publication *The State of Black America*, and a former director of communications for the National Association for the Advancement of Colored People's Legal Defence and Educational Fund. He worked with Rachel Robinson on *Jackie Robinson: An Intimate Portrait*, which examined her late husband's historic achievements and their life together; and with Vernon E. Jordan Jr on a book of his speeches, *Make It Plain: Standing Up and Speaking Out*. Daniels is the author of *Last Chance: The Political Threat to Black America.*

Janice Golding is a research associate at the University of Cape Town's Plant Conservation Unit. A botanical ecologist by training, she is inspired by Africa's biodiversity and social value. She manages the Swiss government's economic portfolio with South Africa in environment, sustainable development and climate change at the Embassy of Switzerland in South Africa. She holds a doctorate from the University of Oxford's Environmental Change Institute.

Gregory F. Houston is a chief research specialist in the Service Delivery, Democracy and Governance research programme at the Human Sciences Research Council in Cape Town, South Africa. He holds a Master's degree in political studies from the University of the Witwatersrand, and a doctorate in political science from the University of Natal. Before joining the HSRC, he was a senior lecturer in the Department of Political Studies at the University of Transkei, where he lectured for twelve years. Houston is the author of *The National Liberation Struggle in South Africa: A Case Study of the United Democratic Front, 1983–87* and co-editor of *Public Participation in Democratic Governance in South Africa*. He has served as executive director of the South African Democracy Education Trust, which has produced six volumes in the series *The Road to Democracy in South Africa*.

Maureen Isaacson works as an editor and researcher for the Foundation for Human Rights in Johannesburg, South Africa. She previously worked as an independent journalist, writer, researcher and editor. She specialises in in-depth profiles, op-ed columns and literary criticism. Isaacson freelances for a range of publications, including *Afropolitan* and *Leadership* magazines. She worked in print journalism for three decades, starting by freelancing for *Business Day* and *The Star* newspapers. She worked for a variety of publications in the *Independent* newspaper stable for twenty-one years, most recently as an assistant editor and as literary editor of the *Sunday Independent*. She has published a collection of short stories, *Holding Back Midnight*, as well as other short stories in a variety of anthologies and journals. She has researched and edited two books: *The Fifties People of South Africa* and *The Finest Photographs from the Old Drum*.

James O.C. Jonah is a former UN Undersecretary General for Political Affairs. He holds a doctorate from the Massachusetts Institute of Technology. He is currently a senior fellow at the Ralph Bunche Institute for International Studies at the City University of New York's Graduate Centre. In 2001, Jonah won a Carnegie Scholar Grant to write his 2006 memoirs: *What Price the Survival of the United Nations? Memoirs of a Veteran International Civil Servant*. Prior to this, he served his country, Sierra Leone, as minister of finance, development and economic planning, and as permanent representative of Sierra Leone to the United Nations.

Ali A. Mazrui is director of the Institute of Global Cultural Studies at the State University of New York. Previously he was head of the Political Science Department and dean of the Faculty of Social Sciences at Makerere University in Uganda, and director of the University of Michigan's Centre for Afro-American and African Studies. In 1986, Mazrui wrote and narrated the influential nine-part documentary *The Africans: A Triple Heritage*, which established his global reputation. The author of more than thirty books and hundreds of essays, he holds a doctorate from Oxford University. He has served in an advisory capacity to numerous organisations, including the United Nations.

Gwendolyn Mikell is Professor of Anthropology at Georgetown University in Washington DC. Previously she was a senior fellow in African studies at the Council on Foreign Relations, president of the United States' African Studies Association, and a visiting fellow at universities and institutes in Ghana, South Africa, Nigeria and Japan, as well as at the Institute for Advanced Studies at Princeton University. In addition to numerous articles in books and journals, her books include *Cocoa and Chaos in Ghana* and *African Feminism: The Politics of Survival in Sub-Saharan Africa*. She is writing a book on the ideas of Nobel peace laureate and former UN Secretary General Kofi Annan. She holds a Bachelor's degree in sociology from the University of Chicago, and a Master's degree and doctorate in anthropology from Columbia University in the United States.

Pearl T. Robinson has authored more than forty articles and book chapters on African and African-American politics. She is co-author of *Stabilizing Nigeria: Sanctions, Incentives, and Support for Civil Society* and *Transformation and Resiliency in Africa*. She is currently a member of the United States' Council on Foreign Relations, and was previously president of the African Studies Association of the USA, and director of Tufts University's International Relations Programme. She has taught at Makerere University in Uganda and the University of Dar es Salaam in Tanzania. Her current projects include an intellectual biography of Nobel peace laureate Ralph Bunche and a documentary film about Islam and female empowerment in Niger titled *Mama Kiota!*

Chris Saunders is an emeritus professor at the University of Cape Town in South Africa. He completed his undergraduate studies there, and his doctorate at the University of Oxford, before returning to teach at the University of Cape Town. Professor Saunders is particularly interested in the recent political history of South Africa and its neighbours, and has written widely on the history and historiography of Southern Africa. He is the author of *The Making of the South African Past and South Africa: A Modern History* and co-editor of *Region-Building in Southern Africa: Progress, Problems and Prospects* and *Southern African Liberation Struggles*.

INDEX